Exam 70-433: *Microsoft* *SQL Server* *2008* *—Database Development*

OBJECTIVE	LOCATION IN BOOK
IMPLEMENTING TABLES AND VIEWS	
Create and alter tables.	Chapter 3, Lesson 1
Create and alter views.	Chapter 5, Lesson 4
Create and alter indexes.	Chapter 6, Lesson 2
Create and modify constraints.	Chapter 3, Lesson 2
Implement data types.	Chapter 3, Lesson 1 Chapter 8, Lesson 1
Implement partitioning solutions.	Chapter 6, Lesson 2
IMPLEMENTING PROGRAMMING OBJECTS	
Create and alter stored procedures.	Chapter 5, Lesson 1
Create and alter user-defined functions (UDFs).	Chapter 5, Lesson 2
Create and alter DML triggers.	Chapter 5, Lesson 3
Create and alter DDL triggers.	Chapter 5, Lesson 3
Create and deploy CLR-based objects.	Chapter 7, Lesson 2
Implement error handling.	Chapter 5, Lesson 1
Manage transactions.	Chapter 2, Lesson 3 Chapter 5, Lesson 1
WORKING WITH QUERY FUNDAMENTALS	
Query data by using SELECT statements.	Chapter 1, Lesson 2
Modify data by using INSERT, UPDATE, and DELETE statements.	Chapter 2, Lesson 1
Return data by using the OUTPUT clause.	Chapter 2, Lesson 2
Modify data by using MERGE statements.	Chapter 2, Lesson 2
Implement aggregate queries.	Chapter 1, Lesson 3
Combine datasets.	Chapter 1, Lesson 4
Apply built-in scalar functions.	Chapter 1, Lesson 5

OBJECTIVE	LOCATION IN BOOK
APPLYING ADDITIONAL QUERY TECHNIQUES	
Implement subqueries.	Chapter 4, Lesson 2
Implement CTE (common table expression) queries.	Chapter 4, Lesson 1
Apply ranking functions.	Chapter 4, Lesson 3
Control execution plans.	Chapter 6, Lesson 1
Manage international considerations.	Chapter 3, Lesson 1
WORKING WITH ADDITIONAL SQL SERVER COMPONENTS	
Integrate Database Mail.	Chapter 9, Lesson 1
Implement full-text search.	Chapter 8, Lesson 2
Implement scripts by using Windows PowerShell and SQL Server Management Objects (SMOs).	Chapter 9, Lesson 2
Implement Service Broker solutions.	Chapter 8, Lesson 3
Track data changes.	Chapter 9, Lesson 3
WORKING WITH XML DATA	
Retrieve relational data as XML.	Chapter 7, Lesson 1
Transform XML data into relational data.	Chapter 7, Lesson 1
Query XML data.	Chapter 7, Lesson 1
Manage XML data.	Chapter 7, Lesson 1
GATHERING PERFORMANCE INFORMATION	
Capture execution plans.	Chapter 6, Lesson 1
Gather trace information by using the SQL Server Profiler.	Chapter 6, Lesson 1
Collect output from the Database Engine Tuning Advisor.	Chapter 6, Lesson 2
Collect information from system metadata.	Chapter 6, Lesson 1 Chapter 6, Lesson 2

Exam Objectives The exam objectives listed here are current as of this book's publication date. Exam objectives are subject to change at any time without prior notice and at Microsoft's sole discretion. Please visit the Microsoft Learning Web site for the most current listing of exam objectives: *http://www.microsoft.com/learning/en/us/exams/70-433.mspx.*

Microsoft

MCTS Self-Paced Training Kit (Exam 70-433): Microsoft® SQL Server® 2008—Database Development

Tobias Thernström
Ann Weber
Mike Hotek
and Grand Masters

PUBLISHED BY
Microsoft Press
A Division of Microsoft Corporation
One Microsoft Way
Redmond, Washington 98052-6399

Library of Congress Control Number: 2009924965

Printed and bound in the United States of America.

3 4 5 6 7 8 9 10 11 12 QGT 5 4 3 2 1 0

Distributed in Canada by H.B. Fenn and Company Ltd.

A CIP catalogue record for this book is available from the British Library.

Microsoft Press books are available through booksellers and distributors worldwide. For further information about international editions, contact your local Microsoft Corporation office or contact Microsoft Press International directly at fax (425) 936-7329. Visit our Web site at www.microsoft.com/mspress. Send comments to tkinput@microsoft.com.

Acquisitions Editor: Ken Jones
Developmental Editor: Laura Sackerman
Project Editor: Melissa von Tschudi-Sutton
Editorial Production: S4Carlisle Publishing Services
Technical Reviewer: Kurt Meyer; Technical Review services provided by Content Master, a member of CM Group, Ltd.
Cover: Tom Draper Design

Body Part No. X15-52839

Contents at a Glance

Contents

What do you think of this book? We want to hear from you!

Microsoft is interested in hearing your feedback so we can continually improve our
books and learning resources for you. To participate in a brief online survey, please visit:

www.microsoft.com/learning/booksurvey/

Chapter 3 Tables, Data Types, and Declarative Data Integrity   81

Chapter 9   An Introduction to Microsoft SQL Server Manageability Features   373

Acknowledgments

Tobias Thernström

First of all, I want to thank my wife, Frida, for bearing with me while I worked on this book. I also want to thank the people at Microsoft Press for turning my Swenglish into English; I know it wasn't easy. I really enjoyed working with Ken, Melissa, Laura, and DeAnn, as well as our great technical reviewer, Kurt! I would also like to extend my thanks to the people at GrandMasters for helping put together the great team that made this book possible. Finally, to my great coauthors, Ann and Mike—without you, there would never have been a book. Thanks, guys. You rock!

Ann Weber

I would like to thank my family and friends for all of the support I received while working on this project. I would also like to thank Richard Kobylka and Lisa Kreissler for believing in me and providing me with this great opportunity. I would be remiss if I did not thank Mike Hotek for sharing the wisdom and knowledge he has gained while authoring many books. His helpfulness and sense of humor kept me going throughout the project. Finally, I would like to thank Laura Sackerman for making my first project with Microsoft Press an easy transition.

Mike Hotek

I'd like to thank all of our readers for your many years of support and encouragement. Thank you to my coauthors, Ann and Tobias—my small contribution wouldn't have made it out the door without all of the work that you put in. Thank you to Richard, DeAnn, and Kurt—your long hours and hard work transformed our technobabble into coherent English. It has been a pleasure working with Melissa, who spent countless hours herding cats to bring this book into being. Laura, this has been our third book together and, as always, it has been a pleasure. To the proverbial "man behind the curtain," Ken Jones—even when the train is barreling down the wrong track without a driver, it always manages to arrive at the right station, which is a testament to the invaluable time and effort you put into every Microsoft Press book.

Introduction

This training kit is designed for IT professionals who plan to take the Microsoft Certified Technology Specialist (MCTS) Exam 70 433, as well as database developers who need to know how to implement, query, and optimize databases using Microsoft SQL Server 2008. It's assumed that before using this training kit, you already have a working knowledge of Microsoft Windows and SQL Server 2008, or that you have experience with previous versions of SQL Server or another database platform.

By using this training kit, you will learn how to do the following:

- Create and manage database objects
- Query and modify data
- Optimize query performance
- Extend database functionality with full-text search, Service Broker, and SQL Server PowerShell
- Integrate Database Mail

Using the CD and DVD

A companion CD and an evaluation software DVD are included with this training kit. The companion CD contains the following:

- **Practice tests**   You can practice for the 70-433 certification exam by using tests created from a pool of about 200 realistic exam questions, which gives you enough different practice tests to ensure that you're prepared.

- **Practice files**   Not all exercises incorporate code, but for each exercise that does, there is one or more files in a folder for the corresponding chapter on the companion CD. You can either type the code from the book or open the corresponding code file in a query window.

- **eBook**   An electronic version (eBook) of this training kit is included for use at times when you don't want to carry the printed book with you. The eBook is in Portable Document Format (PDF), and you can view it by using Adobe Acrobat or Adobe Reader. You can use the eBook to cut and paste code as you read through the text or work through the exercises.

- **Sample chapters**   Sample chapters are included from other Microsoft Press titles on SQL Server 2008. These chapters are in PDF format.

- **Evaluation software**   The evaluation software DVD contains a 180-day evaluation edition of SQL Server 2008 in case you want to use it instead of the full version of SQL Server 2008 to complete the exercises in this book.

DIGITAL CONTENT FOR DIGITAL BOOK READERS

If you bought a digital-only edition of this book, you can enjoy select content from the print edition's companion CD. Visit **http://go.microsoft.com/fwlink/?LinkID=146933** to get your downloadable content. This content is always up-to-date and available to all readers.

How to Install the Sample Databases

CAUTION

Database names are unique within an instance of SQL Server. The sample databases are named *AdventureWorks2008, AdventureWorksDW2008,* and *Northwind.* If you already have databases with these names, you need to make changes to either the names of these sample databases or to the databases that already exist in your instance. If you make changes to the names, you also need to make the corresponding naming adjustments wherever a database name is referenced within this book.

To install the sample databases from the companion CD to your hard disk, perform the following steps:

1. Follow the instructions in the SQL Server Books Online article "How to: Enable FILESTREAM" at *http://msdn.microsoft.com/en-us/library/cc645923.aspx*.

2. Insert the companion CD into your CD-ROM drive.

3. Browse to the \Databases folder and then to the directory of your choice.

4. Copy the Northwind.mdf and Northwind.ldf files to C:\Program Files\Microsoft SQL Server\MSSQL10.MSSQLSERVER\MSSQL\DATA.

5. Copy the AdventureWorksDW2008_Data.mdf and AdventureWorksDW2008_Log.ldf files to C:\Program Files\Microsoft SQL Server\MSSQL10.MSSQLSERVER\MSSQL\DATA.

6. Copy the AdventureWorks2008_Data.mdf and AdventureWorks2008_Log.ldf files with the entire Documents folder to C:\Program Files\Microsoft SQL Server\ MSSQL10.MSSQLSERVER\MSSQL\DATA.

7. In SQL Server Management Studio connect to your SQL Server instance in an Object Explorer window.

8. Right-click the Databases node and select Attach.

9. Click Add, select AdventureWorks2008_Data.mdf, and click OK.

10. Click Add, select AdventureWorksDW2008_Data.mdf, and click OK.

11. Click Add, select Northwind.mdf, and click OK.

12. Click OK. Verify that you have the *AdventureWorks2008, AdventureWorksDW2008,* and *Northwind* databases attached to your instance.

How to Install the Practice Tests

To install the practice test software from the companion CD to your hard disk, perform the following steps:

1. Insert the companion CD into your CD-ROM drive and accept the license agreement that appears onscreen. The CD menu appears.

> **NOTE ALTERNATIVE INSTALLATION INSTRUCTIONS IF AUTORUN IS DISABLED**
>
> If the CD menu or the license agreement doesn't appear, AutoRun might be disabled on your computer. Refer to the Readme.txt file on the companion CD for alternative installation instructions.

2. Click Practice Tests and follow the instructions on the screen.

How to Use the Practice Tests

To start the practice test software, follow these steps:

1. Click Start and select All Programs, Microsoft Press Training Kit Exam Prep. A window appears that shows all the Microsoft Press training kit exam prep suites that are installed on your computer.

2. Double-click the practice test that you want to use.

Practice Test Options

When you start a practice test, you can choose whether to take the test in Certification Mode, Study Mode, or Custom Mode, which are as follows:

- **Certification Mode** Resembles closely the experience of taking a certification exam. The test has a set number of questions, it is timed, and you cannot pause and restart the timer.

- **Study Mode** Creates an untimed test in which you can review the correct answers and the explanations after you answer each question.

- **Custom Mode** Gives you full control over the test options so that you can customize them as you like.

In all modes, the user interface that you see when taking the test is basically the same, but different options are enabled or disabled, depending on the mode. When you review your answer to an individual practice test question, a "References" section is provided. This section lists the location in the training kit where you can find the information that relates to that question, and it provides links to other sources of information. After you click Test Results to score your entire practice test, you can click the Learning Plan tab to see a list of references for every objective.

How to Uninstall the Practice Tests

To uninstall the practice test software for a training kit, browse to Control Panel and use either the Add Or Remove Programs option (in Windows XP and Windows Server 2003) or the Programs And Features option (in Windows Vista and Windows Server 2008).

Microsoft Certified Professional Program

Microsoft certifications provide the best method to prove your command of current Microsoft products and technologies. The exams and corresponding certifications are developed to validate your mastery of critical competencies as you design and develop or implement and support solutions with Microsoft products and technologies. Computer professionals who become Microsoft-certified are recognized as experts and are sought after industry-wide. Certification brings a variety of benefits to the individual and to employers and organizations.

> **MORE INFO**   **LIST OF MICROSOFT CERTIFICATIONS**
>
> For a full list of Microsoft certifications, go to *http://www.microsoft.com/learning/mcp/default.mspx*.

Technical Support

Every effort has been made to ensure the accuracy of this book and the contents of the companion CD. If you have comments, questions, or ideas regarding this book or the companion CD, please send them to Microsoft Press by using either of the following methods:

E-mail:

• tkinput@microsoft.com

Postal Mail:

• *Microsoft Press*

Attn: MCTS Self-Paced Training Kit (Exam 70-433): Microsoft SQL Server 2008—Database Development, *Editor*

One Microsoft Way

Redmond, WA 98052-6399

For additional support information regarding this book and the companion CD (including answers to commonly asked questions about installation and use), visit the Microsoft Press Technical Support Web site at *http://www.microsoft.com/learning/support/books*. To connect directly to the Microsoft Knowledge Base and enter a query, visit *http://support.microsoft.com/search*. For support information regarding Microsoft software, please connect to *http://support.microsoft.com*.

Evaluation Edition Software

The 180-day evaluation edition provided with this training kit is not the full retail product and is provided only for the purposes of training and evaluation. Microsoft and Microsoft Technical Support do not support this evaluation edition.

Information about any issues relating to the use of this evaluation edition with this training kit is posted in the Support section of the Microsoft Press Web site (*http://www.microsoft.com/learning/support/books*). For information about ordering the full version of any Microsoft software, please call Microsoft Sales at (800) 426-9400 or visit *http://www.microsoft.com*.

CHAPTER 1

Data Retrieval

O ne of the primary functions that you need to perform on your Microsoft SQL Server databases is retrieving data. Because querying data is a fundamental function on databases, this book starts with coverage of this important topic. Data retrieval is accomplished by using the *SELECT* statement with a large variety of operators and clauses that expand on the functionality provided by a simple *SELECT* statement.

Exam objectives in this chapter:

- Query data by using *SELECT* statements.
- Implement aggregate queries.
- Combine datasets.
- Apply built-in scalar functions.

Lessons in this chapter:

Before You Begin

To complete the lessons in this chapter, you must have:

- A basic understanding of SQL Server data types
- A basic understanding of relational database concepts
- A basic understanding of object and schema naming standards, including multi-part names such as *Schema.Table*

- A general understanding of SQL programming concepts, such as batches, scripts, looping, and remarks.

- Knowledge about how to open and execute queries in SQL Server Management Studio (SSMS).

- Microsoft SQL Server 2008 Developer, Enterprise, or Enterprise Evaluation, with the *AdventureWorks2008*, *AdventureWorksDW2008*, and *Northwind* sample databases installed. You can download the *AdventureWorks2008* and *AdventureWorksDW2008* from the Codeplex Web site at *http://www.codeplex.com/ MSFTDBProdSamples/Release/ProjectReleases.aspx?ReleaseId=18407*. The Northwind database can currently be found at *http://www.microsoft.com/downloads/details .aspx?FamilyID=06616212-0356-46A0-8DA2-EEBC53A68034&displaylang=en*. For *Northwind*, the .msi file will simply extract the files to your hard drive. Use SSMS to attach the *Northwind* database.

> **NOTE** **SAMPLE DATABASE**
>
> Unless otherwise specified, the samples and practices in this chapter refer to the *AdventureWorks2008* database.

Lesson 1: Querying Data

The primary function of a database is to store data and provide access to that data. In the SQL programming language, the *SELECT* statement provides the data retrieval functionality.

> **After this lesson, you will be able to:**
> - Write basic *SELECT* statements.
> - Manipulate the query result set.
>
> **Estimated lesson time: 30 minutes**

SELECT Statement Syntax

The most basic *SELECT* statement must include at least a *SELECT* clause and a *FROM* clause. The most basic *SELECT* statement retrieves all columns and all rows from a table. The following code sample retrieves all rows and columns from the *Employee* table in the *HumanResources* schema.

```
SELECT * FROM HumanResources.Employee;
```

To narrow the result set and only return relevant columns, replace the asterisk (*) with the required column names, as in the code sample here:

```
SELECT LoginID, JobTitle, BirthDate
, MaritalStatus, Gender
FROM HumanResources.Employee;
```

> **BEST PRACTICES** **CODING BEST PRACTICE**
>
> When breaking lines for readability, it is a good idea to place commas at the beginning of the next line, rather than the end of the previous line, as shown in the preceding code sample. When you do this, you can remark out a line more easily for testing or troubleshooting. This practice also decreases the chances of parsing errors caused by missing or extra commas.

The default behavior of the *SELECT* statement is to return all rows in the table or all rows matching the *WHERE* clause. If you want to exclude rows that have exact duplications of the data, you can use *SELECT DISTINCT*. Figure 1-1 shows each distinct color that exists in the *Production.Product* table. Without the keyword *DISTINCT,* the color associated with every row from the table would be returned, increasing the size of the result set and making it more difficult to read.

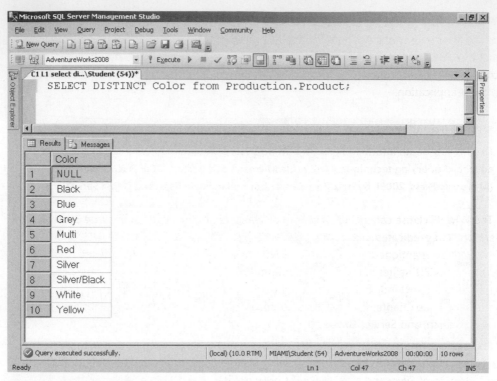

FIGURE 1-1 *SELECT DISTINCT* option

A *WHERE* clause can also be added to the *SELECT* statement to limit the rows that are returned. For example, if you want to view only colors and not see that there are *NULL* rows in the preceding sample, you can use the following code:

```
SELECT DISTINCT Color from Production.Product
WHERE Color IS NOT NULL;
```

> **NOTE WORKING WITH *NULL* VALUES**
>
> A *NULL* value is the absence of data in a column. When the *ANSI_NULLS* setting is set to *ON,* the default configuration, you cannot equate values to *NULL*. If you try, the server returns "unknown". For example, in the previous code, if you replaced "IS NOT" with "<>" , the query would not return any rows in a default configuration. If you executed the following commands together, you would get the same result set as the previous sample code:
>
> ```
> SET ANSI_NULLS OFF;
>
> SELECT DISTINCT Color from Production.Product
> WHERE Color <> NULL;
> ```

Defining a *WHERE* Clause

As shown in the previous example, the *WHERE* clause is used in most cases to limit the number of rows returned in the result set. Including well-written *WHERE* clauses typically increases query performance by limiting the amount of data that needs to be sent back to the client application.

> **MORE INFO**   **UNDERSTANDING QUERY PROCESSING AND PERFORMANCE**
>
> For more in-depth information about how SQL Server processes queries and about advanced querying techniques, see *Inside Microsoft SQL Server 2008: T-SQL Querying* (Microsoft Press, 2009), by Itzik Ben-Gan, Lubor Kollar, Steve Kass, and Dejan Sarka.

The *WHERE* clause can include a variety of search conditions that can include Boolean operators and predicates such as *LIKE , BETWEEN, EXISTS, IS NULL, IS NOT NULL,* and *CONTAINS*. As mentioned earlier, the *IS (IS NOT) NULL* clause returns rows based on the existence of *NULL* values in the named column. The *CONTAINS* clause is available only when you create a full text index on the column being compared. For more information about full text searches, see Chapter 8, "Extending Microsoft SQL Server Functionality with the Spatial, Full-Text Search, and Service Broker."

Boolean operators, which include *AND, OR,* and *NOT,* can be used to define more than one criterion in a *WHERE* clause. The following sample code returns only products that have a color attribute of *Silver* and also have a list price greater than $200:

```
SELECT * FROM Production.Product
WHERE Color = 'Silver' AND ListPrice > 200
```

The following sample assumes that the *Product* table includes newly added products that do not yet have a list price assigned to them. The following sample code includes *Silver* products with a price over $200, as well as the new *Silver* products with a list price of $0 (the default list price for new products added). If the parentheses were not added, the query would return *Silver* products with a price over $200 and all colors of products with a list price of $0 because of the order in which the conditions are evaluated, which is based on the Boolean order of operations:

```
SELECT * FROM Production.Product
WHERE Color = 'Silver'
   AND (ListPrice > 200 OR ListPrice = 0)
```

> **IMPORTANT**   **ORDER OF OPERATIONS**
>
> When the database engine parses and compiles a query, conditions that include Boolean operators are evaluated in the following order: *NOT, AND, OR*. This order of operations is important to understand because misunderstanding this can cause the query to return an unintended result set. You can use parentheses to control the order of operations.

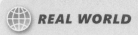

Using the *AND* operator typically results in a smaller result set, thus improving performance. The *NOT* operator typically hurts performance because the query optimizer cannot use indexes for the *WHERE* clause when a *NOT* operator is specified. For indexes to be utilized when an *OR* operator is specified, all columns referenced by the *OR* condition must be included in an index or none of the indexes are used.

The *LIKE* clause allows you to match a character string found in a column to a specified pattern in the *WHERE* clause. The *LIKE* clause uses the following wildcard characters:

- **Percent (%)**   Replaces any number of characters (including 0 characters) in the string. For example, *%at* would match *at, cat, hat,* and *that.*
- **Underscore(_)**   Replaces exactly one character in the string. For example, *_at* would match *cat* and *hat*, but it would not match *that* or *at.*
- **Square Brackets ([ ])**   Replaces any one character within a set or a range of characters. A set is frequently displayed as a straight list of characters, for example, *[abcd]*; but the characters can be separated by commas to add clarity, for example, *[a,b,c,d].* A range is separated by a dash, for example, *[a–d].* Each of these three options includes all rows where the specified character is an *a, b, c,* or *d.*
- **Caret (^)**   Any character not within a set or range of characters. For example, *[^a-d]* would be equal to *[e–z].*

NOTE **PERFORMANCE WITH LEADING WILDCARD CHARACTERS AND *NOT* LOGIC**

Neither leading wildcard characters nor *NOT* logic allow the query optimizer to use indexes to optimize the search. For optimal performance, you should avoid using the *NOT* keyword and leading wildcard symbols.

The following code sample returns all employees whose job title starts with the word *market*. Because we are using a case-insensitive database, capitalization is not considered as part of the search criteria:

```
SELECT BusinessEntityID, JobTitle
FROM HumanResources.Employee
WHERE JobTitle LIKE 'Market%';
```

To search for all employees where the word *market* appears anywhere in the job title, you would change the *LIKE* expression to '%Market%'.

The result set shown in Figure 1-2 contains all employees whose job titles start with the letter *C* or the letter *E*.

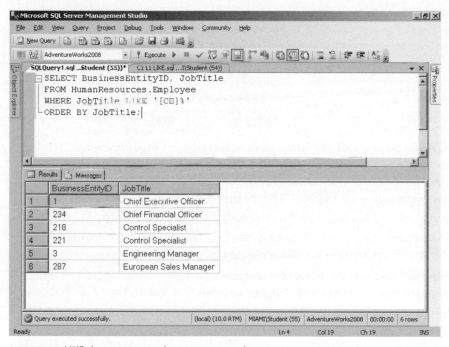

FIGURE 1-2 *LIKE* clause representing a set comparison

Figure 1-3 shows the same query, but it defines a range rather than a set and returns all employees whose job titles start with the letters *C*, *D*, or *E*.

The *BETWEEN* clause returns all rows based on a range of values. The following code sample returns all rows from the *Production.Product* table where the list price is between $50 and $80. Note that the list price can be used in the *WHERE* clause even though it is not listed in the *SELECT* clause:

```
SELECT ProductNumber, Name, Color
FROM Production.Product
WHERE ListPrice BETWEEN 50 AND 80
```

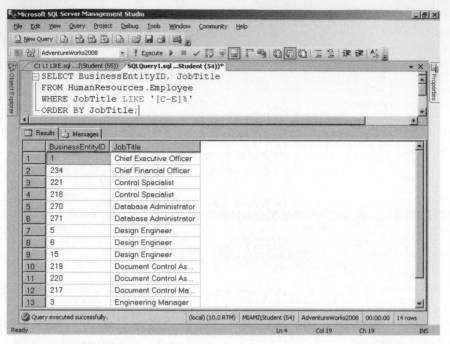

FIGURE 1-3 *LIKE* clause representing a range comparison

IMPORTANT **INCLUSIVE** *BETWEEN*

It is important to remember that the *BETWEEN* clause is inclusive of the outer values specified in the range. For example, *BETWEEN 1 AND 5* includes 1, 1.001, 1.11, and so on through 4.9, 4.99, and 5.0. This can sometimes be confusing when working with alphanumeric fields. If you are querying a book title column and you search *BETWEEN 'S' AND 'Z'*, all book titles starting with *S,* even if only the single letter *S,* are returned, but at the other end of the range, a book with a title of simply *Z* is returned, but *Zebras 101* is not returned.

The *EXISTS* clause defines a subquery to be used to determine if rows exist in the subquery result set.

MORE INFO **SUBQUERIES**

Subqueries are covered in detail in Chapter 4, "Using Additional Query Techniques."

Manipulating Result Sets

Although your organization is likely to use Reporting Services or other report-generating software to provide reports to users, you are still required to manipulate result sets to improve readability or programmability. You can accomplish this by incorporating aliases, string literals, and concatenation.

You can define a table alias to be used when it is not desirable to repeatedly type the table name throughout the query. In addition, table aliases may be required in certain commands such as self-joins. Self-joins are covered in Lesson 2 , "Joining Related Tables." You can also define an alias for a column so that the result set displays the new column name.

The following query uses both column aliases and a table alias:

```
SELECT PP.FirstName AS 'First Name', PP.LastName AS 'Last Name'
, PP.PersonType AS 'Person Category'
FROM Person.Person AS PP
ORDER BY PersonType
```

This query uses an additional clause that affects how the result set is displayed. The *ORDER BY* clause indicates one or more columns that should be used to sort the result set. The preceding query uses the default option of *ORDER BY ASC*, which orders the result set from the lowest to highest values. Sometimes, especially with numeric values, you might want to see the highest values first. When you want to see the highest values first, you would use the *ORDER BY DESC* clause. The sort order and collation defined for the column affect how the results are sorted.

> **MORE INFO** **COLLATIONS AND SORT ORDER**
>
> For more information about collations and sort orders, see Chapter 3, "Tables, Data Types, and Declarative Data Integrity."

When you define a select list, you can include expressions in the result set. You can define column titles for these expressions by using an alias. Concatenations allow you to combine multiple columns and string literals into a single column. The following example creates a single column out of the first and last name columns in the *Person* table. It also adds a space between the first and last name:

```
SELECT PP.FirstName + ' ' + PP.LastName AS 'Name', PP.PersonType AS 'Category'
FROM Person.Person AS PP
ORDER BY PersonType
```

> **NOTE** **EXPRESSION**
>
> When looking through SQL Server Books Online and other Transact-SQL (T-SQL) syntax help, you frequently see the term *expression*. In SQL Server Books Online, an expression is defined as "a combination of symbols and operators that evaluate to a single data value."

In the *Person* table, the *PersonType* column contains "EM" for employees. Figure 1-4 shows a command that builds off the command shown previously and adds a column spelling out *Employee* in a column titled *Description* for each row. The query also restricts the result set to rows containing a *PersonType* of "EM".

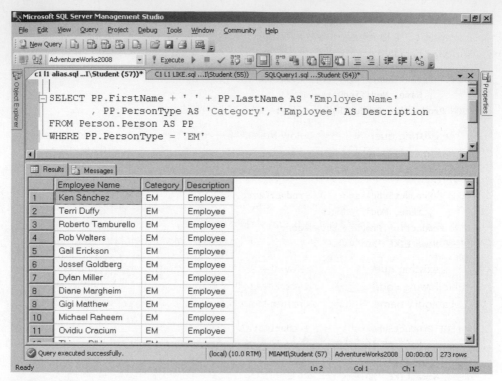

FIGURE 1-4 Using a string literal

PRACTICE **Querying Data**

In this practice session, you retrieve data from the *ProductSubcategory* table. You use the *WHERE* clause, the *LIKE* operator, and the *ORDER BY* clause to manipulate the result set.

EXERCISE Write a *SELECT* Statement

In this exercise, you write a basic *SELECT* statement that retrieves all rows and columns from the *ProductSubcategory* table. You then modify the statement to modify the result set returned.

1. If necessary, start SSMS, connect to your SQL Server instance, and open a new query window.

2. In the existing query window, type and execute the following code to specify the *AdventureWorks2008* database, and then return all rows and all columns in the *ProductSubcategory* table:

```
USE AdventureWorks2008;

SELECT * FROM Production.ProductSubcategory;
```

3. In the existing query window, below the existing code, type, highlight, and execute the following code to return only the *ProductSubcategoryID*, *ProductCategoryID*, *Name*, and *ModifiedDate* columns:

```
SELECT ProductSubcategoryID, ProductCategoryID
      , Name, ModifiedDate
FROM Production.ProductSubcategory;
```

4. In the existing query window, below the existing code, type, highlight, and execute the following code to return rows where the word *bike* is found somewhere in the *Name* column:

```
SELECT ProductSubcategoryID, ProductCategoryID
      , Name, ModifiedDate
FROM Production.ProductSubcategory
WHERE Name LIKE '%Bike%';
```

5. In the existing query window, below the existing code, type, highlight, and execute the following code to add a column alias to the *Name* column to clarify it as the subcategory name. Notice the change to the column title in the result set:

```
SELECT ProductSubcategoryID, ProductCategoryID
      , Name AS 'Subcategory Name', ModifiedDate
FROM Production.ProductSubcategory
WHERE Name LIKE '%Bike%';
```

6. In the existing query window, below the existing code, type, highlight, and execute the following code to sort the result set by the subcategory name:

```
SELECT ProductSubcategoryID, ProductCategoryID
      , Name AS 'Subcategory Name', ModifiedDate
FROM Production.ProductSubcategory
WHERE Name LIKE '%Bike%'
ORDER BY [Subcategory Name];
```

7. Save the script and close the query window.

8. Leave SSMS open for the next practice.

Lesson Summary

- The *SELECT* statement can be used to retrieve data from a table or view.
- The *SELECT* statement result set can be filtered by adding a *WHERE* clause.
- The *SELECT* statement result set can be sorted by using the *ORDER BY* clause.
- Concatenation, aliases, and string literals can be used to manipulate and format the result set.

Lesson 2: Joining Related Tables

With normalized databases, information required for a single result set may be located in two or more tables within the database.

> **After this lesson, you will be able to:**
>
> - Write queries that use the *INNER*, *OUTER*, *FULL*, and *CROSS JOIN* operators.
> - Explain the difference between the different *JOIN* operators.
>
> **Estimated lesson time: 45 minutes**

Using the *JOIN* Operator

The *JOIN* operator allows you to return data from columns stored in multiple related tables. Although actual relationships, implemented by creating *PRIMARY KEY* and *FOREIGN KEY* constraints, are not required, there does need to be at least one column in each of the tables that has the same meaning for the results to be meaningful.

If a column with the same column name exists in more than one table in the query, you must qualify the column with the table name when defining the select list or listing columns in the *WHERE* clause or other clauses within the *SELECT* statement. For example, the *Name* column exists in the *Production.Product*, *Production.Subcategory*, and *Production.Category* tables. If you write a query joining these tables and you want to include the *Name* columns in the select list or elsewhere in the query, you need to qualify them as *Production.Product* .*Name,* and so on. You can use table aliases to avoid lengthy code caused by long schema and object names. The following example shows the use of aliases:

```
SELECT FirstName, LastName, JobTitle, VacationHours, SickLeaveHours
FROM HumanResources.Employee E INNER JOIN Person.Person P
ON E.BusinessEntityID = P.BusinessEntityID;
```

When defining a *JOIN* condition, you need to define the tables to be joined, the join type, and a join condition, which is made up of the columns on which the tables are joined and the logical operator. *INNER JOIN* is the default join type when only the keyword *JOIN* is specified.

Defining Inner Joins

Inner joins return only the rows that match in the join condition. Although an inner join can be specified in either the *FROM* or the *WHERE* clause, it is recommended to specify the *JOIN* in the *FROM* clause. All samples and practices in this book follow this recommendation.

The following sample returns the employee's first and last name from the *Person.Person* table and their job title, sick hours, and vacation hours from the *HumanResources.Employee* table. Aliases are not used in this sample. Notice that the columns in the select list do not require qualification because they are unique across both tables. Because the column name *BusinessEntityID* is used in both tables, it must be qualified with a table name each time it is referenced:

```
SELECT FirstName, LastName, JobTitle, VacationHours, SickLeaveHours
FROM HumanResources.Employee INNER JOIN Person.Person
ON HumanResources.Employee.BusinessEntityID = Person.Person.BusinessEntityID;
```

Because an inner join was defined, rows from the *HumanResources.Employee* table that do not have a matching row in the *Person.Person* table are not returned. The reverse is also true, in that rows from the *Person.Person* table that are not matched in the *HumanResources .Employee* table are not returned. The way to overcome this behavior is to use an *OUTER JOIN* operator.

Defining Outer Joins

An outer join can be used to return all rows from one table and only information from rows that are in common from the other table, or it can return all rows from all tables in the *JOIN* clause. The word *OUTER* can be omitted from the syntax, but you must specify *LEFT, RIGHT,* or *FULL*.

The *LEFT* and *RIGHT* operators can be used to specify from which table all the rows are returned. When you specify *LEFT OUTER JOIN*, all rows are returned from the table to the left of the keyword *JOIN*. This table is referred to as the *outer table*. You can accomplish the same thing with either a *LEFT* or *RIGHT* operator by changing the order in which the table names are referenced. For example, the following sample code returns all rows from the *Person.Person* table, along with the corresponding information from the matching rows in the *HumanResources.Employee* table. Figure 1-5 shows the result set from this query. Notice the *NULL* values in the *JobTitle, VacationHours,* and *SickLeaveHours* columns from the *HumanResources.Employee* table. These values are not available for rows in the *Person.Person* table that do not have corresponding information in the *HumanResources.Employee* table. Because the *HumanResources.Employee* table does not allow *NULL* values for these columns, it is obvious which rows were added to the result set by changing the *INNER JOIN* to a *RIGHT OUTER JOIN*. If *NULL* values were allowed, you would not be able to use the presence of *NULL* values alone to determine which rows were added by changing the join type:

```
SELECT FirstName, LastName, JobTitle, VacationHours, SickLeaveHours
FROM HumanResources.Employee E RIGHT OUTER JOIN Person.Person P
ON E.BusinessEntityID = P.BusinessEntityID;
```

The same result set can be achieved by using a *LEFT OUTER JOIN* by reordering the table names, as in the following query:

```
SELECT FirstName, LastName, JobTitle, VacationHours, SickLeaveHours
FROM  Person.Person P LEFT OUTER JOIN HumanResources.Employee E
ON E.BusinessEntityID = P.BusinessEntityID;
```

Results | Messages

	FirstName	LastName	JobTitle	VacationHo...	SickLeaveHo...
1	Syed	Abbas	Pacific Sales Manager	20	30
2	Catherine	Abel	NULL	NULL	NULL
3	Kim	Abercrombie	NULL	NULL	NULL
4	Kim	Abercrombie	NULL	NULL	NULL
5	Kim	Abercrombie	Production Technician - WC60	24	32
6	Hazem	Abolrous	Quality Assurance Manager	80	60
7	Sam	Abolrous	NULL	NULL	NULL
8	Humberto	Acevedo	NULL	NULL	NULL
9	Gustavo	Achong	NULL	NULL	NULL
10	Pilar	Ackerman	NULL	NULL	NULL
11	Pilar	Ackerman	Shipping and Receiving Supervisor	93	66
12	Aaron	Adams	NULL	NULL	NULL
13	Adam	Adams	NULL	NULL	NULL

Query executed successfully. | (local) (10.0 RTM) | MIAMI\Student (54) | AdventureWorks2008 | 00:00:00 | 19972 rows

FIGURE 1-5 *RIGHT OUTER* result set

A *FULL OUTER JOIN* displays every row from every table in the *JOIN* clause. This can be helpful in finding unmatched rows when relational integrity is not being enforced on the tables. If there are foreign key constraints on the join column, a *FULL OUTER JOIN* provides the same result set as a *LEFT OUTER JOIN* with the table where the foreign key is defined on the left side of the *JOIN* keyword. This is because every value in the foreign key column must have a matching row in the primary key column for the constraint to be satisfied. In addition, when foreign key constraints are defined, an *OUTER JOIN* defined with the primary key table being defined as the outer table provides the same results as an *INNER JOIN*.

MORE INFO **CONSTRAINTS**

For more information about constraints, see Chapter 3.

Defining Cross Joins

Cross joins provide what is referred to as a Cartesian product of the two tables. Every row from the first table is joined with every row from the second table in the *JOIN* clause. There are only a few situations where this type of join is used. The *CROSS JOIN* syntax is the same as all the other join types.

Working with More Than Two Tables

You can join more than two tables to access the required columns for your query. A general performance recommendation is to try and avoid *JOIN* operations that include more than four or five tables. You should always test new *JOIN* statements, especially those containing a large number of tables or rows, on a nonproduction server to avoid problems caused by long-running, resource-intensive queries.

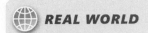

REAL WORLD

Ann Weber

I was working with a small group within a major university that offered technical classes to faculty, staff, and sometimes students of the university. They purchased a database application to manage their class schedule, including student enrollments, instructors, classrooms, and resources. The database created by the application was fully normalized and was locked so that modifications to the schema could not be made. The training coordinator wanted to write a query that would return the course number, course title, classroom assigned, instructor assigned, and the number of seats still available. To accomplish this, she needed to join 11 tables because of the structure of the database. Because she had the permissions required, she developed a Web-based application that included her *SELECT* statement joining 11 tables. Because of many factors, including limited resources on the server, additional overhead caused by the Web-based application, and locking contention that her query caused, there were many problems with several databases housed on this server while she ran her query. After this situation, she temporarily lost her privileges to write new queries directly against the production server. Luckily, shortly after this time, they upgraded their database to SQL Server 2005 and the company from which they purchased the database added permissions for them to create indexed views, which helped solve the 11-table join problem.

The most common type of *JOIN* operation involving more than two tables is an *INNER JOIN*. The following sample expands on the *INNER JOIN* sample from earlier in this lesson and adds an e-mail address from the *Person.EmailAddress* table:

```
SELECT FirstName, LastName, JobTitle, VacationHours, SickLeaveHours, EmailAddress
FROM HumanResources.Employee INNER JOIN Person.Person
    ON HumanResources.Employee.BusinessEntityID = Person.Person.BusinessEntityID
INNER JOIN Person.EmailAddress
    ON Person.Person.BusinessEntityID = Person.EmailAddress.BusinessEntityID
```

CAUTION **WORKING WITH MORE THAN TWO TABLES**

You need to be especially careful to verify result sets when working with the *OUTER JOIN* operator with more than two tables involved. The Database Engine builds temporary result sets from the first *JOIN* operation, and then uses that result set for the next *JOIN* operation. Depending on the order defined and the operators specified, you may get different results.

Defining a Self-Join

A *self-join* is when a single table is referenced more than once in the *JOIN* clause because it uses a different alias each time it refers to the table. There are two main situations when self-joins are beneficial. The first is when your database includes a self-referencing table.

The following sample from the *AdventureWorksDW2008* database displays each employee's name with his or her direct supervisor's name. The aliases ("E" for the reference to the employee information and "DS" to reference the direct supervisor information) were used to make the query easier to understand. The *ParentEmployeeKey* in each employee's record points to their direct supervisor's *EmployeeKey* field:

```
SELECT E.FirstName + ' ' + E.LastName AS 'Employee Name'
, DS.FirstName + ' ' + DS.LastName AS 'Direct Supervisor'
FROM DimEmployee E INNER JOIN DimEmployee DS
ON E.ParentEmployeeKey = DS.EmployeeKey;
```

Because this table includes multiple layers of supervisors, you could also use a common table expression (CTE) to build a recursive output.

> **MORE INFO** **COMMON TABLE EXPRESSIONS**
>
> For more information about CTE, see Chapter 4.

PRACTICE Joining Related Tables

In this practice session, you write queries that expand on the query developed in the Lesson 1 practice. The resulting query includes product, subcategory, and category names for products included in any subcategory that includes the word *bike*.

In addition, you write a query to join the *PurchaseOrderHeader* table to itself to provide a list of pairs of purchase orders. Each row includes two purchase orders that have identical vendors and shipping methods.

EXERCISE 1 Join Tables

In this exercise, you work with the *Product*, *ProductCategory*, and *ProductSubcategory* tables. You enhance this query so that it includes the product, subcategory, and category names of products in a subcategory that includes the word *bike*.

1. Open a new query window in SSMS.

2. In the existing query window, type and execute the following command to return information from the *ProductSubcategory* table, where the subcategory name includes the word *bike*:

```
USE AdventureWorks2008;
SELECT ProductSubcategoryID, ProductCategoryID
     , Name AS 'Subcategory Name'
FROM Production.ProductSubcategory
WHERE Name LIKE '%Bike%'
ORDER BY [Subcategory Name];
```

3. Notice that the result set includes a product category number but not a category name. In the existing query window, below the existing code, type, highlight, and execute the following code to join the *ProductCategory* table to the *ProductSubcategory* table to

retrieve the *Name* column from the *ProductCategory* table. You use an inner join because you are looking only for rows that are in common between the two tables:

```
SELECT ProductSubcategoryID, Production.ProductCategory.ProductCategoryID
      , Production.ProductSubcategory.Name AS 'Subcategory Name'
      , Production.ProductCategory.Name AS 'Category Name'
FROM Production.ProductSubcategory
INNER JOIN Production.ProductCategory
ON Production.ProductCategory.ProductCategoryID =
   Production.ProductSubcategory.ProductCategoryID
WHERE Production.ProductSubcategory.Name LIKE '%Bike%'
ORDER BY [Subcategory Name];
```

4. You now add in the *Product* table so that you can see what products exist in each of these subcategories. In the existing query window, below the existing code, type, highlight, and execute the following code to join the product table into the existing query:

```
SELECT P.ProductID AS 'Product ID'
      , PSC.ProductSubcategoryID AS 'Subcategory ID'
      , PC.ProductCategoryID AS 'Category ID'
      , P.Name AS 'Product Name'
      , PSC.Name AS 'Subcategory Name'
      , PC.Name AS 'Category Name'
FROM Production.ProductSubcategory AS PSC
INNER JOIN Production.ProductCategory AS PC
ON PC.ProductCategoryID = PSC.ProductCategoryID
INNER JOIN Production.Product AS P
ON P.ProductSubcategoryID = PSC.ProductSubcategoryID
WHERE PSC.Name LIKE '%Bike%'
ORDER BY [Subcategory Name];
```

Again, you use an inner join because only rows in common between the three tables need to be retrieved. In addition, because the schema and table names are long and are making the code difficult to read, you add table aliases to the query and reference the columns with the alias name.

EXERCISE 2 Perform a Self-Join

In this exercise, you build a query that returns unique pairs of purchase orders that have the same vendor and shipping method. The report should not include the same pair of purchase order IDs more than once.

1. Open a new query window.

2. In the existing query window, type and execute the following command to return pairs of purchase orders that have the same vendor and shipping method:

```
USE AdventureWorks2008;
SELECT a.PurchaseOrderID
      , b.PurchaseOrderID
```

```
        , a.VendorID
        , a.ShipMethodID
FROM Purchasing.PurchaseOrderHeader AS a
JOIN Purchasing.PurchaseOrderHeader AS b
ON a.VendorID = b.VendorID
   AND a.ShipMethodID = b.ShipMethodID
WHERE a.PurchaseOrderID < b.PurchaseOrderID;
```

3. In the existing query window, below the existing code, type, highlight, and execute the following code to make the result set easier to read by replacing the vendor IDs and shipping method IDs with their names:

```
SELECT a.PurchaseOrderID
       , b.PurchaseOrderID
       , v.Name
       , s.Name
FROM Purchasing.PurchaseOrderHeader AS a
JOIN Purchasing.PurchaseOrderHeader AS b
  ON a.VendorID = b.VendorID
    AND a.ShipMethodID = b.ShipMethodID
JOIN Purchasing.Vendor AS v
  ON a.VendorID = v.BusinessEntityID
JOIN Purchasing.ShipMethod AS s
  ON a.ShipMethodID = s.ShipMethodID
WHERE a.PurchaseOrderID < b.PurchaseOrderID;
```

4. Save the script and close the query window. Leave SSMS open for the next practice.

Lesson Summary

- The *JOIN* clause allows you to retrieve columns from related tables and group the results into a single result set.
- *JOIN* types include *INNER*, *LEFT OUTER*, *RIGHT OUTER*, *FULL OUTER*, and *CROSS*.
- *JOIN* operators can combine more than two tables.
- A table can be joined to itself by defining different aliases for each reference to the table.

Lesson 3: Implementing Aggregate Queries

Aggregate functions allow you to apply calculations on values in a column. Adding the *GROUP BY* clause allows you to provide aggregate on subsets of the data.

> **After this lesson, you will be able to:**
> - Describe the purpose of the aggregate functions available.
> - Group aggregate data by using the *GROUP BY* statement.
>
> **Estimated lesson time: 45 minutes**

Working with Aggregate Functions

Aggregate functions perform calculations on a set of data and return a scalar (single) value. The following aggregate functions are available in SQL Server 2008:

- **AVG**   Returns the average of all values in the data set.
- **CHECKSUM_AGG**   Returns the checksum of all values in the data set.
- **COUNT**   Returns the number of values contained in the data set. *COUNT(*)* returns the number of rows in the set. When a column is specified, such as *COUNT(FaxNo)*, the value returned reflects the number of rows that contain data in that column. *NULL* values are ignored. In addition, *COUNT DISTINCT* returns the number of unique non-*NULL* values in the data set.
- **COUNT_BIG**   Works the same as *COUNT*, but it returns the *bigint* data type, while *COUNT* returns only the *int* data type.
- **GROUPING**   Returns 1 or 0 and identifies rows as aggregate or detail rows when the *GROUP BY* statement is used. A value of 1 indicates an aggregate row, while 0 indicates details.
- **MAX**   Returns the highest value in the data set for numeric, data, and character-based fields.
- **MIN**   Returns the lowest value in the data set for numeric, data, and character-based fields.
- **SUM**   Returns the total of the values in the data set. You can specify *ALL* or *DISTINCT* to produce either the sum of all values or only distinct values in the data set.
- **STDEV**   Returns the statistical standard deviation of the values in the data set.
- **STDEVP**   Returns the statistical standard deviation for the population of the values in the data set.
- **VAR**   Returns the statistical variance of the values in the data set.
- **VARP**   Returns the statistical variance for the population of the values in the data set.

NULL values are ignored for all the aggregate functions. It is important to understand this so that you can verify the data is being properly interpreted. For example, in a table that maintains test scores, there is a big difference between *NULL* and 0 when you use the *AVG* or *MIN* aggregates. If the test is excused and should not be included in the calculation, the *NULL* value does not have a negative impact on the accuracy of the calculation, but if the test should be averaged in, the database integrity checks should make sure that 0 is entered rather than *NULL*.

The following sample returns the average, maximum, and minimum list prices of all products in the *Production.Product* table. Products that are either new and have not been priced or that are not sold to consumers have a list price of 0. To provide more accurate aggregates, these products are removed from the result set:

```
SELECT AVG(Listprice) AS 'Average'
      , MIN(Listprice) AS 'Minimum'
      , MAX(Listprice) AS 'Maximum'
FROM Production.Product
WHERE ListPrice <> 0;
```

Using the *GROUP BY* Clause

Frequently, the *GROUP BY* clause is included in queries with aggregate functions. When an aggregate function is included in the *SELECT* clause, all other expressions in the *SELECT* clause must either be aggregate functions or included in a *GROUP BY* clause.

The *GROUP BY* clause allows you to define subtotals for the aggregate data. For example, the following command returns the average, minimum, and maximum list prices for products that belong to each product subcategory:

```
SELECT Production.Product.ProductSubcategoryID
      , AVG(Listprice) AS 'Average'
      , MIN(Listprice) AS 'Minimum'
      , MAX(Listprice) AS 'Maximum'
FROM Production.Product
WHERE ListPrice <> 0
GROUP BY Product.ProductSubcategoryID;
```

The result set for the preceding query is shown in Figure 1-6. The top row, where the *ProductSubcategoryID* is listed as *NULL*, is the summary row that provides the average, minimum, and maximum list prices of products without a *ProductSubcategoryID*.

Using the *WITH ROLLUP* and *WITH CUBE* Operators

To be able to see subtotals for more than one column, you can add the *WITH ROLLUP* or *WITH CUBE* operator. These operators provide a grand total, along with subtotals based on the columns included in the *GROUP BY* statement. The order in which the columns are specified changes the summary data returned in the result set for the *WITH ROLLUP* function.

	ProductSubcategor...	Average	Minimum	Maximum
1	NULL	159.1333	133.34	196.92
2	1	1683.365	539.99	3399.99
3	2	1597.45	539.99	3578.27
4	3	1425.2481	742.35	2384.07
5	4	73.89	44.54	120.27
6	5	92.24	53.99	121.49
7	6	106.50	106.50	106.50
8	7	20.24	20.24	20.24
9	8	278.99	175.49	404.99
10	0	106.475	91.49	121.46
11	10	184.40	148.22	229.49
12	11	87.0733	34.20	124.73
13	12	678.2535	249.79	1364.50
14	13	64.0185	40.49	80.99
15	14	780.0436	337.22	1431.50
16	15	39.6333	27.12	52.64

Query executed successfully.   (local) (10.0 RTM) MIAMI\Student (56) AdventureWorks2008 00:00:00 38 rows

FIGURE 1-6 Basic *GROUP BY* sample result set

For example, the query shown here returns the average, minimum, and maximum list prices for each subcategory within each category. Because both the subcategory and category ID columns are listed in the *SELECT* clause, they must both be listed in the *GROUP BY* clause as well. Because the *Production.ProductCategory.ProductCategoryID* column is listed first in the *GROUP BY* statement, a summary row is included that shows the specified aggregates for all subcategories in that category together. If the *Product.ProductSubcategoryID* column had been listed first, the summary rows would return the aggregate values across all categories for each subcategory. In the sample data, each subcategory is related to only one category, minimizing the usefulness of this particular result set:

```
SELECT Production.ProductCategory.ProductCategoryID
      , Production.Product.ProductSubcategoryID
      , AVG(Listprice) AS 'Average'
      , MIN(Listprice) AS 'Minimum'
      , MAX(Listprice) AS 'Maximum'
FROM Production.Product
JOIN Production.ProductSubcategory
ON Production.ProductSubcategory.ProductSubcategoryID =
   Production.Product.ProductSubcategoryID
JOIN Production.ProductCategory
ON Production.ProductSubcategory.ProductCategoryID =
   Production.ProductCategory.ProductCategoryID
WHERE ListPrice <> 0
GROUP BY Production.ProductCategory.ProductCategoryID, Product.ProductSubcategoryID
WITH ROLLUP
```

The partial result set pictured in Figure 1-7 shows the average, minimum, and maximum prices for product subcategory 25 in the first row pictured (row 27). The average, minimum, and maximum prices for category 3 are listed in row 28 and are signified by the *NULL* value

	ProductCategoryID	ProductSubcategor...	Average	Minimum	Maximum
27	3	25	63.50	63.50	63.50
28	3	NULL	50.9914	8.99	89.99
29	4	26	120.00	120.00	120.00
30	4	27	159.00	159.00	159.00
31	4	28	7.99	4.99	9.99
32	4	29	7.95	7.95	7.95
33	4	30	21.98	21.98	21.98
34	4	31	34.99	34.99	34.99
35	4	32	54.99	54.99	54.99
36	4	33	31.3233	13.99	44.99
37	4	34	25.00	25.00	25.00
38	4	35	125.00	125.00	125.00
39	4	36	22.49	19.99	24.99
40	4	37	19.4827	2.29	35.00
41	4	NULL	34.3489	2.29	159.00
42	NULL	NULL	744.5952	2.29	3578.27

Query executed successfully.   (local) (10.0 RTM)   MIAMI\Student (59)   AdventureWorks2008   00:00:00   42 rows

FIGURE 1-7 *GROUP BY* results with the *WITH ROLLUP* operator

listed for the *ProductSubcateogryID* column. The average, minimum, and maximum prices across all categories and subcategories are listed in row 42 and are signified by the *NULL* values in both the *ProductCategoryID* and the *ProductSubcategoryID* columns. If the *WITH ROLLUP* operator had not been specified, the summary rows found in rows 28 and 41 would not have been included in the result set.

> **NOTE   CHECKSUM_AGG COMPATIBILITY**
>
> The *CHECKSUM_AGG* aggregate function is not compatible with *ROLLUP, CUBE,* or *GROUPING SETS*.

The *WITH CUBE* operator can be used when summary information needs to be included for more than one column. Because each subcategory exists in only one category, the *WITH CUBE* operator does not make sense with this sample. But if I were listing the average price for each product on a particular order and from within each subcategory, I could use the *WITH CUBE* operator to return the summary information based on each order ID and on each subcategory ID. I would also get the grand total row included in the result set.

> **BEST PRACTICES   ENHANCING *GROUP BY* PERFORMANCE**
>
> Avoid using the *WITH CUBE* operator on large tables where more than three columns exist in the *GROUP BY* clause. The *WITH CUBE* operator returns summary information for every column listed in the *GROUP BY* clause. These result sets can grow very quickly when additional columns are added to the *GROUP BY* clause and may slow performance drastically.

Using the *GROUPING* Aggregate Function

When there are *NULL* values appearing in a column being returned by the *GROUP BY* clause, it can be difficult to find and interpret the summary rows produced. The *GROUPING* aggregate function can be added to the *SELECT* clause to show which rows hold summary information and which rows hold detail information that may include *NULL* values. The *GROUPING* aggregate function returns a 1, which indicates an aggregate or summary row, or a 0, which indicates a detail row.

Although these result sets can become overwhelming and difficult to read, if the results are being further processed by an application, an application can easily use the 1s and 0s returned to determine which rows include summary data and then perform the appropriate operations.

The following sample includes *GROUPING* columns with the *ROLLUP* query used in the previous sample. Note that in the partial result set shown in Figure 1-8, summary data is not included for all product categories in a subcategory. Either the columns in the *GROUP BY* clause would need to be reversed, or the *WITH CUBE* operator would need to be specified for summary data to appear in this column:

```
SELECT Production.ProductCategory.ProductCategoryID
      ,GROUPING (Production.ProductCategory.ProductCategoryID)
      , Production.Product.ProductSubcategoryID
      ,GROUPING (Production.Product.ProductSubcategoryID)
      , AVG(Listprice) AS 'Average'
      , MIN(Listprice) AS 'Minimum'
      , MAX(Listprice) AS 'Maximum'
FROM Production.Product
JOIN Production.ProductSubcategory
ON Production.ProductSubcategory.ProductSubcategoryID =
    Production.Product.ProductSubcategoryID
JOIN Production.ProductCategory
ON Production.ProductSubcategory.ProductCategoryID =
    Production.ProductCategory.ProductCategoryID
WHERE ListPrice <> 0
GROUP BY Production.ProductCategory.ProductCategoryID, Product.ProductSubcategoryID
WITH ROLLUP;
```

	ProductCategoryID	(No column na...	ProductSubcategor...	(No column na...	Average	Minimum	M
26	3	0	24	0	74.99	74.99	
27	3	0	25	0	63.50	63.50	
28	3	0	NULL	1	50.9914	8.99	
29	4	0	26	0	120.00	120.00	
30	4	0	27	0	159.00	159.00	
31	4	0	28	0	7.99	4.99	
32	4	0	29	0	7.95	7.95	
33	4	0	30	0	21.98	21.98	
34	4	0	31	0	34.99	34.99	
35	4	0	32	0	54.99	54.99	
36	4	0	33	0	31.3233	13.99	
37	4	0	34	0	25.00	25.00	
38	4	0	35	0	125.00	125.00	
39	4	0	36	0	22.49	19.99	
40	4	0	37	0	19.4827	2.29	
41	4	0	NULL	1	34.3489	2.29	
42	NULL	1	NULL	1	744.5952	2.29	

Query executed successfully. (local) (10.0 RTM) MIAMI\Student (55) AdventureWorks2008 00:00:00 42 rows

FIGURE 1-8 Results with the *GROUPING* function added

Using *GROUPING SETS*

GROUPING SETS were added in SQL Server 2008 to give you greater flexibility when defining *SELECT* statements that include aggregate functions. Depending on how the *GROUPING SETS* are defined, they can be equivalent to a standard *ROLLUP* or *CUBE* operation, to several *GROUP BY* operations combined with the *UNION ALL* operator, or a subset of the data that would typically be returned by a *ROLLUP* or *CUBE* operator.

> **MORE INFO** *GROUPING SETS* EQUIVALENTS
>
> For a complete list of commands that are equivalent to different combinations of *GROUPING SETS*, see "GROUPING SETS Equivalents," in SQL Server Books Online.

GROUPING SETS Samples

The samples in this section provide you with an idea of some of the options available when defining *GROUPING SETS*.

The following sample includes two separate queries that produce identical result sets, but the *GROUPING SETS* query shown first is much cleaner and easier to read. The remark between the queries has been made bold to make the second query (noted as the Equivalent code) easier to locate:

```
SELECT Production.ProductCategory.ProductCategoryID
     , Production.Product.ProductSubcategoryID
     , AVG(Listprice) AS 'Average'
FROM Production.Product
JOIN Production.ProductSubcategory
ON Production.ProductSubcategory.ProductSubcategoryID =
   Production.Product.ProductSubcategoryID
JOIN Production.ProductCategory
ON Production.ProductSubcategory.ProductCategoryID =
   Production.ProductCategory.ProductCategoryID
WHERE ListPrice <> 0
GROUP BY GROUPING SETS ((Production.ProductCategory.ProductCategoryID),
   (Product.ProductSubcategoryID))

--Equivalent code
SELECT NULL AS 'ProductCategoryID', Production.Product.ProductSubcategoryID
     , AVG(Listprice) AS 'Average'
FROM Production.Product
JOIN Production.ProductSubcategory
ON Production.ProductSubcategory.ProductSubcategoryID =
   Production.Product.ProductSubcategoryID
JOIN Production.ProductCategory
ON Production.ProductSubcategory.ProductCategoryID =
   Production.ProductCategory.ProductCategoryID
```

```
WHERE ListPrice <> 0
GROUP BY (Production.Product.ProductSubcategoryID)
UNION ALL
SELECT Production.ProductCategory.ProductCategoryID, NULL
      , AVG(Listprice) AS 'Average'
FROM Production.Product
JOIN Production.ProductSubcategory
ON Production.ProductSubcategory.ProductSubcategoryID =
   Production.Product.ProductSubcategoryID
JOIN Production.ProductCategory
ON Production.ProductSubcategory.ProductCategoryID =
   Production.ProductCategory.ProductCategoryID
WHERE ListPrice <> 0
GROUP BY (Production.ProductCategory.ProductCategoryID)
```

The partial result set produced by either of these two commands is displayed in Figure 1-9.

	ProductCategoryID	ProductSubcategor...	Average
26	NULL	26	120.00
27	NULL	27	159.00
28	NULL	28	7.99
29	NULL	29	7.95
30	NULL	30	21.98
31	NULL	31	34.99
32	NULL	32	54.99
33	NULL	33	31.3233
34	NULL	34	25.00
35	NULL	35	125.00
36	NULL	36	22.49
37	NULL	37	19.4827
38	1	NULL	1586.737
39	2	NULL	469.8602
40	3	NULL	50.9914
41	4	NULL	34.3489

Query executed successfully. (local) (10.0 RTM) MIAMI\Student (54) AdventureWorks2008 00:00:00 41 rows

FIGURE 1-9 Sample *GROUPING SETS* results

> **NOTE UNION ALL OPERATOR**
>
> A full description of the *UNION ALL* operator is located in Lesson 4, "Combining Datasets."

The next sample provides the same result set as the previous one, but it also adds a rollup row that produces the summary of both columns:

```
SELECT Production.ProductCategory.ProductCategoryID
     , Production.Product.ProductSubcategoryID
     , AVG(Listprice) AS 'Average'
```

```
FROM Production.Product
JOIN Production.ProductSubcategory
ON Production.ProductSubcategory.ProductSubcategoryID =
    Production.Product.ProductSubcategoryID
JOIN Production.ProductCategory
ON Production.ProductSubcategory.ProductCategoryID =
    Production.ProductCategory.ProductCategoryID
WHERE ListPrice <> 0
GROUP BY GROUPING SETS (ROLLUP(Production.ProductCategory.ProductCategoryID),
    (Product.ProductSubcategoryID));
```

The partial result set displayed in Figure 1-10 shows the new rollup row on row 38.

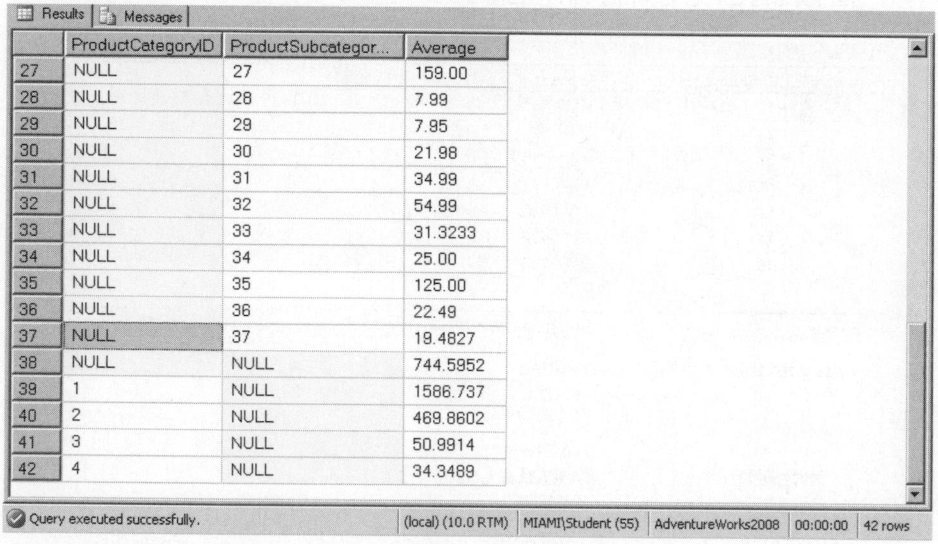

FIGURE 1-10 Sample *GROUPING SETS* with a *ROLLUP* result set

Using the *HAVING* Clause

Although you can still use *WHERE* clauses to limit the result set based on values that exist in the columns specified in the *FROM* clause, the *HAVING* clause allows you to filter based on the results of the calculations performed by the aggregate functions.

The following query uses a *HAVING* clause that returns only product subcategories where the minimum price is greater than $200:

```
SELECT Production.ProductCategory.ProductCategoryID
    , Production.Product.ProductSubcategoryID
    , AVG(Listprice) AS 'Average'
    , MIN(Listprice) AS 'Minimum'
    , MAX(Listprice) AS 'Maximum'
```

```
FROM Production.Product
JOIN Production.ProductSubcategory
ON Production.ProductSubcategory.ProductSubcategoryID =
    Production.Product.ProductSubcategoryID
JOIN Production.ProductCategory
ON Production.ProductSubcategory.ProductCategoryID =
    Production.ProductCategory.ProductCategoryID
WHERE ListPrice <> 0
GROUP BY Production.ProductCategory.ProductCategoryID, Product.ProductSubcategoryID
WITH ROLLUP
HAVING MIN(ListPrice) > 200;
```

The result set for this query is shown in Figure 1-11.

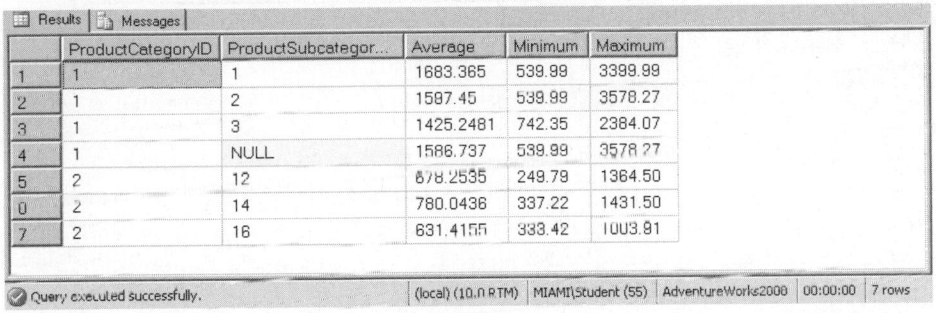

	ProductCategoryID	ProductSubcategor...	Average	Minimum	Maximum
1	1	1	1683.365	539.99	3399.99
2	1	2	1597.45	539.99	3578.27
3	1	3	1425.2481	742.35	2384.07
4	1	NULL	1586.737	539.99	3578.27
5	2	12	878.2535	249.79	1364.50
6	2	14	780.0436	337.22	1431.50
7	2	16	631.4155	333.42	1003.81

Query executed successfully.   (local) (10.0 RTM) | MIAMI\Student (55) | AdventureWorks2008 | 00:00:00 | 7 rows

FIGURE 1-11 Results with the *HAVING* clause added

PRACTICE   **Implementing Aggregate Queries**

In this practice session, you create aggregate queries that progress from returning the results of a system aggregate function to returning aggregates grouped by a variety of columns and including *GROUPING SETS*.

EXERCISE   Use the *GROUP BY* Statement

In this exercise, you use aggregate functions and the *GROUP BY* clause with a variety of operators, such as *ROLLUP* and *HAVING*, that provide summary and detail information in the result set.

1. Open a new query window in SSMS.

2. In the existing query window, type and execute the following code to return the grand total of all products ordered on all lines of all sales orders:

```
USE AdventureWorks2008;
SELECT SUM(LineTotal) FROM Sales.SalesOrderDetail;
```

3. In the existing query window, below the existing code, type, highlight, and execute the following code to return the total list price for each combination of sales order IDs and product IDs. Then, review the result set.

```
SELECT SalesOrderID, ProductID, SUM(Linetotal) AS 'Total'
FROM Sales.SalesOrderDetail
GROUP BY SalesOrderID, ProductID
ORDER BY SalesOrderID;
```

4. In the existing query window, below the existing code, type, highlight, and execute the following code to provide a grand total, as well as a subtotal of all products on each sales order. Then, review the result set:

```
SELECT SalesOrderID, ProductID, SUM(Linetotal) AS 'Total'
FROM Sales.SalesOrderDetail
GROUP BY SalesOrderID, ProductID
WITH ROLLUP
ORDER BY SalesOrderID;
```

5. In the existing query window, below the existing code, type, highlight, and execute the following code to reverse the order of the columns listed in the *GROUP BY* clause and provide the subtotal of each product across all sales orders and a grand total. The sort order has been changed to make the results easier to review. After executing the query, review the result set:

```
SELECT SalesOrderID, ProductID, SUM(Linetotal) AS 'Total'
FROM Sales.SalesOrderDetail
GROUP BY ProductID, SalesOrderID
WITH ROLLUP
ORDER BY ProductID;
```

6. In the existing query window, below the existing code, type, highlight, and execute the following code to provide subtotal information on both the sales order IDs and the product IDs. Review the result set:

```
SELECT SalesOrderID, ProductID, SUM(Linetotal) AS 'Total'
FROM Sales.SalesOrderDetail
GROUP BY ProductID, SalesOrderID
WITH CUBE
ORDER BY SalesOrderID, ProductID;
```

7. In the existing query window, below the existing code, type, highlight, and execute the following code to limit the result set to line totals that exceed 10,000. Review the results:

```
SELECT SalesOrderID, ProductID, SUM(Linetotal) AS 'Total'
FROM Sales.SalesOrderDetail
GROUP BY ProductID, SalesOrderID
```

```
WITH CUBE
HAVING SUM(Linetotal) > 10000
ORDER BY SalesOrderID, ProductID;
```

8. In the existing query window, below the existing code, type, highlight, and execute the following code to create a grouping set on the *SalesOrderID* and *ProductID* columns without any rollup operations. Review the result set:

```
SELECT SalesOrderID, ProductID, SUM(Linetotal) AS 'Total'
FROM Sales.SalesOrderDetail
GROUP BY GROUPING SETS (ProductID, SalesOrderID )
ORDER BY SalesOrderID, ProductID
```

9. Save the script and close the query window, but leave SSMS open for the next practice.

Lesson Summary

- Aggregate functions perform calculations on expressions that are provided as input to the function.
- Use the *GROUP BY* clause when aggregates should be applied based on the data in specific rows rather than the entire table.
- Include all columns listed in a *SELECT, WHERE*, or *ORDER BY* clause in the *GROUP BY* clause.
- Use *ROLLUP* and *CUBE* to provide additional summary information.
- Use the *GROUPING* function to show which rows hold summary data provided by the *ROLLUP* or *CUBE* operators.
- Use *GROUPING SETS* to provide greater flexibility and readability to your *GROUP BY* queries.

Lesson 4: Combining Datasets

SQL Server 2008 provides several operators that provide you with the ability to combine or compare the results from multiple *SELECT* statements. The *UNION* operator has been available from the first version of SQL Server to provide the ability to combine the result sets from multiple queries. On the other hand, the *EXCEPT* and *INTERSECT* operators were introduced in SQL Server 2005 to provide the ability to compare the results from two queries and provide a new result set based on whether or not there are rows in common between the result sets.

In addition, datasets can be manipulated by using the *APPLY* operator to apply a table-valued function against each row of the query results from what is defined as the outer table.

> **NOTE USER-DEFINED FUNCTIONS**
>
> SQL Server 2008 provides you with the ability to create user-defined functions (UDFs). Scalar functions return a single value of a specified data type, while inline table-valued functions and multi-statement table-valued functions return a table data type. For more information, see Chapter 5, "Programming Microsoft SQL Server with T-SQL User-Defined Stored Procedures, Functions, Triggers, and Views."

> **After this lesson, you will be able to:**
> - Write queries that use the *UNION* operator to combine result sets.
> - Write queries that use the *EXCEPT* and *INTERSECT* operators to compare the results from multiple queries.
>
> **Estimated lesson time: 30 minutes**

The *UNION*, *EXCEPT*, and *INTERSECT* operators can be specified between two or more queries to provide a single result set. While the *UNION* operator combines the result sets from the multiple queries into a single result set, the *EXCEPT* and *INTERSECT* operators compare the result sets of two queries to determine what subset of rows should be included in the final result set.

Using the *UNION* Operator

The *UNION* operator allows you to combine the result sets created by multiple *SELECT* statements into a single result set. Although the syntax for the *UNION* operator is straightforward (you add the word *UNION* or *UNION ALL* between each *SELECT* statement), you must follow some basic rules if you want the query to succeed. When specifying the *UNION* operator, both queries must return the same number of columns. In addition, each data type in the corresponding columns must be compatible. For example, if the first column in one *SELECT* statement has an *integer* data type and the first column of the second *SELECT* statement has a *character* data type, the integer field must be converted for the command to succeed.

In the *Northwind* database, customers have an alphanumeric customer ID field and employees have a numeric ID field. If you want to retrieve these columns as a single result set, the *EmployeeID* field would need to be converted, as in this sample query:

```
SELECT CONVERT(Char(8),Employees.EmployeeID) FROM Employees
UNION
SELECT Customers.CustomerID FROM Customers
```

In addition to the rules listed previously, there are some other rules that you should be aware of. First, the column titles are taken from the first query listed. Therefore, you should define aliases in the first *SELECT* statement. In addition, *ORDER BY* clauses should be defined at the end of the last *SELECT* statement. The *ORDER BY* clause can refer to aliases defined in the first *SELECT* statement. Finally, if rows should be filtered, each *SELECT* statement should include its own *WHERE* clause.

The *ALL* keyword specifies that all rows, including duplicate rows, should be returned. By default, duplicate rows are not returned.

The next example also uses the *Employees* and *Customers* tables from the *Northwind* database to create a single result set that merges customers and employees into a single result set containing a name, company name, and phone number:

```
SELECT FirstName + ' ' + LastName AS 'Contact Name'
       , 'Northwind Traders' AS 'Company'
       , Employees.HomePhone AS 'Phone'
FROM Employees
UNION
SELECT ContactName, CompanyName, Phone
FROM Customers
ORDER BY 'Contact Name';
```

Using the *EXCEPT* and *INTERSECT* Commands

Unlike the *UNION* operator, which returns a combination of the rows from various *SELECT* statements, the *EXCEPT* and *INTERSECT* operators compare the result sets from two separate queries and provide a subset of the information.

The *EXCEPT* operator returns all rows that exist in the table to the left of the operator and that do not have matching rows in the table to the right. In the following example from the *AdventureWorksDW2008* database, employees who have never placed a reseller sales order are listed in the result set:

```
SELECT EmployeeKey
FROM DimEmployee
EXCEPT
SELECT EmployeeKey
FROM FactResellerSales
```

Like the *UNION* statement, the same number of columns with compatible data types must be defined in both queries. To accomplish this, you can join the tables and use the *EXCEPT* operator. The following sample adds an employee's name and title to the query listed in the previous sample:

```
SELECT EmployeeKey, FirstName, LastName, Title
FROM DimEmployee
EXCEPT
SELECT FRS.EmployeeKey, DE.FirstName, DE.LastName, DE.Title
FROM FactResellerSales FRS
    JOIN DimEmployee DE
    ON DE.EmployeeKey = FRS.EmployeeKey
ORDER BY Title;
```

On the other hand, if we want to see only employees who have placed orders for reseller sales, we can use the *INTERSECT* command, as shown in this sample:

```
SELECT EmployeeKey, FirstName, LastName, Title
FROM DimEmployee
INTERSECT
SELECT FRS.EmployeeKey, DE.FirstName, DE.LastName, DE.Title
FROM FactResellerSales FRS
    JOIN DimEmployee DE
    ON DE.EmployeeKey = FRS.EmployeeKey
ORDER BY Title;
```

Using the *APPLY* Operator

The *APPLY* operator is different from the other operators discussed so far because it uses the results from a query to a table or view as what is called the *left input,* and the results of a table-valued function as what is called the *right input.*

The *APPLY* operator has two forms, *CROSS APPLY* and *OUTER APPLY. CROSS APPLY* returns only rows from the left output, which produces data from the table-valued function. The *OUTER APPLY* returns all rows from the left, outer table. Like an *OUTER JOIN* statement, *NULL* values are included for the columns where the function does not produce data. This sample returns the first name, last name, job title, type of contact entry, and e-mail address for all contacts in the database by combining the results from the *Person.EmailAddress* table with the *ufnGetContactInformation* UDF. The *BusinessEntityID* value from each row in the table result set is the input required by the *ufnGetContactInformation* function:

```
SELECT GCI.FirstName, GCI.LastName
    , GCI.JobTitle, GCI.BusinessEntityType
    , PE.EmailAddress
FROM Person.EmailAddress AS PE
CROSS APPLY
dbo.ufnGetContactInformation(PE.BusinessEntityID) AS GCI;
```

NOTE LONG-RUNNING QUERY

Please note that this query may take a long time to run.

In the previous sample, the query returns 19,683 rows. When *CROSS APPLY* is replaced with *OUTER APPLY*, all 19,972 rows in the *EmailAddress* table are returned, even though some of them do not have data returned by the function. Figure 1-12 shows the result set of the *OUTER APPLY* displaying *NULL* in all columns returned by the function.

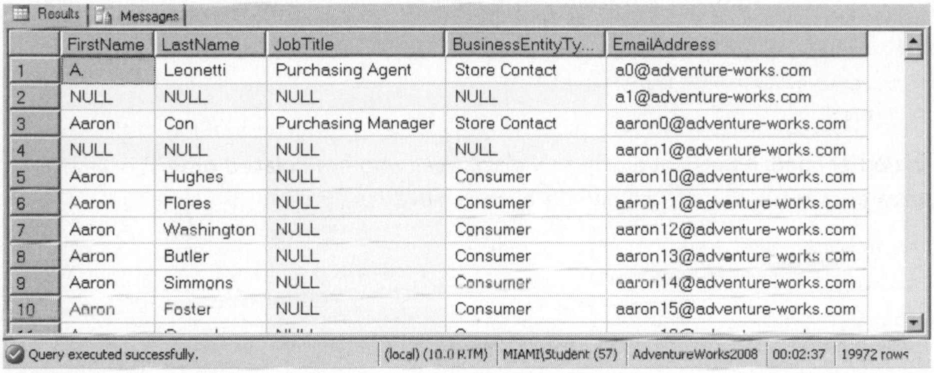

	FirstName	LastName	JobTitle	BusinessEntityTy...	EmailAddress
1	A.	Leonetti	Purchasing Agent	Store Contact	a0@adventure-works.com
2	NULL	NULL	NULL	NULL	a1@adventure-works.com
3	Aaron	Con	Purchasing Manager	Store Contact	aaron0@adventure-works.com
4	NULL	NULL	NULL	NULL	aaron1@adventure-works.com
5	Aaron	Hughes	NULL	Consumer	aaron10@adventure-works.com
6	Aaron	Flores	NULL	Consumer	aaron11@adventure-works.com
7	Aaron	Washington	NULL	Consumer	aaron12@adventure-works.com
8	Aaron	Butler	NULL	Consumer	aaron13@adventure-works.com
9	Aaron	Simmons	NULL	Consumer	aaron14@adventure-works.com
10	Aaron	Foster	NULL	Consumer	aaron15@adventure-works.com

Results
Messages
Query executed successfully.
(local) (10.0 RTM)
MIAMI\Student (57)
AdventureWorks2008
00:02:37
19972 rows

FIGURE 1-12 *OUTER APPLY* results

PRACTICE Combining Data Sets

In this practice session, you use the *UNION*, *EXCEPT*, and *INTERSECT* operators in the *AdventureWorks2008* and *AdventureWorksDW2008* databases.

EXERCISE 1 Use the *UNION* Operator

In this exercise, you combine the result sets from the *FactInternetSales* and the *FactResellerSales* tables in the *AdventureWorksDW2008* database.

1. Open a new query window in SSMS.
2. In the existing query window, type and execute the following command to display all orders from both the reseller and Internet sales fact tables. Because the Internet sales fact table does not have a column that would correlate with the reseller name from the reseller sales table, a string literal of 'N/A' is included to respond to the requirement of the command when both *SELECT* statements have the same number of columns. In addition, the reseller name is retrieved from the *DimReseller* table:

```
USE AdventureWorksDW2008;
SELECT SalesOrderNumber, SalesOrderLineNumber
, SalesAmount, TaxAmt, 'N/A' FROM FactInternetSales
UNION ALL
```

```
SELECT SalesOrderNumber, SalesOrderLineNumber
, SalesAmount, TaxAmt, ResellerName FROM FactResellerSales
     JOIN DimReseller
     ON DimReseller.ResellerKey = FactResellerSales.ResellerKey
ORDER BY SalesOrderNumber;
```

3. Save the script and close the query window.

EXERCISE 2   Use the *EXCEPT* and *INTERSECT* Operators

In this exercise, you use the *EXCEPT* and *INTERSECT* operators to compare results from the *Production.Product* and *Sales.SalesOrderDetail* tables in the *AdventureWorks2008* database.

1. Open a new query window.

2. In the existing query window, type and execute the following command to display the product ID and name for all active products that have not had any sales. Products with a list price of $0 are not included because they are not currently available for sale.

```
USE AdventureWorks2008;

SELECT ProductID, Name, ListPrice FROM Production.Product
WHERE ListPrice <> 0
EXCEPT
SELECT SOD.ProductID, Name, p.listprice FROM Sales.SalesOrderDetail SOD
JOIN Production.Product P
ON P.ProductID = SOD.ProductID
ORDER BY ProductID;
```

3. In the existing query window, below the existing code, type, highlight, and execute the following code to display those products that have been included on a product order:

```
SELECT ProductID, Name, ListPrice FROM Production.Product
INTERSECT
SELECT SOD.ProductID, Name, p.listprice FROM Sales.SalesOrderDetail SOD
JOIN Production.Product P
ON P.ProductID = SOD.ProductID
ORDER BY ProductID;
```

4. Because of the data integrity checks in this database, the *SELECT* command in step 3 returns the same result set as a *SELECT DISTINCT* command run against the *SalesOrderDetail* table because every product that is sold is included in the *Product* table. You can execute the following command and compare with the result set from step 3 to verify this:

```
SELECT DISTINCT SOD.ProductID, Name, p.listprice
FROM Sales.SalesOrderDetail SOD
     JOIN Production.Product P
     ON P.ProductID = SOD.ProductID
ORDER BY ProductID;
```

5. Save the script and close the query window.

Lesson Summary

- The *UNION* operator combines result sets from two or more *SELECT* statements.

- The *EXCEPT* operator returns rows that are in the left *SELECT* statement and do not have matching rows in the right *SELECT* statement.

- The *INTERSECT* operator returns only rows that are shared by the two *SELECT* statements.

- The *APPLY* operator uses the results from a query as input to apply a table-valued function to each row in the result set.

- *OUTER APPLY* returns all rows from the outer table along with the results returned by the function when rows match, while *CROSS APPLY* returns only the rows from the outer table where a match exists within the function results.

Lesson 5: Applying Built-in Scalar Functions

SQL Server 2008 provides a large number of built-in functions in a variety of categories. You can use many of these functions to enhance your queries. You also can use many of these functions to perform actions such as inserting data, creating tables, and creating constraints, as discussed later in this book.

> **MORE INFO** **FUNCTIONS**
>
> For a complete list of function categories that link to descriptions of each function, see "Functions (Database Engine)" in SQL Server Books Online.

> **After this lesson, you will be able to:**
> - Describe uses for built-in scalar functions.
> - Describe a variety of built-in scalar functions along with the functionality they provide.
>
> **Estimated lesson time: 45 minutes**

Using the Built-in Scalar Functions

Built-in functions can be used in the *SELECT* or *WHERE* clause of a *SELECT* statement, but for optimal performance, you should avoid using functions in the *WHERE* clause. When you use a built-in function, you frequently follow the function name with parentheses, even when there is no parameter. In many instances, empty parentheses tell the database engine to use the current value. For example, the *db_id* function returns the database ID for the database that is currently active in the system. Because of this behavior, many of the system functions are what is called *nondeterministic,* meaning that the result may vary and the system does not have a list of predetermined values to supply for the results of the function. The *ISNULL* function, on the other hand, is deterministic because the value to be supplied is contained within the definition when the *ISNULL* function is called.

Although a discussion of all the functions available is beyond the scope of this chapter, you will see a number of samples with descriptions of the functionality provided for some of the more commonly used functions.

Built-in Function Samples

A large number of functions are available. Microsoft has organized these functions into groups based on their definitions or functionality.

Date and Time Functions

A variety of functions is available when you are working with dates. New to SQL Server 2008, the *SYSDATETIME, SYSDATETIMEOFFSET,* and *SYSUTCDATETIME* functions all retrieve the current system time from the server, accurate to within 100 nanoseconds. Sample results are shown in Figure 1-13.

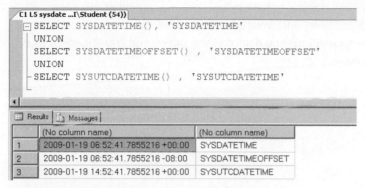

FIGURE 1-13 Sample results for system date functions

If you do not need the precision of these functions, the following functions return the *datetime* data type rather than the *datetime2(7)* and *datetimeoffset(7)* data types returned with these functions. Although the *GETDATE* and *GETUTCDATE* date functions use the same format of including parentheses after the function name, the *CURRENT_TIMESTAMP* function does not. The *CURRENT_TIMESTAMP* and *GETDATE* functions produce the same results.

Using these less precise date and time functions can improve performance because they return a smaller data set. Figure 1-14 shows the results using these less precise functions.

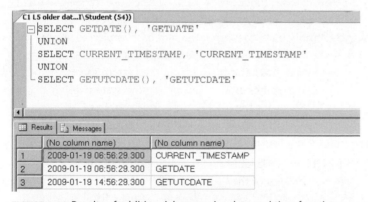

FIGURE 1-14 Results of additional, less precise date and time functions

In addition to the functions that return the current date and time, there are functions that return date and time parts, such as *DATEPART* and *DATENAME*. The *DATENAME* function returns the name of the part specified, such as "January" for the month. In contrast, the *DATEPART* function returns the numeric value of the part specified. For example, "1" is returned for January. There are also functions to perform mathematical operations on dates, such as *DATEADD* and *DATEDIFF*.

The *DATEADD* and *DATEDIFF* functions require a date part to be defined. A variety of keywords and symbols can be used to specify the date part. For example, a year can be specified as *YEAR*, *YY*, or *YYYY*. Day can be represented as *DAY* or *DD*, and so on. Figure 1-15 shows the result of several queries using date functions.

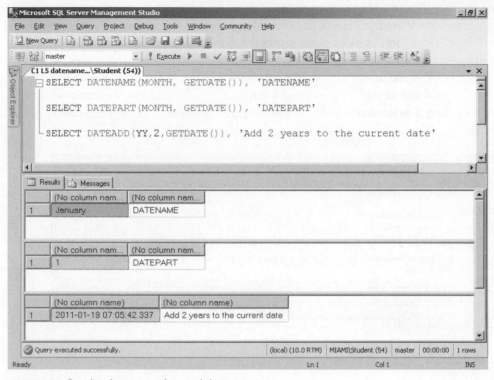

FIGURE 1-15 Queries that return date and time parts

The *DATEDIFF* syntax follows:

```
DATEDIFF (datepart, startdate, enddate)
```

The *startdate* is subtracted from the *enddate*. For example, if the following code was run on January 19, 2009, the result for the first query would be -8, representing that 8 year boundaries had been crossed between the start and end dates provided. The result for the second query would be -18 representing that 18 day boundaries had been crossed between the start and end dates. By reversing the start and end dates in each query, positive values are returned in the result set:

```
SELECT DATEDIFF(YEAR, GETDATE(), '1/1/2001')
SELECT DATEDIFF(DD, GETDATE(), '1/1/2009')
```

> **MORE INFO**   **DATE AND TIME FUNCTIONS**
>
> For a complete list of data types and functions that are used to work with date fields, see "Date and Time Data Types and Functions (Transact-SQL)," in SQL Server Books Online.

System Functions

In addition to the date and time functions, system functions that manipulate the data format are commonly used. The *CAST* and *CONVERT* functions are used to convert an expression from one data type to another. The *CONVERT* statement can also be used to format a date. Figure 1-16 shows a number of date conversions. It is important, especially in an international organization, to understand how users interpret dates. For example, in the United States, most users would interpret the date "01/05/07" as January 5, 2007, while in France, users would interpret it as May 1, 2007, and in Japan, users would interpret it as May 7, 2001. If you do not specify a specific date format, the format is determined by whether a localized version of SQL Server is installed. When a localized version is installed, the formatting is determined by the default language configured on the computer running SQL Server.

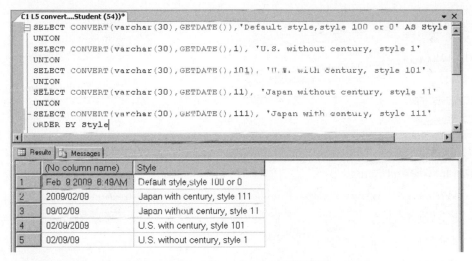

FIGURE 1-16 Different date styles retrieved by using the *CONVERT* function

---

MORE INFO   INTERNATIONAL CONSIDERATIONS

For more information about managing international considerations, see Chapter 3.

Additional system functions are beneficial when programming and troubleshooting. The *@@ERROR* function returns the most recent error number in the current session, while *@@TRANCOUNT* returns the number of current active transactions in the current session. These functions were known as global variables in early versions of SQL Server. Unlike many of the previous samples, the syntax for these commands does not include parentheses. The *@@ERROR* statement must be executed immediately following the command that raised the error.

String Functions

String functions perform an operation on string expressions. Listed here are several of the more common string functions:

- **LEFT, RIGHT**   Returns the specified number of characters from the specified side (left or right) of the expression.

- **UPPER, LOWER**   Returns the specified case (uppercase or lowercase) for all characters in the expression.

- **SUBSTRING**   Receives an expression as input and returns a certain number of characters after a starting point. For example, *SUBSTRING(FirstName,1,3)* starts at the first character of the value in the *FirstName* column and returns the next three characters.

- **REPLACE**   Replaces one string with another within a defined string.

- **LEN**   Returns the number of characters within a defined string. If you would like the number of bytes rather than characters, you should use the *DATALENGTH* function.

Additional Functions

The following functions are also commonly required:

- **DATALENGTH**   Returns the number of bytes required to represent an expression. Can be used with any data type, but is especially useful with *varchar*, *varbinary*, and *nvarchar*, *binary*, and *image* data types.

- **PATINDEX**   Returns the starting position of the first occurrence of a specified pattern within a defined string.

- **CHARINDEX**   Returns the starting position, if found, of a defined string within another defined string. The function also accepts an optional input of *start_location*, which defines the point within the second expression at which the comparisons should begin.

PRACTICE   **Using Built-in Scalar Functions**

In this practice session, you use a variety of built-in scalar functions to add meaning and formatting to your result sets.

EXERCISE   Write Queries That Include Built-in Functions

In this exercise, you use the *DATENAME, DATEPART, DATEDIFF, LEFT, REPLACE,* and *CONVERT* functions.

1. Open a new query window in SSMS.

2. In the existing query window, type and execute the following code to retrieve the day of the week on which each order was placed, arranged by the day of the week:

```
USE AdventureWorks2008;
SELECT SalesOrderID, DATENAME(DW, orderdate) AS 'Day of Week'
FROM Sales.SalesOrderHeader
ORDER BY DATEPart(DW, orderdate);
```

3. In the existing query window, below the existing code, type, highlight, and execute the following code to retrieve the number of days that passed between when an order was placed and when it was shipped:

```
SELECT SalesOrderID, DATEDIFF(DD, Orderdate, ShipDate ) AS 'Days lapsed'
FROM Sales.SalesOrderHeader;
```

4. In the existing query window, below the existing code, type, highlight, and execute the following code to return a column named *Employee Code* that is made up of the first three characters of each employee's first name and first three characters of their last name:

```
SELECT LEFT(FirstName, 3) + LEFT(LastName, 3)AS 'Employee Code'
FROM Person.Person;
```

5. In the existing query window, below the existing code, type, highlight, and execute the following code to replace the word *bike* with the word *bicycle* in all product descriptions:

```
SELECT REPLACE(Description, 'bike', 'bicycle')
FROM Production.ProductDescription;
```

6. In the existing query window, below the existing code, type, highlight, and execute the following code to return each employee's name and employee number in a single column. To accomplish this, you must convert the *BusinessEntityID* (which represents the employee number) column to a character data type:

```
SELECT FirstName + ' ' + Lastname + ' Employee Number: '
       + CONVERT(char, E.BusinessEntityID)
FROM HumanResources.Employee AS E
JOIN Person.Person AS P
ON P.BusinessEntityID = E.BusinessEntityID;
```

7. In the existing query window, below the existing code, type, highlight, and execute the following code to return the order number and order date. Format the date so that the time information is not included:

```
SELECT SalesOrderNumber, CONVERT(varchar(30), OrderDate, 107)
FROM Sales.SalesOrderHeader;
```

8. Modify the date style to additional formats such as 11, 03, 111, 114, and 103. Notice that 114 does not provide the required information, while 03 and 11 would be confusing to any user not familiar with those formats.

9. Save the script and close SSMS.

Lesson Summary

- Use built-in functions to provide more meaningful result sets.
- Use date and time functions to manipulate and return date information.
- Use string functions to format or return information about string expressions.

Chapter Review

To practice and reinforce the skills you learned in this chapter further, you can perform the following tasks:

- Review the chapter summary.
- Review the list of key terms introduced in this chapter.
- Complete the case scenarios. These scenarios set up a real-world situation involving the topics of this chapter and asks you to create solutions.
- Complete the suggested practices.
- Take a practice test.

Chapter Summary

- The *SELECT* statement provides the ability to retrieve data from a database. The simplest *SELECT* statement includes a *SELECT* clause and a *FROM* clause. A *WHERE* clause can limit the number of rows returned in the result set.

- Use *JOIN* operators to combine columns from multiple related tables to add clarity and greater functionality to your *SELECT* statements. Use *INNER JOIN* to retrieve only those rows that have a matched row in each table based on the *ON* predicate. Use *LEFT* or *RIGHT OUTER JOIN* to return all rows from the outer table and those rows in common from the inner table. Use *FULL OUTER JOIN* to define both tables as outer tables, returning all rows.

- Use aggregate functions and the *GROUP BY* clause to provide summary data. Use *ROLLUP* and *CUBE* to provide additional summary information. Use the *GROUPING* function to show which rows hold summary data provided by the *ROLLUP* or *CUBE* operators. Use *GROUPING SETS* to provide greater flexibility and readability to your *GROUP BY* queries.

- Use the *UNION, INTERSECT,* and *EXCEPT* operators to combine and compare result sets.

- Use built-in functions to provide additional formatting and context to the data included in your result sets. These can include any of the groups of functions defined in SQL Server 2008, but some of the most common functions are string and date/time functions.

Key Terms

Do you know what these key terms mean? You can check your answers by looking up the terms in the glossary at the end of the book.

- Function
- Scalar function
- User-defined function (UDF)
- Aggregate function

- Table-valued function
- *UNION*
- *JOIN*
- *INNER JOIN*
- *OUTER JOIN*

Case Scenarios

In the following case scenarios, you apply what you have learned in this chapter. You can find answers to these questions in the "Answers" section at the end of this book.

Case Scenario 1: Retrieving Data

You are a database developer for Wide World Importers. You are responsible for a sales database for the company. This database is normalized to third normal form.

An application developer who is fairly new to SQL Server is developing a Web application that retrieves information from the database. Although he feels confident in his ability to use his reference tools to develop the required queries, he has asked for a set of sample queries from which he can extrapolate and build the required queries.

You need to provide a Web developer with a sampling of queries demonstrating the required functionality. The application needs to include queries that return information on products (including their names and descriptions) that were imported based on the date the order was placed or completed. The sales department would like to provide an option in the application to display dates in different formats. In addition, the salespeople would like to be able to sort data based on the number of days between when the order was placed and when it was completed. Finally, users should be able to return data from different time periods, such as the past month, quarter, or year.

Answer the following question for your manager:

What functions and clauses should you include in the sample queries to provide the application developer with samples to help him with his application development?

Case Scenario 2: Grouping Data

The application developer from Case Scenario 1 has implemented the first stage of the Web application successfully based on the queries you provided. The customer has now asked that he include summary data detailing how many total products were sold, as well as how many total products were sold from a particular category. Each row in the *SalesOrderDetail* table refers to only one product ID and the *Qty* column includes the quantity ordered of that item on the order number.

Answer the following question for your manager:

What functions and clauses should you include in the sample queries to provide the application developer with samples to help him with his application development?

Suggested Practices

To help you master the exam objectives presented in this chapter, do all the following practices.

Query Data by Using *SELECT* Statements

- **Practice 1** Write and execute a variety of *SELECT* statements including *WHERE* clauses using Boolean operators and *LIKE* and the *ORDER BY* clause. Review and compare the output from the different statements.

Combine Datasets

- **Practice 1** Write and execute a variety of *SELECT* statements that include the *JOIN* operator. Be sure to compare the results of *INNER*, *LEFT* or *RIGHT OUTER*, and *FULL OUTER* joins.

- **Practice 2** Write and execute a variety of *SELECT* statements that use the *UNION*, *EXCEPT, INTERSECT, CROSS APPLY*, and *OUTER APPLY* operators.

Implement Aggregate Queries

- **Practice 1** Write and execute a variety of *SELECT* statements that use aggregate functions with the *GROUP BY* clause and *GROUPING* operator.

Apply Built-in Scalar Functions

- **Practice 1** Write and execute a variety of queries that return values from built-in functions including a variety of date and time functions, *CAST* and *CONVERT*, *REPLACE, LEN* and *DATALENGTH, PATINDEX*, and *CHARINDEX*.

Take a Practice Test

The practice tests on this book's companion CD offer many options. For example, you can test yourself on just one exam objective, or you can test yourself on all the 70-433 certification exam content. You can set up the test so that it closely simulates the experience of taking a certification exam, or you can set it up in study mode so that you can look at the correct answers and explanations after you answer each question.

> **MORE INFO** **PRACTICE TESTS**
>
> For details about all the practice test options available, see the section titled "How to Use the Practice Tests," in the Introduction to this book.

CHAPTER 2

Modifying Data—The *INSERT, UPDATE, DELETE,* and *MERGE* Statements

One of the basic functions required for any database is the ability to add, remove, and modify data. In the SQL programming language, data manipulation language (DML) serves this purpose. The *INSERT, UPDATE,* and *DELETE* commands provide you with the ability to manipulate data based on provided input or based on information found elsewhere in the database.

In Microsoft SQL Server 2005, the *OUTPUT* clause was introduced to allow you to return information from each row affected by an *INSERT, UPDATE,* or *DELETE* statement. In SQL Server 2008, the *MERGE* statement was introduced to enhance the ability to perform *INSERT, UPDATE,* and *DELETE* statements on a table based on the results of a query to a joined table. These two features add flexibility to your DML statements.

To ensure data consistency and reliability, SQL Server provides the ability to execute statements as part of a transaction. A *transaction* is a group of commands that succeeds or fails as a whole. One of the most referenced examples of a transaction is the transfer of funds from a savings account to a checking account. At a minimum, two steps need to occur: a debit from savings and a credit to checking. A transaction would ensure that if only part of the transaction was completed when the system failed, the entire transaction would return to its initial state.

> **MORE INFO ERROR HANDLING**
>
> For information about using transactions within stored procedures and about error handling, see Chapter 5, "Programming Microsoft SQL Server with T-SQL User-Defined Stored Procedures, Functions, Triggers, and Views."

Exam objectives in this chapter:

- Modify data by using *INSERT, UPDATE,* and *DELETE* statements.
- Return data by using the *OUTPUT* clause.

- Modify data by using *MERGE* statements.
- Manage transactions.

Lessons in this chapter:

Before You Begin

To complete the lessons in this chapter, you must have:

- A basic understanding of relational database design concepts and terminology
- A basic understanding of SQL Server data types
- A general understanding of *SELECT* statement syntax
- Knowledge about how SQL Server Management Studio (SSMS) functions. as well as the ability to open new query windows and existing query files from within SSMS
- SQL Server 2008 Developer Edition, Enterprise Edition, or Enterprise Evaluation Edition, with the *AdventureWorks2008* and *Northwind* sample databases installed

 REAL WORLD

Ann Weber

Transactions are key to providing a consistent and reliable view of the data to all users at all times. As a consultant and as a trainer, I have come across numerous difficulties caused by poorly written transactions. One of the most frustrating errors I came across was when a company had long transactions that would cause deadlock situations to arise from time to time in the application. Shortening and reordering the order that tables were accessed within the transactions would have minimized the number of deadlock errors that occurred. But even more frustrating was the fact that the code did not handle the errors. The users would lose all the data they had been entering (which may have taken them up to 15 minutes to complete) and they would receive the following error message: "Transaction (Process ID *xx*) was deadlocked on lock resources with another process and has been chosen as the deadlock victim. Rerun the transaction." Even if you do not expect deadlock situations to occur, you need to program for the possibility. Users should never see this kind of message. The client needed to capture the user's input before opening the transaction, intercept the deadlock error, and attempt to resend the user's input before finally sending a user-friendly message stating that the insert failed and to please try again later.

Lesson 1: Modifying Data by Using *INSERT*, *UPDATE*, and *DELETE* Statements

The *INSERT*, *UPDATE*, and *DELETE* statements allow you to add, remove, and modify data in your databases. These statements can be used in a variety of ways to allow you to specify fixed values. The table schema (also known as the *table definition*) affects the values that may or may not be defined, modified, and removed in *INSERT*, *UPDATE*, and *DELETE* statements. For example, the *IDENTITY* property is used to create an identity column that automatically assigns incremental values in the identity column each time a new row is inserted. Because of this, under normal circumstances, you cannot enter a value for an identity column when executing an *INSERT* or *UPDATE* statement. You can overcome this limitation by issuing the *SET IDENTITY_INSERT ON* command in the current connection. *NULL* definitions and constraints also have an effect on DML statements.

> **MORE INFO** **CONSTRAINTS AND *IDENTITY* COLUMNS**
>
> For more information about table schemas, constraints, and the *IDENTITY* property, see Chapter 3, "Tables, Data Types, and Declarative Data Integrity."

> **After this lesson, you will be able to:**
> - Use the *INSERT* statement to add new rows to your tables.
> - Use the *UPDATE* statement to modify rows in your tables.
> - Use the *DELETE* statement to remove rows from your tables.
>
> **Estimated lesson time: 45 minutes**

 REAL WORLD

Ann Weber

DML statements are a core functionality in SQL Server. As a trainer and consultant, I have come across many cases of data loss caused by improperly constructed *UPDATE* or *DELETE* statements. To minimize the possibility of data loss when issuing DML commands, you can follow several precautions. First, develop and test all code on a nonproduction server. Second, build the logic for the *UPDATE*, *INSERT*, or *DELETE* command as a *SELECT* statement to verify the correct result set is being returned. In addition, either execute the command as part of an explicit transaction and do not commit the transaction until you verify success, or turn on implicit transactions while you are building ad hoc queries to change data. Remember that with implicit transactions, a DML statement automatically starts a transaction, but you must execute a *COMMIT* or *ROLLBACK* statement manually.

The fact that implicit transactions are disabled by default on a server running SQL Server has caught many Oracle developers off guard. Unless you change the SQL Server default settings or explicitly start a transaction, there is no way to roll back a command once it has been executed. Implicit transactions actions are always enabled on Oracle servers. If you would like to have the same functionality in SQL Server, enable the *SET_IMPLICIT_TRANSACTIONS* connection property for each connection created.

Inserting Data

The *INSERT* statement provides you with the ability to add new rows to a table. Depending on the schema of the table, you may need to provide data for all or only a portion of the columns in the table. *DEFAULT* constraints, *IDENTITY* properties, and *NULL* settings may all affect the data requirements of your *INSERT* statements.

INSERT Statement Syntax

The *INSERT* command syntax is as follows:

```
[ WITH <common_table_expression> [ ,...n ] ]
INSERT
    [ TOP ( expression ) [ PERCENT ] ]
    [ INTO ]
    { <object> | rowset_function_limited
      [ WITH ( <Table_Hint_Limited> [ ...n ] ) ]
    }
{
    [ ( column_list ) ]
    [ <OUTPUT Clause> ]
    { VALUES ( { DEFAULT | NULL | expression } [ ,...n ] ) [ ,...n ]
    | derived_table
    | execute_statement
    | <dml_table_source>
    | DEFAULT VALUES
    }
}
[; ]
```

MORE INFO **THE *WITH <COMMON TABLE EXPRESSION>* CLAUSE AND THE *OUTPUT* CLAUSE**

For more information about the *WITH* clause and common table expressions, see Chapter 4, "Using Additional Query Techniques." For more information about the *WITH* clause, see Lesson 2, "Enhancing DML Functionality with the *OUTPUT* Clause and *MERGE* Statement," later in this chapter.

Using the *INSERT* Statement

When inserting data, you can include data for all columns or a partial list of columns. When inserting data for all columns, you do not have to specify the column names in the *INSERT* statement, as in the sample here:

```
INSERT INTO Sales.SalesReason
VALUES ('Item Closeout', 'Other', getdate());
```

In this command, *SalesReasonID* is not entered because it is an identity column and is inserted automatically by the SQL Server engine.

The *ModifiedDate* column of the *SalesReason* table has a *DEFAULT* constraint associated with it that specifies the *getdate()* function. Because of this, the following command produces the same results as the previous command:

```
INSERT INTO Sales.SalesReason
VALUES ('Item Closeout', 'Other', DEFAULT);
```

> **NOTE** **OPTIONAL *INTO* KEYWORD**
>
> The *INTO* keyword is optional in all *INSERT* statements.

If a column supports *NULL* values, you can use the keyword *NULL* to insert a row with missing data in one or more columns, as shown in bold type in the following example:

```
INSERT INTO Sales.SpecialOffer
VALUES ('Temporary Holiday Discount', .10, 'Seasonal Discount'
    , 'Reseller', GETDATE(), DATEADD(dd, 30, getdate())
    , 1, NULL, DEFAULT, DEFAULT);
```

If you want to specify only certain columns, you can reference the column names when writing the *INSERT* statement, as in the following example:

```
INSERT INTO Sales.SpecialOffer
(Description, DiscountPct, Type, Category, StartDate
    , EndDate, MinQty)
VALUES ('Temporary Holiday Discount', .10, 'Seasonal Discount'
    , 'Reseller', GETDATE(), DATEADD(dd, 30, getdate())
    , 1);
```

Using the *INSERT ... SELECT* statement allows you to append rows to an existing table based on data selected from a different table. The following command takes rows from the *Employees* table and appends them to the *Customers* table. Because the number and data type of columns in the result set must match the destination table, concatenation is used to provide the correct number of columns. The following *SUBSTRING* command retrieves the first five letters of the employee's last name to build a customer ID that is similar to those in the *Customers* table:

```
INSERT INTO Customers
SELECT SUBSTRING(lastname,1,5), 'Northwind Traders', FirstName + ' ' + LastName
     , 'Employee', Address, City, Region, PostalCode
     , Country, HomePhone, NULL
FROM Employees
```

> **NOTE DATABASE**
>
> The sample that has just been discussed uses the *Northwind* database.

Finally, the *SELECT INTO* statement allows you to create a new temporary or permanent table populated with the results of the defined *SELECT* statement. The following command creates a temporary table named *#EmployeeDepartment* that includes each employee's name, job title, and department information:

```
SELECT IDENTITY (int, 1,1) AS EmpID, FirstName, LastName, JobTitle
  , Name AS 'Department', GroupName as 'Division'
INTO #EmployeeDepartment
FROM  HumanResources.Employee JOIN Person.Person
  ON HumanResources.Employee.BusinessEntityID = Person.Person.BusinessEntityID
  JOIN HumanResources.EmployeeDepartmentHistory
  ON    HumanResources.Employee.BusinessEntityID =
        HumanResources.EmployeeDepartmentHistory.BusinessEntityID
  JOIN HumanResources.Department
  ON HumanResources.Department.DepartmentID =
     HumanResources.EmployeeDepartmentHistory.DepartmentID
  WHERE HumanResources.EmployeeDepartmentHistory.EndDate IS NULL
  ORDER BY Department, Division
```

Updating Data

Over time, existing data in the database changes and requires modification. The *UPDATE* command allows you to change the value of one or more columns in one or more rows of a table. Adding a value to a column that is currently *NULL* and removing a value from a column are both considered *UPDATE* statements, not *INSERT* or *DELETE* statements. It is important to remember that an *INSERT* statement adds an entirely new row to the table and that a *DELETE* statement removes a complete row from the table.

UPDATE Statement Syntax

The *UPDATE* statement full syntax is as follows:

```
[ WITH <common_table_expression> [...n] ]
UPDATE
    [ TOP ( expression ) [ PERCENT ] ]
```

```
    { <object> | rowset_function_limited
    [ WITH ( <Table_Hint_Limited> [ ...n ] ) ]
    }
SET
        { column_name = { expression | DEFAULT | NULL }
          | { udt_column_name.{ { property_name = expression
                               | field_name = expression }
                               | method_name ( argument [ ,...n ] )
                   }
          }
        | column_name { .WRITE ( expression , @Offset , @Length ) }
        | @variable = expression
        | @variable = column = expression
        | column_name { += | -= | *= | /= | %= | &= | ^= | |= } expression
        | @variable { += | -= | *= | /= | %= | &= | ^= | |= } expression
        | @variable = column { += | -= | *= | /= | %= | &= | ^= | |= } expression
        } [ ,...n ]
[ <OUTPUT Clause> ]
    [ FROM{ <table_source> } [ ,...n ] ]
    [ WHERE { <search_condition>
           | { [ CURRENT OF
                { { [ GLOBAL ] cursor_name }
                  | cursor_variable_name
                }
              ]
            }
         }
    ]
    [ OPTION ( <query_hint> [ ,...n ] ) ]
[ ; ]
```

Using the *UPDATE* Statement

In its simplest form, the *UPDATE* statement requires only the name of the object (table or view) being updated and the value to be set. The *WHERE* clause defines which rows are updated by the command. Because a single *UPDATE* statement has the ability to update all rows in a table with a single command, programming techniques such as stored procedures and triggers need to be designed to detect and handle multiple-row updates.

The following command updates every row in the *CurrencyRate* table and adds 0.005 to the current end-of-day rate:

```
UPDATE Sales.CurrencyRate
SET EndOfDayRate = EndOfDayRate + .005;
```

If you need to update only specific rows, you must define a *WHERE* clause to restrict the row set. The following command sets the sales reason name to "N/A," for *SalesReasonID* 10 in the *SalesReason* table:

```
UPDATE Sales.SalesReason
SET Name = 'N/A'
WHERE SalesReasonID = 10;
```

You can also update the information in a target table based on information in a table joined to the target table by using the *FROM* clause. For example, the following command increases the unit price of all red products by 5 percent:

```
UPDATE Sales.SalesOrderDetail
SET UnitPrice = UnitPrice * 1.05
FROM SALES.SalesOrderDetail JOIN Production.Product
  ON SALES.SalesOrderDetail.ProductID = Production.Product.ProductID
WHERE Production.Product.Color = 'Red'
```

> **BEST PRACTICES**   **TESTING DATA MODIFICATIONS**
>
> Build the logic of an *UPDATE* or *DELETE* statement as a *SELECT* statement and verify its logic before modifying it to run as an *UPDATE* or *DELETE* statement. In addition, execute data modifications as part of an explicit transaction to enable a rollback of unintended modifications. Transactions are covered in Lesson 3, "Managing Transactions," later in this chapter.

Deleting Data

The *DELETE* statement allows you to remove from the database rows that are no longer required. With the *DELETE* statement, entire rows of data are removed from the table. If you want to simply remove a value from a column in a given row, you should use an *UPDATE* statement.

DELETE Statement Syntax

The *DELETE* statement full syntax is as follows:

```
[ WITH <common_table_expression> [ ,...n ] ]
DELETE
    [ TOP ( expression ) [ PERCENT ] ]
    [ FROM ]
    { <object> | rowset_function_limited
      [ WITH ( <table_hint_limited> [ ...n ] ) ]
    }
    [ <OUTPUT Clause> ]
    [ FROM <table_source> [ ,...n ] ]
    [ WHERE { <search_condition>
            | { [ CURRENT OF
                  { { [ GLOBAL ] cursor_name }
                    | cursor_variable_name
                  }
```

```
                ]
              }
           }
      ]
      [ OPTION ( <Query Hint> [ ,...n ] ) ]
[; ]


<object> ::=
{
    [ server_name.database_name.schema_name.
      | database_name. [ schema_name ] .
      | schema_name.
    ]
        table_or_view_name
}
```

> **NOTE** **CURSORS**
>
> The *CURRENT OF, GLOBAL, cursor_name,* and *cursor_variable_name* options are applicable only when using cursors. The discussion of cursors is beyond the scope of this book. For more information about cursors, see the article "Transact-SQL Cursors" in SQL Server Books Online.

Using the *DELETE* Statement

The syntax for the *DELETE* statement is the simplest of the three DML statements. Like the *UPDATE* statement, it is important to remember to include the *WHERE* clause when writing a *DELETE* statement. If you execute a *DELETE* statement without a *WHERE* clause, all rows from the table are deleted.

To delete all rows from a table, the syntax is simply

```
DELETE FROM <tablename>
```

> **NOTE** **OPTIONAL *FROM* KEYWORD**
>
> The *FROM* keyword is optional in the *DELETE* statement syntax.

To limit the rows removed, add a *WHERE* clause to the *DELETE* statement. The following example removes all rows in the *Employees* table for the employee who has an employee ID of 7:

```
DELETE FROM EMPLOYEES
WHERE EmployeeID = 7
```

> **NOTE** **DATABASE**
>
> This sample uses the *Northwind* database, but it does not actually succeed in the sample database due to a foreign key constraint with the *Orders* table.

Like the *INSERT* and *UPDATE* commands, the *DELETE* command can remove rows in one table based on information returned from a joined table. To accomplish this, you define a second *FROM* clause. The following command removes rows from the *Order Details* table where the order was placed before July 10, 1996, and the order has shipped:

```
DELETE FROM [Order Details]
FROM ORDERS JOIN [Order Details]
    ON Orders.OrderID = [Order Details].OrderID
WHERE OrderDate < '07-10-1996' AND ShippedDate IS NOT NULL
```

Using the *TRUNCATE TABLE* Statement

Like a *DELETE* statement without a *WHERE* clause, the *TRUNCATE TABLE* statement can also be used to remove all data from a table. The *TRUNCATE TABLE* statement differs from the *DELETE* statement in several ways. First, the *DELETE* statement logs information on each row deleted, while the *TRUNCATE TABLE* statement only creates entries for the deallocation of the data pages. Second, because of the minimal logging, along with how the Database Engine removes the data from the table, the *TRUNCATE TABLE* statement executes more quickly and requires fewer resources on the server. Finally, if an identity column exists in the table, the *TRUNCATE TABLE* command resets the identity seed value.

The syntax for the *TRUNCATE TABLE* statement is simply

```
TRUNCATE TABLE <tablename>
```

Neither the *DELETE* statement without a *WHERE* clause nor the *TRUNCATE TABLE* statement affect the schema structure of the table or related objects.

<hr/>

PRACTICE **Modifying Data**

In this practice, you insert data into the *Credit* table in the *Sales* database by using a variety of methods. You also update and delete data from the *Credit* table.

EXERCISE 1 Insert Data

In this exercise, you insert data into the *Credit* table and verify the results.

1. If necessary, start SSMS and connect to your SQL Server instance.
2. Open, review, and execute the Lesson01 PracticeSetup.sql file, which can be found among the accompanying sample files in the Practice folder, to create the *Sales* database and the *Credit* table for these exercises.
3. Close the current query window.
4. Open a new query window, and type and execute the following command to review the columns in the *Sales* table. No rows exist in this table at this time:

    ```
    USE Sales;
    GO
    SELECT * FROM Credit;
    ```

5. In the current query window, below the existing text, type, highlight, and execute the following command to add a new row to the *Credit* table by specifying values for each column based on its relative location in the table schema:

```
INSERT INTO Credit
VALUES ('Izak', 'Cohen', 5000, 'izak@adatum.com');
```

> ***MORE INFO*** **IDENTITY COLUMNS**
>
> You cannot specify a value for *CustomerID* because it is defined as an identity column. For more information on the *IDENTITY* property, see Chapter 3.

6. In the current query window, below the existing text, type, highlight, and execute the following command to add a new row to the *Credit* table by specifying values for each column based on its relative location, where data is not provided to every column. A value of "0", the default value defined when the table was created, is entered for the credit limit:

```
INSERT INTO Credit
VALUES ('David', 'Hamilton', DEFAULT, NULL);
```

7. In the current query window, below the existing text, type, highlight, and execute the following command to add a new row to the *Credit* table by specifying values for each column based on its relative location, where data is not provided to every column. This command fails because the number of columns specified does not match the table definition:

```
INSERT INTO Credit
VALUES ('Don', 'Hall', 5000);
```

8. To correct this error, delete the previous command and type, highlight, and execute the following command. This command specifies the columns and column order to be expected in the *VALUES* clause and adds two new rows to the table:

```
INSERT INTO Credit
(firstname, lastname, creditlimit)
VALUES ('Don', 'Hall', 5000);
INSERT INTO Credit
(firstname, lastname, creditlimit)
VALUES ('Punya', 'Palit',10000);
```

9. In the current query window, below the existing text, type, highlight, and execute the following command to review the rows added to the *Credit* table:

```
SELECT * FROM CREDIT;
```

10. Save the script and close the query window. Leave SSMS open for the next exercise.

EXERCISE 2 Update Data

In this exercise, you update the data that you entered into the *Credit* table in Exercise 1. You then verify the results of each *UPDATE* statement.

1. Open a new query window, and type and execute the following command to add an e-mail address for Punya Palit (CustomerID 4):

```
USE Sales;
GO
UPDATE Credit
SET Email = 'punya@adatum.com'
WHERE CustomerID = 4;
```

2. In the current query window, below the existing text, type, highlight, and execute the following command to review the row modified in step 1:

```
SELECT * FROM Credit WHERE CustomerID = 4;
```

3. In the current query window, below the existing text, type, highlight, and execute the following command to add 500 to the *CreditLimit* value in every row:

```
UPDATE Credit
SET CreditLimit = CreditLimit + 500;
```

4. In the current query window, below the existing text, type, highlight, and execute the following command to review the rows modified in step 3. Notice that all the credit limits have been increased by 500:

```
SELECT * FROM Credit;
```

5. Save the script and close the query window. Leave SSMS open for the next exercise.

EXERCISE 3 Delete Data

In this exercise, you delete the data that you entered into the *Credit* table in Exercise 1. You also verify the functionality of the *TRUNCATE TABLE* statement.

1. Open a new query window, and type and execute the following command to delete the row for Punya Palit (CustomerID 4):

```
USE SALES;
GO
DELETE FROM Credit
WHERE CustomerID = 4;
```

2. In the current query window, below the existing text, type, highlight, and execute the following command to review the remaining rows:

```
SELECT * FROM Credit;
```

3. In the current query window, below the existing text, type, highlight, and execute the following command to delete all rows from the *Credit* table and verify the results:

```
DELETE FROM Credit;
GO
SELECT * FROM Credit;
```

4. In the current query window, below the existing text, type, highlight, and execute the following command to add a new row to the credit table and verify the results. Notice that the *CustomerID* value is the next incremented value even though the previous rows were all deleted:

```
INSERT INTO Credit
(firstname, lastname, creditlimit)
VALUES ('Punya', 'Palit',10000);


SELECT * FROM Credit;
```

5. In the current query window, below the existing text, type, highlight, and execute the following command to truncate the table and reset the *CustomerID Identity* property to the original seed value:

```
TRUNCATE TABLE Credit;
```

6. In the current query window, below the existing text, type, highlight, and execute the following command to add a new row to the credit table and verify the results. Notice that the *CustomerID* value is "1", the original seed value:

```
INSERT INTO Credit
(firstname, lastname, creditlimit)
VALUES ('Punya', 'Palit',10000);


SELECT * FROM Credit;
```

7. Save the script and close the query window.

8. Verify that you have closed all the query windows opened during this practice, and then open, review, and execute the Lesson01 PracticeCleanup.sql file, which can be found among the accompanying sample files in the Chapter 2/Lesson 1 folder.

Lesson Summary

- The *INSERT* statement allows you to add new rows to a table.
- The *UPDATE* statement allows you to make changes to the existing data in a table. It allows you not only to modify the value in a column, it also allows you to add or remove a value from a single column in the table without affecting the rest of the row being modified.
- The *DELETE* statement allows you to remove one or more rows from a table.

Lesson 2: Enhancing DML Functionality with the *OUTPUT* Clause and *MERGE* Statement

You can use the *OUTPUT* clause and *MERGE* statement to enhance the functionality provided by DML statements. The *OUTPUT* clause allows you to return information from rows affected by an *INSERT, UPDATE,* or *DELETE* statement. With this functionality, you can perform additional tasks more cleanly based on the information provided. These tasks can include confirmation e-mails, data auditing, and similar duties.

The *MERGE* statement provides you with the ability to perform an *INSERT, UPDATE,* or *DELETE* operation on a target table based on a set of rules that are determined by a row comparison between the target table and a source table.

> **After this lesson, you will be able to:**
>
> - Use the *OUTPUT* clause to return information from inserted, deleted, or modified rows.
> - Use the *MERGE* statement to perform *INSERTS, UPDATES,* or *DELETES* based on a comparison between two tables.
>
> **Estimated lesson time: 30 minutes**

Using the *OUTPUT* Clause

The *OUTPUT* clause gives you the ability to access the inserted and deleted tables that in versions previous to SQL Server 2005 were accessible only through triggers. Because of this, some of the functionality that was previously performed through triggers can be handled by stored procedures instead, removing the need for certain triggers.

> **MORE INFO**   **TRIGGERS AND STORED PROCEDURES**
>
> There are both benefits and limitations to consider when deciding whether to provide functionality through stored procedures and triggers. For more information about triggers and stored procedures, see Chapter 5.

OUTPUT Clause Syntax

The *OUTPUT* clause syntax can be included with any *INSERT, UPDATE,* or *DELETE* statement. The syntax specific to the *OUTPUT* clause follows:

```
<OUTPUT_CLAUSE> ::=
{
    [ OUTPUT <dml_select_list> INTO { @table_variable | output_table } [ ( column_list )
] ]
    [ OUTPUT <dml_select_list> ]
}
```

```
<dml_select_list> ::=
{ <column_name> | scalar_expression } [ [AS] column_alias_identifier ]
    [ ,...n ]

<column_name> ::=
{ DELETED | INSERTED | from_table_name } . { * | column_name }
    | $action
```

OUTPUT Clause Samples

There are many functions that can be fulfilled by using the OUTPUT clause. Several examples are included next.

> **NOTE DATABASE AND SAMPLE SCRIPTS**
>
> The OUTPUT clause query samples use the Northwind database. You can find scripts to create the sample data along with the queries presented in the text among the accompanying sample files in the Chapter2/TextSamples folder.

Many environments need to record data inserts to an audit table. For the following example, the company wants to be able to run reports identifying how many rows are inserted during different periods of time. The business requirements specify that the date the row was inserted, along with the primary key identifier from the source table, should be included in a special auditing table that is used to run these reports. One way to accomplish this is with the OUTPUT clause. For this example, the Audit table includes an AuditID column, which is an identity column; an InsertedDate column, which contains the date the row was inserted; and the InsertedID column, which contains the primary key value from the row inserted into the table being audited. The following command adds a new row to the Employees table, and also adds a corresponding row with the current date and time and the EmployeeID for the new employee into the Audit table:

```
INSERT INTO Employees
(LastName, FirstName, Title)
OUTPUT getdate(), inserted.EmployeeID INTO Audit
VALUES ('Ralls', 'Kim', 'Support Rep');
```

Another scenario involves data archiving. For example, suppose that a company wants to move all records for orders placed before December 1, 1997, from the Order Details table to the OrderDetailsArchive table. You can delete the rows from the Order Details table and move them to the OrderDetailsArchive table in a single step by using the following DELETE statement with the OUTPUT clause:

```
DELETE FROM [Order Details]
OUTPUT deleted.* INTO OrderDetailsArchive
FROM Orders join [Order Details]
ON Orders.OrderID = [Order Details].OrderID
WHERE OrderDate < '12-01-1997';
```

The final scenario is for a company that would like to see the before and after state of the *CategoryName* column whenever updates are made to this column. This information, along with the modification date and the login ID for the employee that made each change, is gathered in a table named *CategoryChanges*. The following command adds information to a *CategoryChanges* table that includes the following columns: *ChangeID*, *CategoryID*, *OldCategoryName*, *NewCategoryName*, *ModifiedDate*, and *LoginID*. The command also modifies a category name and adds a row to the *CategoryChanges* table:

```
UPDATE Categories
SET CategoryName = 'Dried Produce'
OUTPUT inserted.CategoryID, deleted.CategoryName
    , inserted.CategoryName, getdate(), SUSER_SNAME()
    INTO CategoryChanges
WHERE CategoryID = 7;
```

Using the *MERGE* Statement

The *MERGE* statement, along with change data capture (CDC), which were both introduced in SQL Server 2008, greatly enhance the functionality for data warehouses and staging databases. The *MERGE* statement gives you the ability to compare rows in a source and destination table. You can then define the appropriate *INSERT*, *UPDATE*, or *DELETE* command to be performed based on the results of the comparison.

> **MORE INFO** **CHANGE DATA CAPTURE (CDC)**
>
> For more information about CDC, see Chapter 9, "An Introduction to Microsoft SQL Server Manageability Features."

MERGE Statement Syntax

The syntax of the *MERGE* statement is as follows:

```
[ WITH <common_table_expression> [,...n] ]
MERGE
    [ TOP ( expression ) [ PERCENT ] ]
    [ INTO ] target_table [ WITH ( <merge_hint> ) ] [ [ AS ] table_alias ]
    USING <table_source>
    ON <merge_search_condition>
    [ WHEN MATCHED [ AND <clause_search_condition> ]
        THEN <merge_matched> ]
    [ WHEN NOT MATCHED [ BY TARGET ] [ AND <clause_search_condition> ]
        THEN <merge_not_matched> ]
    [ WHEN NOT MATCHED BY SOURCE [ AND <clause_search_condition> ]
        THEN <merge_matched> ]
    [ <output_clause> ]
    [ OPTION ( <query_hint> [ ,...n ] ) ]
;
```

The following options can be defined as part of the *MERGE* statement syntax:

- **[INTO] <target_table>**   Defines the table or view where the rows returned by the *WHEN* clauses will be inserted, updated, or deleted. This table or view is also used to match data against rows in the *<table_source>* based on the *<clause_search_ condition>*. If the *<target_table>* is a view, all conditions for updating a view must be met for the *MERGE* statement to succeed.

- **[AS] table_alias**   Defines an alias that can be used to minimize typing or make a command more readable by shortening table names referenced multiple times within the command.

- **USING <table_source>**   Defines the table, view, or expression from which the rows that are matched to the target table come.

- **ON <merge_search_condition>**   Specifies the conditions that should be used to define whether the rows in the two tables match. Similar to the *ON* clause in a *JOIN* operation, this could simply be `<table1_id> = <table2_id>`.

- **WHEN MATCHED THEN <merge_matched>**   Defines the action to be performed on the rows in the target table where a match exists between the source and target rows based on the *ON <merge_search_condition>* clause and any additional conditions specified as part of the *WHEN MATCHED THEN <merge_matched>* clause. For an *UPDATE* to succeed, the source row must match only one target row. A single *MERGE* statement can have up to two *WHEN MATCHED* clauses joined by an *AND* operator. When two *WHEN MATCHED* clauses are defined, one must perform an *UPDATE* and one a *DELETE*. In addition, the second *WHEN MATCHED* clause is performed only where the first is not. For example, assume the target table includes only rows for products that are in stock. It does not include rows for products with 0 or negative inventory. The source table includes stock inventory changes and additions and subtractions from stock (represented as positive and negative integers). The first *WHEN MATCHED* clause includes a condition of adding the quantities of matched rows and then verifying if they are greater than 0. If yes, the quantity in the target table is set to the sum of the source quantity and the target quantity. The second *WHEN MATCHED* clause has a condition of the sum being less than or equal to 0 and if that is so, it deletes the row from the target table.

- **WHEN NOT MATCHED [BY TARGET] THEN <merge_not_matched>**   Specifies that a row be inserted into the target table if a matched row is not found and if any additional conditions defined in the *WHEN NOT MATCHED [BY TARGET]* clause. Only one *WHEN NOT MATCHED [BY TARGET]* clause may exist in a *MERGE* statement.

- **WHEN NOT MATCHED BY SOURCE THEN <merge_matched>**   Defines an *UPDATE* or *DELETE* action on rows that exist in the target table but not in the source. Like the *WHEN MATCHED* clause, a *MERGE* statement can include up to two *WHEN NOT MATCHED BY SOURCE* clauses, and when two exist, one must be defined as an *UPDATE* and the other is defined as a *DELETE*. When no rows are returned by the source table, columns in the source table cannot be referenced in the *<merge_matched>* clause or an error 207 (invalid column name) is returned.

MERGE Statement Samples

A common merge scenario is moving data from one table to another. For example, suppose that a company needs to copy information from the *SalesOrderDetail* table in the *AdventureWorks2008* database to the *SalesOrderDetailHistory* table. The *SalesOrderDetailHistory* table includes a column called *Cancelled* in addition to the columns defined in the *SalesOrderDetail* table. Instead of using timestamps or some other method to identify what rows have changed since the last time information was moved, the *MERGE* statement can compare the two tables and insert only new rows, rather than having to insert all rows or maintaining *Timestamp* columns. The use of CDC makes this process even more efficient. The *MERGE* statement here inserts any new rows into the *SalesOrderDetailHistory* table and adds a value of "True" to the *Cancelled* column for any rows that no longer exist in the source table. Because business rules and data constraints prohibit updates to the *SalesOrderDetails* table, row modifications are not checked or propagated:

```
MERGE INTO Sales.SalesOrderDetailHistory AS SODH
  USING Sales.SalesOrderDetail AS SOD
  ON SODH.salesorderid = SOD.salesorderid
  AND SODH.SalesOrderDetailID = SOD.SalesOrderDetailID
WHEN NOT MATCHED BY TARGET THEN
  INSERT (Linetotal, SalesOrderID, SalesOrderDetailID, CarrierTrackingNumber, OrderQty
  , ProductID, SpecialOfferID, UnitPrice, UnitPriceDiscount
  , rowguid, ModifiedDate, Cancelled)
VALUES (Linetotal, SalesOrderID, SalesOrderDetailID, CarrierTrackingNumber, OrderQty
  , ProductID, SpecialOfferID, UnitPrice, UnitPriceDiscount
  , rowguid, ModifiedDate,DEFAULT)
WHEN NOT MATCHED BY SOURCE THEN
  UPDATE SET SODH.Cancelled = 'True';
```

You can use the *OUTPUT* clause in conjunction with the *$action* variable to report information on whether inserts, updates, or deletes were performed during the execution of the *MERGE* statement, as shown in Figure 2-1.

PRACTICE **Implementing Extended DML Functionality**

In this practice, you use the *OUTPUT* clause to report the before and after states of the quantity column when a row is updated in the *SalesOrderDetail* table. You also use the *MERGE* statement in conjunction with the *OUTPUT* clause to maintain information in a *SalesOrderDetailHistory* table and track changes performed by the *MERGE* statement in the *MergeAudit* table.

EXERCISE 1 Use the *OUTPUT* Clause

In this exercise, you test a script that uses the *OUTPUT* clause to build a table variable with information determined by the results of an *UPDATE* command. You perform this update as part of a transaction so that you can roll back changes after the test has been successfully completed. Transactions are covered in detail in Lesson 3, later in this chapter.

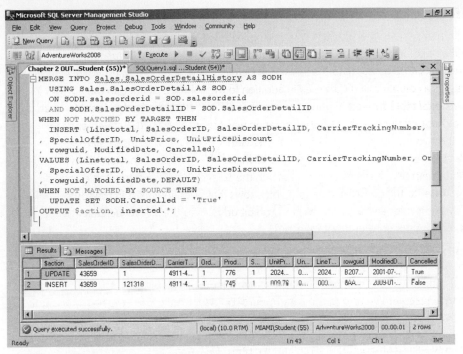

```
Microsoft SQL Server Management Studio                                    _|5|x|
File  Edit  View  Query  Project  Debug  Tools  Window  Community  Help
New Query

AdventureWorks2008  ▼  Execute ▶ ■ ✓

Chapter 2 OUT...Student (55))*  SQLQuery1.sql...Student (54))*            ▼ × 

MERGE INTO Sales.SalesOrderDetailHistory AS SODH
    USING Sales.SalesOrderDetail AS SOD
    ON SODH.salesorderid = SOD.salesorderid
    AND SODH.SalesOrderDetailID = SOD.SalesOrderDetailID
WHEN NOT MATCHED BY TARGET THEN
    INSERT (Linetotal, SalesOrderID, SalesOrderDetailID, CarrierTrackingNumber,
    , SpecialOfferID, UnitPrice, UnitPriceDiscount
    , rowguid, ModifiedDate, Cancelled)
VALUES (Linetotal, SalesOrderID, SalesOrderDetailID, CarrierTrackingNumber, Or
    , SpecialOfferID, UnitPrice, UnitPriceDiscount
    , rowguid, ModifiedDate,DEFAULT)
WHEN NOT MATCHED BY SOURCE THEN
    UPDATE SET SODH.Cancelled = 'True'
OUTPUT $action, inserted.*;
```

	$action	SalesOrderID	SalesOrderD...	CarrierT...	Ord...	Prod...	S...	UnitPr...	Un...	LineT...	rowguid	ModifiedD...	Cancelled
1	UPDATE	43659	1	4911-4...	1	776	1	2024...	0...	2024...	B207...	2001-07-...	True
2	INSERT	43659	121318	4911-4...	1	745	1	009.76	0...	000...	84A...	2009-01-...	False

```
Query executed successfully.     (local) (10.0 RTM)  MIAMI\Student (55)  AdventureWorks2008  00:00:01  2 rows
Ready                                                Ln 43        Col 1        Ch 1              INS
```

FIGURE 2-1 Results of running the *OUTPUT* $action clause

1. If necessary, start SSMS, connect to your SQL Server instance, and open a new query window.

2. In the new query window, type and execute the following command to declare a table type variable, update a row in the *SalesOrderDetail* table, and output the results to the table variable:

```
USE AdventureWorks2008;

BEGIN TRANSACTION;

DECLARE @testoutput TABLE
    (SalesOrderID int, SalesOrderDetailID int
    , QtyBefore int, QtyAfter int
    , ModifiedDate datetime2, UserNmae varchar(30))
UPDATE Sales.SalesOrderDetail
SET OrderQty = 2
OUTPUT inserted.SalesOrderID, inserted.SalesOrderDetailID
        , deleted.OrderQty, inserted.OrderQty
        , GETDATE(), SUSER_SNAME()
        INTO @testoutput
WHERE SalesOrderID = 43659 and SalesOrderDetailID = 1;

SELECT * FROM @testoutput;
```

3. Verify that a row is returned with the required data.

4. In the existing query window, below the existing code, type, highlight, and execute the following command to undo the change that you made to the *SalesOrderDetail* row:

```
ROLLBACK TRANSACTION;
```

5. Save the script and close the query window. Leave SSMS open for the next exercise.

EXERCISE 2   Use the *MERGE* Statement and *OUTPUT* Clause

In this exercise, you execute a script that creates a *SalesOrderDetailHistory* table in the *AdventureWorks2008* database. You then use the *MERGE* statement and the *OUTPUT* clause to maintain the data in the *SalesOrderDetailHistory* table, as well as provide auditing information about the modifications made to the *SalesOrderDetailHistory* table.

1. In SSMS, open a new query window.

2. Open, review, and execute the Lesson02 PracticeSetup.sql file, which can be found among the accompanying sample files in the Practice folder to create the *SalesOrderDetailHistory* table from the *SalesOrderDetail* table. The script also adds the *Cancelled* column and sets the initial values to *False*. Finally, the script adds an audit table to hold information about modifications performed by the *MERGE* statement.

3. Review the result set and notice that all the rows from the *SalesOrderDetail* table have been copied to the new *SalesOrderDetailHistory* table. This exercise deals with *SalesOrderID* 43659, so review the rows relating to 43659.

4. Open a new query window.

5. In the new query window, type and execute the following command to start a new transaction, and insert a row into the *SalesOrderDetail* table, modify the *OrderQty* of a row, and delete a row from the *SalesOrderDetail* table:

```
USE AdventureWorks2008;

BEGIN TRANSACTION;

DELETE FROM Sales.SalesOrderDetail
WHERE SalesOrderID = 43659 AND SalesOrderDetailID = 1
INSERT INTO Sales.SalesOrderDetail
  (SalesOrderID, CarrierTrackingNumber, OrderQty, ProductID
  , SpecialOfferID, UnitPrice, UnitPriceDiscount
  , rowguid, ModifiedDate)
VALUES (43659, '4911-403-C-98', 1, 745
  , 1, 809.76, 0.00
  , DEFAULT, DEFAULT)
UPDATE Sales.SalesOrderDetail
SET OrderQty = 2
WHERE SalesOrderID = 43659 AND SalesOrderDetailID = 2;
```

6. In the existing query window, below the existing code, type, highlight, and execute the following code to merge the changes into the *Sales.SalesOrderDetailHistory* table as well as add the required information about the merge to the *MergeAudit* table:

```
SET IDENTITY_INSERT Sales.SalesOrderDetailHistory ON;

MERGE INTO Sales.SalesOrderDetailHistory AS SODH
  USING Sales.SalesOrderDetail AS SOD
  ON SODH.SalesOrderID = SOD.SalesOrderId
  AND SODH.SalesOrderDetailID = SOD.SalesOrderDetailID
WHEN NOT MATCHED BY TARGET THEN
  INSERT (Linetotal, SalesOrderID, SalesOrderDetailID
          , CarrierTrackingNumber, OrderQty, ProductID
          , SpecialOfferID, UnitPrice, UnitPriceDiscount
          , rowguid, ModifiedDate, Cancelled)
  VALUES (Linetotal, SalesOrderID, SalesOrderDetailID
          , CarrierTrackingNumber, OrderQty, ProductID
          , SpecialOfferID, UnitPrice, UnitPriceDiscount
          , rowguid, ModifiedDate,DEFAULT)
WHEN NOT MATCHED BY SOURCE THEN
  UPDATE SET SODH.Cancelled = 'True'
WHEN MATCHED AND
    (SODH.OrderQty <> SOD.OrderQty
    OR SODH.SpecialOfferID <> SOD.SpecialOfferID
            OR SODH.UnitPrice <> SOD.Unitprice
            OR SODH.UnitPriceDiscount <> SOD.UnitPriceDiscount)
    THEN
    UPDATE SET SODH.OrderQty = SOD.OrderQty
            , SODH.SpecialOfferID = SOD.SpecialOfferID
            , SODH.UnitPrice = SOD.Unitprice
            , SODH.UnitPriceDiscount = SOD.UnitPriceDiscount
            , SODH.Linetotal = SOD.Linetotal
OUTPUT inserted.salesorderid,inserted.salesorderdetailid, getdate(), $action
INTO MergeAudit ;

SELECT * from Sales.SalesOrderDetailHistory
WHERE Salesorderid = 43659;

SELECT * FROM MergeAudit;
```

7. In the existing query window, below the existing code, type, highlight, and execute the following command to undo the changes that you made:

```
ROLLBACK TRANSACTION;
```

8. Save the script and close the query window.

9. Verify that you have closed all the query windows opened during this practice, and then open, review, and execute the Lesson02 PracticeCleanup.sql file, which can be found among the accompanying sample files in the Chapter 2/Lesson 2 folder.

Lesson Summary

- The *OUTPUT* clause allows you to redirect information to the calling application, or to an object such as a table or a table variable, about the *INSERT*, *UPDATE*, or *DELETE* statement performed.

- The *MERGE* statement allows you to perform DML actions on a target table based on whether or not a row matches information found in a source table.

Lesson 3: Managing Transactions

Because data manipulation is a prominent function in Online Transaction Processing (OLTP) databases, transactions are important in managing and maintaining consistent data.

After this lesson, you will be able to:

- Describe why transactions are used in SQL Server 2008.
- Describe implicit transactions and set a session to support implicit transactions.
- Define explicit transactions.
- Describe how *ROLLBACK* functions in different situations, such as with savepoints or nested transactions.
- Describe the different modes of locks assigned to resources within SQL Server.
- Describe transaction isolation levels.
- Set transaction isolation levels.

Estimated lesson time: 60 minutes

Understanding Transactions

Transactions are frequently defined as a set of actions that succeed or fail as a whole. To be more specific, transactions can provide four major functions to the data manipulation processes that access the database:

- **Atomicity**   When two or more pieces of information are involved in a transaction, either all the pieces are committed or none of them are committed.
- **Consistency**   At the end of a transaction, either a new and valid form of the data exists or the data is returned to its original state. Returning data to its original state is part of the rollback functionality provided by SQL Server transactions.
- **Isolation**   During a transaction (before it is committed or rolled back), the data must remain in an isolated state and not be accessible to other transactions. In SQL Server, the isolation level can be controlled for each transaction, as described later in this lesson.
- **Durability**   After a transaction is committed, the final state of the data is still available even if the server fails or is restarted. This functionality is provided through checkpoints and the database recovery process performed at startup in SQL Server.

   The acronym ACID is used to represent these four functions.

By default in SQL Server, each *INSERT*, *UPDATE*, or *DELETE* statement is an individual transaction that is committed automatically and does not offer rollback functionality.

You can enable implicit transactions within your connection settings so that the Database Engine starts a transaction automatically when any of the following commands are executed: *ALTER TABLE, CREATE, DELETE, DENY, DROP, FETCH, GRANT, INSERT, OPEN, REVOKE, SELECT,*

TRUNCATE TABLE, or *UPDATE.* The transaction is active until you manually issue a *COMMIT* or *ROLLBACK* statement. You can enable implicit transactions by using the *SET IMPLICIT_ TRANSACTIONS ON* statement, through the Object Linking and Embedding Database (OLE DB) or Open Database Connectivity (ODBC) application programming interfaces (APIs), on the ANSI page of the Query Options window in SSMS, or you can modify the server properties to change the default behavior to enable implicit transactions in all connections, unless they are explicitly set to *OFF* for a specific connection.

Defining Explicit Transactions

Explicit transactions are typically defined within stored procedures. An explicit transaction is started when a *BEGIN TRANSACTION* statement is executed. The transaction is completed by issuing either a *COMMIT TRANSACTION* or *ROLLBACK TRANSACTION* statement. Once a transaction is committed, SQL Server ensures that the data is written to the database even in cases of server failure. A *ROLLBACK* statement returns the data to its state prior to the start of the transaction.

> **NOTE   ROLLBACK FUNCTIONALITY**
>
> Although the *ROLLBACK* statement returns the data to its prior state, some functionalities, such as seed values for identity columns, are not reset.

While a transaction is active, locks are maintained on the resources accessed based on the isolation level of the transaction. When a transaction completes (through *COMMIT* or *ROLLBACK*), all locks are released. Understanding how these locks and isolation levels function is critical to understanding and optimizing code that includes transactions.

Understanding Special *ROLLBACK* Scenarios

When transactions are nested, by issuing multiple *BEGIN TRANSACTION* statements within a session, a *ROLLBACK* statement rolls back to the outermost nested transaction. This is even true if *COMMIT* statements are issued for the inner transactions before the *ROLLBACK* command is issued for the outer transaction. In the following example, the data is rolled back all the way to the transaction starting on line 1, and the inserted row does not exist at all in the table. (The line numbers are only for reference.)

```
1. BEGIN TRANSACTION
2. INSERT INTO TestTable
3. VALUES (1, 'a', 'b');

4.    BEGIN TRANSACTION
5.    UPDATE TestTable
6.    SET Col2 = 'c' WHERE TestID = 1;
7.    COMMIT TRANSACTION;

8. ROLLBACK;
```

If you want to roll back only a portion of a transaction, you can define savepoints by using the *SAVE TRANSACTION savepoint_name* statement and then referencing the savepoint name in the *ROLLBACK* statement. By doing this, you are telling the Database Engine to roll back data changes only to the point where you issued the *SAVE TRANSACTION* statement with the same name.

If you define more than one savepoint with the same name, the *ROLLBACK* statement rolls the data back to the most recent savepoint with the name specified in the *ROLLBACK* statement. If you would like to roll back the entire transaction, issue a *ROLLBACK TRANSACTION* statement with the transaction name or with no name. Remember that issuing a *ROLLBACK TRANSACTION* statement with no name rolls back all nested transactions.

> **IMPORTANT** **ADDITIONAL CODE AND RESTRICTIONS**
>
> You must include a *COMMIT* statement for the saved portion of the transaction and any additional code that may follow the *ROLLBACK TRANSACTION savepoint_name* statement. In addition, you cannot use savepoints with distributed transactions.

Gathering Information About Transactions

It is important to track active transactions, especially when working with nested transactions and savepoints. When working with stored procedures, error handling routines should verify transaction completion (*COMMIT* or *ROLLBACK*) before closing a connection.

You can use the *@@trancount* global variable to see the number of open transactions in the current session.

For a greater level of detail, you can use the following transaction-specific dynamic management objects:

- *sys.dm_tran_active_snapshot_database_transactions*
- *sys.dm_tran_current_snapshot*
- *sys.dm_tran_database_transactions*
- *sys.dm_tran_session_transactions*
- *sys.dm_tran_transactions_snapshot*
- *sys.dm_tran_active_transactions*
- *sys.dm_tran_current_transaction*
- *sys.dm_tran_top_version_generators*
- *sys.dm_tran_version_store*
- *sys.dm_tran_locks*

Like *@@trancount*, the *sys.dm_tran_current_transaction* object provides information on the current transaction within the current session.

The *sys.dm_tran_active_transactions* object returns information about all active transactions on an instance. The transaction ID reported is unique across all databases, but not across all instances on a server. Figure 2-2 shows sample output from *sys.dm_tran_active_transactions* where two transactions, one named *Tran1* and one named *Tran2,* are currently active in two sessions other than the current query session.

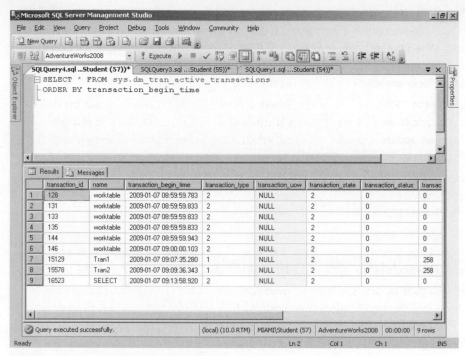

FIGURE 2-2 *sys.dm_tran_active_transactions*

Understanding Locking

To understand fully how transactions interact with one another on a database server, you must first understand isolation levels and locking. In a database environment, there are two general control philosophies about locking. The pessimistic control approach assumes that users could attempt to read and update the same data concurrently and locks are used to prevent problems caused by multiple users accessing the same data concurrently. The optimistic control approach assumes that either users will not be accessing data at the same time or that a certain level of temporary inconsistency is acceptable for concurrent reads during an update, and no read locks are issued so that better concurrency and faster performance can be achieved.

To achieve the required approach, you use a combination of lock hints and isolation levels. Although locking and isolation levels are very interconnected, we discuss locks and how to view locking information on the server first, followed by a discussion of isolation levels.

Locks are typically handled dynamically by the lock manager, a part of the Database Engine, not through applications.

SQL Server assigns locks at different levels to optimize performance, resource management, and concurrency. Locks can be assigned to resources such as rows, pages, indexes, tables, and databases. Depending on the requirements, locks may be assigned to more than one level, creating a hierarchy of related locks.

SQL Server 2008 includes the following locking modes:

- **Shared (S)**   Placed on resources for read (*SELECT*) operations. Shared locks are compatible with other shared locks. Shared locks are not compatible with exclusive locks. When the isolation level is set to *REPEATABLE READ* or higher, or a locking hint is used, the shared locks are retained for the duration of the transaction. Otherwise, shared locks are released as soon as the read is completed.

- **Update (U)**   Placed on resources where a shared (S) lock is required, but the need to upgrade to an exclusive (X) lock is anticipated. Only one transaction at a time can obtain an update lock on a resource. When modification to the resource is required, the update lock is upgraded to an exclusive lock.

- **Exclusive (X)**   Placed on resources for data modification. An exclusive lock is not compatible with any other type of lock. Only the *NOLOCK* hint or the *READ UNCOMMITTED* isolation level overrides an exclusive lock's functionality.

- **Intent (IS, IX, SIX)**   Placed on resources to improve performance and locking efficiency by placing intent (IS, IX, SIX) locks at a high-level object (such as a table) before placing shared (S) or exclusive (X) locks at a lower level (such as the page level).

- **Schema (Sch-M, Sch-S)**   Schema modification (Sch-M) locks are placed on objects during schema modification operations, such as adding a new column to a table. Schema stability (Sch-S) locks are placed on objects while queries are being compiled or executed. Sch-M locks block all other operations until the lock is released. Sch-S locks are not compatible with Sch-M locks.

- **Bulk Update (BU)**   Placed on tables for bulk insert. These locks allow multiple bulk insert threads to access the table but do not allow other processes to access the table. These locks are enabled by either using the *TABLOCK* hint or by using the *sp_tableoption* stored procedure to enable the *Table lock on bulk load* table option.

- **Key-range**   Placed on a range of rows to protect against phantom insertions and deletions in a record set that is being accessed by a transaction. These locks are used by transactions using the *SERIALIZABLE* transaction isolation level.

Understanding Deadlock and Blocking Scenarios

Because transactions at certain isolation levels hold locks until the transaction is completed, transactions can block each other from completing successfully. By default, transactions in SQL Server 2008 wait an indefinite amount of time for a resource to become available unless SQL Server recognizes that a deadlock situation has occurred. In a deadlock situation, two transactions are holding resources that each of the two transactions requires before completion. Because of this, neither transaction is ever able to complete successfully. Based on the estimated cost for SQL Server to roll back each transaction, the lock manager selects a "victim" of the deadlock situation and rolls back that transaction, issuing a 1205 error. Because this error does not attempt to restart the transaction or provide an informative message to users, all 1205 errors should be captured and handled appropriately.

You can use the following best practices to reduce deadlock situations and blocking issues:

- Keep transactions short.
- Collect and verify input data from users before opening a transaction.
- Access resources in the same order whenever possible within transactions.
- Keep transactions in a single batch.
- Where appropriate, use a lower isolation level or row versioning–based isolation level.
- Access the least amount of data possible in the transaction.

To manage blocking issues further, database administrators can adjust the query wait times based on performance analysis. This can be accomplished through the advanced server properties. To locate transactions that are affected by deadlock situations, you can use SQL Server Profiler to produce an Extensible Markup Language (XML) representation of a deadlock chain of events, including the *system process ID (SPID)* of the transactions involved in the deadlock situation.

Understanding Reports on Lock Status

There are many options for viewing lock status within your computer running SQL Server. You can use SQL Profiler to capture lock and blocking information. You can use the System Monitor that is part of the performance console (*perfmon*) to capture statistics on lock wait times, locks per second, and so on. You can use the *sys.dm_tran_locks* dynamic management view (DMV) to gather information on locks being held by transactions. Finally, you can use the Activity Monitor in SSMS to see information on blocking processes.

A representation of Activity Monitor showing a session being blocked by another session is shown in Figure 2-3.

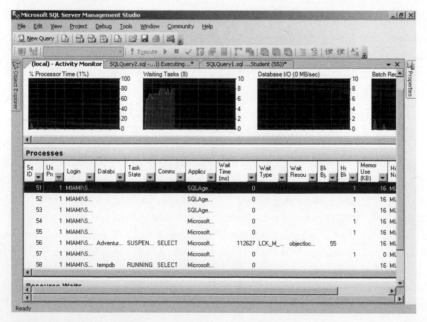

FIGURE 2-3 Activity Monitor

The *sys.dm_tran_locks* DMV provides detailed information about each lock that is currently being held on the instance. You can then use the *sys.dm_tran_active_transactions* DMV to provide additional information about the blocked or blocking transaction. Figures 2-4 and 2-5 show the results of a query of the *sys.dm_tran_locks* and the *sys.dm_tran_active_transactions* DMVs.

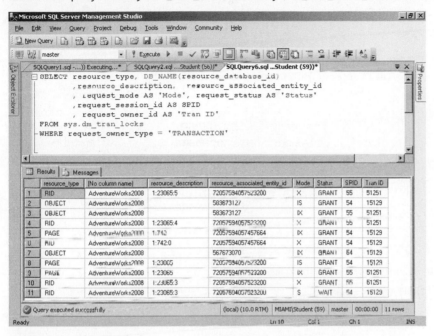

FIGURE 2-4 *sys.dm_tran_locks*

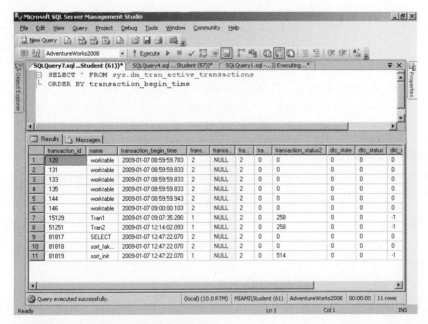

FIGURE 2-5 *sys.dm_tran_active_transactions*

In many of these reports, you see the locking method and the resource that is locked. You might see locks on the following types of resources:

- **Row Identifier (RID)** A row identifier used to define a lock on a single row located in a heap

> **NOTE HEAPS**
>
> A *heap* is the storage method for a table without a clustered index. For more information about indexing, see Chapter 6, "Techniques to Improve Query Performance."

- **KEY** The range of keys in an index used to define a lock on key ranges
- **PAGE** An 8-kilobyte (KB) page from tables or indexes
- **EXTENT** A group of eight contiguous pages within a table or index
- **HoBT** A heap or a balanced tree (B-tree) index
- **TABLE** An entire table, made up of both data and index pages
- **FILE** An entire database file
- **APPLICATION** An application-specified resource
- **METADATA** Used for metadata locks
- **ALLOCATION_UNIT** A single allocation unit
- **DATABASE** An entire database, including all data files

Using SQL Server Extended Events

SQL Server 2008 includes SQL Server Extended Events, such as *FindBlocker* and *lock_count*, which can be used in conjunction with Windows Event logs, SQL Profiler, or System Monitor.

> **MORE INFO EXTENDED EVENTS**
>
> Working with SQL Server Extended Events is beyond the scope of this book. For more information about Extended Events, see the article titled "Advanced Troubleshooting with Extended Events" at *http://technet.microsoft.com/en-us/magazine/dd314391.aspx*. To learn more about or to download a copy of the Extended Events Manager, a C# Microsoft.NET WinForms application that aids in creating and working with Extended Events sessions, see "SQL Server 2008 Extended Events Manager" at *http://www.codeplex.com/ExtendedEventManager*.

Using *DBCC LOG*

SQL Server includes the *DBCC LOG* statement, which is a nondocumented feature that returns information about the information contained in the current transaction log. The syntax is as follows:

```
DBCC LOG (<databasename>, <output identifier>)
```

The output identifier may be set to any of the following levels:

- **0** Returns minimal information, including the current Log Sequence Number (LSN), operation, context, transaction ID, and log block generation

- **1** Returns all the information from the previous level, as well as flags and record length information

- **2** Returns all the information from the previous level, as well as the object name, index name, page ID, and slot ID

- **3** Returns a full set of information about the operation

- **4** Returns a full set of information about the operation, as well as a hex dump of the current transaction log row

Setting Transaction Isolation Levels

The following transaction levels can be set by using the *SET TRANSACTION ISOLATION LEVEL* syntax:

- ***READ UNCOMMITTED*** Allows statements to read rows that were updated by a transaction before the rows are committed to the database. This isolation level minimizes contention but allows dirty reads and nonrepeatable (phantom) reads.

- ***READ COMMITTED*** Allows statements within the current connection and transaction to experience nonrepeatable (phantom) reads but prevents dirty reads (data updated by another connection's open transaction). This is the default setting for SQL Server 2008.

- ***REPEATABLE READ*** Does not allow transactions to read noncommitted modified data (dirty reads) and ensures that shared locks are maintained until the current transaction is completed.

- ***SNAPSHOT*** Requires the *ALLOW_SNAPSHOT_ISOLATION* database option to be set to *ON*. The *SNAPSHOT* isolation level takes a snapshot of the data at the time the data is read into the transaction but does not hold locks on the data. Updates can occur on the data from other transactions, but the current transaction does not see those updates reflected in subsequent reads of the original data. If the current transaction modifies data, those modifications are visible only to the current transaction.

- ***SERIALIZABLE*** Does not allow data to be read that has been modified but not committed by other transactions. In addition, no other transactions can update data that has been read by the current transaction until the current transactions is complete. The *SERIALIZABLE* isolation level protects against phantom reads but causes the highest level of blocking and contention.

MORE INFO **TRANSACTION ISOLATION LEVELS AND LOCKING**

A complete discussion of isolation levels and the effects on locking and blocking is beyond the scope of this book. *Microsoft SQL Server 2008 Internals* (Microsoft Press, 2009), by Kalen Delaney et al., has an extensive discussion about isolation levels.

Command Syntax

Once you have determined the appropriate transaction isolation level, the command syntax is very straightforward, as shown here:

```
SET TRANSACTION ISOLATION LEVEL
    { READ UNCOMMITTED
    | READ COMMITTED
    | REPEATABLE READ
    | SNAPSHOT
    | SERIALIZABLE
    }
[ ; ]
```

Once the *SET TRANSACTION ISOLATION LEVEL* statement has been executed in a session, all transactions within that connection use the defined isolation level.

PRACTICE Defining Explicit Transactions

In this practice, you verify a rollback of nested transactions.

EXERCISE Define Explicit Transactions

In this exercise, you create a very simple table and test how rollbacks affect committed nested transactions.

1. If necessary, start SSMS, connect to your SQL Server instance, and open a new query window.

2. In the query window, type and execute the following code to create a simple table:

```
USE AdventureWorks2008;
CREATE TABLE testtran (col1 int, col2 int);
```

3. Open a new query window, type, highlight, and execute the following code to begin a transaction, verify the data currently in the *testtran* table, add a row to the *testtran* table, and then verify the data now included in the *testtran* table and the number of open transactions:

```
BEGIN TRAN

    SELECT * FROM testtran;

    INSERT INTO testtran VALUES (1,1);

    SELECT * FROM testtran;

    SELECT @@TRANCOUNT;
```

4. In the current query window, below the existing code, type, highlight, and execute the following code to start a nested transaction, insert a second row, and verify the rows in the table and the number of open transactions:

```
BEGIN TRAN

    INSERT INTO testtran VALUES (2,2);
```

```
SELECT * FROM testtran;

SELECT @@TRANCOUNT;
```

5. In the current query window, below the existing code, type, highlight, and execute the following code to commit the inner transaction, and verify the data in the table and that the transaction level has decreased by 1:

```
COMMIT TRAN

SELECT * FROM testtran;

SELECT @@TRANCOUNT;
```

6. In the current query window, below the existing code, type, highlight, and execute the following code to roll back the transactions and verify that both rows were removed from the table and the transaction level has been lowered to 0:

```
ROLLBACK TRAN

SELECT * FROM testtran;

SELECT @@TRANCOUNT;
```

7. Save the script and close the query window.

8. Verify that you have closed all the query windows opened during this practice, and then open, review, and execute the Lesson03 PracticeCleanup.sql file, which can be found among the accompanying sample files in the Chapter 2/Lesson 3 folder.

9. Close SSMS.

Lesson Summary

- A transaction is a set of actions that make up an atomic unit of work and must succeed or fail as a whole

- By default, implicit transactions are not enabled. When implicit transactions are enabled, a number of statements automatically begin a transaction. The developer must execute a *COMMIT* or *ROLLBACK* statement to complete the transaction.

- Explicit transactions start with a *BEGIN TRANSACTION* statement and are completed by either a *ROLLBACK TRANSACTION* or *COMMIT TRANSACTION* statement.

- Issuing a *ROLLBACK* command when transactions are nested rolls back all transactions to the outermost *BEGIN TRANSACTION* statement, regardless of previously issued *COMMIT* statements for nested transactions.

- SQL Server uses a variety of lock modes, including shared (S), exclusive (X), and intent (IS, IX, SIX) to manage data consistency while multiple transactions are being processed concurrently.

- SQL Server 2008 supports the *READ UNCOMMITTED, READ COMMITTED, REPEATABLE READ, SNAPSHOT,* and *SERIALIZABLE* isolation levels.

Chapter Review

To practice and reinforce the skills you learned in this chapter further, you can perform the following tasks:

- Review the chapter summary.
- Review the list of key terms introduced in this chapter.
- Complete the case scenarios. The scenarios set up a real-world situation involving the topics of this chapter and ask you to create solutions.
- Complete the suggested practices.
- Take a practice test.

Chapter Summary

- DML statements such as *INSERT*, *UPDATE*, and *DELETE* allow you to handle the data storage and retrieval requirements of your organization.
- The *MERGE* statement and *OUTPUT* clause allow you to increase the functionality of your OLTP database environment as well as data warehouse and reporting environments. These options, in addition to CDC, provide a means to compare rows and set the *UPDATE, INSERT,* or *DELETE* logic based on those comparisons.
- Transactions and locks provide the means by which many users can access and update data concurrently on a server running SQL Server while receiving a consistent view of the data.

Key Terms

Do you know what these key terms mean? You can check your answers by looking up the terms in the glossary at the end of the book.

- System process ID (SPID)
- Row identifier (RID)
- Atomicity
- Consistency
- Isolation
- Durability

Case Scenarios

In the following case scenarios, you apply what you have learned in this chapter. You can find answers to these questions in the "Answers" section at the end of this book.

Case Scenario 1: Modifying Data

You are a database developer for Wide World Importers. Five of the companies from which your company imports goods have decided to remove their fax capabilities and receive information only via the Internet or e-mail. Corporate data standards require that the fax column either be the numeric value or *NULL*. In addition, even though a column for e-mail addresses exists, these companies have not previously had e-mail addresses in their records. You must add this information. Finally, all updates to the fax, address, or e-mail address must have their before and after states, along with the user name of the person making the change and the date the change was made, recorded in the *ImporterPropertiesAudit* table.

Answer the following question for your manager:

- What statement(s) and or clauses do you need to use to provide the required functionality?

Case Scenario 2: Using Transactions

You are a database developer for Litware, Inc. Litware has had numerous problems with long wait times and many deadlock situations. The database administrator has collected performance information through *perfmon* and SQL Server Profiler and has determined that the majority of the problems seem to involve five long-running stored procedures that include transactions. You have been asked to review the stored procedures and make recommendations for improving the locking and blocking concerns.

Answer the following question for your manager:

- What types of information should you consider when determining your recommendations?

Suggested Practices

To help you master the exam objectives presented in this chapter, do all the following practices.

Modify Data by Using *INSERT*, *UPDATE*, and *DELETE* Statements

- **Practice 1**   Write multiple *INSERT* statements using a variety of options.
- **Practice 2**   Write *UPDATE* and *DELETE* statements, including those based on the results from a joined table.

Return Data by Using the *OUTPUT* Clause

- **Practice 3**   Write a variety of statements that make use of both the *INSERTED* and *DELETED* tables using the *OUTPUT* clause.

Modify Data by Using *MERGE* Statements

- **Practice 4** Write a variety of *MERGE* statements including those using two definitions for the *WHEN NOT MATCHED BY SOURCE THEN <merge_matched>* and *WHEN MATCHED THEN <merge_matched>* statements.

Manage Transactions

- **Practice 5** Practice working with transactions, including nested transactions, savepoints, and rollbacks. Verify *@@trancount* and results along each step of the process.

Take a Practice Test

The practice tests on this book's companion CD offer many options. For example, you can test yourself on just the content covered in this chapter, or you can test yourself on all the 70-433 certification exam content. You can set up the test so that it closely simulates the experience of taking a certification exam, or you can set it up in study mode so that you can look at the correct answers and explanations after you answer each question.

> **MORE INFO** **PRACTICE TESTS**
>
> For details about all the practice test options available, see the section entitled "How to Use the Practice Tests," in the Introduction to this book.

Tables, Data Types, and Declarative Data Integrity

The most basic concept of any relational database management system (RDBMS) is the table. However, tables have evolved significantly since the first RDBMS versions. In this chapter, you examine the possibilities and restrictions that exist when designing your tables. The chapter also covers ways of optimizing your table structures and data integrity.

Exam objectives in this chapter:

- Create and alter tables.
- Implement data types.
- Manage international considerations.
- Create and modify constraints.

Lessons in this chapter:

Before You Begin

To complete the lessons in this chapter, you must have:

- A basic understanding of Transact-SQL (T-SQL)
- A good understanding of data types in any programming language
- Microsoft SQL Server 2008 Developer Edition, Enterprise Edition, or Enterprise Evaluation Edition, and the *AdventureWorks* sample database installed

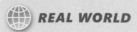 **REAL WORLD**

Tobias Thernström

Without declarative data integrity, your database can end up in a terrible state. I have seen this too many times when working with clients as a consultant. It typically starts with queries behaving oddly. As an example, I once visited a client that complained of an order that he knew should exist in the database and that he claimed had been lost. My first instinct was that it probably was lost because of an accidental delete by the client, but when querying the database, sure enough, there was the order. So why wasn't it showing up in the application? Simple: the query that fetched the order was joined (using an *INNER JOIN*) to a customer in the table containing customers, and the customer was missing! Because they didn't have any foreign key constraint declared between the customer and order tables, the customer had been accidentally deleted even though it had existing (and undelivered) orders.

Lesson 1: Working with Tables and Data Types

Designing, creating, and maintaining tables is one of the most important tasks of a database developer. In this lesson, you walk through these and other tasks related to tables. You also take a look at the data types available in SQL Server 2008.

> **After this lesson, you will be able to:**
> - Know the details of the basic data types that are included in SQL Server 2008.
> - Use these data types correctly.
> - Implement declarative data integrity in your tables.
>
> **Estimated lesson time: 60 minutes**

Data Types

Before you can start creating tables, you must understand the different data types that can be used to define the domains of columns in tables, that is, what data can be entered into the column. There are two different kinds of data types in SQL Server:

- SQL Server system data types
- User-defined types (UDTs) or SQL Common Language Runtime (SQLCLR) types

You start by reviewing the available system data types and then look at the possibility of simplifying the use of data types using UDTs. UDTs are implemented using SQLCLR, which is covered in Chapter 7, "Extending Microsoft SQL Server Functionality with XML, SQLCLR, and *Filestream*."

The available system data types are typically split into several groups, including exact numeric, approximate numeric, character, date and time, and binary.

Character Types

There are quite a few string data types in SQL Server; *char, varchar, nchar, nvarchar, text,* and *ntext*. The *text* and *ntext* types are both deprecated, so avoid using them. They have been replaced by *varchar(max)* and *nvarchar(max)*. All the *-char* types take one parameter, which is the number of characters to support storing. The difference between *char* and *varchar* (as well as between *nchar* and *nvarchar*) is that *char* is fixed-length and *varchar* is variable-length. This means that *char* always allocates enough storage space to store its entire declared length and that *varchar* stores only the actual data entered. The advantage of using *char* over *varchar* is that updates made to a *char* column never require moving the row because the data that is entered always fits in the allocated space. Note that this advantage is almost always outweighed by the fact that *varchar* uses a lot less storage space than *char* [consider *varchar(100)* vs. *char(100)*].

With *char* and *varchar,* a collation is used to specify the code page (character set) to use when storing and interpreting the contents of the columns. The collation is also used to decide how to sort and compare the data stored in these columns. There are 2,397 variations of collations available in SQL Server 2008, three of which are Japanese_ CI_AI, Finnish_Swedish_CI_AI, and Latin1_General_CI_AI. The rest can be found by querying the table-valued function *fn_helpcollations.* The collation Japanese_CI_AI uses the 932 code page to support storing Japanese characters. Both Finnish_Swedish_CI_AI and Latin1_General_CI_AI use the 1252 code page. The _CI_AI part of the collation name specifies whether the collation is case-insensitive (CI) or case-sensitive (CS), as well as accent-insensitive (AI) or accent-sensitive (AS). It is important to know that what is considered an "accent" is different in different languages and, thus, in different collations as well. Take the character ö, for example. In Latin1_General_CI_AI, ö is considered an accented o, meaning that 'o' = 'ö' would return *True;* on the other hand, in Finnish_ Swedish_CI_AI, ö is considered a separate character and 'o' = 'ö' would return *False.*

Finally, what about *nchar* and *nvarchar?* Both of these data types store characters using the Unicode universal code page (UCS-2). This means that if you use *nchar* or *nvarchar,* you can store any type of character regardless of the collation you choose because two bytes are always used to store each character. Contrast this with *varchar* and *char,* which store characters using one or two bytes depending on the collation. Remember that you still need to specify collation because the collation still decides how to sort and compare the data stored in your column.

If you want to use a different collation than the one specified on a column when making a comparison, you can specify it in an expression. Here is an example that shows the *WHERE* clause specifying a collation:

```
... WHERE Name = 'Öqvist' COLLATE Finnish_Swedish_CI_AS
```

Note that by changing the collation in the expression, SQL Server cannot use an index defined on the column to perform a seek operation because that index is sorted according to another collation.

Exact Numeric Types

The exact numeric types are made up of integer (or whole number) types and fixed decimal point types. All exact numeric types always produce the same result, regardless of which kind of processor architecture is being used or the magnitude of the numbers (that is, how large the numbers are). Table 3-1 lists the available exact numeric data types.

TABLE 3-1 Exact Numeric Data Types

DATA TYPE	STORAGE SIZE	POSSIBLE VALUES	COMMENTS
tinyint	1 byte	0 to 255	Equal to the *byte* data type in most programming languages, cannot store negative values
smallint	2 bytes	−32768 to 32767	A signed 16-bit integer

DATA TYPE	STORAGE SIZE	POSSIBLE VALUES	COMMENTS
int	4 bytes	–2,147,483,648 to 2,147,483,647	A signed 32-bit integer
bigint	8 bytes	–2E63 to 2E63 – 1	A signed 64-bit integer
decimal (precision, scale)	5 to 17 bytes depending on precision	–10E38 + 1 to 10E38 – 1	A decimal number containing up to 38 digits
numeric (precision, scale)	Functionally equivalent to the decimal data type		

While the integer data types (*tinyint, smallint, int* and *bigint*) don't accept any parameters, the decimal (and numeric) data types do. When using the decimal data type, you can specify the precision and scale of values stored using the data type. The precision defines the total number of digits that the data type holds, supporting a maximum precision of 38 and the scale defines how many of the digits defined by the precision are used as decimals. A decimal defined as *decimal(38,0)* allows only for whole numbers and a decimal defined as *decimal(38, 38)* allows only for decimals. If you define a column as just *decimal*, without specifying precision and scale, it gets the default precision of 18 and scale of 0. Depending on the precision that you specify, the *decimal* data type requires between 5 and 17 bytes of storage. It is important that you choose the lowest appropriate precision to conserve storage space, as well as memory resources. In Table 3-2, the storage required by the different precisions are listed. Note that the scale selected has no effect on storage requirements.

TABLE 3-2 Decimal Storage Requirements

PRECISION	STORAGE
1 to 9	5 bytes
10 to 19	9 bytes
20 to 28	13 bytes
29 to 38	17 bytes

Approximate Numeric Types

SQL Server supports two data types with floating point or approximate numeric values, *float* and *real*. Like the *decimal* data type described previously, the *float* data type accepts a parameter. The parameter supplied to the *float* data type defines the number of bits that are used to store the mantissa of the floating point number, as shown in Table 3-3. Any parameter value less than or equal to 24 is interpreted as 24, and anything above 24 is interpreted as 53. This means that the mantissa is either 24 or 53 bits, depending on what value you supply to the *float* parameter.

TABLE 3-3 Approximate Numeric Data Types

DATA TYPE	STORAGE SIZE	POSSIBLE VALUES
float (n <= 24)	4 bytes	−3.40E38 to −1.18E-38, 0 and 1.18E-38 to 3.40E38
float (24 > n <= 53)	8 bytes	−1.79E308 to −2.23E-308, 0 and 2.23E-308 to 1.79E308
real	Functionally equivalent to *float(24)*	

Handling Date and Time

Table 3-4 lists the data types that can hold date and time values in SQL Server 2008.

TABLE 3-4 Date and Time Data Types

DATA TYPE	STORAGE SIZE	POSSIBLE VALUES	COMMENTS
datetime	8 bytes	January 1, 1753, through December 31, 9999, with time accuracy down to every third millisecond.	Mainly available for backwards compatibility. Use *datetime2, date, time,* or *datetimeoffset* whenever possible.
smalldatetime	4 bytes	January 1, 1900, through June 6, 2079, with time accuracy down to every minute.	Mainly available for backwards compatibility. Use *datetime2, date, time,* or *datetimeoffset* whenever possible.
datetime2 (fractional seconds precision)	Between 6 and 8 bytes	January 1, 0001, through December 31, 9999, with time accuracy down to the specified fractional seconds precision.	Use when both date and time are required and time zone offset is not required.
datetimeoffset (fractional seconds precision)	Between 8 and 10 bytes	January 1, 0001, through December 31, 9999, with time accuracy down to the specified fractional seconds precision and time zone offset between −14:00 and +14:00.	Use when date, time, and time zone offset are required.

DATA TYPE	STORAGE SIZE	POSSIBLE VALUES	COMMENTS
date	3 bytes	January 1, 0001, through December 31, 9999.	Use when only a date is required.
time (fractional seconds precision)	Between 3 and 5 bytes.	00:00:00 to 23:59:59, with accuracy down to the specified fraction of a second.	Use when only a time is required.

One of the most anticipated features of SQL Server 2008 was the introduction of new *date* and *time* data types. Before SQL Server 2008, the software had two data types for managing date and time: *datetime* and *smalldatetime*. Because both of these data types are still in use in SQL Server 2008 today and it will take a long time before all databases that are upgraded to SQL Server 2008 are converted to the new *date* and *time* data types, it is very important to understand how to use the *smalldatetime* and *datetime* data types. There are two major problems with the *datetime* data type. The first problem is that the date and time are stored together, which may not always be desirable. Take the following query, where you want to retrieve all orders made on August 18, 2008:

```
SELECT
    SalesOrderID
    ,CustomerId
    ,OrderDate
FROM Sales.SalesOrderHeader
WHERE OrderDate = '20080818';
```

This query returns only orders made on August 18, 2008, at exactly 00:00:00. To solve this problem, you must handle the time portion of the *datetime* data type correctly in the query. Doing this brings us to the second problem with the *datetime* data type, which is the precision of the time portion of the data type. The smallest time unit that is supported is every third millisecond (for *smalldatetime,* it is every minute). This means that the last digit in a *datetime* instance (that is, *yyyy-MM-dd hh:mm:ss.xx**x***) can be only 0, 4, or 7. This in turn means that the last supported *datetime* time of day is 23:59:59.997. The time 23:59:59.998 rounds down to 23:59:59.997, and the time 23:59:59:999 rounds up to the next day at 00:00:00.000. This behavior is extremely important to remember when working with the *datetime* data type. Continuing with the example of querying the *Sales.SalesOrderHeader* table for all orders of August 18, 2008, you have to use either one of the following two queries to get the desired result:

```
-- Query #1
SELECT
    SalesOrderID
    ,CustomerId
    ,OrderDate
```

```
FROM Sales.SalesOrderHeader
WHERE OrderDate BETWEEN '2008-08-18T00:00:00' AND '2008-08-18T23:59:59.997';

-- Query #2
SELECT
    SalesOrderID
    ,CustomerId
    ,OrderDate
FROM Sales.SalesOrderHeader
WHERE OrderDate >= '20080818' AND OrderDate < '20080819';
```

Even though both of these queries produce the same result, you should consider using the second query because it also correctly handles the new *datetime2* data type. This is because the *datetime2* data type can store fractions of time down to 100 nanoseconds (or .0000001 of a second), meaning that .997 is not the last millisecond of the day. Whenever you query time data, you should try to use a "less than" predicate to avoid relying on a specific second fraction precision. Finally, when converting a literal string to a *datetime* or *smalldatetime* data type, you should always use the *YYYYMMDD* format for dates without time, and the *YYYY-MM-DDTHH:MI:SS.XXX* format for dates with time. Both of these formats work independent of the language and date formats in effect on your connection.

> **MORE INFO** **DATE FORMATS**
>
> For more information about how to affect the date formats that SQL Server accepts, see the articles "SET DATEFORMAT" and "SET LANGUAGE" in SQL Server Books Online.

The new, and long-awaited, date and time data types in SQL Server 2008 are *datetime2*, *date, time*, and *datetimeoffset*. We start with the simplest data type, which is *date*.

The *date* data type is something very simple and very useful, a data type that can store only dates. Because of this fact, this data type is perfect to use in all cases when no time is required. This simplifies queries because the time issue described earlier doesn't exist and because this data type saves storage space by allocating only 3 bytes. When converting a string literal to the *date* data type, you should always use the *YYYY-MM-DD* format (always including the century).

The *time* data type is available to store a time without a date. For this data type, you can supply an optional parameter specifying the precision or number of decimals for a fraction of a second that you want the time instance to support. The possible values that you can supply are between 0 and 7, that is, between a second being the smallest value (0) and 100 nanoseconds being the smallest value (7). If you do not specify this parameter when declaring the data type, a default of 7 is used. When converting a string literal to the *time* data type, you should always use the *HH:MI:SS.NNNNNNN* format. The storage size used by the *time* data type depends on the precision specified. Table 3-5 lists the storage space used depending on the specified precision.

TABLE 3-5 *Time* Data Type Storage Requirements

PRECISION	STORAGE
0 to 2	3 bytes
3 to 4	4 bytes
5 to 7	5 bytes

The *datetime2* data type is a combination of the *date* and *time* data types, with the same precision parameter for fractional seconds as the *time* data type. When converting a string literal to the *datetime2* data type, you should always use the *YYYY-MM-DD HH:MI:SS. NNNNNNN* format. Table 3-6 lists the storage space used by the *datetime2* data type depending on the precision specified.

TABLE 3-6 *Datetime2* Data Type Storage Requirements

PRECISION	STORAGE
0 to 2	6 bytes
4 to 5	7 bytes
6 to 7	8 bytes

The final date and time data type available in SQL Server 2008 is the *datetimeoffset* data type. In addition to what the *datetime2* data type stores, this data type stores a time zone offset. This can be very useful when it is important to know not only the time that something happened, but also in which time zone it happened. When converting a string literal to the *datetimeoffset* data type, you should always use the *YYYY-MM-DD HH:MI:SS.NNNNNNN +|-HH:MI* format. Table 3-7 lists the storage space used by the *datetimeoffset* data type depending on the precision specified.

TABLE 3-7 *Datetimeoffset* Data Type Storage Requirements

PRECISION	STORAGE
0 to 2	6 bytes
4 to 5	7 bytes
6 to 7	8 bytes

Table Basics

The table is the most central object of any RDBMS. In SQL Server, there are several variations of tables: permanent tables (or just tables), local temporary tables, global temporary tables, and table variables. Besides these variations, there are also table types and table parameters, which will be covered in detail in Chapter 5, "Programming Microsoft SQL Server with T-SQL User-Defined Stored Procedures, Functions, Triggers, and Views."

Creating a Table

Before you can create a table, you need a schema in which to create the table .A *schema* is similar to a namespace in many other programming languages; however, there can be only one level of schemas (that is, schemas cannot reside in other schemas). There are already several schemas that exist in a newly created database: the *dbo, sys,* and *information_schema* schemas. The *dbo* schema is the default schema for new objects, while the *sys* and *information_schema* schemas are used by different system objects.. Before SQL Server 2005, schemas did not exist. Instead of the object residing in a schema the object was owned by a database user (however, the syntax was the same: *<owner>.<object>*) In these versions, *dbo* was recommended to own all objects, but this is not true anymore. Starting with SQL Server 2005, all objects should be created within a user-defined schema. Schemas are created using the *CREATE SCHEMA* statement, as shown in the following example of creating a schema and a table within that schema:

```
CREATE SCHEMA Sales;
GO

CREATE TABLE Sales.Customers (
    CustomerId INT NOT NULL
    ,Name NVARCHAR(50) NOT NULL
);
```

Tables are created either using the *CREATE TABLE* or the *SELECT … INTO* statement (the *SELECT … INTO* statement creates a new table based on a query). The basic syntax of the *CREATE TABLE* statement is shown here:

```
CREATE TABLE
    [ database_name . [ schema_name ] . | schema_name . ] table_name
        ( { <column_definition> | <computed_column_definition>
                | <column_set_definition> }
        [ <table_constraint> ] [ ,...n ] )
    [ ON { partition_scheme_name ( partition_column_name ) | filegroup
        | "default" } ]
    [ { TEXTIMAGE_ON { filegroup | "default" } ]
    [ WITH ( <table_option> [ ,...n ] ) ]
[ ; ]
```

Before we go into the specifics of the syntax, we will look at the rules that apply when naming tables and columns.

Table and Column Names (Identifiers)

Both table and column names are identifiers, and they must adhere to certain rules. Identifiers are either standard or delimited. The requirements of each of these are described next.

STANDARD IDENTIFIERS

Here are the requirements for standard identifiers:

- The first character must be a letter or an underscore (_), not a digit.

> **NOTE EXCEPTION**
>
> The first character can also be an at sign (@) or a number sign (#), but both of these have special meanings, as follows:
>
> - @ defines a variable or parameter.

> **NOTE**
>
> @@ doesn't mean anything other than @, and it should not be used because many system functions begin with @@.
>
> - # defines a temporary object (that is, the object is available only from the current connection).
> - ## defines a global temporary object (that is, the object is available from any connection in the same instance).

- Subsequent characters can include letters, digits, the at sign (@), the dollar sign ($), the number sign (#), and the underscore (_).
- The identifier must not be a T-SQL reserved word.
- Embedded spaces or special characters are not allowed.

DELIMITED IDENTIFIERS

Any identifier that does not adhere to the standard identifier naming rules must be delimited using either quotation marks (") or square brackets ([]). Using quotation marks conforms to the ANSI SQL standard; however, you must be aware that the *SET QUOTED_IDENTIFIER* session setting must be set to *ON* for the quotation marks to be used for delimited identifiers. (Square brackets can always be used for delimited identifiers.) The default setting for *SET QUOTED_IDENTIFIER* is *ON*, but older T-SQL code may require it to be set to *OFF*. Setting *QUOTED_IDENTIFIER* to *OFF* causes SQL Server to interpret the quotation marks as strings instead of identifiers.

The following are examples of identifiers:

```
-- Standard identifiers
CREATE TABLE HR.Employees (
    EmployeeId INT NOT NULL
);


-- Delimited identifiers:
SET QUOTED_IDENTIFIER ON;

CREATE TABLE HR."Organisation Employees" (
    "Employee Id" INT NOT NULL
);
-- or
CREATE TABLE HR.[Organisation Employees] (
    [Employee Id] INT NOT NULL
);
```

Creating the Table

Now, let's look at creating a simple table. Consider this example:

```
CREATE TABLE HR.Employees (
    EmployeeId INT NOT NULL
    ,FirstName NVARCHAR(50) NOT NULL
    ,LastName NVARCHAR(50) NOT NULL
    ,PhoneNumber VARCHAR(15) NULL
    ,BirthDate DATE NOT NULL
);
```

This code creates a table named *Employees* containing five columns. The *CREATE TABLE* statement starts by defining which schema the table should reside in (in this case, *HR*), the table's name (*Employees*) and the table's columns. The columns are defined using three basic properties: column name, data type, and nullability (whether or not the column allows *NULL* values).

Naming Guidelines

When choosing the name of tables and columns, it is important to follow the organization or project's naming guidelines. A few typical naming guidelines are provided here:

- Use PascalCasing (also known as *upper camel casing*).
- Avoid abbreviations.
- A long name that users understand is preferred over a short name that users might not understand.

Choosing Data Types

The data type used for each column is also very important. We have already covered most of the data types available in SQL Server 2008, but this section discusses some guidelines that you should try to follow when deciding which data type to use. They are as follows:

- Always use the data type that requires the least amount of disk space while still providing the functionality that you require.

- It can be very costly (both in development time and server resources) to change a column's data type later on. Do not use a data type if there is a chance that it will not cover your application's future needs.

- In most cases use a variable-length data type, such as *nvarchar*, rather than a fixed-length data type, such as *nchar*.

- One of the few cases where a fixed-length data type is preferred over a variable-length data type is if the column's value changes frequently. If the column's value is updated frequently, the cost of moving the row to a new position where the new value fits may outweigh the cost of the additional storage required by a fixed data type.

- Avoid using the *datetime* and *smalldatetime* because they use more disk space and provide less precision than the new *date, time,* and *datetime2* data types.

- Use the *varchar(max), nvarchar(max),* and *varbinary(max)* data types instead of the *text, ntext,* and *image* data types, which might not be available in future releases of SQL Server.

- Use the *rowversion* data type instead of the *timestamp* data type because the *timestamp* data type may not be available in future releases of SQL Server.

- Only use the *varchar(max), nvarchar(max), varbinary(max),* and *xml* data types if a data type with a specified size cannot be used. This is because using the data types prevents you from being able to rebuild indexes online and because these data types cannot be used in the key of an index.

> **MORE INFO** **INDEXES**
>
> Indexes are covered in detail in Chapter 6, "Techniques to Improve Query Performance."

- Use the *float* or *real* data types only if the precision provided by *decimal* is insufficient.

NULL or NOT NULL?

Deciding on whether to allow *NULLs* in a column can be a problem. Many people have very strong opinions about *NULLs*—they either accept them or they are strongly against them.

The decision whether to allow *NULLs* is actually easy to make: In general, never allow them because it is the simplest way to design the table. Allowing *NULLs* where you don't need to do so greatly increases the potential for problems when querying your tables.

If the value for the column is optional (that is, not all rows have a value), the column must allow *NULLs*. You should never use another value instead of *NULL* (such as –1 for integers), which might cause you lots of problems in your queries. This is because –1 means "minus one" and not "unknown," which is the definition of *NULL*. For example, if you use the *AVG* function, it includes -1 values in the calculation, but *AVG* would omit the *NULL* values.

Alternatively, add a new table with a one-to-one relationship to the table you are designing and store the potentially unknown value in the other table. If a row shouldn't have a value, you simply don't insert a row into the other table. Consider this example:

```
CREATE TABLE HR.Employees (
    EmployeeId INT NOT NULL
    ,FirstName NVARCHAR(50) NOT NULL
    ,LastName NVARCHAR(50) NOT NULL
    ,BirthDate DATE NOT NULL
);
CREATE TABLE HR.EmployeePhoneNumbers (
    EmployeeId INT NOT NULL
    ,PhoneNumber VARCHAR(15) NOT NULL
);
-- Employee with phone number:
INSERT HR.Employees (EmployeeId, FirstName, LastName, BirthDate)
    VALUES (1, N'John', N'Kane', '1970-02-20');


INSERT HR.EmployeePhoneNumbers (EmployeeId, PhoneNumber)
    VALUES (1, N'+1-425-555-1234');


-- Employee without phone number:
INSERT HR.Employees (EmployeeId, FirstName, LastName, BirthDate)
    VALUES (2, N'Jane', N'Dow', '1965-05-30');
```

This implementation is not used very often because it increases the need for queries with *OUTER JOINS* or subqueries to retrieve the "nullable" columns from the other table. This, in turn, increases the risk for performance problems and also adds more complexity to queries than just allowing *NULL* values in the original table.

Identity

All tables should have one column or a combination of columns that uniquely identifies rows in the table. This is called the *primary key*, and it is covered in Lesson 2, "Declarative Data Integrity," later in this chapter. Most of the time, it is difficult to select a column of data whose values make a good primary key, typically because values are not guaranteed to be unique or because the values might change frequently. Instead of using such a column, called a *natural key,* you can use a technical or automatically generated key. In SQL Server, the *IDENTITY* property is used to designate one column per table whose value should be automatically increased or decreased as new rows are added. The syntax for creating an identity column is *<column name> <data type> IDENTITY(<seed>, <increment>) NOT NULL*. The seed is the starting point for generating numbers, and the increment is the value by which the key is incremented (or decremented, if negative). An identity column cannot allow *NULL* values. The following example creates the *HR.Employees* table and defines the *EmployeeId* column with an identity that starts at 1000 and increments by a value of 2 for each row:

```
CREATE TABLE HR.Employees (
    EmployeeId INT IDENTITY(1000, 2) NOT NULL
    ,FirstName NVARCHAR(50) NOT NULL
    ,LastName NVARCHAR(50) NOT NULL
    ,BirthDate DATE NOT NULL
);
```

Note that the *IDENTITY* property can be specified only when creating a new column. An existing column cannot be modified to use the *IDENTITY* property. To change an existing column, the existing column must be dropped and the identity column added in its place.

The identity column can be used only on data types that store whole numbers, which include both the *integer* data types and the *decimal* data type with a scale set to 0.

Another important point to note with identity columns is that they are not guaranteed to generate complete sequences. If an insert fails, it still uses the identity value, creating a hole in the sequence. Consider this example:

```
INSERT HR.Employees (FirstName, LastName, BirthDate)
    VALUES ('John', 'Kane', '1970-01-30');
-- EmployeeID generated: 1000
GO

INSERT HR.Employees (FirstName, LastName, BirthDate)
    VALUES ('John', 'Kane', '1970-01-32');
-- Fails because of invalid date
GO

INSERT HR.Employees (FirstName, LastName, BirthDate)
    VALUES ('Jane', 'Dow', '1972-03-30');
-- EmployeeID generated: 1004 (1002 is missed)
GO
```

In this example, the second *INSERT* fails and the key 1002 is skipped, so Jane Dow is inserted with the key 1004.

Compression

SQL Server 2008 introduces the possibility of compressing the data in tables and indexes if you use SQL Server 2008 Enterprise Edition. Data compression is implemented in two levels: row and page. The following statement configures a table to use page-level compression:

```
ALTER TABLE HR.Employees
    REBUILD
    WITH (DATA_COMPRESSION = PAGE);
```

If you turn on row-level compression, SQL Server changes the format used to store rows. In simple terms, this row format converts all data types to variable-length data types. It also uses no storage space to store *NULL* values. The more fixed-length data types (such as *datetime2, int, decimal,* and *nchar*) that you use in a table, the more likely you are to benefit from row-level compression.

Page-level compression includes row-level compression and adds page-level compression using page dictionary and column prefixing. Page dictionary simply introduces pointers between rows in the same page to avoid storing redundant data. Consider the following simplified page storing names:

```
Row 01: John Kane
Row 02: John Woods
Row 03: John Kane
```

If this page used page dictionary, it would look like this:

```
Row 01: John Kane
Row 02: John Woods
Row 03: 01
```

Here, the value in Row 03 points to the value in Row 01, saving several bytes in storage. Page compression also includes column prefixing, which is similar to page dictionary but can reuse parts of values.

When considering whether to use row- or page-level compression, it is very important to verify the amount of space actually saved by turning on the compression.

Lesson Summary

- Creating tables is about more than just defining columns. It is very important to choose the right data type and to implement data integrity.
- You need to know the details of how the different data types behave before you can use them correctly.
- Data integrity needs be a part of your table definition from the beginning to make sure that you protect your data from faults.

Creating Tables and Data Types

In this practice, you create tables and data types and modify existing tables. Because the exercises build sequentially, it is important to do them in the order specified.

EXERCISE 1 Create a New Table

In this exercise, you create a table that can store customer information.

1. Open Microsoft SQL Server Management Studio (SSMS) and connect to an instance of SQL Server 2008.

2. In a new query window, type and execute the following SQL statements to create the *TestDB* database and the *Test* schema:

```
CREATE DATABASE TestDB;
GO

USE TestDB;
GO

CREATE SCHEMA Test;
GO
```

3. In the query window, create a new table with the following properties:

   ■ It should be named *Customers*.

   ■ It should exist in the *Test* schema.

   ■ It should have the following columns:

      • *CustomerId*, which is a whole number between 1 and 100,000. This column should also be given increasing values automatically. The first value should be 1,000, and then each subsequent row should be given a new value increased by 1. You should use the data type that uses the minimum storage space required.

      • *Name*, which is a string that can contain Unicode characters and be up to 70 characters long.

      • *CreatedDateTime*, which is the date and time when the customer was added to the database.

      • *CreditLimit*, which is an exact numeric value that must allow up to five decimals and values less than 10,000,000.

   All columns except the *CustomerId* column should allow *NULL* values.

   The correct statement follows—but don't look at it before you have tried to create the table yourself.

Type, highlight, and execute the following statement:

```
CREATE TABLE Test.Customers (
    CustomerId INT IDENTITY(1000, 1) NOT NULL
    ,Name NVARCHAR(70) NULL
    ,CreatedDateTime DATETIME2 NULL
    ,CreditLimit DECIMAL(12,5) NULL
);
```

EXERCISE 2   Create New Data Types

In this exercise, you create two new data types that can be used in a database application to minimize errors when using different data types for the same type of data.

1. If necessary, open SSMS and connect to the appropriate instance of SQL Server 2008.

2. In a new query window, type and execute the following SQL statement to use the *TestDB* database:

```
USE TestDB;
```

3. In the query window, create a new data type with the following properties:
   - It should be called *NAME*.
   - It should exist in the *Test* schema.
   - It should be a string that can contain Unicode characters and be up to 70 characters long.

   The correct statement follows—but don't look at it before you have tried to create the data type yourself.

   Type, highlight, and execute the following statement:

```
CREATE TYPE Test.NAME FROM NVARCHAR(70);
```

4. In the query window, create a new data type with the following properties:
   - It should be named *CURRENCYVALUE*.
   - It should exist in the *Test* schema.
   - It should be an exact numeric value that must allow up to five decimals and values up to 999,999,999.99999.

   The correct statement follows—but don't look at it before you have tried to create the data type yourself.

   Type, highlight, and execute the following statement:

```
CREATE TYPE Test.CURRENCYVALUE FROM DECIMAL(14,5);
```

EXERCISE 3   Modifying an Existing Table

In this exercise, you modify the table that you created in Exercise 1 to use the data types that you created in Exercise 2.

1. If necessary, open SSMS and connect to the appropriate instance of SQL Server 2008.

2. In a new query window, type and execute the following SQL statement to use the *TestDB* database.

   ```
   USE TestDB;
   ```

3. In the query window, modify the *Test.Customers* table with the following changes:

   - Modify the *Name* column to use the *Test.NAME* data type and to not allow *NULL* values.

   - Modify the *CreditLimit* column to use the *Test.CURRENCYVALUE* data type.

   - Modify the *CreatedDateTime* column to not allow *NULL* values.

   The correct set of statements follows—but don't look at it before you have tried to modify the table yourself.

   Type, highlight, and execute the following statements:

   ```
   ALTER TABLE Test.Customers
       ALTER COLUMN Name Test.NAME NOT NULL;

   ALTER TABLE Test.Customers
       ALTER COLUMN CreditLimit Test.CURRENCYVALUE NULL;

   ALTER TABLE Test.Customers
       ALTER COLUMN CreatedDateTime DATETIME2 NOT NULL;
   ```

EXERCISE 4 Implement Data Compression

In this exercise, you populate the *Test.Customers* table with 100,000 rows and then compare the disk usage of the table depending on the data compression level used. Note that data compression is available only in the Developer, Enterprise, and Enterprise Evaluation editions of SQL Server 2008.

1. If necessary, open SSMS and connect to the appropriate instance of SQL Server 2008.

2. In a new query window, type and execute the following SQL statement to use the *TestDB* database.

   ```
   USE TestDB;
   ```

3. In the query window, type, highlight, and execute the following query to populate the *Test.Customers* table with 100,000 rows:

   ```
   INSERT Test.Customers (Name, CreatedDateTime, CreditLimit)
       SELECT TOP(100000)
           so1.name
           ,SYSDATETIME()
           ,CASE
   ```

```
            WHEN ABS(so1.object_id) > 100000000 THEN NULL
            ELSE ABS(so1.object_id)
        END
    FROM sys.all_objects AS so1
    CROSS JOIN sys.all_objects AS so2;
```

4. In the query window, type, highlight, and execute the following statements to rebuild the table using no compression and report the space usage of the table:

```
ALTER TABLE Test.Customers
    REBUILD WITH (DATA_COMPRESSION = NONE);


EXEC sp_spaceused
    @objname = 'Test.Customers'
    ,@updateusage = 'true';
```

Note the total disk space reserved for the table, as reported by the *sp_spaceused* stored procedure.

5. In the query window, type, highlight and execute the following query to rebuild the table using row compression and report the space usage of the table:

```
ALTER TABLE Test.Customers
    REBUILD WITH (DATA_COMPRESSION = ROW);


EXEC sp_spaceused
    @objname = 'Test.Customers'
    ,@updateusage = 'true';
```

Note the total disk space reserved for the table.

6. In the query window, type, highlight, and execute the following query to rebuild the table using page compression and report the space usage of the table:

```
ALTER TABLE Test.Customers
    REBUILD WITH (DATA_COMPRESSION = PAGE);


EXEC sp_spaceused
    @objname = 'Test.Customers'
    ,@updateusage = 'true';
```

Note the total disk space reserved for the table.

7. To clean up after this practice, close all open query windows in SSMS, open a new query window, and execute the following SQL statement:

```
USE master;
GO

DROP DATABASE TestDB;
```

Lesson 2: Declarative Data Integrity

Validating data is one of the most common tasks in software development. As a result, validation routines tend to be spread throughout an application's architecture. You are likely to find data validation in the following technologies:

- Microsoft Windows Forms or Windows Presentation Foundation (WPF) applications
- ASP.NET pages and Silverlight applications
- JavaScript embedded in Hypertext Markup Language (HTML)
- Business components (such as .NET library assemblies or COM components)
- Databases

It is very common to find that too few validation routines are created in a database. This is because many developers tend to trust that the validation is performed before the data actually arrives in the database. This lesson covers what type of validation you can and probably should perform in a database and how you can implement it.

> **After this lesson, you will be able to:**
> - Implement declarative data integrity on your tables.
> - Define primary key constraints.
> - Define foreign key constraints.
> - Define unique constraints.
> - Define check constraints.
>
> **Estimated lesson time: 60 minutes**

Validating Data

There are two ways to validate data integrity in SQL Server, either using declarative data integrity or procedural data integrity.

Declarative data integrity is a set of rules that are applied to a table and its columns using the *CREATE TABLE* or *ALTER TABLE* statements. These rules are called *constraints*.

> **NOTE DON'T USE RULES!**
> You can also implement declarative data integrity using rules (with the CREATE RULE statement); however, rules should not be used because they will be removed from SQL Server in a future release.

Procedural data integrity is implemented either by letting a stored procedure validate data or by creating triggers that check the data before or after a data manipulation language (DML) statement (such as *INSERT, UPDATE* or *DELETE*) is issued. Stored procedures and triggers are covered in Chapter 5.

In general, declarative data integrity is the simplest integrity check to integrate because it requires very little development effort. This also makes it less likely to produce bugs because it contains less code than procedural data integrity. On the other hand, procedural data integrity typically allows for more advanced integrity checks. The typical database application needs to use both declarative and procedural data integrity. In this lesson, we cover declarative data integrity.

Implementing Declarative Data Integrity

Declarative data integrity is implemented using constraints. There are five types of constraints: *PRIMARY KEY, UNIQUE, FOREIGN KEY, CHECK,* and *DEFAULT.*

PRIMARY KEY AND UNIQUE CONSTRAINTS

Both primary keys and *unique constraints* identify a column or combination of columns that uniquely identifies a row in a table. This is enforced through the creation of a unique index; that is, an index that does not allow duplicate values. Because of this, a primary key and unique constraints have the same size limitations as the key of an index, that is, it cannot contain more than 16 columns or 900 bytes of data.

If nothing else is specifed, the index that is created for a primary key is a *clustered* index and the index for a unique constraint is a *non-clustered* index. However, you can change this behavior by specifying the type of index to create in the *ALTER TABLE* or *CREATE TABLE* statement, as follows:

```
-- Primary key as a clustered index.
ALTER TABLE MyTable
    ADD PRIMARY KEY (MyTableID);


-- Primary key as a nonclustered index.
ALTER TABLE MyTable
    ADD PRIMARY KEY NONCLUSTERED (MyTableID);
```

Because primary keys and unique constraints are both constraints and indexes, you can find information about them in both the *sys.key_constraints* and *sys.indexes* catalog views.

> ***NOTE*** **COMPUTED COLUMNS**
>
> **You can create both primary key and unique constraints on computed columns.**

FOREIGN KEY CONSTRAINTS

Foreign key constraints identify a column or combination of columns whose values must exist in another column or combination of columns in the same table or another table in the same database. Foreign key constraints manage referential integrity between tables or within a single table. To implement a foreign key constraint, you must follow these rules:

- The columns being referenced must have exactly the same data type (and collation, for string columns) as the local columns.
- The columns being referenced must have a unique index created on them. This is typically implemented using either a primary key or a unique constraint.
- Because the foreign key must reference a unique index, the foreign key columns have the same size limitations as that of the primary key and unique constraints.

You can also create foreign key constraints on computed columns. You can find information about which foreign key constraints exist in your database by querying the *sys.foreign_keys* and *sys.foreign_key_columns* catalog views.

Foreign keys are usually queried frequently in user queries and in joins, as well as when SQL Server needs to verify referential integrity when deleting or updating primary key rows. This means that foreign keys usually greatly benefit from being indexed. Indexing is covered in greater detail in Chapter 6.

When a foreign key constraint notices a referential integrity violation because of a *DELETE* or an *UPDATE* of a row that it references, the default reaction is to raise an error message and roll back the statement that violated the constraint. If this is not the result you want, you can change the default action for the foreign key to delete the referenced row, update the referenced column, or both. There are four actions to choose from:

- *NO ACTION* (the default)
- *SET NULL*
- *SET DEFAULT*
- *CASCADE*

An example implementation is shown here:

```
CREATE TABLE Test.Customers
(
   CustomerID INT PRIMARY KEY
);
CREATE TABLE Test.Orders
(
   OrderID INT PRIMARY KEY
   ,CustomerID INT NULL
        REFERENCES Test.Customers
             ON DELETE SET NULL
             ON UPDATE CASCADE
);
```

The default behavior of the foreign key is *NO ACTION*. If the foreign key finds a violation and *NO ACTION* is specified, SQL Server rolls back the statement that violated the constraint and raises an error message.

SET NULL and *SET DEFAULT* cause all the referenced values to be set to either *NULL* (for *SET NULL*) or *DEFAULT* (for *SET DEFAULT;* that is, the default defined on the column) instead of raising an error and rolling back the statement. In the relationship between the *Orders* and *Customers* tables shown in the code sample, if a customer is deleted, the *CustomerID* column is set to *NULL* for all orders belonging to that customer and no error message is sent to the calling application.

The *CASCADE* action causes SQL Server to delete referenced rows for a *DELETE* statement (*ON DELETE*) and update the referenced values (*ON UPDATE*) for an *UPDATE* statement. Using the same code sample, if the *CustomerID* column is changed for a row in the *Customers* table, all corresponding rows in the *Orders* table are updated with the same *CustomerID* to reflect the change. If *ON DELETE CASCADE* is specified for the foreign key constraint and a row in the *Customers* table is deleted, all referencing rows in the *Orders* table are deleted. This might sound reasonable, but it might not be possible to implement *CASCADE* for all foreign key constraints because cyclic references are not supported. For example, in the following script, an error is raised when you try to add the foreign key *FKCustomersLastOrder* because it introduces a cyclic reference. If a customer is deleted, all referencing orders must be deleted, and all customers referencing those orders through the *LastOrderID* column must also be deleted:

```
CREATE TABLE Test.Customers (
    CustomerID INT PRIMARY KEY
    ,LastOrderID INT NULL
);

CREATE TABLE Test.Orders (
    OrderID INT PRIMARY KEY
    ,CustomerID INT NOT NULL
        REFERENCES Test.Customers
            ON DELETE CASCADE
            ON UPDATE NO ACTION
);

ALTER TABLE Test.Customers ADD
    CONSTRAINT FKCustomersLastOrder
    FOREIGN KEY (LastOrderID)
        REFERENCES Test.Orders (OrderID)
            ON DELETE CASCADE
            ON UPDATE NO ACTION;
```

In the previous example, consider what happens if a customer is deleted—all the customer's orders are also deleted. This might be fine, but consider the following code:

```
CREATE TABLE Test.Countries (
    CountryID INT PRIMARY KEY
);

CREATE TABLE Test.Cities (
    CityID INT PRIMARY KEY
    ,CountryID INT NOT NULL
        REFFRENCES Test.Countries
            ON DELETE CASCADE
);

CREATE TABLE Test.Customers (
    CustomerID INT PRIMARY KEY
    ,CityID INT NOT NULL
        RFFERENCES Test.Cities
            ON DELETE CASCADE
);

CREATE TABLE Test.Orders (
    OrderID INT PRIMARY KEY
    ,CustomerID INT NOT NULL
        REFERENCES Test.Customers
            ON DELETE CASCADE
);
```

In this example, if you delete a country, all cities in that country, all customers in those cities, and all orders belonging to those customers are also deleted. Be cautious—you might be deleting more than you think. Consider someone executing the query DELETE Test.Countries WHERE CountryID = 1; from SSMS. The person might think he is deleting only one row in the *Countries* table, when he or she might actually be deleting millions of rows. The time it takes to execute this *DELETE* statement depends on how many rows are being deleted. When it finishes, SSMS returns the following message:

```
(1 row(s) affected)
```

This message is returned even if millions of rows were deleted because the message tells us only how many rows were deleted directly by the executed statement. There is nothing wrong with this behavior, but it is definitely something you should consider.

> **NOTE TRIGGERS**
>
> If you have defined foreign keys with cascading actions, any AFTER triggers on the affected tables are still executed, but they are executed after the whole chain of cascading actions have completed. If an error occurs while the cascading action chain is being executed, the entire chain is rolled back and no AFTER triggers are executed for that chain.

CHECK CONSTRAINTS

Check constraints are a set of rules that must be validated prior to data being allowed into a table. Advantages to using check constraints include the following:

- They are simple to implement. (They are very similar to a WHERE clause.)
- They are checked automatically.
- They can improve performance.

A sample check constraint that verifies that a *Product* must have a non-negative price is shown here:

```
ALTER TABLE Products
  ADD CHECK(Price >= 0.0);
```

The simplicity of check constraints is a great advantage over using triggers. However, there are some disadvantages as well, such as the following:

- Error messages from check constraints are system-generated and cannot be replaced by a more user-friendly error message.
- A check constraint cannot "see" the previous value of a column. This means that it cannot be used for some types of data integrity rules, such as "Updates to the price column cannot increase or decrease the price by more than 10 percent."

One important aspect of check constraints is that they reject values that evaluate to *False* rather than accepting values that evaluate to *True*. That might seem like the same thing, but in SQL Server, it is not, because of an issue related to *NULL* values that is important to acknowledge. For example, if you have a check constraint that states that `Price > 10.0`, you can still insert a *NULL* value into the *Price* column. This value is allowed because any comparison made with *NULL* returns *NULL*—it is neither *True* nor *False*. If you don't want the check constraint to allow the *NULL* value, you can either dissallow *NULL* in the *Price* column by specifying the *NOT NULL* constraint for the column or by changing the check constraint to read `Price > 10.0 AND Price IS NOT NULL`.

EXTENDING CHECK CONSTRAINTS WITH USER-DEFINED FUNCTIONS

User-defined functions (UDFs) created both in T-SQL and managed code (also referred to as .NET or CLR UDFs) can be an integral part of check constraints and are therefore discussed briefly here. They are covered in more detail in Chapter 5.

The expression in a check constraint can contain most of the logic that you can use in a *WHERE* clause (including *NOT, AND,* and *OR*). It can call scalar UDFs and reference other columns in the same table; however, it is not allowed to contain subqueries directly. Because you can write your own scalar functions in either T-SQL or managed code, you can apply advanced logic inside your check constraints and, through them, even use subqueries.

The following example creates a UDF called *fnIsPhoneNumber* in managed code (shown in both Microsoft Visual Basic and C#) to verify that a string contains a valid U.S. phone number by applying a regular expression:

```vb
'VB
<Microsoft.SqlServer.Server.SqlFunction(IsDeterministic:=True, _
    DataAccess:=DataAccessKind.None)> _
Public Shared Function fnIsPhoneNumber(ByVal phoneNumber As SqlString) _
    As SqlBoolean
    If (phoneNumber.IsNull) Then
        Return SqlBoolean.Null
    End If
    Return System.Text.RegularExpressions.Regex.IsMatch(phoneNumber.Value, _
        "^\([1-9]\d{2}\)\s?\d{3}\-\d{4}$")
End Function
```

```csharp
// C#
[SqlFunction(IsDeterministic = true, DataAccess=DataAccessKind.None)]
static public SqlBoolean fnIsPhoneNumber(SqlString phoneNumber)
{
    if (phoneNumber.IsNull){
        return SqlBoolean.Null;
    }
    return System.Text.RegularExpressions.Regex
        .IsMatch(phoneNumber.Value, @"^\([1-9]\d{2}\)\s?\d{3}\-\d{4}$");
}
```

> **MORE INFO** **UDFs**
>
> UDFs are explained in detail in Chapter 7, "Extending Microsoft SQL Server Functionality with XML, SQLCLR, and Filestream."

The following code creates a table and the check constraint that references the UDF:

```sql
CREATE TABLE Test.Contacts (
     ContactID INT IDENTITY PRIMARY KEY
    ,Name NVARCHAR(50) NOT NULL
    ,PhoneNumber VARCHAR(20) NULL
    ,CONSTRAINT CKContactsPhoneNumber
        CHECK(dbo.fnIsPhoneNumber(PhoneNumber) = CAST(1 AS BIT))
);

-- Allowed:
INSERT Test.Contacts (Name, PhoneNumber)
     VALUES ('Tobias', '(425)555-1111');
INSERT Test.Contacts (Name, PhoneNumber)
     VALUES ('Chris', NULL);

-- Disallowed, will raise an error:
INSERT Test.Contacts (Name, PhoneNumber)
     VALUES ('Ann', '(42)555-2222');
```

When is this check constraint executed? Only when needed. The optimizer runs the check constraint only if columns referenced in the check constraints are referenced by the executed DML statement. For *INSERTs*, this is always true because an *INSERT* always affects all columns (even if you insert a *NULL* value). For *UPDATES*, the check constraint is executed only if a column contained in the check constraint is referenced by the update.

> **NOTE PERFORMANCE**
>
> Adding a lot of logic to your check constraints can hurt performance. A good approach is to add the necessary constraints and then run a performance test to verify that the performance is sufficent.

USING A UDF WITH A SUBQUERY

It is possible to include subqueries in check constraints by placing them inside a UDF. This practice can result in poor performance because the subquery is executed once for each row affected by an *UPDATE* or *INSERT* statement against the table. Imagine you want to extend the previous example to also validate the telephone area codes using a subquery. The supported area codes are stored in a separate table called *Test.AreaCodes*. Here is the extended version of the UDF:

```vb
' VB
<Microsoft.SqlServer.Server.SqlFunction(IsDeterministic:=True, _
    DataAccess:=DataAccessKind.Read)> _
Public Shared Function fnIsPhoneNumber2(ByVal phoneNumber As SqlString) _
    As SqlBoolean

    If (phoneNumber.IsNull) Then
        Return SqlBoolean.Null
    End If

    If Not System.Text.RegularExpressions.Regex.IsMatch(phoneNumber.Value, _
        "^\([1-9]\d{2}\)\s?\d{3}\-\d{4}$") Then
        Return False
    Else

        Dim areaCode As String = phoneNumber.Value.Substring(1, 3)

        Using conn As SqlConnection = New SqlConnection("context connection=true;")
            Using cmd As SqlCommand = conn.CreateCommand()
                cmd.CommandText = _
                    "IF EXISTS(SELECT * FROM Test.AreaCodes " & _
                    "    WHERE AreaCode = @AreaCode) " & _
                    "  SELECT CAST(1 AS BIT) AS Found " & _
                    "ELSE " & _
                    "  SELECT CAST(0 AS BIT) AS Found"
```

```
            cmd.Parameters.Add("@AreaCode", SqlDbType.Char, 3).Value = areaCode
            conn.Open()
            Return CType(cmd.ExecuteScalar(), Boolean)
        End Using
    End Using
    End If
End Function


// C#
[SqlFunction(IsDeterministic = true, DataAccess=DataAccessKind.Read)]
static public SqlBoolean fnIsPhoneNumber2(SqlString phoneNumber)
{
    if(phoneNumber.IsNull)
        return SqlBoolean.Null;

    if(!System.Text.RegularExpressions.Regex
        .IsMatch(phoneNumber.Value, @"^\([1-9]\d{2}\)\s?\d{3}\-\d{4}$")){
        return false;
    }else{
        string areaCode = phoneNumber.Value.Substring(1,3);
        using(SqlConnection conn = new SqlConnection(
            @"context connection=true;"))
        {
            using(SqlCommand cmd = conn.CreateCommand())
            {
                cmd.CommandText = @"IF EXISTS(SELECT * FROM Test.AreaCodes
                                    WHERE AreaCode = @AreaCode)
                                SELECT CAST(1 AS BIT) AS Found
                            ELSE
                                SELECT CAST(0 AS BIT) AS Found";
                cmd.Parameters.Add("@AreaCode", SqlDbType.Char, 3)
                    .Value = areaCode;
                conn.Open();
                return (bool)cmd.ExecuteScalar();
            }
        }
    }
}
```

The following code creates a table and the check constraint referencing the UDF:

```
CREATE TABLE Test.AreaCodes (
  AreaCode CHAR(3) NOT NULL PRIMARY KEY
);
-- The only allowed area code.
INSERT Test.AreaCodes (AreaCode) VALUES ('425');
```

```
CREATE TABLE Test.Contacts (
    ContactID INT IDENTITY PRIMARY KEY
    ,Name NVARCHAR(50) NOT NULL
    ,PhoneNumber VARCHAR(20) NULL
    ,CONSTRAINT CKContactsPhoneNumber
        CHECK(dbo.fnIsPhoneNumber2(PhoneNumber) = CAST(1 AS BIT))
);

-- Allowed:
INSERT Test.Contacts (Name, PhoneNumber)
    VALUES ('Ann', '(425)555-1111');
INSERT Test.Contacts (Name, PhoneNumber)
    VALUES ('Chris', NULL);

-- Disallowed because of invalid area code:
INSERT Test.Contacts (Name, PhoneNumber)
    VALUES ('Tobias', '(111)555-2222');
```

A very imporant consideration when using subqueries in check constraints is that, while the check constraint is verified for *UPDATEs* and *INSERTs* to the table, it is not verified when deleting rows in the table that the subquery references. The data that the check constraint validated against on the *INSERT* or *UPDATE* can be deleted without raising an error. For example, the following *DELETE* statement does not result in an error:

```
DELETE Test.AreaCodes WHERE AreaCode = '425';
```

However, after executing the *DELETE* statement, the following *UPDATE* statement raises an error:

```
UPDATE Test.Contacts SET PhoneNumber = PhoneNumber;
```

This behavior is highly undesirable because you might think you have the same protection that you have with foreign keys, which protect you against the *DELETE* statement as well. In SQL Server 2008 (and 2005), you can often replace this logic by using a foreign key, as described in the next section.

USING A FOREIGN KEY WITH A SUBQUERY

Let's implement the validation of the phone number as a combination of a check constraint and a foreign key constraint. You use the first version of the UDF (the one without the subquery) with a foreign key. How can you implement the foreign key? You want it to check the area code only against the *Test.AreaCodes* table, not the entire phone number. You do this by implementing a computed column that returns only the area code portion of the phone number. You need to do a couple of things to make it possible to create the foreign key shown in the example.

The result of the expression in the *AreaCode* column must be of the same data type as the column that the foreign key references, *CHAR(3)*. You ensure this by calling the *CAST* function in the *AreaCode* expression.

The column must also be marked as *PERSISTED,* which means that SQL Server physically stores the result of the computed column's expression in the data row instead of calculating it each time it is referenced in a query. It is recalculated every time the column is updated. One of the reasons for this requirement is that it affects performance; you don't want SQL Server to execute the *SUBSTRING* function each time the foreign key needs to be validated.

The following script creates the new version of the *Test.Contacts* table, including the added foreign key constraint:

```
CREATE TABLE Test.Contacts (
    ContactID INT IDENTITY PRIMARY KEY
    ,Name NVARCHAR(50) NOT NULL
    ,PhoneNumber VARCHAR(20) NULL
    ,CONSTRAINT CKContactsPhoneNumber
        CHECK(dbo.fnIsPhoneNumber(PhoneNumber) = 1)
    ,AreaCode AS CAST(SUBSTRING(PhoneNumber, 2, 3) AS CHAR(3)) PERSISTED
    ,CONSTRAINT FKContactsAreaCodes
        FOREIGN KEY (AreaCode)
        REFERENCES Test.AreaCodes
);
```

As you can see, the *AreaCode* column in the *Contacts* table is just a subset of the *PhoneNumber* column.

What happens if you insert a *NULL* value into the *PhoneNumber* column? The *SUBSTRING* function returns *NULL*, and *NULL* is accepted by the foreign key and interpreted as a value that does not reference the *AreaCodes* table.

CHECK AND FOREIGN KEY CONSTRAINTS VS. QUERY PERFORMANCE

Can check and foreign key constraints improve query performance? Don't they just protect us against invalid data, and in doing so, somewhat degrade performance? The answers to these questions are "Yes, they can," and "No, they don't."

Because foreign keys and check constraints are declared rules, the optimizer can use them to create more efficient query plans. This usually involves skipping some part of the query plan because for example, the optmizer can see that because of a foreign key constraint, it is unnecessary to execute that particular part of the plan. The following code sample is a simple example of this behavior with a foreign key constraint. Consider the following two tables and the foreign key *FKOrdersCustomers*:

```
CREATE TABLE Test.Customers (
    CustomerID INT PRIMARY KEY
);

CREATE TABLE Test.Orders (
    OrderID INT PRIMARY KEY
    ,CustomerID INT NOT NULL
        CONSTRAINT FKOrdersCustomers
            REFERENCES Test.Customers (CustomerID)
);
```

Now, let's look at what SQL Server actually does when you query these tables with the foreign key in place. To do this, in SSMS, from the Query menu, choose Include Actual Execution Plan, or, alternatively, press Ctrl-M.

The following query returns all orders that have a valid customer reference:

```
SELECT o.* FROM Test.Orders AS o
WHERE EXISTS (SELECT * FROM Test.Customers AS c
                    WHERE c.CustomerID = o.CustomerID);
```

The execution plan that SQL Server uses to execute this query is shown in Figure 3-1. In the execution plan, you can see that the *Test.Customers* table is not accessed; the only table being accessed is *Test.Orders*. This is because the optimizer knows that it is not necessary to execute the *EXISTS* operator in this query because the foreign key constraint requires all orders to refer to an existing customer, which is what the *WHERE* clause checks.

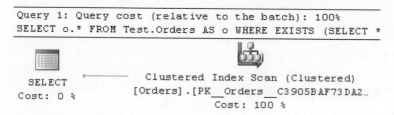

FIGURE 3-1 An actual execution plan in SSMS

Now turn off the foreign key by executing the following statement:

```
ALTER TABLE Test.Orders NOCHECK CONSTRAINT FKOrdersCustomers;
```

After executing the same query again, you get a new execution plan, as shown in Figure 3-2. The optimizer executes the *EXISTS* operator (in this case, the Nested Loops icon in the execution plan) to return only those orders that actually have a valid reference to the *Test.Customers* table. Because you turned off the foreign key constraint, SQL Server could not be sure that all orders actually have valid customer references. Therefore, it had to execute the *EXISTS* operator. For a large table, this can make a huge difference in performance.

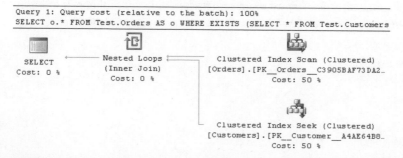

FIGURE 3-2 An actual execution plan in SSMS when the foreign key constraint is turned off

Now turn on the foreign key again by executing the following statement, then rerun the query:

```
ALTER TABLE Test.Orders
    CHECK CONSTRAINT FKOrdersCustomers;
```

After running the query this time, you end up with the same plan again—the plan shown in Figure 3-2. How can this be? You turned the constraint back on, so now SQL Server should be sure that all orders have valid customer references. However, this is actually not the case. This is because the foreign key is considered to be "not trusted". The optimizer does not take into account a constraint that is not trusted (which applies only to foreign key and check constraints). Your foreign key is no longer trusted because, while it was turned off, someone could have inserted or updated an order row with an invalid *CustomerID*. Turning the constraint back on does not verify existing data. You can verify that the foreign key is indeed not trusted by executing the following query:

```
SELECT name, is_not_trusted FROM sys.foreign_keys
    WHERE name = 'FKOrdersCustomers';
```

You find that the *is_not_trusted* column contains the value 1, indicating that the constraint is not trusted. To make it trusted, you need to modify the earlier *turn on* statement by adding the *WITH CHECK* option to it, as shown in the following example:

```
ALTER TABLE Test.Orders
    WITH CHECK
    CHECK CONSTRAINT FKOrdersCustomers;
```

This option tells SQL Server to verify that all rows in the table comply with the constraint prior to turning it back on. If any rows do not comply with the constraint, an error message is returned and the *ALTER TABLE* statement is rolled back.

If you execute the query again, you find that you are back to the first execution plan (the one shown in Figure 3-1) and, if you execute the query against the *sys.foreign_keys* catalog view again, you find that the *is_not_trusted* column now returns the value 0. The constraint is once again trusted.

One last note on this implementation: you can change the script for the *Test.Customers* and *Test.Orders* tables, as shown in the following example, so that the *CustomerID* column in the *Test.Orders* table allows for *NULL* values—that is, it is not declared with the *NOT NULL* constraint:

```
CREATE TABLE Test.Customers (
    CustomerID INT PRIMARY KEY
);

CREATE TABLE Test.Orders (
    OrderID INT PRIMARY KEY
    ,CustomerID INT NULL
        CONSTRAINT FKOrdersCustomers
            REFERENCES Test.Customers (CustomerID)
);
```

If you execute the same query against this table structure, you get the execution plan from Figure 3-2. This means that the *EXISTS* operator is being executed even if you have the trusted foreign key constraint in place. To persuade the optimizer to go back to the plan that didn't execute the *EXISTS* operator, you need to change the query as shown in the following example:

```
SELECT o.* FROM Test.Orders AS o
WHERE EXISTS (SELECT * FROM Test.Customers AS c
                    WHERE c.CustomerID = o.CustomerID)
   AND o.CustomerID IS NOT NULL;
```

This informs SQL Server that no orders with a *CustomerID* of *NULL* should be returned, which brings you back to the plan from Figure 3-1.

PRACTICE Implementing Constraints

In this practice, you add constraints when adding a new table. You also modify an existing table by adding constraints to it. Because the exercises build on each other sequentially, it is important to do them in the order specified.

EXERCISE 1 Create a New Table with Constraints

In this exercise, you create two tables that will be used to store a list of customers and their respective orders. You also define basic constraints on the two tables.

1. If necessary, open SSMS and connect to an instance of SQL Server 2008.

2. In a new query window, type and execute the following SQL statements to create the *TestDB* database with the *Test* schema:

```
CREATE DATABASE TestDB;
GO

USE TestDB;
GO

CREATE SCHEMA Test;
GO
```

3. In the query window, create a new table with the following properties:

   - It should be named *Customers*.

   - It should exist in the *Test* schema.

   - It should have the following columns:

     - *CustomerId,* which must be a whole number between 1 and 100,000. This column should also be given increasing values automatically. Use the data type that requires the least storage space. The first value should be 1,000, and then each following row should be given a new value increased by 1. This value should be the table's primary key.

- *Name*, which should be a string that can be up to 50 characters long.

■ No columns should allow *NULL* values.

The correct statement follows—but don't look at it before you have tried to create the table yourself.

Type, highlight, and execute the following statement:

```
CREATE TABLE Test.Customers (
    CustomerId INT IDENTITY(1000, 1) NOT NULL
        CONSTRAINT PKCustomers
            PRIMARY KEY
    ,Name NVARCHAR(50) NOT NULL
);
```

4. In the query window, create a new table with the following properties:

■ It should be named *Orders*.

■ It should exist in the *Test* schema.

■ It should have the following columns:

- *OrderId*, which must be a whole number between 1 and 100,000. This column should also be given increasing values automatically. Use the data type that requires the least storage space. The first value should be 1,000, and then each following row should be given a new value increased by 1. This value should be the table's primary key.

- *OrderDate*, which must be a date.

If no value is provided, today's date should be added automatically.

- *CustomerId*, which must reference a row with the same value in the *CustomerId* column of the *Test.Customers* table.

■ No columns should allow *NULL* values.

The correct statement follows—but don't look at it before you have tried to create the table yourself.

Type, highlight, and execute the following statement:

```
CREATE TABLE Test.Orders (
    OrderId INT IDENTITY(1000, 1) NOT NULL
    ,OrderDate DATE NOT NULL DEFAULT SYSDATETIME()
    ,CustomerId INT NOT NULL
        CONSTRAINT FKOrdersCustomerId
            REFERENCES Test.Customers (CustomerId)
);
```

EXERCISE 2 Add More Constraints

In this exercise, you add further constraints to the tables that you created in Exercise 1.

1. If necessary, open SSMS and connect to the appropriate instance of SQL Server 2008.

2. In a new query window, type and execute the following SQL statements to use the *TestDB* database:

```
USE TestDB;
GO
```

3. In the query window, add a constraint that verifies that the *Name* column in the *Test.Customers* table must start with a letter and be at least three characters long.

   The correct statement follows—but don't look at it before you have tried to create the constraint yourself.

   Type, highlight, and execute the following statement:

```
ALTER TABLE Test.Customers
    ADD CONSTRAINT CKCustomerName
     CHECK(Name LIKE N'[A-Z]__%');
```

4. In the query window, add a constraint that verifies that the *OrderDate* column in the *Test.Orders* table must contain today's date.

   The correct statement follows—but don't look at it before you have tried to create the constraint yourself.

   Type, highlight, and execute the following statement:

```
ALTER TABLE Test.Orders
    ADD CONSTRAINT CKOrdersOrderDate
     CHECK(OrderDate = CAST(SYSDATETIME() AS DATE));
```

5. To clean up after this lab, close all open query windows in SSMS, open a new query window, and execute the following SQL statements:

```
USE master;
GO

DROP DATABASE TestDB;
```

Chapter Review

To practice and reinforce the skills you learned in this chapter further, you can perform the following tasks:

- Review the chapter summary.
- Review the list of key terms introduced in this chapter.
- Complete the case scenario. This scenario sets up a real-world situation involving the topics of this chapter and asks you to create solutions.
- Complete the suggested practices.
- Take a practice test.

Chapter Summary

- Always consider which data types you are using because changing your mind later can be more difficult than you think.
- Consider using user-defined data types to simplify selecting the correct data type when creating tables and to avoid data type mismatches in your database.
- Having appropriate names, as defined in a naming guidelines document for objects and columns, is very important to make sure that the naming in your database is consistent.
- Consider compressing large tables to save disk space and memory, as well as possibly increasing performance.
- Implement constraints to verify data integrity.
- Implement constraints to support the optimizer.
- Consider using UDFs in check constraints to implement advanced data integrity.

Key Terms

- Constraint
- Primary key
- Unique constraint
- Foreign key constraint
- Check constraint
- Identity

Case Scenario

In the following case scenario, you apply what you have learned about in this chapter. You can find answers to these questions in the "Answers" section at the end of this book.

Case Scenario: Constraints and Data Types

You are a database developer for Contoso Corporation. You have been given the responsibility to add both check and foreign key constraints to the *Products* table, which contains a large amount of incorrect data. You need to add the constraints to the table to prevent any more incorrect data from being inserted or updated in the table.

You also need to create a new table named *ProductLog*, which will use an identity column as its primary key and which will contain a huge number of rows. For this reason, you must choose the largest data type that is supported by the *IDENTITY* property for this column.

Answer the following questions for your manager:

1. How should you add the constraints to the *Products* table?
2. Which data type should you use for the *ProductLog* table?

Suggested Practices

To help you master the exam objectives presented in this chapter, do all the following practices:

Create and Alter Tables

- **Practice 1**   Create the tables needed to store information about your DVD collection.

Implement Data Types

- **Practice 2**   Create all alias types (user-defined data types) needed by the columns defined in Practice 1.

Manage International Considerations

- **Practice 3**   Change the tables defined in Practice 1 to use the alias types that you created in Practice 2.

Create and Modify Constraints

- **Practice 4**   Implement referential integrity on the tables that you defined in Practice 1 using primary key and foreign key constraints.

- **Practice 5**   Implement any check and unique constraints that you think are appropriate to verify the data integrity in the tables defined in Practice 1.

Take a Practice Test

The practice tests on this book's companion CD offer many options. For example, you can test yourself on just the content covered in this chapter, or you can test yourself on all the 70-433 certification exam content. You can set up the test so that it closely simulates the experience of taking a certification exam, or you can set it up in study mode so that you can look at the correct answers and explanations after you answer each question.

> **MORE INFO** **PRACTICE TESTS**
>
> For details about all the practice test options available, see the section entitled "How to Use the Practice Tests," in the Introduction to this book.

Using Additional Query Techniques

Within many applications you need to construct queries that go beyond a basic *SELECT* statement, such as creating running totals, finding gaps in sequences, traversing a recursive hierarchy, or ranking data within a set. In this chapter, you will learn how to extend the querying techniques that you have learned within this book to encompass subqueries, common table expressions (CTEs), and ranking functions.

Exam objectives in this chapter:

- Implement subqueries.
- Implement CTE (common table expression) queries.
- Apply ranking functions.

Lessons in this chapter:

Before You Begin

To complete the lessons in this chapter, you must have:

- SQL Server 2008 installed
- The *AdventureWorks* database installed

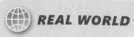

REAL WORLD

Michael Hotek

One of the more common requirements that I come across, especially with data warehouses, is to find where data is missing. You might be expecting sales figures from a store on a daily basis, defects from a manufacturing line every hour, or inventory levels from a series of sequentially numbered bins. When trying to solve "missing gaps" problems, many developers turn to some kind of cursor operation. Either a database cursor is used, or the data is pulled back into an application that sorts the data and then moves across every record, keeping track of the previous and subsequent values to find all the missing values.

One particular problem that I see is finding gaps in a sequence. I had to solve this type of problem several years ago for a customer who was trying to place advertisements automatically within a time sequence where you had to repeatedly find gaps that matched a set of criteria. The existing solution used a lot of trial and error with nested cursors. Using subqueries and unequal joins solved the problem with a 90 percent reduction in time and resources.

A colleague of mine sent me an e-mail with a solution to the problem of figuring out a correlation between billboard postings and wildfires that used multiple *WHILE* loops and table variables. While the code worked and produced the required result, it could have been collapsed into a set of noncorrelated subqueries with unequal joins that would perform much better against a large result set. (Clint, I hope you found my solution useful.)

Even as I was writing this chapter, another customer needed to validate data sets in a data warehouse to find data that was missing from the loads.

While the one-row-at-a-time solutions get the job done, finding gaps within a large set of data can require a significant amount of time. Instead of using a cursor approach or multiple *WHILE* loops, you can solve the problem very efficiently either by using subqueries with unequal joins or by combining ranking functions with CTEs.

Lesson 1: Building Recursive Queries with CTEs

CTEs provide a capability that is very similar to a derived table (derived tables are explained in Lesson 2 in this chapter). However, CTEs also allow you to iterate across a result set to solve one of the more difficult challenges within Transact-SQL (T-SQL), efficiently executing a recursive query. In this lesson, you learn how to build CTEs to solve recursive query problems.

> **After this lesson, you will be able to:**
> - Apply CTEs to recursive query problems.
>
> **Estimated lesson time: 20 minutes**

Common Table Expressions

A CTE is defined with two parts:

- A *WITH* clause containing a *SELECT* statement that generates a valid table
- An outer *SELECT* statement that references the table expression

The following CTE returns the number of employees that have a given title:

```
WITH EmpTitle AS
(SELECT JobTitle, count(*) numtitles
        FROM HumanResources.Employee
        GROUP BY JobTitle)
SELECT b.BusinessEntityID, b.JobTitle, a.numtitles
FROM EmpTitle a INNER JOIN HumanResources.Employee b ON a.JobTitle = b.JobTitle;
GO
```

A *recursive* CTE expands the definition of the table expression and consists of two parts:

- An anchor query, which is the source of the recursion, along with a UNION ALL statement and a second query, which recurses across the anchor query.
- An outer query, which references the routine and specifies the number of recursion levels

For example, the following query allows you to specify an employee and then return each level of management above the employee in the organization across a maximum of 25 organization levels:

```
DECLARE @EmployeeToGetOrgFor   INT = 126;

WITH EMP_cte(BusinessEntityID, OrganizationNode, FirstName, LastName,
    JobTitle, RecursionLevel)
AS (SELECT e.BusinessEntityID, e.OrganizationNode, p.FirstName,
        p.LastName, e.JobTitle, 0
    FROM HumanResources.Employee e INNER JOIN Person.Person as p
        ON p.BusinessEntityID = e.BusinessEntityID
    WHERE e.BusinessEntityID = @EmployeeToGetOrgFor
    UNION ALL
```

```
        SELECT e.BusinessEntityID, e.OrganizationNode, p.FirstName, p.LastName,
            e.JobTitle, RecursionLevel + 1
        FROM HumanResources.Employee e INNER JOIN EMP_cte
            ON e.OrganizationNode = EMP_cte.OrganizationNode.GetAncestor(1)
            INNER JOIN Person.Person p  ON p.BusinessEntityID = e.BusinessEntityID)

SELECT EMP_cte.RecursionLevel, EMP_cte.BusinessEntityID,
    EMP_cte.FirstName, EMP_cte.LastName,
    EMP_cte.OrganizationNode.ToString() AS OrganizationNode,
    p.FirstName AS 'ManagerFirstName', p.LastName AS 'ManagerLastName'
FROM EMP_cte INNER JOIN HumanResources.Employee e
    ON EMP_cte.OrganizationNode.GetAncestor(1) = e.OrganizationNode
    INNER JOIN Person.Person p ON p.BusinessEntityID = e.BusinessEntityID
ORDER BY RecursionLevel, EMP_cte.OrganizationNode.ToString()
OPTION (MAXRECURSION 25);
```

The first query within the *WITH* clause defines the anchor result set. The second query is executed recursively up to the maximum recursion level against the anchor query. The recursion is accomplished by the inner join on the CTE, as follows:

```
INNER JOIN EMP_cte
```

The outer query is then used to return the results of the recursive operation along with any additional data that is needed. The *OPTION* clause in the outer query specifies the maximum number of recursion levels that are allowed.

> **CAUTION   RECURSION LEVELS**
>
> If the iterative query does not reach the bottom of the hierarchy by the time the *MAXRECURSION* value has been exhausted, you receive an error message.

EXAM TIP

Because the *WITH* keyword is used in multiple ways within T-SQL, any statements preceding the *WITH* keyword are required to be terminated with a semicolon.

 Quick Check

1. What are the two parts of a CTE?
2. What are the two parts of a recursive CTE?

Quick Check Answers

1. A CTE has a *WITH* clause that contains a *SELECT* statement, which defines a table, along with an outer *SELECT* statement, which references the CTE.
2. A recursive CTE has an anchor query, which is the source of the recursion, along with a *UNION ALL* statement and a second query, which recurses across the anchor query; and an outer query, which references the CTE and specifies the maximum recursion levels.

In this practice, you use a recursive CTE to expand the bill of materials for a component within the *AdventureWorks* database.

EXERCISE   Create a Recursive CTE

In this exercise, you use a recursive CTE to expand the bill of materials for a component within the *AdventureWorks* database.

1. Open a new query window, type and execute the following query:

```
DECLARE @date              date = '4/18/2000',
        @productassembly   int = 749;


WITH BOM(ProductAssemblyID, ComponentID, AssemblyDescription, PerAssemblyQty,
    ComponentCost, ListPrice, BOMLevel, RecursionLevel)
AS (SELECT b.ProductAssemblyID, b.ComponentID, p.Name, b.PerAssemblyQty,
        p.StandardCost, p.ListPrice, b.BOMLevel, 0
    FROM Production.BillOfMaterials b INNER JOIN Production.Product p
        ON b.ComponentID = p.ProductID
    WHERE b.ProductAssemblyID = @productassembly
        AND @date >= b.StartDate
        AND @date <= ISNULL(b.EndDate, @date)
    UNION ALL
    SELECT b.ProductAssemblyID, b.ComponentID, p.Name, b.PerAssemblyQty,
        p.StandardCost, p.ListPrice, b.BOMLevel, RecursionLevel + 1
    FROM BOM cte INNER JOIN Production.BillOfMaterials b
            ON b.ProductAssemblyID = cte.ComponentID
        INNER JOIN Production.Product p ON b.ComponentID = p.ProductID
    WHERE @date >= b.StartDate
        AND @date <= ISNULL(b.EndDate, @date))


SELECT b.ProductAssemblyID, b.ComponentID, b.AssemblyDescription,
SUM(b.PerAssemblyQty) AS ComponentQty , b.ComponentCost, b.ListPrice,
    b.BOMLevel, b.RecursionLevel
FROM BOM b
GROUP BY b.ComponentID, b.AssemblyDescription, b.ProductAssemblyID,
    b.BOMLevel, b.RecursionLevel, b.ComponentCost, b.ListPrice
ORDER BY b.BOMLevel, b.ProductAssemblyID, b.ComponentID
OPTION (MAXRECURSION 25)
GO
```

2. Rerun the query with the date changed to 10/16/2000 and observe the results.

3. Inspect the contents of the *Production.BillOfMaterials* table and observe the changes to components over time to see why the two queries return such different results.

Lesson Summary

- A recursive CTE contains two *SELECT* statements within the *WITH* clause, separated by the *UNION ALL* keyword. The first query defines the anchor for the recursion, and the second query defines the data set that is to be iterated across.

- If a CTE is contained within a batch, all statements preceding the *WITH* clause must be terminated with a semicolon.

- The outer query references the CTE and specifies the maximum recursion.

Lesson 2: Implementing Subqueries

Subqueries allow you to nest one query within another to build complex routines, as well as retrieve data sets that would be impossible to construct without resorting to a multistep process that writes intermediate results out to temporary objects.

You can construct queries with two types of subqueries: correlated and noncorrelated. A noncorrelated subquery is independent of the outer query within which it is contained. A correlated subquery depends upon and references columns from the outer query.

Either type of subquery can return a scalar or multiple values. Scalar-valued subqueries can be placed anywhere within a *SELECT* statement where one or zero values are expected. A multivalued subquery can be used anywhere a set of values is expected.

In this lesson, you learn how to implement correlated and noncorrelated subqueries.

> **After this lesson, you will be able to:**
> - Implement correlated subqueries.
> - Implement noncorrelated subqueries.
>
> **Estimated lesson time: 20 minutes**

Noncorrelated Subqueries

The main purpose of a noncorrelated subquery is to allow you to write code that is more dynamic and does not require that a user knows all the intermediate values that currently exist in the database. For example, if you wanted to return a list of customers that were assigned to a specific region, you first have to know the list of cities or states from which to retrieve the requested list. However, a table would exist within your database that specifies which cities or states are assigned to a given region and a noncorrelated subquery could be used to make your query resilient to changes in the way a region is organized. Here is an example of how it might work:

```
SELECT a.CustomerID, a.FirstName, a.LastName, b.Address, b.City, b.StateProvince
FROM Customer.Customer a INNER JOIN Customer.CustomerAddress b
    ON a.CustomerID = b.CustomerID
WHERE b.City IN (SELECT c.City FROM Customer.CityRegion c INNER JOIN Customer.Region d
                    ON c.RegionID = d.RegionID
                WHERE d.Region = 'RegionX')
```

As another example, suppose that you wanted to return all the products with a list price greater than the average list price for all products. Instead of having to retrieve the average list price separately, store the value in a variable, and then use the variable in a second *SELECT* statement, you could use the following query:

```
SELECT a.ProductID, a.Name, a.ListPrice
FROM Production.Product a
WHERE a.ListPrice > (SELECT AVG(b.ListPrice) FROM Production.Product b)
```

Derived Tables

If you want to return a list of employees and the number of employees who have the same title, you might try to execute the following query:

```
SELECT BusinessEntityID, JobTitle, count(*)
FROM HumanResources.Employee
GROUP BY BusinessEntityID, JobTitle
```

Now you have a problem. You need to calculate the number of employees with a given job title and *then* return a list of employees along with how many other employees have the same job title. But to meet the requirements of the *GROUP BY*, you have to include all the nonaggregate columns in the *GROUP BY* clause. You are faced with a dilemma because it appears that your query can't be satisfied.

The issue with your query is the order of operations. You have to first calculate the number of people with a given job title. Then, based on that result, join it back to the *Employee* table to get a list of employees and how many other employees have the same title.

Instead of resorting to temporary tables to store the intermediate result set, T-SQL can solve this dilemma by taking advantage of an interesting feature of a *FROM* clause; namely, it accepts a table source. A table is constructed of rows and columns. When you execute a *SELECT* statement, you get a result set that consists of rows and columns. Therefore, it seems possible that you could actually put an entire *SELECT* statement into the *FROM* clause because the only requirement is to have a source that has the structure of a table.

When you embed a *SELECT* statement into a *FROM* clause, you are using a feature referred to as *derived tables* or *virtual tables*. A *SELECT* statement returns a result set, but no name exists for the result set to be referenced within a query. You get around the lack of a name by wrapping the entire *SELECT* statement in parentheses and specifying an alias. The solution to your original problem then becomes the following:

```
SELECT b.BusinessEntityID, b.JobTitle, a.numtitles
FROM (SELECT JobTitle, count(*) numtitles
        FROM HumanResources.Employee
        GROUP BY JobTitle) a
    INNER JOIN HumanResources.Employee b ON a.JobTitle = b.JobTitle
```

SQL Server first executes the *SELECT...GROUP BY* statement, loads the results into memory, and "tags" the results with the specified alias. You can then reference any column within the derived table in the remainder of the *SELECT* statement just as if you were working with a physical table. Keep in mind that any aggregate, concatenation, or computation within the derived table must have an alias specified because it is not possible to construct a table with a column that has no name.

The main benefit of a derived table is the fact that the result set resides entirely in memory, which allows faster data access than if the result set were on a storage device. In almost all cases, any routine that uses a temporary table to store an intermediate result set that is used by a subsequent query can use a derived table instead.

Running Aggregates

By combining derived tables with unequal joins, you can calculate a variety of cumulative aggregates. The following query returns a running aggregate of orders for each salesperson:

```
SELECT SH3.SalesPersonID, SH3.OrderDate, SH3.DailyTotal, SUM(SH4.DailyTotal)
RunningTotal
FROM (SELECT SH1.SalesPersonID, SH1.OrderDate, SUM(SH1.TotalDue) DailyTotal
        FROM Sales.SalesOrderHeader SH1
        WHERE SH1.SalesPersonID IS NOT NULL
        GROUP BY SH1.SalesPersonID, SH1.OrderDate) SH3
INNER JOIN (SELECT SH2.SalesPersonID, SH2.OrderDate, SUM(SH2.TotalDue) DailyTotal
        FROM Sales.SalesOrderHeader SH2
        WHERE SH2.SalesPersonID IS NOT NULL
        GROUP BY SH2.SalesPersonID, SH2.OrderDate) SH4
ON SH3.SalesPersonID = SH4.SalesPersonID
    AND SH3.OrderDate >= SH4.OrderDate
GROUP BY SH3.SalesPersonID, SH3.OrderDate, SH3.DailyTotal
ORDER BY SH3.SalesPersonID, SH3.OrderDate
```

The derived tables are used to combine all orders for salespeople who have more than one order on a single day. The join on *SalesPersonID* ensures that you are accumulating rows for only a single salesperson. The unequal join allows the aggregate to consider only the rows for a salesperson where the order date is earlier than the order date currently being considered within the result set.

By adding a *HAVING* clause, you can expand a running aggregate to encompass a variety of situations, such as displaying a running sales total only for salespeople who have already met their quota or sales aggregated across a sliding window.

Correlated Subqueries

In a correlated subquery, the inner query depends upon the values from the outer query. This causes the inner query to be executed repeatedly based on input from the outer query. The following query returns products and their corresponding list price for all products that have been sold:

```
SELECT a.ProductID, a.ListPrice
FROM Production.Product a
WHERE EXISTS (SELECT 1 FROM Sales.SalesOrderDetail b
            WHERE b.ProductID = a.ProductID)
```

Using a join or any other *WHERE* clause would return the product every time it were sold; however, that would detail how many times a product had sold instead of detailing products that have sold at least once. The *EXISTS* argument also improves the performance of the query because SQL Server has to find only a single occurrence within the table for the *WHERE* clause to be true. As soon as a value is located, SQL Server quits looking at the remainder of the rows because the return value would not change from that point forward.

EXAM TIP

For the exam, you are going to need to read a query and, based solely on the *SELECT* statement, determine whether the query can be used to solve the business problem presented.

 Quick Check

1. What is the difference between a correlated and a noncorrelated subquery?
2. What is a derived table?

Quick Check Answers

1. A noncorrelated subquery is a query that is embedded within another query but does not reference any columns from the outer query. A correlated subquery is embedded within another query and references columns within the outer query.
2. A derived table is a *SELECT* statement that is embedded within a *FROM* clause.

PRACTICE **Finding Sequence Gaps**

In this practice, you use subqueries to find gaps in a sequence.

EXERCISE Find Sequence Gaps

In the following exercise, you use subqueries to find gaps in a sequence.

1. Open a new query window, type and execute the following code to load a table with test data:

```
CREATE TABLE #orderdates
(CustomerID    INT       NOT NULL,
OrderDate      DATETIME NOT NULL);

DECLARE @startDate       datetime,
        @endDate         datetime,
        @CustomerID      int

SET @CustomerID = 1
```

```
WHILE @CustomerID < 100
BEGIN
    SELECT @startDate = 'Jan 01, 2007',
           @endDate = DATEADD(yy, 1, @startDate);

    WITH dates AS
    (SELECT @startDate AS begindate
     UNION ALL
     SELECT DATEADD(dd,1,begindate) FROM dates
         WHERE begindate < dateadd(dd,-1,@endDate ) )

    INSERT INTO #orderdates
    SELECT @CustomerID, begindate FROM dates
    OPTION (MAXRECURSION 0);

    SET @CustomerID = @CustomerID + 1
END

SELECT * FROM #orderdates;
```

2. In the existing query window, type, highlight, and execute the following code to introduce gaps within the sequence:

```
--Now delete some of the rows to produce gaps
DELETE #orderdates
WHERE DATEDIFF(dd, 0, OrderDate)%11 = 0 ;

--Produce a couple of multi-day gaps
DELETE FROM #orderdates
WHERE OrderDate IN ('1/4/2007','2/17/2007')
      AND CustomerID%3 = 0

SELECT * FROM #orderdates;
```

3. In the existing query window, type, highlight, and execute the following code to retrieve a list of all the sequence gaps:

```
SELECT CustomerID, StartGap, EndGap,
    DATEDIFF(dd,StartGap,EndGap) + 1 AS NumberMissingDays
FROM
    (SELECT t1.CustomerID, t1.OrderDate AS StartGap, MIN(t2.OrderDate) AS EndGap
       FROM
        (SELECT CustomerID, DATEADD(dd, 1, OrderDate) AS OrderDate
         FROM #orderdates tbl1
         WHERE NOT EXISTS(SELECT * FROM #orderdates tbl2
                          WHERE DATEDIFF(dd, tbl1.OrderDate, tbl2.OrderDate) = 1
                              AND tbl1.CustomerID = tbl2.CustomerID)
          AND OrderDate <> (SELECT MAX(OrderDate) FROM #orderdates)) t1
```

```
INNER JOIN
(SELECT CustomerID, DATEADD(dd, -1, OrderDate) AS OrderDate
  FROM #orderdates tbl1
   WHERE NOT EXISTS(SELECT * FROM #orderdates tbl2
                     WHERE DATEDIFF(dd, tbl2.OrderDate, tbl1.OrderDate) = 1
                        AND tbl1.CustomerID = tbl2.CustomerID)
   AND OrderDate <> (SELECT MIN(OrderDate) FROM #orderdates)) t2
  ON t1.OrderDate <= t2.OrderDate AND t1.CustomerID = t2.CustomerID
 GROUP BY t1.CustomerID, t1.OrderDate) a
 ORDER BY CustomerID, StartGap;
```

Lesson Summary

- Noncorrelated subqueries are independent queries that are embedded within an outer query and are used to retrieve a scalar value or list of values that can be consumed by the outer query to make code more dynamic.

- Correlated subqueries are queries that are embedded within an outer query but reference values within the outer query.

Lesson 3: Applying Ranking Functions

Ranking functions are used to provide simple analytics such as statistical ordering or segmentation. In this lesson, you learn how to use the four ranking functions that ship with SQL Server 2008.

> **After this lesson, you will be able to:**
> - Use ranking functions in your queries.
>
> **Estimated lesson time: 20 minutes**

Ranking Data

T-SQL has four functions that can be used for ranking data: *ROW_NUMBER, RANK, DENSE_RANK,* and *NTILE*.

The *ROW_NUMBER* function assigns a number from 1 to *n* based on a user-specified sorting order. *ROW_NUMBER* does not account for ties within the result set, so if you have rows with the same values within the column(s) that you are ordering by, repeated calls to the database for the same result set can produce different row numbering.

The following example returns the salesperson along with his or her year-to-date sales and is numbered in descending order according to the year-to-date sales amount:

```
SELECT p.FirstName, p.LastName, ROW_NUMBER() OVER(ORDER BY s.SalesYTD DESC) AS 'RowNumber',
    s.SalesYTD, a.PostalCode
FROM Sales.SalesPerson s INNER JOIN Person.Person p
        ON s.BusinessEntityID = p.BusinessEntityID
    INNER JOIN Person.BusinessEntityAddress ba ON p.BusinessEntityID = ba.BusinessEntityID
    INNER JOIN Person.Address a ON a.AddressID = ba.AddressID
WHERE s.TerritoryID IS NOT NULL
```

You can also use the *ROW_NUMBER* function with an aggregate to provide a sequence number within each group. You generate a number within each group by providing an optional *PARTITION BY* clause as follows:

```
SELECT p.FirstName, p.LastName,
    ROW_NUMBER() OVER (PARTITION BY s.TerritoryID ORDER BY SalesYTD DESC) AS 'RowNumber',
        s.SalesYTD, s.TerritoryID
FROM Sales.SalesPerson s INNER JOIN Person.Person p
        ON s.BusinessEntityID = p.BusinessEntityID
    INNER JOIN Person.BusinessEntityAddress ba ON p.BusinessEntityID = ba.BusinessEntityID
    INNER JOIN Person.Address a ON a.AddressID = ba.AddressID
WHERE s.TerritoryID IS NOT NULL
```

If you need to number a result set but also deal with ties, you can use the *RANK* function. If the result set does not have any ties, *RANK* produces the same results as *ROW_NUMBER*.

However, if there are ties, *RANK* assigns the same value to each row that is tied and then skips to the next value, leaving a gap in the sequence corresponding to the number of rows that were tied. The following examples show how *RANK* is applied to duplicates as well as within each aggregate grouping:

```
SELECT a.ProductID, b.Name, a.LocationID, a.Quantity,
    RANK() OVER (PARTITION BY a.LocationID ORDER BY a.Quantity DESC) AS 'Rank'
FROM Production.ProductInventory a INNER JOIN Production.Product b
    ON a.ProductID = b.ProductID
ORDER BY b.Name


SELECT a.ProductID, b.Name, a.LocationID, a.Quantity,
    RANK() OVER (PARTITION BY a.LocationID ORDER BY a.Quantity DESC) AS 'Rank'
FROM Production.ProductInventory a INNER JOIN Production.Product b
    ON a.ProductID = b.ProductID
ORDER BY 'Rank'
```

If you do not want any gaps in a sequence, you can use the *DENSE_RANK* function. *DENSE_RANK* assigns the same value to each duplicate but does not produce gaps in the sequence. The following two examples show the same result set when *DENSE_RANK* is applied:

```
SELECT a.ProductID, b.Name, a.LocationID, a.Quantity,
    DENSE_RANK() OVER (PARTITION BY a.LocationID ORDER BY a.Quantity DESC) AS 'DenseRank'
FROM Production.ProductInventory a INNER JOIN Production.Product b
    ON a.ProductID = b.ProductID
ORDER BY b.Name


SELECT a.ProductID, b.Name, a.LocationID, a.Quantity,
    DENSE_RANK() OVER (PARTITION BY a.LocationID ORDER BY a.Quantity DESC) AS DenseRank
FROM Production.ProductInventory a INNER JOIN Production.Product b
    ON a.ProductID = b.ProductID
ORDER BY DenseRank
```

NTILE is used to divide a result set into approximately equal groups. For example, if you wanted to split a result set into six groups with approximately the same number of rows in each group, you could use *NTILE(6)*. The following examples show how *NTILE* can be used to segment a result set:

```
SELECT p.FirstName, p.LastName,
    NTILE(4) OVER(ORDER BY s.SalesYTD DESC) AS QuarterGroup,
    s.SalesYTD, a.PostalCode
FROM Sales.SalesPerson s INNER JOIN Person.Person p
        ON s.BusinessEntityID = p.BusinessEntityID
    INNER JOIN Person.BusinessEntityAddress ba ON p.BusinessEntityID = ba.BusinessEntityID
    INNER JOIN Person.Address a ON a.AddressID = ba.AddressID
WHERE s.TerritoryID IS NOT NULL
```

```
SELECT p.FirstName, p.LastName,
    NTILE(2) OVER(PARTITION BY s.TerritoryID ORDER BY s.SalesYTD DESC) AS QuarterGroup,
        s.SalesYTD, s.TerritoryID
FROM Sales.SalesPerson s INNER JOIN Person.Person p
        ON s.BusinessEntityID = p.BusinessEntityID
    INNER JOIN Person.BusinessEntityAddress ba ON p.BusinessEntityID = ba.BusinessEntityID
    INNER JOIN Person.Address a ON a.AddressID = ba.AddressID
WHERE s.TerritoryID IS NOT NULL
```

EXAM TIP

In addition to understanding the application of the four ranking functions, you need to understand when *RANK/DENSE_RANK* produce the same results as *ROW_NUMBER*, as well as what the difference is between *RANK* and *DENSE_RANK*.

✔ Quick Check

1. What is the difference between *RANK* and *DENSE_RANK*?
2. When do *ROW_NUMBER, RANK,* and *DENSE_RANK* produce the same results?

Quick Check Answers

1. *RANK* assigns the same number to ties but leaves a gap in the sequence corresponding to the number of rows that were tied. *DENSE_RANK* assigns the same number to ties but does not create a gap in a sequence.
2. *ROW_NUMBER, RANK,* and *DENSE_RANK* produce the same results when the column being sorted by does not contain any duplicate values within the result set.

PRACTICE   **Finding Gaps in a Sequence**

In this practice, you enhance the solution of the practice in Lesson 2, "Implementing Subqueries," using ranking functions with a CTE to improve performance.

EXERCISE

In this exercise, you will enhance the solution of the practice in Lesson 2 using ranking functions with a CTE to improve performance.

1. Open a new query window, type and execute the following code to load a table with test data:

```
CREATE TABLE #orderdates
(CustomerID    INT      NOT NULL,
OrderDate      DATETIME NOT NULL);
```

```
DECLARE @startDate      datetime,
        @endDate        datetime,
        @CustomerID     int

SET @CustomerID = 1

WHILE @CustomerID < 100
BEGIN
    SELECT @startDate = 'Jan 01, 2007',
           @endDate = DATEADD(yy, 1, @startDate);

    WITH dates AS
    (SELECT @startDate AS begindate
     UNION ALL
     SELECT DATEADD(dd,1,begindate) FROM dates
        WHERE begindate < dateadd(dd,-1,@endDate ) )

    INSERT INTO #orderdates
    SELECT @CustomerID, begindate FROM dates
    OPTION (MAXRECURSION 0);

    SET @CustomerID = @CustomerID + 1
END

SELECT * FROM #orderdates;
```

2. In the existing query window, type, highlight, and execute the following code to introduce gaps within the sequence:

```
--Now delete some of the rows to produce gaps
DELETE #orderdates
WHERE DATEDIFF(dd, 0, OrderDate)%11 = 0 ;

--Produce a couple of multi-day gaps
DELETE FROM #orderdates
WHERE OrderDate IN ('1/4/2007','2/17/2007')
      AND CustomerID%3 = 0

SELECT * FROM #orderdates;
```

3. In the existing query window, type, highlight, and execute the following code to retrieve a list of all the sequence gaps:

```
WITH OrderDatesCTE(CustomerID, RowNum, OrderDate) AS
(SELECT CustomerID,
    ROW_NUMBER() OVER(PARTITION BY CustomerID ORDER BY OrderDate) AS RowNum,
OrderDate
 FROM #orderdates)
```

```
SELECT a.CustomerID, DATEADD(dd, 1, a.OrderDate) AS StartGap,
    DATEADD(dd, -1, b.OrderDate) AS EndGap,
    DATEDIFF(dd,DATEADD(dd, 1, a.OrderDate),DATEADD(dd, -1, b.OrderDate)) + 1
        AS NumberMissingDays
  FROM OrderDatesCTE a INNER JOIN OrderDatesCTE b
  ON a.CustomerID = b.CustomerID and a.RowNum = b.RowNum - 1
  WHERE DATEDIFF(dd, a.OrderDate, DATEADD(dd, -1, b.OrderDate)) <> 0
ORDER BY a.CustomerID, a.OrderDate
```

Lesson Summary

- *ROW_NUMBER* is used to number rows sequentially in a result set but might not produce identical results if there are ties in the column(s) used for sorting.

- *RANK* numbers a tie with identical values but can produce gaps in a sequence.

- *DENSE_RANK* numbers ties with identical values but does not produce gaps in the sequence.

- *NTILE* allows you to divide a result set into approximately equal-sized groups.

Chapter Review

To practice and reinforce the skills you learned in this chapter further, you can perform the following tasks:

- Review the chapter summary.
- Review the list of key terms introduced in this chapter.
- Complete the case scenarios. These scenarios set up real-world situations involving the topics in this chapter and ask you to create a solution.
- Complete the suggested practices.
- Take a practice test.

Chapter Summary

- Recursive CTEs can be used to solve a variety of problems that require traversal of a hierarchy more efficiently than cursor-based approaches.
- Subqueries allow you to embed one query within another query. A noncorrelated subquery is independent of the outer query, whereas a correlated subquery references columns in the outer query.
- Ranking functions can be used to solve a variety of problems that require ordering of a result set, such as pagination and finding gaps within a sequence.

Key Terms

Do you know what these key terms mean? You can check your answers by looking up the terms in the glossary at the end of the book.

- Correlated subquery
- Noncorrelated subquery
- Recursive CTE

Case Scenario

In the following case scenario, you apply what you've learned in this chapter. You can find answers to these questions in the "Answers" section at the end of this book.

Case Scenario: Improving Query Performance

Blue Yonder Airlines is implementing a new data warehouse that receives daily loads. A report needs to be produced every day to notify management if any of the subsidiaries does not upload its data. At the same time, severe performance problems are occurring within the production environment. You have been brought in to design the data load and reporting requirements of the data warehouse, as well as to solve the performance issues within the transactional databases. During your analysis, you find that every stored procedure is based on the use of cursors and temporary tables. Cursors are used to iterate across result sets to find missing data, fill empty seats on an airplane, or calculate sales figures. Temporary tables are used primarily to hold intermediate result sets before a final result is returned.

Answer the following question for your manager:

- What can you do to resolve the issues at Blue Yonder Airlines?

Suggested Practices

To help you master the exam objectives presented in this chapter, complete the following tasks.

Build Recursive Queries with CTEs

- **Practice 1**   Replace the cursor-based solutions for navigating hierarchies in your applications with recursive CTEs.

Implement Subqueries

- **Practice 1**   Replace the cursor-based solutions that you use to calculate running totals in your applications with subqueries.

- **Practice 2**   Find code that makes multiple calls to solve a problem within your applications. Change the code to retrieve all the values in a set that can then be substituted into a *WHERE* clause as a noncorrelated subquery.

- **Practice 3**   Remove temporary tables that are used to store intermediate result sets in your applications and replace them with derived tables.

Apply Ranking Functions

- **Practice 1**   Replace a cursor-based solution that you use to find sequence gaps in one of your applications with a CTE combined with a *ROW_NUMBER* function.

Take a Practice Test

The practice tests on this book's companion CD offer many options. For example, you can test yourself on just one exam objective, or you can test yourself on all the 70-433 certification exam content. You can set up the test so that it closely simulates the experience of taking a certification exam, or you can set it up in study mode so that you can look at the correct answers and explanations after you answer each question.

> **MORE INFO PRACTICE TESTS**
>
> For details about all the practice test options available, see the section entitled "How to Use the Practice Tests," in the Introduction to this book.

Programming Microsoft SQL Server with T-SQL User-Defined Stored Procedures, Functions, Triggers, and Views

Microsoft SQL Server 2008 allows you to create three types of programmable objects: stored procedures, functions, and triggers. Instead of executing a single statement or command at a time, you can build objects that contain blocks of code using a rich programming language complete with variables, parameters, control flow, and error handling. SQL Server ships with hundreds of functions and allows you to create your own functions to encapsulate frequently executed data retrieval operations. Just as application developers use public properties and methods to expose application programming interfaces (APIs) to build the object-oriented, client-server, Web-enabled, service-oriented, and cloud-computing applications in use throughout organizations, stored procedures provide an abstraction API to the tables and data contained within your databases, which allows developers to focus on writing code instead of understanding the intricacies of the database design. Triggers are a special form of stored procedure that are executed automatically when data manipulation language (DML) or data definition language (DDL) commands are executed.

In addition to the three types of programmable objects, you can store *SELECT* statements within a database by using views.

In this chapter, you learn how to build stored procedures, functions, triggers, and views for your applications. You also learn how to manage transactions and implement error-handling routines. Although programmable objects can be written using either Transact-SQL (T-SQL) or Common Language Runtime (CLR) languages, in this chapter you learn how to create objects using T-SQL.

Exam objectives in this chapter:

- Create and alter stored procedures.
- Create and alter user-defined functions (UDFs).
- Create and alter DML triggers.
- Create and alter DDL triggers.
- Create and deploy CLR-based objects.
- Implement error handling.
- Manage transactions.
- Create and alter views.

Lessons in this chapter:

Before You Begin

To complete the lessons in this chapter, you must have:

- SQL Server 2008 installed
- The *AdventureWorks* database installed

> **MORE INFO** **CLR OBJECTS**
>
> You can create triggers, functions, and stored procedures using any supported CLR language. The creation and management of CLR objects is covered in Chapter 7, "Extending Microsoft SQL Server Functionality with XML, Filestream, and SQLCLR."

>   **REAL WORLD**
>
> Michael Hotek
>
> For decades, companies have been creating frameworks and code generation tools that are supposed to "shield" developers from needing to understand databases or Structured Query Language (SQL). While many of these frameworks and code generation tools have allowed developers to quickly create large volumes of database access code, unless the code generated undergoes significant modification, very little will perform well enough to meet the needs of business applications.

At one company where I was working on a project, one of the developers couldn't wait to use one of these new code generators that was designed to shield the developers from needing to understand the databases they were using. Within the application, the developer wrote about four lines of code that would retrieve a single row from a table based on an input value for one of the columns of a table. This could have been done with a simple SELECT statement, which could have been encapsulated inside a stored procedure. However, what the application submitted to SQL Server created a function that contained the SELECT statement, a SELECT statement to access the function, code to drop the function at the end of the process, and 30 to 40 lines of T-SQL to perform error handling validation and ensure that the function was properly created and then dropped.

Had the developer simply written the stored procedure and then called the stored procedure in the code, he would have needed to write a total of eight lines of code, and each user request would execute a total of three statements. Using the code generated by the code generator, however, required an object to be created and then destroyed along with the execution of more than 70 lines of code for each user request.

Although the code generator did all the work so that the developer "didn't have to worry about it," performance comparisons showed that the automatically generated code required six times as many resources and took 245 percent longer to execute than if the developer had just written a stored procedure.

T-SQL is a very simple language to learn and has been around, with much the same syntax, for more than 50 years. Every time I hear about the next code generation tool that someone created to free developers from needing to understand how to access a database, the thing that always comes to mind is reinventing the wheel. T-SQL is a much simpler language than any of the development platforms in use. Just like the wheel, which has been around for more than 5,000 years with very little in the way of innovation, SQL will long outlive any application development language you will ever use, while at the same time being the most efficient way to access a relational database.

Lesson 1: Stored Procedures

Stored procedures provide an abstraction layer that shields applications from the underlying database structure. As the backbone of any SQL Server application, stored procedures allow you to make changes to the database structure and manage performance without needing to rewrite applications or deploy application updates. In this lesson, you learn how to create stored procedures to provide the programmatic interface necessary for writing easily maintained and efficient database applications.

> **After this lesson, you will be able to:**
> - Create and alter stored procedures.
> - Implement error handling.
> - Manage transactions.
>
> **Estimated lesson time: 20 minutes**

Creating Stored Procedures

A *stored procedure* is one or more statements that has been given a name and stored within a database. Almost any command within the T-SQL language can be included in a stored procedure, making procedures suitable for applications and for performing myriad administrative actions. The only commands that cannot be used in a stored procedure are the following:

- *USE* <database name>
- *SET SHOWPLAN_TEXT*
- *SET SHOWPLAN_ALL*
- *SET PARSEONLY*
- *SET SHOWPLAN_XML*
- *CREATE AGGREGATE*
- *CREATE RULE*
- *CREATE DEFAULT*
- *CREATE SCHEMA*
- *CREATE FUNCTION* or *ALTER FUNCTION*
- *CREATE TRIGGER* or *ALTER TRIGGER*
- *CREATE PROCEDURE* or *ALTER PROCEDURE*
- *CREATE VIEW* or *ALTER VIEW*

The first time that a stored procedure is accessed, SQL Server generates compile and execution plans that are stored in the query cache and reused for subsequent executions. Therefore, you can receive a slight performance benefit when using a stored procedure by avoiding the need to parse, compile, and generate a query plan on subsequent executions of a stored procedure. However, the main purpose of a stored procedure is to provide a security layer and an API to your databases that isolate applications from changes to the database structure.

The generic syntax to create a stored procedure is

```
CREATE { PROC | PROCEDURE } [schema_name.] procedure_name [ ; number ]
    [ { @parameter [ type_schema_name. ] data_type }
        [ VARYING ] [ = default ] [ OUT | OUTPUT ] [READONLY]
    ] [ ,...n ]
[ WITH <procedure_option> [ ,...n ] ]
[ FOR REPLICATION ]
AS { <sql_statement> [;][ ...n ] | <method_specifier> } [;]
<procedure_option> ::=
    [ ENCRYPTION ] [ RECOMPILE ] [ EXECUTE AS Clause ]
```

When you specify the *ENCRYPTION* option, available for triggers, functions, procedures, and views, SQL Server applies a bitwise *OR* to the code in the object. The *ENCRYPTION* option is a carryover from early versions of SQL Server and the option causes quite a bit of confusion. When you specify the *ENCRYPTION* option, you are not applying an encryption routine to hide your code. The algorithm that SQL Server uses is a simple bitwise *OR* that only obfuscates the code in the object. If you look at the definition of the object, it appears as unintelligible text. However, a very simple, publicly available routine reverses the obfuscation. SQL Server does not allow you to hide the code in triggers, functions, views, and stored procedures, and anyone with *VIEW DEFINITION* authority on the object can retrieve the code you have written.

> **CAUTION ENCRYPTING MODULES**
>
> SQL Server is not a digital rights management (DRM) system. The text of the module is not encrypted; rather, it is obfuscated. Any user with access to database metadata can reverse-engineer the obfuscated text easily. The *ENCRYPTION* option is not meant to prevent a user from reading the code within your modules.

If you want to modify the contents of a stored procedure or the procedure options, you can use the *ALTER PROCEDURE* statement.

What sets a stored procedure apart from a simple batch of T-SQL are all the code structures that can be employed, such as variables, parameterization, error handling, and control flow constructs.

Commenting Code

One of the hallmarks of well-constructed code is appropriate comments that simplify future maintenance.

T-SQL has two different constructs for commenting code, as follows:

```
--This is a single line comment


/*
This is a
multi-line comment
*/
```

Variables, Parameters, and Return Codes

SQL Server provides three types of objects that are designed to pass values within your code, as well as return a scalar value to a calling routine.

Variables

Variables provide a way to manipulate, store, and pass data within a stored procedure, as well as between stored procedures and functions. SQL Server has two types of variables: local and global. A *local variable* is designated by a single at sign (@) while a *global variable* is designated by a double at sign (@@). In addition, you can create, read, and write local variables, but you can only read the values from global variables. Table 5-1 lists some of the more common global variables.

TABLE 5-1 Global Variables

GLOBAL VARIABLE	DEFINITION
@@ERROR	Error code from the last statement executed
@@IDENTITY	Value of the last identity value inserted within the connection
@@ROWCOUNT	The number of rows affected by the last statement
@@TRANCOUNT	The number of open transactions within the connection
@@VERSION	The version of SQL Server

BEST PRACTICES **IDENTITIES**

The @@*IDENTITY* variable contains the last identity value inserted for the connection. If you call multiple code modules that insert identity values, the last value inserted is always contained in @@*IDENTITY*. For example, if you call a procedure that inserts a row into *TableA*, which has a trigger that inserts rows into *TableB*, *TableC*, and *TableD*, with each insert generating a new identity value, the value of @@*IDENTITY* that is retrieved following the insert into *TableA* corresponds to the identity value inserted into *TableD*. Because of this limitation, the use of @@*IDENTITY* is very strongly discouraged. Use the *SCOPE_IDENTITY()* function instead, which returns the last identity value inserted in the scope of the current statement.

You instantiate a variable with the *DECLARE* clause, where you specify the name and the data type of the variable. A variable can be defined using any data type except *text*, *ntext*, and *image*. For example:

```
DECLARE @intvariable    INT,
        @datevariable   DATE,
        @spatialvar     GEOGRAPHY,
        @levelvar       HIERARCHYID



DECLARE @tablevar       TABLE
(ID       INT         NOT NULL,
Customer  VARCHAR(50) NOT NULL)
```

NOTE **DEPRECATED DATA TYPES**

Text, *ntext*, and *image* data types have been deprecated and should not be used.

While a single *DECLARE* statement can be used to instantiate multiple variables, the instantiation of a table variable must be in a separate *DECLARE* statement.

You can assign either a static value or a single value returned from a *SELECT* statement to a variable. Either a *SET* or a *SELECT* can be used to assign a value; however, if you are executing a query to assign a value, you must use a *SELECT* statement. *SELECT* is also used to return the value of a variable.

In addition to assigning a value using either a *SET* or *SELECT* statement, you can also assign a value at the time a variable is instantiated. Here are some examples of setting variables in various ways:

```
DECLARE @intvariable    INT = 2,
        @datevariable   DATE = GETDATE(),
        @maxorderdate   DATE = (SELECT MAX(OrderDate) FROM Orders.OrderHeader),
        @counter1       INT,
        @counter2       INT

SET @counter1 = 1
SELECT @counter2 = -1

SELECT @intvariable, @datevariable, @maxorderdate, @counter1, @counter2
```

> **CAUTION   VARIABLE ASSIGNMENT**
>
> One of the most common mistakes is to forget that, with the exception of a table variable, variables contain scalar values. If you assign the results of a *SELECT* statement to a variable, you must ensure that only a single row is returned from the *SELECT* statement. If the *SELECT* statement returns more than one row, the variable is set to the value corresponding to the last row in the result set and all other values in the result set are discarded.

A variable can be used to perform calculations, control processing, or populate a search argument (*SARG*) in a query. You can perform calculations with variables using either a *SET* or a *SELECT* statement. SQL Server 2008 introduces a more compact way of assigning values to variables using a calculation:

```
--SQL Server 2005 and earlier
DECLARE @var    INT

SET @var = 1
SET @var = @var + 1
SELECT @var
SET @var = @var * 2
SELECT @var
SET @var = @var / 4
SELECT @var
GO

--SQL Server 2008
DECLARE @var    INT
```

```
SET @var = 1
SET @var += 1
SELECT @var
SET @var *= 2
SELECT @var
SET @var /= 4
SELECT @var
GO
```

Parameters

Parameters are local variables that are used to pass values into a stored procedure when it is executed. During execution, any parameters are used just like variables and can be read and written. You declare a parameter as in this example:

```
CREATE PROCEDURE <procedure name> @parm1  INT, @parm2 VARCHAR(20) = 'Default value'
AS
    --Code block
```

You can create two types of parameters: input and output. An output parameter is designated by using the keyword *OUTPUT*:

```
CREATE PROCEDURE <procedure name> @parm1  INT, @parm2 VARCHAR(20) = 'Default value',
    @orderid    INT OUTPUT
AS
    --Code block
```

Output parameters are used when you need to return a single value to an application. If you need to return an entire result set, you include a *SELECT* statement in the stored procedure that generates the results and returns the result set to the application as shown here:

```
CREATE PROCEDURE <procedure name> @parm1  INT, @parm2 VARCHAR(20) = 'Default value'
AS
    --This will return the results of this query to an application
    SELECT SalesOrderID, CustomerID, OrderDate, SubTotal, TaxAmt, Freight, TotalDue
    FROM Sales.SalesOrderHeader
```

Control Flow Constructs

Stored procedures have several control flow constructs that can be used:

- *RETURN*
- *IF...ELSE*
- *BEGIN...END*
- *WHILE*
- *BREAK/CONTINUE*
- *WAITFOR*
- *GOTO*

A return code can be passed back to an application to indicate the execution status of the procedure. Return codes are not intended to send data but are used to report execution status. *RETURN* terminates the execution of the procedure and returns control back to the calling application. Any statements after the *RETURN* statement are not executed, as shown here:

```
CREATE PROCEDURE <procedure name> @parm1  INT, @parm2 VARCHAR(20) = 'Default value'
AS
    --This will return the value 1 back to the caller of the stored procedure
    RETURN 1


    --Any code from this point on will not be executed
```

IF...ELSE provides the ability to conditionally execute code. The *IF* statement checks the condition supplied and executes the next statement when the condition evaluates to True. The optional *ELSE* statement allows you to execute code when the condition check evaluates to False. Here is an example:

```
DECLARE @var    INT

SET @var = 1

IF @var = 1
    PRINT 'This is the code executed when true.'
ELSE
    PRINT 'This is the code executed when false.'
```

Regardless of the branch your code takes for an *IF...ELSE*, only the next statement is conditionally executed, as demonstrated in this example:

```
DECLARE @var    INT

SET @var = 1

IF @var = 2
    PRINT 'This is the code executed when true.'
    PRINT 'This will always execute.'
```

Because an *IF* statement conditionally executes only the next line of code, you have a problem when you want to execute an entire block of code conditionally. The *BEGIN...END* statement allows you to delimit code blocks that should execute as a unit, as shown here:

```
DECLARE @var    INT

SET @var = 1

IF @var = 2
BEGIN
    PRINT 'This is the code executed when true.'
    PRINT 'This code is also executed only when the condition is true.'
END
```

WHILE is used to iteratively execute a block of code so long as a specified condition is true. Here is an example:

```
DECLARE @var1    INT,
        @var2    VARCHAR(30)

SET @var1 = 1

WHILE @var1 <= 10
BEGIN
    SET @var2 = 'Iteration #' + CAST(@var1 AS VARCHAR(2))

    PRINT @var2

    SET @var1 += 1
END
```

BEST PRACTICES **STATEMENT EXECUTION**

One of the most common mistakes you can make when writing code blocks that use an *IF* or a *WHILE* is forgetting that SQL Server executes the next statement only conditionally. To avoid the most common coding mistakes, it is strongly recommended that you always use a *BEGIN...END* with an *IF* or *WHILE*, even when you are going to execute only a single line of code conditionally. Not only does it make the code more readable, but it also helps prevent bugs when your code is modified in the future.

BREAK is used in conjunction with a *WHILE* loop. If you need to terminate execution within a *WHILE* loop, you can use the *BREAK* statement to end the loop iteration. Once *BREAK* is executed, the next line of code following the *WHILE* loop is executed. *CONTINUE* is used within a *WHILE* loop to have the code continue to execute from the beginning of the loop.

NOTE **BREAK AND CONTINUE**

BREAK and *CONTINUE* statements are almost never used. A *WHILE* loop terminates as soon as the condition for the *WHILE* loop is no longer true. Instead of embedding a conditional test along with a *BREAK* statement, *WHILE* loops are normally controlled through the use of an appropriate condition for the *WHILE*. In addition, so long as the conditional for the *WHILE* is true, the loop continues executing. Therefore, you should never need to use a *CONTINUE* statement.

WAITFOR is used to allow the code execution to pause. *WAITFOR* has three different permutations: *WAITFOR DELAY*, *WAITFOR TIME*, and *WAITFOR RECEIVE*. *WAITFOR RECEIVE* is used in conjunction with Service Broker, which you learn about in Chapter 8, "Extending SQL Server Functionality with the Spatial, Full-Text Search, and Service Broker." *WAITFOR TIME* pauses the execution of code until a specified time is reached. *WAITFOR DELAY* pauses the execution of code for a specified length of time:

```
DECLARE @var1   INT,
        @var2   VARCHAR(30)


SET @var1 = 1


--Pause for 2 seconds
WAITFOR DELAY '00:00:02'


WHILE @var1 <= 10
BEGIN
    SET @var2 = 'Iteration #' + CAST(@var1 AS VARCHAR(2))

    PRINT @var2

    SET @var1 += 1
END
```

GOTO allows you to pass the execution to a label embedded within the procedure. Code constructs such as *GOTO* are discouraged in all programming languages.

Error Messages

Error messages in SQL Server have three components:

- Error number
- Severity level
- Error message

The error number is an integer value. Error messages that ship with SQL Server are numbered from 1 to 49999.

SQL Server defines 26 severity levels numbered from 0 through 25. Any error with a severity level of 16 or higher is logged automatically to the SQL Server error log and the Windows Application Event Log. Errors with a severity level of 19 to 25 can be specified only by members of the *sysadmin* fixed server role. Errors with a severity level of 20 to 25 are considered fatal and cause the connection to be terminated and any open transactions to be rolled back.

The error message can be up to 255 Unicode characters long and allows up to two parameters to be passed.

You can create your own custom error messages, which must be numbered 50001 and higher. (The number 50000 is reserved to designate a message whose number is not specified.) Error messages can be localized for each language that SQL Server supports; however, you must create an English version of the message before creating a non-English version.

You create a custom error message by executing *sp_addmessage* as follows:

```
sp_addmessage [ @msgnum = ] msg_id ,        [ @severity = ] severity , [ @msgtext = ] 'msg'
    [ , [ @lang = ] 'language' ]
    [ , [ @with_log = ] 'with_log' ]
    [ , [ @replace = ] 'replace' ]
```

The following example creates a custom message in the English language with an error number of 50001 and a severity of 16:

```
EXEC sp_addmessage 50001, 16,
    N'The approved credit must be between 100 and 10,000';
GO
```

The following example creates a custom message in both English and French that accepts two parameters with a message number of 50002 and a severity of 16:

```
EXEC sp_addmessage @msgnum = 50002, @severity = 16,
    @msgtext = N'The product named %s already exists in %d.',
    @lang = 'us_english';

EXEC sp_addmessage @msgnum = 50002, @severity = 16,
    @msgtext = N' %1! de produit existent déjà dans %2!',
    @lang = 'French';
GO
```

The first message parameter is designated as *%s*, while the second parameter is designated as *%d*. The *%s* and *%d* parameters are used only with U.S. English–based messages. All other languages use *%1!* to designate the first parameter and *%2!* to designate the second parameter.

You send an error message by executing the *RAISERROR* command, using the following syntax:

```
RAISERROR ( { msg_id | msg_str | @local_variable }
    { ,severity ,state }
    [ ,argument [ ,...n ] ] )
    [ WITH option [ ,...n ] ]
```

You can view the messages available for the SQL Server instance by querying the *sys.messages* catalog view. Custom error messages can be modified by executing the *sp_altermessage* system stored procedure. You can drop a custom error message by executing the *sp_dropmessage* system stored procedure.

Error Handling

If you always wrote bug-free code that was always accessed in a well-defined, predictable manner, you would never have any errors. However, all your code is always subject to failure. An application could attempt to pass parameters that are invalid, business rules could be violated, or your code might not be designed to handle the calls made from a series of new applications. Therefore, you need to include error handling in your stored procedures, which allows the source of a problem to be diagnosed and fixed in a user-friendly way.

Prior to SQL Server 2005, the only way of performing error handling was to test the value of the @@ERROR global variable. When each statement is executed, SQL Server records the status of the result in @@ERROR. If an error occurred, @@ERROR contains the error number. If the statement was successful, @@ERROR contains a 0. You then need to query the variable to determine whether a statement succeeded or failed. Unfortunately, the simple act of executing a SELECT statement to retrieve the value of @@ERROR also sets the value of the variable, thereby overwriting any previous error value. Using @@ERROR to perform error handling is very cumbersome, requiring you to embed checks after each statement along with an error handling routine for each statement.

To provide a more structured way of handling errors that is very similar to the error handling routines of other programming languages, you can now use a TRY...CATCH block.

The TRY...CATCH block has two components. The TRY block is used to wrap any code in which you might receive an error that you want to trap and handle. The CATCH block is used to handle the error.

The following code creates an error due to the violation of a primary key constraint. You might expect this code to leave an empty table behind due to the error in the transaction; however, you find that the first and third INSERT statements succeed and leave two rows in the table:

```
--Transaction errors
CREATE TABLE dbo.mytable
(ID              INT                NOT NULL PRIMARY KEY)

BEGIN TRAN
    INSERT INTO dbo.mytable VALUES(1)
    INSERT INTO dbo.mytable VALUES(1)
    INSERT INTO dbo.mytable VALUES(2)
COMMIT TRAN

SELECT * FROM dbo.mytable
```

The reason that you have two rows inserted into the table is because by default, SQL Server does not roll back a transaction that has an error. If you want the transaction to either complete entirely or fail entirely, you can use the SET command to change the XACT_ABORT setting on your connection, as follows:

```
TRUNCATE TABLE dbo.mytable

SET XACT_ABORT ON;
BEGIN TRAN
    INSERT INTO dbo.mytable VALUES(1)
```

```
        INSERT INTO dbo.mytable VALUES(1)
        INSERT INTO dbo.mytable VALUES(2)
COMMIT TRAN
SET XACT_ABORT OFF;

SELECT * FROM dbo.mytable
```

Although the *SET XACT_ABORT ON* statement accomplishes your goal, when you change the settings for a connection, you can have unpredictable results for an application if your code does not reset the options properly. A better solution is to use a structured error handler to trap and decide how to handle the error.

The way a *TRY...CATCH* is implemented in SQL Server 2008 is as follows:

- If an error with a severity less than 20 is encountered within the *TRY* block, control passes to the corresponding *CATCH* block.

- If an error is encountered in the *CATCH* block, the transaction is aborted and the error is returned to the calling application unless the *CATCH* block is nested within another *TRY* block.

- The *CATCH* block must immediately follow the *TRY* block.

- Within the *CATCH* block, you can commit or roll back the current transaction unless the transaction is in an uncommitable state.

- A *RAISERROR* executed in the *TRY* block immediately passes control to the *CATCH* block without returning an error message to the application.

- A *RAISERROR* executed in the *CATCH* block closes the transaction and returns control to the calling application with the specified error message.

- If a *RAISERROR* is not executed within the *CATCH* block, the calling application never receives an error message.

> **NOTE   TRAPPING ERRORS**
>
> A *TRY...CATCH* block does not trap errors that cause the connection to be terminated, such as a fatal error or a sysadmin executing the *KILL* command. You also cannot trap errors that occur due to compilation errors, syntax errors, or nonexistent objects. Therefore, you cannot use a *TRY...CATCH* block to test for an object's existence.

The following code implements structured error handling for the previous code block:

```
--TRY...CATCH
TRUNCATE TABLE dbo.mytable

BEGIN TRY
    BEGIN TRAN
        INSERT INTO dbo.mytable VALUES(1)
        INSERT INTO dbo.mytable VALUES(1)
        INSERT INTO dbo.mytable VALUES(2)
```

```
        COMMIT TRAN
END TRY

BEGIN CATCH
    ROLLBACK TRAN
    PRINT 'Catch'
END CATCH

SELECT * FROM dbo.mytable
```

One of the more important aspects of a *TRY...CATCH* block is that no error messages are sent to an application unless a *RAISERROR* is executed within the *CATCH* block. Within the *CATCH* block, you have access to the following functions:

- **ERROR_NUMBER()**   The error number of the error thrown
- **ERROR_MESSAGE()**   The text of the error message
- **ERROR_SEVERITY()**   The severity level of the error message
- **ERROR_STATE()**   The state of the error
- **ERROR_PROCEDURE()**   The function, trigger, or procedure name that was executing when the error occurred
- **ERROR_LINE()**   The line of code within the function, trigger, or procedure that caused the error

> **BEST PRACTICES**   **RETURNING SYSTEM ERROR MESSAGES**
>
> If you implement a *TRY...CATCH* block, any errors, including system errors, are not returned to the calling application. The only way to return an error message to a calling application is to execute a *RAISERROR* statement. However, you can only specify a user-defined error message or dynamically construct an error message using *RAISERROR*. Therefore, you have a slight problem if you want to return a system-generated error to a calling application. If you want to return a system error message, you should dynamically build a message that includes the system error message information, which is returned with a *RAISERROR* statement that does not supply a message ID. That way, any system-generated messages are always returned with an error number of 50000.

Within the *CATCH* block, you can determine the current transaction nesting level with the *@@TRANCOUNT* global variable. You can also retrieve the state of the innermost transaction with the *XACT_STATE* function. The *XACT_STATE* function can return the following values:

- **1**   An open transaction exists that can be either committed or rolled back.
- **0**   There is no open transaction.
- **–1**   An open transaction exists, but it is in a doomed state. Due to the type of error that was raised, the transaction can only be rolled back.

XACT_ABORT behaves differently when used in conjunction with a *TRY* block. Instead of terminating the transaction, control is transferred to the *CATCH* block. However, if

XACT_ABORT is turned on, any error is fatal. The transaction is left in a doomed state and *XACT_STATE* returns –1. Therefore, you cannot commit a transaction inside a *CATCH* block if *XACT_ABORT* is turned on.

EXAM TIP

Make sure you understand how *TRY...CATCH* blocks handle errors, as well as how *XACT_ABORT* behaves within a *TRY...CATCH* block.

Executing Stored Procedures

You access a stored procedure by using an *EXEC* statement. If a stored procedure does not have any input parameters, the only code required is

```
EXEC <stored procedure>
```

If a stored procedure has input parameters, you can pass in the parameters either by name or by position:

```
--Execute by name
EXEC <stored procedure> @parm1=<value>, @parm2=<value>,...
--Execute by position
EXEC <stored procedure> <value>, <value>,...
```

Passing parameters to a stored procedure by position results in code that is more compact; however, it is more prone to errors. When parameters are passed to a stored procedure by name, changes in the order of parameters within the procedure do not require changes elsewhere in your applications. Regardless of whether you are passing parameters by position or by name, you need to specify a value for each parameter that does not have a default value.

BEST PRACTICES **EXECUTING STORED PROCEDURES**

If the stored procedure being executed is the first line in the batch, the *EXEC* keyword is optional. However, the *EXEC* keyword is required for a stored procedure call anywhere else in the batch. Even if the only code before the stored procedure is a comment, the *EXEC* keyword is still required. To avoid confusion and ensure that your code always runs, regardless of the structure of the batch, you should always include the *EXEC* keyword.

To use an output parameter, you need to specify the *OUT* or *OUTPUT* keyword following each output parameter:

```
--Using output parameters
DECLARE @variable1    <data type>,
        @variable2    <data type>
    ...

EXEC <stored procedure> @parameter1, @variable1 OUTPUT, @variable2 OUT
```

If you need to capture the return code from a stored procedure, you must store it in a variable, as follows:

```
--Capturing a return code
DECLARE @variable1     <data type>,
        @variable2     <data type>,
        @returncode    INT


EXEC @returncode = <stored procedure> @parameter1, @variable1 OUTPUT, @variable2 OUT
```

Dynamic Execution

While dynamic command execution is very rare within stored procedures that applications use, many administrative procedures need to construct commands and dynamically execute them. T-SQL has two ways to execute dynamically constructed statements: *EXEC(<command>)* and *sp_executesql <command>*. The following shows how to use each method.

```
EXEC('SELECT OrderID, CustomerID FROM Sales.SalesOrderHeader WHERE OrderID = 1')
GO


DECLARE @var    VARCHAR(MAX)
SET @var = 'SELECT OrderID, CustomerID FROM Sales.SalesOrderHeader WHERE OrderID = 1'
EXEC(@var)
GO


EXEC sp_executesql N'SELECT OrderID, CustomerID
                     FROM Sales.SalesOrderHeader WHERE OrderID = 1'
GO


DECLARE @var    NVARCHAR(MAX)
SET @var = 'SELECT OrderID, CustomerID FROM Sales.SalesOrderHeader WHERE OrderID = 1'
EXEC sp_executesql @var
GO
```

> **IMPORTANT APPLICATION SECURITY AND SQL INJECTION ATTACKS**
>
> Any time you are building a string for dynamic execution, you have the potential of an SQL injection attack. You should always validate any parameters passed to the stored procedure that will be used for a dynamically created command. You should also use the *sp_executesql* system stored procedure with parameter substitution to avoid many of the SQL injection problems that could be created. SQL injection is beyond the scope of this book, but you should read the many articles published on SQL injection and understand the risks before writing code that takes advantage of dynamic execution.

Module Execution Context

Functions and stored procedures allow you to modify the security context under which the object is running by using the *EXECUTE AS* option. *EXECUTE AS* has three possible arguments:

- **LOGIN**   Executes under the context of the specified login.
- **USER**   Executes under the security context of the specified database user. This account can't be a role, group, certificate, or asymmetric key.
- **CALLER**   Executes under the security context of the routine that called the module.

The *EXECUTE AS* clause also has two additional arguments: *NO REVERT* and *COOKIE INTO*. The *NO REVERT* option specifies that once the security context is changed, it can't be changed back. The *COOKIE INTO* option sets a cookie that allows the security context to be returned to a specific, previous security context.

Cursors

SQL Server is built to process sets of data. However, there are times when you need to process data one row at a time. The result of a *SELECT* statement is returned to a server-side object called a *cursor,* which allows you to access one row at a time within the result set and even allows scrolling forward as well as backward through the result set.

> **NOTE   CURSOR PERFORMANCE**
>
> SQL Server is built and optimized for set-based operations. A cursor causes the engine to perform row-based processing. A cursor never performs as well as an equivalent set-based process.

Cursors have five components. *DECLARE* is used to define the *SELECT* statement that is the basis for the rows in the cursor. *OPEN* causes the *SELECT* statement to be executed and load the rows into a memory structure. *FETCH* is used to retrieve one row at a time from the cursor. *CLOSE* is used to close the processing on the cursor. *DEALLOCATE* is used to remove the cursor and release the memory structures containing the cursor result set.

> **IMPORTANT   DEALLOCATING CURSORS**
>
> If a cursor is used within a stored procedure, it is not necessary to close and deallocate the cursor. When the stored procedure exits, SQL Server automatically closes and deallocates any cursors created within the procedure to reclaim memory space.

> **NOTE   CURSOR USAGE**
>
> If you write a cursor that performs the same operation against every row retrieved by the cursor, you should rewrite the process to use a more efficient set-based operation.

The generic syntax for declaring a cursor is

```
DECLARE cursor_name CURSOR [ LOCAL | GLOBAL ]
    [ FORWARD_ONLY | SCROLL ]
    [ STATIC | KEYSET | DYNAMIC | FAST_FORWARD ]
    [ READ_ONLY | SCROLL_LOCKS | OPTIMISTIC ]
    [ TYPE_WARNING ]
    FOR select_statement
    [ FOR UPDATE [ OF column_name [ ,...n ] ] ]
```

The following statements show three different ways of declaring the same cursor:

```
DECLARE curproducts CURSOR FAST_FORWARD FOR
    SELECT ProductID, ProductName, ListPrice FROM Products.Product
GO


DECLARE curproducts CURSOR READ_ONLY FOR
    SELECT ProductID, ProductName, ListPrice FROM Products.Product
GO


DECLARE curproducts CURSOR FOR
    SELECT ProductID, ProductName, ListPrice FROM Products.Product
FOR READ ONLY
GO
```

Once the cursor has been declared, you issue an *OPEN* command to execute the *SELECT* statement:

```
OPEN curproducts
```

You then need to retrieve data from the row in the cursor by using a *FETCH* statement. When you execute *FETCH* for the first time, a pointer is placed at the first row in the cursor result set. Each time a *FETCH* is executed, the cursor pointer is advanced one row in the result set until you run out of rows in the result set. Each execution of *FETCH* also sets a value for the global variable *@@FETCH_STATUS*. You usually use a *WHILE* loop to iterate across the cursor, fetching a row each iteration through the loop. You iterate the *WHILE* loop so long as *@@FETCH_STATUS* = 0. Here is an example:.

```
DECLARE @ProductID      INT,
        @ProductName    VARCHAR(50),
        @ListPrice      MONEY


DECLARE curproducts CURSOR FOR
    SELECT ProductID, ProductName, ListPrice FROM Products.Product
FOR READ ONLY

OPEN curproducts

FETCH curproducts INTO @ProductID, @ProductName, @ListPrice
```

```
WHILE @@FETCH_STATUS = 0
BEGIN
    SELECT @ProductID, @ProductName, @ListPrice
    FETCH curproducts INTO @ProductID, @ProductName, @ListPrice
END

CLOSE curproducts
DEALLOCATE curproducts
```

> **NOTE** **SET-BASED PROCESSING**
>
> If you are writing stored procedures that have cursors (especially multilevel cursors), you should reevaluate the process you are trying to write. You can probably replace the cursors with a set-based process that is more efficient.

You can declare four different types of cursors:

- **FAST_FORWARD** The fastest performing cursor type because it allows you only to move forward one row at a time. Scrolling (discussed later in this section) is not supported. A FAST_FORWARD cursor is the same as declaring a FORWARD_ONLY, READ_ONLY cursor. FAST_FORWARD is the default option for cursors.

- **STATIC** The result set is retrieved and stored in a temporary table in the *tempdb* database. All fetches go against the temporary table and modifications to the underlying tables for the cursor are not visible. A STATIC cursor supports scrolling, but modifications are not allowed.

- **KEYSET** The set of keys that uniquely identify each row in the cursor result set is stored in a temporary table in *tempdb*. As you scroll within the cursor, non-key columns are retrieved from the underlying tables. Therefore, any modifications to rows are reflected as the cursor is scrolled. Any inserts into the underlying table are not accessible to the cursor. If you attempt to access a row that has been deleted, @@FETCH_STATUS returns –2.

- **DYNAMIC** The most expensive cursor to use. The cursor reflects all changes made to the underlying result set, including newly inserted rows as the cursor is scrolled. The position and order of rows within the cursor can change each time a fetch is made. The FETCH ABSOLUTE option is not available for dynamic cursors.

By default, all cursors are updatable. To make modifications to underlying table rows, you can execute an UPDATE or DELETE statement with the WHERE CURRENT OF <cursor name> clause to modify or delete the row in the underlying table that the cursor pointer is currently accessing.

> **IMPORTANT** **CURSOR OPTIONS**
>
> If all you are going to do is read data within a cursor, make certain that you are declaring the cursor as read-only. Read-only cursors require less overhead than updatable cursors.

Access to rows within a cursor can be restricted by using the *FORWARD_ONLY* and *SCROLL* options. If a cursor is declared as *FORWARD_ONLY*, each row can be read only once as the cursor pointer advances through the result set. If you declare a cursor using the *SCROLL* option, the *FETCH* statement has the following options:

- **FETCH FIRST**   Fetches the first row in the result set.
- **FETCH LAST**   Fetches the last row in the result set.
- **FETCH NEXT**   Fetches the next row in the result set based on the current position of the pointer. *FETCH NEXT* is equivalent to just executing *FETCH,* which also moves forward one row at a time within the cursor result set.
- **FETCH PRIOR**   Fetches the row in the result set just before the current position of the cursor pointer.
- **FETCH ABSOLUTE n**   Fetches the *n*th row from the beginning of the result set.
- **FETCH RELATIVE n**   Fetches the *n*th row forward in the cursor result set from the current position of the cursor pointer.

T-SQL has three concurrency options available for cursors:

- **READ_ONLY**   SQL Server does not acquire a lock on the underlying row in the table because a cursor marked as *READ_ONLY* cannot be updated.
- **SCROLL_LOCKS**   A lock is acquired as each row is read into the cursor, guaranteeing that any transaction executed against the cursor succeeds.
- **OPTIMISTIC**   A lock is not acquired. SQL Server instead uses either a timestamp or a calculated checksum in the event that a timestamp column does not exist to detect if the data has changed since being read into the cursor. If the data has changed, the modification fails.

Compilation and Recompilation

When a stored procedure is created, SQL Server checks the syntax but does not validate any of the objects referenced within the procedure. The first time you execute a stored procedure, SQL Server parses and compiles the code. When the procedure is compiled for the first time, a check is made to ensure that all objects referenced either exist or will be created within the procedure prior to being accessed.

At compilation time, a query plan is generated and stored in the query cache. This compile plan is reentrant and is reused each time the procedure is executed. Each concurrent execution of a stored procedure also generates a query plan for execution, which is called the *execution plan.* Execution plans are also stored in the query cache, but they are non-reentrant. Once a connection has finished executing the procedure, the execution plan stored in the query cache can be assigned to the next connection that executes the procedure. Therefore, a single stored procedure that is heavily used can have a single compile plan along with many execution plans in the query cache, each of which consumes memory.

Under most circumstances, storing the compile plan for reuse eliminates the resources that need to be used to generate a query plan each time the procedure is executed. However, if the stored procedure contains multiple code paths depending on the results of condition checking, dramatically different query plans could be generated for the procedure. By reusing the same query plan for each execution, performance can suffer in some cases.

If a stored procedure generates a different query plan the majority of the time that it is executed, you should create the procedure using the *RECOMPILE* option. When the *RECOMPILE* option is enabled for a stored procedure, SQL Server does not cache and reuse a query plan.

In addition to the *RECOMPILE* option, SQL Server can detect if statistics are out of date during the execution of a procedure. If SQL Server determines that the query plan could be less than optimal during the execution of a procedure, execution will stop while a new query plan is generated for the next statement to execute within the procedure. Prior to SQL Server 2005, the query plan for the entire stored procedure would be regenerated. However, since SQL Server 2005, recompilation occurs at the statement level.

> **BEST PRACTICES** **RECOMPILATION**
>
> One of the advantages of procedures and functions is the ability of SQL Server to cache query plans for subsequent executions of the code. While you want to maximize caching, there are times when subsequent executions could require different query plans for optimal execution. When the query plan generated depends upon the values used for each execution, you should use the *RECOMPILE* option to force SQL Server to optimize the procedure or function each time it is executed.

However, a more efficient method is to split the stored procedure into multiple procedures. For example, you could have a procedure similar to the following, where executing each branch of the *IF* statement produces dramatically different query plans:

```
CREATE PROCEDURE PROC1
AS
    IF <some condition>
    BEGIN
        <code block A>
    END
    ELSE
    BEGIN
        <code block B>
    END
GO
```

You can take advantage of the query cache while avoiding suboptimal query plans by creating a stored procedure for each branch of the conditional test, as follows:

```
CREATE PROCEDURE PROCA
AS
<code block A>
GO
CREATE PROCEDURE PROCB
```

```
AS
<code block B>
GO
CREATE PROCEDURE PROC1
AS
    IF <some condition>
    BEGIN
        EXEC PROCA
    END
    ELSE
    BEGIN
        EXEC PROCB
    END
GO
```

When *PROC1* is executed, a very simple compile plan is generated, which can be reused regardless of the code path taken. When *PROCA* is executed the first time, SQL Server parses, compiles, and caches the compile plan, which can be reused each time code path A is executed. Similarly, the first time *PROCB* is executed, a compile plan is cached, which can then be subsequently reused as well.

32-bit vs. 64-bit SQL Server

When the subject of whether to deploy a 32-bit or 64-bit version of SQL Server comes up, many people mistakenly assume that 64-bit is automatically going to improve the performance of their applications. Applications that achieve the greatest improvements are those that are memory bound within the query cache, not the data cache.

The query cache contains executable code, which on a 32-bit platform cannot reside in memory above 4 gigabytes (GB), while at the same time, SQL Server limits the maximum size of the query cache to approximately 20 percent of the memory allocated to the SQL Server instance. Applications with large numbers of concurrent users can quickly use up all the memory available to the query cache between the compile and execution plans, thereby causing any additional requests to wait until memory can be freed up in the query cache.

By installing the 64-bit version of SQL Server, you remove the 4-GB limit for executable code and allow more space to become available to the query cache. With increased memory space available, more concurrent executions can be handled by the instance, thereby improving performance.

PRACTICE   Creating a Stored Procedure

In the following practice, you create stored procedures.

EXERCISE   Create a Stored Procedure

In this exercise, you create two stored procedures to compare the processing efficiency of a set-oriented routine and a cursor-based routine.

1. Open a new query window and change the context to the *AdventureWorks* database.

2. In the existing query window, type, highlight, and execute the following code to create a cursor-based stored procedure to modify all the employee hire dates:

```
CREATE PROCEDURE HumanResources.UpdateAllEmployeeHireDateInefficiently
AS
BEGIN TRY
    SET XACT_ABORT ON

    DECLARE curemployee CURSOR FOR SELECT EmployeeID FROM HumanResources.Employee
    OPEN curemployee
    FETCH FROM curemployee

    WHILE @@FETCH_STATUS = 0
    BEGIN
        UPDATE HumanResources.Employee
        SET HireDate = GETDATE()
        WHERE CURRENT OF curemployee

        FETCH FROM curemployee
    END
END TRY
```

```
BEGIN CATCH
    ROLLBACK TRANSACTION
    PRINT 'An error occured, transaction rolled back'
END CATCH
GO
```

3. In the existing query window, type, highlight, and execute the following code to create a stored procedure to modify all the employee hire dates using a set-based approach:

```
CREATE PROCEDURE HumanResources.UpdateAllEmployeeHireDateEfficiently
AS
DECLARE @now    DATETIME = GETDATE()

BEGIN TRY
    SET XACT_ABORT ON

    UPDATE HumanResources.Employee
    SET HireDate = @now
END TRY
BEGIN CATCH
    ROLLBACK TRANSACTION
    PRINT 'An error occured, transaction rolled back'
END CATCH
GO
```

4. Compare the execution of the two procedures by executing the following code:

```
EXEC HumanResources.UpdateAllEmployeeHireDateInefficiently
GO
EXEC HumanResources.UpdateAllEmployeeHireDateEfficiently
GO
```

Lesson Summary

-   A stored procedure is a batch of T-SQL code that is given a name and is stored within a database.
-   You can pass parameters to a stored procedure either by name or by position. You can also return data from a stored procedure using output parameters.
-   You can use the *EXECUTE AS* clause to cause a stored procedure to execute under a specific security context.
-   Cursors allow you to process data on a row by row basis; however, if you are making the same modification to every row within a cursor, a set-oriented approach is more efficient.
-   A *TRY...CATCH* block delivers structured error handling to your procedures.

Lesson 2: User-Defined Functions

Functions are programmable objects that are used to perform calculations that can be returned to a calling application or integrated into a result set. Functions can access data and return results, but they cannot make any modifications. In this lesson, you learn how to create user-defined functions using the T-SQL language.

> **After this lesson, you will be able to:**
>
> - Create and alter user-defined functions (UDFs).
>
> **Estimated lesson time: 20 minutes**

System Functions

SQL Server ships with a vast array of functions that you can use to perform many operations. The built-in functions can be broken down into 15 different categories, as shown in Table 5-2.

TABLE 5-2 System Functions

OPTION	PURPOSE
Aggregate	Combine multiple values. Examples include *SUM, AVG, COUNT_BIG,* and *VAR*.
Configuration	Return system configuration information. Examples include *@@VERSION, @@SERVERNAME,* and *@@LANGUAGE*.
Cryptographic	Support encryption and decryption.
Cursor	Return state information about a cursor. Examples include *@@FETCH_ STATUS* and *@@CURSOR_ROWS*.
Date and time	Return portions of a date/time or calculate dates and times. Examples include *DATEADD, DATEPART, DATEDIFF,* and *GETDATE*.
Management	Return information to manage portions of SQL Server. Examples include *sys.dm_db_index_physical_stats, sys.dm_db_index_operational_ stats,* and *fn_trace_gettable*.
Mathematical	Perform mathematical operations. Examples include *SIN, COS, TAN, LOG, PI,* and *ROUND*.
Metadata	Return information about database objects. Examples include *OBJECT_NAME, OBJECT_ID, DATABASEPROPERTYEX,* and *DB_NAME*.
Ranking	Return values used in ranking result sets. Ranking functions are described in Chapter 9, "An Introduction to SQL Server Manageability Features."
Rowset	Return a result set that can be joined to other tables. Examples include *CONTAINS* and *FREETEXT*.

OPTION	PURPOSE
Security	Return security information about users and roles. Examples include *SUSER_SNAME, Has_perms_by_name,* and *USER_NAME.*
String	Manipulate *CHAR* and *VARCHAR* data. Examples include *POS, CHARINDEX, SOUNDEX, REPLACE, STUFF,* and *RTRIM.*
System	Return information about a variety of system, database, and object settings as well as data. Examples include *DATALENGTH, HOST_NAME, ISDATE, ISNULL, SCOPE_IDENTITY, CAST,* and *CONVERT.*
System statistics	Return operational information about a SQL Server instance. Examples include *fn_virtualfilestats* and *@@CONNECTIONS.*
Text and image	Manipulate text and image data. Examples include *TEXTPTR* and *TEXTVALID.* Text and image data types have been deprecated and you should not use either of these functions in applications.

Most of the system functions are stored in the *mssqlsystemresource* database or *master* database, or they are made available within code libraries that support the T-SQL language.

User-Defined Functions

You can create your own functions, referred to as *user-defined functions,* and store the functions in any database for which you have *CREATE FUNCTION* authority.

While functions are used to perform calculations, a function is not allowed to change the state of a database or SQL Server instance. Functions cannot do any of the following:

- Perform an action that changes the state of an instance or database
- Modify data in a table
- Call a function that has an external effect, such as the *RAND* function
- Create or access temporary tables
- Execute code dynamically

Functions can either return a scalar value or a table value. Table-valued functions can be of two different types: inline and multi-statement.

The general syntax for a scalar function is

```
CREATE FUNCTION [ schema_name. ] function_name
( [ { @parameter_name [ AS ][ type_schema_name. ] parameter_data_type
    [ = default ] [ READONLY ] }   [ ,...n ]  ])
RETURNS return_data_type
    [ WITH <function_option> [ ,...n ] ]
    [ AS ]
```

```
BEGIN
    <function_body>
    RETURN scalar_expression
END
```

An inline table-valued function contains a single *SELECT* statement that returns a table. Because an inline table-valued function does not perform any other operations, the optimizer treats an inline table-valued function just like a view.

The general syntax for an inline table-valued function is

```
CREATE FUNCTION [ schema_name. ] function_name
( [ { @parameter_name [ AS ] [ type_schema_name. ] parameter_data_type
    [ = default ] [ READONLY ] }   [ ,...n ] ])
RETURNS TABLE
    [ WITH <function_option> [ ,...n ] ]
    [ AS ]
    RETURN [ ( ] select_stmt [ ) ]
```

The general syntax for a multi-statement table-valued function is

```
CREATE FUNCTION [ schema_name. ] function_name
( [ { @parameter_name [ AS ] [ type_schema_name. ] parameter_data_type
    [ = default ] [READONLY] }   [ ,...n ] ])
RETURNS @return_variable TABLE <table_type_definition>
    [ WITH <function_option> [ ,...n ] ]
    [ AS ]
    BEGIN
        <function_body>
        RETURN
    END
```

The code within every function is required to complete with a *RETURN* statement. For a scalar function, you return a single value. For an inline table-valued function, you return a *SELECT* statement. For a multi-statement table-valued function, you include only the *RETURN* keyword at the end of the function. With the exception of an inline table-valued function, all the code within the function is required to be enclosed in a *BEGIN...END* block.

Regardless of the type of function, four options can be specified: *ENCRYPTION, SCHEMABINDING, RETURNS NULL ON NULL INPUT/CALLED ON NULL INPUT,* and *EXECUTE AS*. The *ENCRYPTION, SCHEMABINDING,* and *EXECUTE AS* options are also available for stored procedures. In addition, *SCHEMABINDING* can be specified for triggers and views.

> **NOTE** **THE *ENCRYPTION* OPTION**
>
> The *ENCRYPTION* option behaves the same regardless of whether you are creating a stored procedure, function, trigger, or view.

The *SCHEMABINDING* option is applied to ensure that you can't drop dependent objects. For example, if you were to create a function that performed a *SELECT* against the *Sales.SalesOrderHeader* table, it would usually be possible to drop the table without receiving an error. The next time the function is executed, you would receive an error that the *Sales.SalesOrderHeader* table did not exist. To prevent objects that a programmable object relies on from being dropped or altered, you specify the *SCHEMABINDING* option. If you attempt to drop or modify the dependent object, SQL Server prevents the change. To drop or alter a dependent object, you first have to drop the programmable object that depends on the object you want to drop or alter.

> **NOTE THE *SCHEMABINDING* OPTION**
>
> The *SCHEMABINDING* option is available for functions and views.

The option that is unique to a function is *RETURNS NULL ON NULL INPUT/CALLED ON NULL INPUT*. The default value is *CALLED ON NULL INPUT*. Under the default setting, if you specify a *NULL* parameter, the function still is called and any code within the function is executed. If you specify *RETURNS NULL ON NULL INPUT*, when you specify *NULL* for an input parameter, the function is not executed, and *NULL* is returned immediately to the calling routine. If you have a function that should be executed only if you have passed non-*NULL* parameters, you should specify the *RETURNS NULL ON NULL INPUT* option so that you can avoid executing extraneous code.

Retrieving Data from a Function

You retrieve data from a function by using a *SELECT* statement. Functions can be used in any of the following:

- A *SELECT* list
- A *WHERE* clause
- An expression
- A *CHECK* or *DEFAULT* constraint
- A *FROM* clause with the *CROSS/OUTER APPLY* function

How a function is used can have a dramatic impact on the performance of the queries that you execute.

A function in the *SELECT* list is used to calculate an aggregate or perform a computation on one or more columns of the tables in the *FROM* clause. A function in the *WHERE* clause is used to restrict a result set based on the results of the function.

Functions can be nested inside each other so long as the return value of an inner function matches the input parameter of the outer function. For example, a common string-parsing routine might contain code as follows: DATALENGTH(POS(CHARINDEX(REPLACE(...)))).

Functions in the *CHECK* and *DEFAULT* constraints are used to extend the static computations available. For example, if you want to validate the area code for a phone number against a list of area codes stored within a table, you can use a function to perform the validation that would not typically be possible because a *CHECK* constraint doesn't accept a *SELECT* statement.

EXAM TIP

An inline table-valued function behaves like and is interchangeable with a view.

 Quick Check

1. What are the three types of functions that you can create?
2. What are the required elements of a function?

Quick Check Answers

1. You can create a scalar function, which returns a single value, an inline table-valued function, which contains a single *SELECT* statement and is treated the same as a view, and a multi-statement table-valued function, which returns a table.

2. Every function ends with a *RETURN* statement. Scalar functions include the value to be returned immediately following the *RETURN* statement. Inline table-valued functions include the *SELECT* statement for the result set to return immediately following the *RETURN* statement. Multi-statement table-valued functions just terminate with a *RETURN*. With the exception of inline table-valued functions, the entire function body is required to be enclosed in a *BEGIN...END* block.

In this practice, you create and use three different types of functions.

EXERCISE 1   Create a Scalar Function

In this exercise, you create and use a scalar function to return the current inventory of a product.

1. Open a new query window, type and execute the following code to create the function:

```
CREATE FUNCTION Production.udf_GetProductInventory (@ProductID INT)
RETURNS INT
AS
--There are several locations for a product during each stage
-- of manufacturing.  We only want finished goods.
--A product can also be stored on multiple shelves and bins, so
-- we need to sum the quantities.
BEGIN
    DECLARE @Inventory  INT

    SELECT @Inventory = SUM(a.Quantity)
    FROM Production.ProductInventory a INNER JOIN Production.Location b
        ON a.LocationID = b.LocationID
    WHERE a.ProductID = @ProductID
        AND b.Name IN ('Miscellaneous Storage','Finished Goods Storage')

    IF (@Inventory IS NULL)
    BEGIN
        SET @Inventory = 0
    END
    RETURN @Inventory
END
GO
```

2. In the existing query window, type, highlight, and execute the following code to return results from the function:

```
SELECT Production.udf_GetProductInventory (325)
GO
```

3. In the existing query window, type, highlight, and execute the following code to verify the results:

```
SELECT SUM(a.Quantity)
FROM Production.ProductInventory a INNER JOIN Production.Location b
    ON a.LocationID = b.LocationID
WHERE a.ProductID = 325
    AND b.Name IN ('Miscellaneous Storage','Finished Goods Storage')
GO
```

EXERCISE 2   Create an Inline Table-Valued Function

In this exercise, you create and use an inline table-valued function to return all orders that have not yet shipped.

1. Open a new query window, type, highlight, and execute the following code to create an unshipped order:

```
UPDATE Sales.SalesOrderHeader
SET ShipDate = NULL
WHERE SalesOrderID = 75123
GO
```

2. In the existing query window, type, highlight, and execute the following code to create the function:

```
CREATE FUNCTION Sales.GetUnshippedOrders()
RETURNS TABLE
AS
RETURN SELECT a.SalesOrderID, a.CustomerID, a.OrderDate, a.DueDate,
              c.Name, b.OrderQty
       FROM Sales.SalesOrderHeader a INNER JOIN Sales.SalesOrderDetail b
           ON a.SalesOrderID = b.SalesOrderID
           INNER JOIN Production.Product c ON b.ProductID = c.ProductID
       WHERE a.ShipDate IS NULL
GO
```

3. Test the function. Turn on the display of the actual execution plan to verify that SQL Server did not execute the function but instead substituted the function body into the *SELECT* statement. In the existing query window, type, highlight, and execute the following code:

```
SELECT c.FirstName, c.MiddleName, c.LastName
FROM Sales.GetUnshippedOrders() a INNER JOIN Sales.Customer b
    ON a.CustomerID = b.CustomerID
    INNER JOIN Person.Person c ON b.PersonID = c.BusinessEntityID
GO
```

4. In the existing query window, type, highlight, and execute the following code to reset the data to the original values:

```
UPDATE Sales.SalesOrderHeader
SET ShipDate = '08/07/2004'
WHERE SalesOrderID = 75123
GO
```

EXERCISE 3   Create a Multi-Statement Table-Valued Function

In this exercise, you create and use a multi-statement table-valued function to return the most recent order for a customer.

1. Open a new query window, type, highlight, and execute the following code to create the function:

```
CREATE FUNCTION Sales.GetLastShippedCustomerOrder (@CustomerID INT)
RETURNS @CustomerOrder TABLE
(SalesOrderID    INT            NOT NULL,
 CustomerID      INT            NOT NULL,
 OrderDate       DATETIME       NOT NULL,
 DueDate         DATETIME       NOT NULL,
 Name            NVARCHAR(50)   NOT NULL,
 OrderQty        INT            NOT NULL)
AS
BEGIN
    DECLARE @MaxOrderDate   DATETIME

    SELECT @MaxOrderDate = MAX(OrderDate)
    FROM Sales.SalesOrderHeader
    WHERE CustomerID = @CustomerID

    INSERT @CustomerOrder
    SELECT a.SalesOrderID, a.CustomerID, a.OrderDate, a.DueDate,
           c.Name, b.OrderQty
    FROM Sales.SalesOrderHeader a INNER JOIN Sales.SalesOrderDetail b
        ON a.SalesOrderID = b.SalesOrderID
        INNER JOIN Production.Product c ON b.ProductID = c.ProductID
    WHERE a.OrderDate = @MaxOrderDate
        AND a.CustomerID = @CustomerID
    RETURN
END
GO
```

2. In the existing query window, type, highlight, and execute the following code to test the function:

```
SELECT * FROM Sales.GetLastShippedCustomerOrder(11000)
GO
SELECT * FROM Sales.SalesOrderHeader WHERE CustomerID = 11000
GO
```

Lesson Summary

- You can create scalar functions, inline table-valued functions, and multi-statement table-valued functions.
- With the exception of inline table-valued functions, the function body must be enclosed within a *BEGIN...END* block.
- All functions must terminate with a *RETURN* statement.
- Functions are not allowed to change the state of a database or of a SQL Server instance.

Lesson 3: Triggers

Triggers are a special type of stored procedure that automatically execute when a DML or DDL statement associated with the trigger is executed. In this lesson, you learn how to create DML triggers that execute when you add, modify, or remove rows in a table. You also learn how to create DDL triggers that execute when DDL commands are executed or users log in to a SQL Server instance.

> **After this lesson, you will be able to:**
> - Create and alter DML triggers.
> - Create and alter DDL triggers.
>
> **Estimated lesson time: 20 minutes**

DML Triggers

Although a trigger is a programmable object that you create, you can't execute a trigger directly. *DML triggers* are created against a table or a view and are defined for a specific event: *INSERT*, *UPDATE*, or *DELETE*. When you execute the event for which a trigger is defined, SQL Server automatically executes the code within the trigger, which also is known as "firing" the trigger.

The generic syntax for creating a trigger is

```
CREATE TRIGGER [ schema_name . ]trigger_name
ON { table | view }
[ WITH <dml_trigger_option> [ ,...n ] ]
{ FOR | AFTER | INSTEAD OF }
{ [ INSERT ] [ , ] [ UPDATE ] [ , ] [ DELETE ] }
[ WITH APPEND ]
[ NOT FOR REPLICATION ]
AS { sql_statement  [ ; ] [ ,...n ] | EXTERNAL NAME <method specifier [ ; ] > }
```

When a trigger is defined as *AFTER*, the trigger fires after the modification has passed all constraints. If a modification fails a constraint, such as a check constraint, primary key constraint, or foreign key constraint, the trigger is not executed.

> **NOTE MULTIPLE TRIGGERS FOR THE SAME ACTION**
>
> *AFTER* triggers are defined only for tables, and multiple *AFTER* triggers can be defined for the same action. If you have multiple triggers created for the same action, you can specify the first and last triggers to fire by using the *sp_settriggerorder* system stored procedure. However, any other triggers for the same action are executed in random order.

A trigger defined with the *INSTEAD OF* clause causes the trigger code to be executed as a replacement for *INSERT, UPDATE,* or *DELETE*. You can define a single *INSTEAD OF* trigger for a given action. Although *INSTEAD OF* triggers can be created against both tables and views, *INSTEAD OF* triggers are almost always created against views.

Regardless of the number of rows that are affected, a trigger fires only once for an action.

The *NOT FOR REPLICATION* option controls the behavior of the trigger when the replication engine is applying changes. By default, any *INSERT, UPDATE,* or *DELETE* executed on a subscriber by the replication engine causes the corresponding trigger to fire. If you do not want the triggers on the subscriber to fire when the replication engine is applying changes, you can specify the *NOT FOR REPLICATION* option. If a change is being made by any process other than the replication engine, the trigger still fires.

When a trigger is executed, two special tables named *inserted* and *deleted* are available. These are the same *inserted* and *deleted* tables that were explained in Chapter 2, "Modifying Data—The *INSERT, UPDATE, DELETE,* and *MERGE* Statements."

DDL Triggers

DDL triggers can execute either when a DDL statement is executed or when the user logs on to the SQL Server instance.

The general syntax for creating a DDL trigger is as follows:

```
CREATE TRIGGER trigger_name
ON { ALL SERVER | DATABASE }
[ WITH <ddl_trigger_option> [ ,...n ] ]
{ FOR | AFTER } { event_type | event_group } [ ,...n ]
AS { sql_statement [ ; ] [ ,...n ] | EXTERNAL NAME < method specifier > [ ; ] }

<ddl_trigger_option> ::=
  [ ENCRYPTION ]  [ EXECUTE AS Clause ]

<method_specifier> ::=
  assembly_name.class_name.method_name
```

DDL triggers can be scoped at either the database or instance level. To scope a DDL trigger at the instance level, you use the *ON ALL SERVER* option. To scope a DDL trigger at the database level, you use the *ON DATABASE* option.

The following is an example of a DDL trigger:

```
CREATE TRIGGER tddl_tabledropalterprevent
ON DATABASE
FOR DROP_TABLE, ALTER_TABLE
AS
  PRINT 'You are attempting to drop or alter tables in production!'
  ROLLBACK;
```

The value for the event type is derived from the DDL statement being executed. Table 5-3 shows several examples.

TABLE 5-3 DDL Trigger Event Types

DDL COMMAND	EVENT TYPE
CREATE DATABASE	CREATE_DATABASE
DROP LOGIN	DROP_LOGIN
UPDATE STATISTICS	UPDATE_STATISTICS
DROP TRIGGER	DROP_TRIGGER
ALTER TABLE	ALTER_TABLE

Event types roll up within a command hierarchy called *event groups*. For example, the *CREATE_TABLE, ALTER_TABLE,* and *DROP_TABLE* event types are contained within the *DDL_TABLE_EVENTS* event group. Event types and event groups allow you to create flexible and compact DDL triggers.

While DML triggers have access to the *inserted* and *deleted* tables, DDL triggers have access to the *EVENTDATA* function. *EVENTDATA* returns the following Extensible Markup

Language (XML) document, which can be queried by using the *value()* method available through *XQUERY*:

```
<EVENT_INSTANCE>
    <EventType>type</EventType>
    <PostTime>date-time</PostTime>
    <SPID>spid</SPID>
    <ServerName>name</ServerName>
    <LoginName>name</LoginName>
    <UserName>name</UserName>
    <DatabaseName>name</DatabaseName>
    <SchemaName>name</SchemaName>
    <ObjectName>name</ObjectName>
    <ObjectType>type</ObjectType>
    <TSQLCommand>command</TSQLCommand>
</EVENT_INSTANCE>
```

The XML document available varies based on the event type that caused the DDL trigger to fire. The XML schemas for each DDL event are documented at *http://schemas.microsoft.com/sqlserver*. For example, for a *CREATE_TABLE, ALTER_TABLE,* or *DROP_TABLE* event, you can use the following query to retrieve the database, schema, object, and command executed:

```
SELECT EVENTDATA().value
       ('(/EVENT_INSTANCE/DatabaseName)[1]','nvarchar(max)'),
       EVENTDATA().value
       ('(/EVENT_INSTANCE/SchemaName)[1]','nvarchar(max)'),
       EVENTDATA().value
       ('(/EVENT_INSTANCE/ObjectName)[1]','nvarchar(max)'),
       EVENTDATA().value
       ('(/EVENT_INSTANCE/TSQLCommand)[1]','nvarchar(max)')
```

Logon Triggers

In addition to responding to DDL events, you can create a trigger to fire for a logon to the SQL Server instance. *Logon triggers* are fired after authentication succeeds but before the user session is actually established. You cannot return any messages to a user from within a logon trigger.

The generic syntax for a logon trigger is

```
CREATE TRIGGER trigger_name
ON ALL SERVER
[ WITH <logon_trigger_option> [ ,...n ] ]
{ FOR | AFTER } LOGON
AS { sql_statement  [ ; ] [ ,...n ] | EXTERNAL NAME < method specifier >  [ ; ] }
<logon_trigger_option> ::= [ ENCRYPTION ] [ EXECUTE AS Clause ]
```

Logon triggers are used to audit and restrict access. For example, you could limit the number of connections that a user is allowed to make to the instance. If you execute a *ROLLBACK* statement within a logon trigger, the connection to the instance terminates.

EXAM TIP

For the exam, make sure you know how to retrieve information from within a DDL trigger using the *EVENTDATA* function.

✔ **Quick Check**

1. What are the three types of triggers that can be created?
2. How do you access information about the cause of an event within a DDL trigger?

Quick Check Answers

1. You can create DML, DDL, and logon triggers.
2. You query the XML document returned by the *EVENTDATA* function within DDL and logon triggers to retrieve information about the event that caused the trigger to fire. Each event has a different XML schema. All the SQL Server schemas are documented at *http://schemas.microsoft.com/sqlserver*.

PRACTICE **Creating Triggers**

In this practice, you create DML, DDL, and logon triggers.

EXERCISE 1 **Create a DML Trigger**

In this exercise, you create a DML trigger to maintain an audit trail of changes.

1. Open a new query window, type and execute the following code to create a basic audit trail table:

```
CREATE TABLE Production.ProductAuditTrail
(AuditID      INT         IDENTITY(1,1),
AuditDate    DATETIME    NOT NULL,
ChangeUser   SYSNAME     NOT NULL,
```

```
ProductID      INT      NOT NULL,
BeforeListPrice MONEY   NOT NULL,
AfterListPrice  MONEY   NOT NULL)
GO
```

2. In the existing query window, type, highlight, and execute the following code to create an audit trigger:

```
CREATE TRIGGER tu_ProductAuditTrail
ON Production.Product
FOR UPDATE
AS
INSERT INTO Production.ProductAuditTrail
(AuditDate, ChangeUser, ProductID, BeforeListPrice, AfterListPrice)
SELECT GETDATE(), SUSER_SNAME(), i.ProductID, d.ListPrice, i.ListPrice
FROM inserted i INNER JOIN deleted d ON i.ProductID = d.ProductID
GO
```

3. In the existing query window, type, highlight, and execute the following code to test the audit trigger:

```
SELECT * FROM Production.ProductAuditTrail
GO
UPDATE Production.Product
SET ListPrice = ListPrice + 1
WHERE ProductID = 514
GO
SELECT * FROM Production.ProductAuditTrail
GO
```

EXERCISE 2   Create a DDL Trigger

In this exercise, you create a DDL trigger to prevent dropping tables.

1. Open a new query window, type, highlight, and execute the following code to create the DDL trigger:

```
CREATE TRIGGER ddl_preventtabledrop
ON DATABASE
FOR DROP_TABLE
AS
PRINT 'Prevention of an accidental table drop.'
PRINT 'You are attempting to drop a table in a production database.'
PRINT 'If you really want to drop this table, please disable the DDL trigger.'
PRINT 'Once the table has been dropped, please re-enable the DDL trigger.'
ROLLBACK TRANSACTION
GO
```

2. In the existing query window, type, highlight, and execute the following code to test the DDL trigger:

```
CREATE TABLE dbo.Test
(ID      INT     NOT NULL)
GO


SELECT * FROM dbo.Test
GO


DROP TABLE dbo.Test
GO


SELECT * FROM dbo.Test
GO
```

3. In the existing query window, type, highlight, and execute the following code to disable the trigger and test that the drop of the table is successful:

```
DISABLE TRIGGER ddl_preventtabledrop ON DATABASE
GO


DROP TABLE dbo.Test
GO


SELECT * FROM dbo.Test
GO


ENABLE TRIGGER ddl_preventtabledrop ON DATABASE
GO
```

EXERCISE 3   Create a Logon Trigger

In this exercise, you create a logon trigger that can be used to lock out users from a SQL Server instance.

1. Open a new query window, type, highlight, and execute the following code to create a logon trigger:

```
CREATE TRIGGER ddl_preventlogon
ON ALL SERVER
FOR LOGON
AS
IF IS_SRVROLEMEMBER('sysadmin',ORIGINAL_LOGIN()) = 0
BEGIN
    ROLLBACK
END
GO
```

2. In the existing query window, type, highlight, and execute the following code to create a login for testing:

```
CREATE LOGIN TriggerTest WITH PASSWORD = '<InsertStrongPasswordHere>'
GO
```

3. Attempt to log on using the account that you just created.

4. Disable the trigger, and then attempt to log on again:

```
DISABLE TRIGGER ddl_preventlogon ON ALL SERVER
GO
```

Lesson Summary

- Triggers are specialized stored procedures that automatically execute in response to a DDL or DML event.

- You can create three types of triggers: DML, DDL, and logon triggers.

- A DML trigger executes when an *INSERT*, *UPDATE*, or *DELETE* statement for which the trigger is coded occurs.

- A DDL trigger executes when a DDL statement for which the trigger is coded occurs.

- A logon trigger executes when there is a logon attempt.

- You can access the *inserted* and *deleted* tables within a DML trigger.

- You can access the XML document provided by the *EVENTDATA* function within a DDL or logon trigger.

Lesson 4: Views

In Chapter 1, "Data Retrieval," and Chapter 4, "Using Additional Query Techniques," you learned about the various ways that a *SELECT* statement can be constructed to retrieve data. While some of the *SELECT* statements that you create are used for a specific, one-time activity, some *SELECT* statements are used again and again within your environment. Some of the queries that you reuse within your environment contain complex business logic, as well as complex T-SQL code that you do not want to have to re-create each time the query is needed. SQL Server allows you to store a *SELECT* statement within a database using an object called a *view*. In this lesson, you learn how to create views, modify data through a view, and index a view to improve query performance.

> **After this lesson, you will be able to**
> - Create and alter views.
>
> **Estimated lesson time: 20 minutes**

Creating a View

A *view* is simply a *SELECT* statement that has been given a name and stored in a database. The main advantage of a view is that once it's created, it acts like a table for any other *SELECT* statements that you want to write.

The generic syntax to create a view is

```
CREATE VIEW [ schema_name . ] view_name [ (column [ ,...n ] ) ]
[ WITH <view_attribute> [ ,...n ] ]
AS select_statement
[ WITH CHECK OPTION ] [ ; ]
```

The *SELECT* statement defined for the view can reference tables, other views, and functions, but cannot do any of the following:

- Contain the *COMPUTE* or *COMPUTE BY* clause
- Create a permanent or temporary table by using the *INTO* keyword
- Use an *OPTION* clause
- Reference a temporary table
- Reference any type of variable
- Contain an *ORDER BY* clause unless a *TOP* operator is also specified

The view can contain multiple *SELECT* statements so long as you use the *UNION* or *UNION ALL* operators.

The view attributes that can be specified are *ENCRYPTION*, *SCHEMABINDING*, and *VIEW_METADATA*. The *ENCRYPTION* and *SCHEMABINDING* attributes behave the same way as has been discussed already in this chapter. The *VIEW_METADATA* option is used when creating an updatable view and causes SQL Server to return to client applications metadata about the view, instead of about the tables underlying the view.

Modifying Data Through a View

You can modify data through a view so long as the following requirements are met:

- The data modification must reference exactly one table.
- Columns in the view must reference columns in a table directly.
- The column cannot be derived from an aggregate.
- The column cannot be computed as the result of a *UNION/UNION ALL, CROSSJOIN, EXCEPT,* or *INTERSECT.*
- The column being modified cannot be affected by the *DISTINCT, GROUP BY,* or *HAVING* clause.
- The *TOP* operator is not used.

> **NOTE** **UPDATABLE VIEWS**
>
> If a view does not meet the requirements to be updatable, you can create an *INSTEAD OF* trigger on the view. The *INSTEAD OF* trigger executes for the DML operation you are performing instead of sending the DML through the view.

Because the definition of a view can contain a *WHERE* clause, it's possible to make a modification through the view that is not visible when you retrieve data from the view. The *WITH CHECK OPTION* clause requires that the only data manipulation that can occur through the view must also be retrievable when you select from the view.

> **EXAM TIP**
>
> For the exam, you should understand the requirements to update data through a view.

Partitioned Views

As discussed in Chapter 6, "Techniques to Improve Query Efficiency," you can implement partitioning to split a large table across multiple storage structures. Instead of using the built-in partitioning feature of SQL Server, you can also partition a large table manually by decomposing a single table into multiple tables with the same structure. When you manually partition a table, you can bring all the data back together using a view.

Views that unify multiple tables of the same structure are referred to as *partitioned views*. A partitioned view implements a *UNION ALL* of all member tables with the same structure. A partitioned view has the following conditions:

- All columns of the member tables should be contained in the select list of the view.
- Columns in the same ordinal position of each *SELECT* statement need to be of exactly the same data type and collation.

- At least one column that corresponds to a *CHECK* constraint, unique to each member table, should be in the same ordinal position of each *SELECT* statement.

- The constraints must form unique, non-overlapping data sets in each member table.

- The same column cannot be used multiple times in the select list.

- The partitioning column, defined by the *CHECK* constraint, must be part of the primary key.

- The partitioning column cannot be computed, be a *timestamp* data type, have a *DEFAULT* constraint, or be an identity column.

- The same member table cannot appear twice within the view definition.

- Member tables cannot have indexes on computed columns.

- The primary key of each table must have the same number of columns for each member table.

- All member tables must have the same *ANSI_PADDING* setting.

While this list may seem to be rather restrictive, the intent is to ensure that each member table within a partitioned view contains a unique set of data. If you were allowed to place the same primary key value in multiple member tables, the partitioned view would display duplicates and create confusion within applications, and you would not be able to resolve an update to a single row.

One of the advantages of partitioning a table manually is that you can use additional hardware resources that are not available to the built-in partitioning feature. Because manually partitioning a table produces multiple member tables, you can decide which database and SQL Server instance each table resides within. When you split member tables of a partitioned view across SQL Server instances, you create a special case called a *distributed partitioned view*.

A distributed partitioned view has much the same structure as a partitioned view, except each member table is referenced with a four-part name and uses linked servers to combine all the member tables.

> **MORE INFO**   **UPDATING PARTITIONED VIEWS**
>
> Even though both forms of a partitioned view use a *UNION ALL* statement, you can perform updates to a partitioned view. Partitioned views place additional restrictions on the view definition, as well as any transactions, as outlined in the SQL Server Books Online article "CREATE VIEW (Transact-SQL)" at *http://msdn.microsoft.com/en-us/library/ms187956.aspx*.

Creating an Indexed View

In addition to making data modifications through a view, you can also create an index on a view. However, an index cannot be created on a partitioned view because the member tables can span databases and SQL Server instances.

When a regular view is created, SQL Server stores only the definition of the view, which is then substituted by the optimizer for *SELECT* statements issued against the view.

An index can be built against a list of values in a column. When you index a view, SQL Server executes the *SELECT* statement defined by the view, stores the result set, and then builds the index. Any subsequent DML issued against any of the tables the view is defined against causes SQL Server to update the stored result set incrementally, as well as maintain the index, if necessary. Because SQL Server physically stores and maintains the result set, or "materializes" the data, an indexed view is sometimes referred to as a *materialized view*.

Indexed views have a very long list of requirements. The requirements for an indexed view derive from the fact that the data has to be materialized to disk in an unchanging manner and the data within the index also has to be fixed.

Some of the requirements for creating an indexed view are as follows:

- The *SELECT* statement cannot reference other views.
- All functions must be deterministic.
- *AVG, MIN, MAX, STDEV, STDEVP, VAR*, and *VARP* are not allowed.
- The index created must be both clustered and unique.
- *ANSI_NULLS* must have been set to *ON* when the view and any tables referenced by the view were created.
- The view must be created with the *SCHEMABINDING* option.
- The *SELECT* statement must not contain subqueries, outer joins, *EXCEPT, INTERSECT, TOP, UNION, ORDER BY, DISTINCT, COMPUTE/COMPUTE BY, CROSS/OUTER APPLY, PIVOT*, or *UNPIVOT*.

> **MORE INFO** **INDEXED VIEW RESTRICTIONS**
>
> The complete list of restrictions for creating an indexed view can be found in the SQL Server Books Online article "Creating Indexed Views," at *http://msdn.microsoft.com/en-us/library/ms191432.aspx*.

Meeting the requirements for creating an indexed view may seem prohibitive. However, the main advantage of an indexed view is that the data is already materialized and does not have to be calculated on the fly, as with a regular view. Indexed views can provide a significant performance gain when you have queries that combine large volumes of data, such as with aggregates. Indexed views have to be maintained when changes occur to the underlying tables, so an indexed view shouldn't be created against tables that receive large volumes of data modifications.

EXAM TIP

For the exam, you should understand the requirements to create an indexed view, as well as how an indexed view can improve performance of your applications.

Determinism

A function that returns the same value every time it is called, given the same input parameters, is a *deterministic function*. A function that could return a different value each time it is called, given the same input parameters, is a *nondeterministic function*. An example of a deterministic function is *SUBSTRING* because it returns the same value every time for the same input parameters. Examples of nondeterministic functions are *RAND* and *GETDATE* because each one could return a different value each time it is called.

Functions can be used in computed columns, as well as within views. You can also create an index on a computed column as well as indexing a view. To create an index, the results of a function must be deterministic, such that the set of values for the index is fixed. Also, because creating an index on a view causes the results of the view to be materialized and stored, to index a view, every function within the view must be deterministic.

Query Substitution

When a nonmaterialized view is referenced, SQL Server replaces the name of the view with the actual *SELECT* statement defined by the view, rewrites the query as if you had not referenced the view at all, and then submits the rewritten query to the optimizer.

You might have a view with the following definition:

```
CREATE VIEW Customers.CustomerOrders
AS
SELECT CASE WHEN a.CompanyName IS NOT NULL THEN a.CompanyName
        ELSE a.FirstName + ' ' + a.LastName END CustomerName,
    b.AddressLine1, b.AddressLine2, b.AddressLine3, b.City, d.StateProvinceAbbrev,
    e.CountryName, c.OrderDate, c.GrandTotal, c.FinalShipDate
FROM Customers.Customer a INNER JOIN Customers.CustomerAddress b
        ON a.CustomerID = b.CustomerID
INNER JOIN Orders.OrderHeader c ON a.CustomerID = c.CustomerID
INNER JOIN LookupTables.StateProvince d ON b.StateProvinceID = d.StateProvinceID
INNER JOIN LookupTables.Country e ON b.CountryID = e.CountryID
GO
```

You might then issue the following *SELECT* statement:

```
SELECT CustomerName, AddressLine1, AddressLine2, AddressLine3,
    City, StateProvinceAbbrev,
    CountryName, OrderDate, GrandTotal, FinalShipDate
FROM Customers.CustomerOrders
GO
```

But SQL Server actually submits the following query to the optimizer:

```
SELECT CASE WHEN a.CompanyName IS NOT NULL THEN a.CompanyName
        ELSE a.FirstName + ' ' + a.LastName END CustomerName,
    b.AddressLine1, b.AddressLine2, b.AddressLine3, b.City, d.StateProvinceAbbrev,
    e.CountryName, c.OrderDate, c.GrandTotal, c.FinalShipDate
```

```
FROM Customers.Customer a INNER JOIN Customers.CustomerAddress b
        ON a.CustomerID = b.CustomerID
INNER JOIN Orders.OrderHeader c ON a.CustomerID = c.CustomerID
INNER JOIN LookupTables.StateProvince d ON b.StateProvinceID = d.StateProvinceID
INNER JOIN LookupTables.Country e ON b.CountryID = e.CountryID
GO
```

When an index is created against a view, the data is materialized. Queries that reference the indexed view do not substitute the definition of the view but instead return the results directly from the indexed view. The results can be returned directly because in terms of storage, the indexed view is in fact a table that the storage engine maintains.

In SQL Server Enterprise Edition, query substitution goes one step further when an indexed view is present. Normally, the optimizer selects indexes created against tables referenced within a query if it determines that a given index improves query performance. In SQL Server Enterprise Edition, if the optimizer determines that the data can be retrieved more efficiently through the indexed view, it then builds a query plan that ignores the base tables referenced by the query and instead retrieves data from the indexed view instead of the tables.

EXAM TIP

For the exam, you should understand how SQL Server treats views and indexed views in each edition.

 Quick Check

1. What types of views can be created?
2. What types of indexes can be created on a view?

Quick Check Answers

1. You can create a regular view that is just a stored *SELECT* statement. You can also create a partitioned view that uses the *UNION ALL* keywords to combine multiple member tables.
2. You can index a view by creating a unique, clustered index.

PRACTICE **Creating Views**

In this practice, you create an updatable view to return the orders that have not yet shipped.

EXERCISE 1 **Create a View**

In this exercise, you create a view to return the orders that have not yet shipped.

1. Modify an order to have an unshipped state by typing and executing the following code in a new query window:

```
UPDATE Sales.SalesOrderHeader
SET ShipDate = NULL
WHERE SalesOrderID = 75123
GO
```

2. In the existing query window, type, highlight, and execute the following code to create the view:

```
CREATE VIEW Sales.v_UnshippedOrders
AS
SELECT SalesOrderID, RevisionNumber, OrderDate, DueDate, ShipDate,
    Status, OnlineOrderFlag, SalesOrderNumber, PurchaseOrderNumber,
    AccountNumber, CustomerID, SalesPersonID, TerritoryID,
    BillToAddressID, ShipToAddressID, ShipMethodID, CreditCardID,
    CreditCardApprovalCode, CurrencyRateID, SubTotal, TaxAmt, Freight,
    TotalDue, Comment, rowguid, ModifiedDate
FROM Sales.SalesOrderHeader
WHERE ShipDate IS NULL
GO
```

3. In the existing query window, type, highlight, and execute the following code to test the view and then reset the order you modified:

```
SELECT * FROM Sales.v_UnshippedOrders
GO

UPDATE Sales.SalesOrderHeader
SET ShipDate = '08/07/2004'
WHERE SalesOrderID = 75123
GO
```

Lesson Summary

- A view is a name for a *SELECT* statement stored within a database.
- A view has to return a single result set and cannot reference variables or temporary tables.
- You can update data through a view so long as the data modification can be resolved to a specific set of rows in an underlying table.
- If a view does not meet the requirements for allowing data modifications, you can create an *INSTEAD OF* trigger to process the data modification instead.
- You can combine multiple tables that have been physically partitioned using a *UNION ALL* statement to create a partitioned view.
- A distributed partitioned view uses linked servers to combine multiple member tables across SQL Server instances.
- You can create a unique, clustered index on a view to materialize the result set for improved query performance.

Chapter Review

To practice and reinforce the skills you learned in this chapter further, you can perform the following tasks:

- Review the chapter summary.
- Review the list of key terms introduced in this chapter.
- Complete the case scenario. These scenarios set up real-world situations involving the topics in this chapter and ask you to create a solution.
- Complete the suggested practices.
- Take a practice test.

Chapter Summary

- SQL Server allows you to create four programmable objects: functions, stored procedures, triggers, and views.
- Functions can return a scalar value or a result set but are not allowed to change the state of a database or SQL Server instance.
- Stored procedures provide a programming API that abstracts the database structure from applications.
- A stored procedure can contain almost any command within the T-SQL language.
- Triggers are created for tables and views and automatically execute in response to an *INSERT*, *UPDATE*, or *DELETE*.
- Views allow you to assign a name to a *SELECT* statement that produces a single result set and that is stored within a database.

Key Terms

Do you know what these key terms mean? You can check your answers by looking up the terms in the glossary at the end of the book.

- Cursor
- DDL trigger
- Deterministic function
- DML trigger
- Distributed partitioned view
- Event group
- Execution context
- Impersonation
- Indexed view

- Materialized view
- Module
- Nondeterministic function
- Parameter
- Partitioned view
- Schema binding
- Stored procedure
- Variable

Case Scenario

In the following case scenario, you apply what you've learned in this chapter. You can find answers to these questions in the "Answers" section at the end of this book.

Case Scenario: Improving Application Performance

Fabrikam, a large manufacturer and wholesaler of thousands of products for the consumer and industrial plastics industry, has hired you to fix a variety of problems within its core applications.

The manager of application development has identified 22 core applications that run Fabrikam's business lines. Users have complained that almost all these applications have slow performance. The application development team has attempted to address the performance issues, but because all the queries are generated at run time and submitted as ad hoc queries to SQL Server, implementing changes has been extremely difficult. Several attempts to release new code have resulted in applications crashing, requiring the code release to be rolled back.

The production database servers are configured to allow administrative access to the entire development team. There have been numerous incidents in the past four months where objects have been deleted from the production server instead of the deletion occuring against a development server.

There are three applications that all the developers are afraid to modify because the database involved contains very complex code written by a developer who is no longer with the company. No documentation exists for any of the applications.

Answer the following questions for your manager:

1. How do you fix the performance tuning problem?
2. How do you fix the problem with accidentally dropping objects on the production database?
3. How do you fix the problem of the complex code that is preventing any changes to three core applications?

Suggested Practices

To help you master the exam objectives presented in this chapter, complete the following tasks.

Create a Stored Procedure

- **Practice 1** Locate all the ad hoc SQL within your applications and move the code into stored procedures. Rewrite the application to use the stored procedures.

Create a Function

- **Practice 1** Locate a block of nontrivial code that performs a calculation or returns a result set but does not modify the state of a database or SQL Server instance. Encapsulate the code in a function so that the code does not have to be re-created each time you need to reference this calculation.

Create a Trigger

- **Practice 1** Create a DDL trigger to prevent anyone from accidentally dropping objects in your production environment.

Create a View

- **Practice 1** Locate a complicated *SELECT* statement in an application. Create a view to encapsulate this complex *SELECT* statement. Modify the application to reference the view.

- **Practice 2** Locate a deterministic view that is executed frequently and turn it into an indexed view. Observe the performance difference of the indexed view.

Take a Practice Test

The practice tests on this book's companion CD offer many options. For example, you can test yourself on just one exam objective, or you can test yourself on all the 70-433 certification exam content. You can set up the test so that it closely simulates the experience of taking a certification exam, or you can set it up in study mode so that you can look at the correct answers and explanations after you answer each question.

> **MORE INFO** **PRACTICE TESTS**
>
> For details about all the practice test options available, see the section entitled "How to Use the Practice Tests" in the Introduction to this book.

Techniques to Improve Query Performance

After you have designed your database and application, you typically want to make sure that it can deliver the performance that your application users demand. This chapter covers what you can do to find performance problems in your database and how to solve the problems you uncover. Microsoft SQL Server 2008 is an extremely capable and efficient database engine, but it still requires you to do some performance tuning if you have a very large database, complicated queries, a high number of queries being served, or a combination of these factors.

Exam objectives in this chapter:

- Create and alter indexes.
- Implement partitioning solutions.
- Control execution plans.
- Capture execution plans.
- Gather trace information by using the SQL Server Profiler.
- Collect output from the Database Engine Tuning Advisor.
- Collect information from system metadata.

Lessons in this chapter:

Before You Begin

To complete the lessons in this chapter, you must have:

- A basic understanding of Transact-SQL (T-SQL).
- SQL Server 2008 Developer Edition, Enterprise Edition, or Enterprise Evaluation Edition, with the *AdventureWorks* sample database installed.

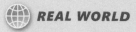

REAL WORLD

Tobias Thernström

Tuning queries is not just about understanding how queries, indexes, and related items work. You must understand how all parts of SQL Server work together. A couple of years ago, I did a consulting job for a big publishing company where long delays in the database happened when orders were received. The company had already investigated their indexing and were not able to find any obvious problems. I started by running SQL Trace to find what was actually taking so much time and found that a simple *INSERT* statement was causing the delays. I then verified that the *INSERT* was not blocked by any locks. Finally, I checked whether the table had any triggers defined on it. It turned out that the table did in fact have an *AFTER INSERT* trigger defined on it. After reviewing the trigger, it was obvious that the trigger was causing the massive delays; the trigger was actually performing aggregations based on the entire order table. After verifying with the customer that a new approach would still solve the business problem, we went ahead and removed the trigger and created an agent that ran every 10 minutes and performed the exact same function as the trigger used to do, for every *INSERT*. By removing the trigger, the *INSERT* statements were now executing with little to no delay. I bring up this point so that you will think about whether other issues are involved that affect performance rather than just the query itself or the index structures that it uses.

Lesson 1: Tuning Queries

Tuning queries is an important task for a database developer. Throughout this lesson, you learn about several options for optimizing queries.

> **After this lesson, you will be able to:**
> - Know more about what affects query performance.
> - Know how to measure query performance.
> - Know how to write more efficient queries.
>
> **Estimated lesson time: 60 minutes**

Evaluating Query Performance

One of the most important aspects of tuning queries is measuring performance. When measuring performance, you need to know what to actually measure—that is, what metric to use. In SQL Server, there are three main metrics to consider: query cost, page reads, and query execution time.

Query Cost

The query cost is typically (but not always, as you will soon see) a good metric to use when comparing query performance. It is an internal metric used in SQL Server that takes into account both CPU and input/output (I/O) resources used by the query. The lower the query cost, theoretically, the better the query performance is. The query cost is not affected by issues such as resource contention or waiting for locks. The query cost is typically a good performance measurement, but when certain items are used in a query, such as scalar user-defined functions (UDFs) and Common Language Runtime (CLR) routines, the cost for these items is not calculated, which renders the query cost lower than a truly accurate assessment. This is why it is called *estimated* query cost.

Page Reads

Page reads represents the number of 8-kilobyte (KB) data pages accessed by the SQL Server storage engine while executing a query. You can retrieve this metric by executing *SET STATISTICS IO ON*. This causes each query execution to output something similar to the following in the Messages tab of the query window:

```
Table 'Customer'. Scan count 2, logical reads 136, physical reads 0, read-ahead
    reads 0, lob logical reads 0, lob physical reads 0, lob read-ahead reads 0.
Table 'SalesOrderHeader'. Scan count 121, logical reads 822, physical reads 5,
    read-ahead reads 0, lob logical reads 0, lob physical reads 0, lob read-ahead reads 0.
```

The total page reads of this output is 136 + 822, which is the sum of the values labeled "logical reads." *Logical reads* are the number of pages read from memory. The logical reads represent the total number of data pages read from any index on the *SalesOrderHeader* table. The other items tell you how many of the logical reads were read from the hard drive (physical and read-ahead reads), the number of passes through an index or heap it took to respond to the query (scan count), and how many of the page reads were used to retrieve Large Object (LOB) data. LOB data is stored outside the row for the data types *varchar(max)*, *nvarchar(max)*, *varbinary(max)*, *text*, *ntext*, *image,* and *XML*. The page reads metric does not take into account the amount of CPU resources used when executing the query. This is why page reads are typically not as appropriate a performance measurement as the query cost. This metric also has the same problem with scalar UDFs and CLR routines as the query cost, which is that page reads caused by these routines are not included in the output of *STATISTICS IO*.

Query Execution Time

The execution time of the query is the most volatile metric. It is affected by blocking (locks), as well as resource contention on the server. That said, it is particularly important to always include the query execution time metric in performance comparisons because it can help you spot problems missed by the other performance metrics (page reads and query cost). If you execute *SET STATISTICS TIME ON*, SQL Server returns the execution time in milliseconds for each query execution.

Examining the Theoretical Query Execution Order

It is vital to have a basic understanding of the theoretical execution order of a *SELECT* statement when working with query tuning. This helps you understand what SQL Server actually needs to do to produce the query results.

The theoretical execution order is referred to as "theoretical" because the optimizer might change the actual execution order to optimize performance. An alternative execution order is used only if the query results would be the same were the theoretical execution order to be used.

The execution order needs to be split into two branches because it differs if the *UNION* clause is included in the query or not. A simplified version of the first branch, without *UNION,* is described in Table 6-1, showing the order in which clauses are processed.

TABLE 6-1 Theoretical Execution Order—Excluding the *UNION* Clause

	CLAUSES	RESULTS
1.	*FROM, JOIN, APPLY,* and *ON*	The join is executed and the first query filter (the *ON* clause) is applied.
2.	*WHERE*	The second query filter is applied.
3.	*GROUP BY* and aggregate functions (such as *SUM, AVG,* and so on) that are included in the query	Grouping and aggregation calculations are performed.

CLAUSES	RESULTS
4. *HAVING*	The third query filter (filtering of the results of aggregate functions) is applied.
5. *SELECT*	Columns that should be returned by the query are selected.
6. *ORDER BY*	Results are sorted.
7. *TOP*	The fourth (and last) query filter is applied; this causes the query to return only the first *X* rows from the results thus far.
8. *FOR XML*	The tabular result returned by the *SELECT* statement is converted to Extensible Markup Language (XML).

Queries that use the *UNION* clause use the theoretical execution order shown in Table 6-2.

TABLE 6-2 Theoretical Execution Order—Including the *UNION* Clause

CLAUSES	RESULTS
1. *FROM, JOIN, APPLY,* and *ON*	The join is executed and the first query filter (the *ON* clause) is applied.
2. *WHERE*	The second query filter is applied.
3. *GROUP BY* and aggregate functions (such as *SUM, AVG,* etc.) that are included in the query	Grouping and aggregation calculations are performed.
4. *HAVING*	The third query filter (filtering of the results of aggregate functions) is applied.
5. *TOP*	The fourth (and last) query filter is applied; this causes the query to return only the first *X* rows from the results thus far. (Note that in this case, the *TOP* clause is executed *before* the *ORDER BY* clause.)
6. *UNION* and *SELECT*	The results of each *SELECT* statement included in the query are concatenated; columns that should be returned by the query are selected.
7. *ORDER BY*	The results are sorted.
8. *FOR XML*	The tabular result returned by the *SELECT* with *UNION* statement is converted to XML.

The cause of the difference in the execution order is the introduction of the *TOP* clause (in SQL Server 7.0), which is not part of the ANSI/ISO SQL standard. The standard-compliant behavior of the *UNION* clause allows only one *ORDER BY* clause, which must be placed in the last *SELECT* statement of the query and must sort the entire query result. This means the *TOP* clause in any but the final *SELECT* statement of a *UNION* query returns the top *X* items *before* they are sorted. This may sound like a minor point, but it is important to be aware of. For example, compare the result of two queries, both of which are intended to return the two most expensive red products and the two most expensive black products. The first query, shown here, produces an incorrect result:

```
USE AdventureWorks;

SELECT TOP(2) ProductID, Name, Color, ListPrice
FROM Production.Product
WHERE Color = 'Black'
UNION
SELECT TOP(2) ProductID, Name, Color, ListPrice
FROM Production.Product
WHERE Color = 'Red'
ORDER BY ListPrice DESC;
```

Here is the (incorrect) result of this first query:

```
ProductID    Name                          Color ListPrice
-----------  ----------------------------  ----- ----------
706          HL Road Frame - Red, 58       Red   1431,50
707          Sport-100 Helmet, Red         Red   34,99
317          LL Crankarm                   Black 0,00
318          ML Crankarm                   Black 0,00
```

The second query, shown here, generates the intended result:

```
USE AdventureWorks;

WITH a AS (
    SELECT TOP(2) ProductID, Name, Color, ListPrice
    FROM Production.Product
    WHERE Color = 'Black'
    ORDER BY ListPrice DESC
), b AS (
    SELECT TOP(2) ProductID, Name, Color, ListPrice
    FROM Production.Product
    WHERE Color = 'Red'
    ORDER BY ListPrice DESC
)
SELECT * FROM a
UNION ALL
SELECT * FROM b;
```

Here are the (correct) results of this second query:

```
ProductID    Name                              Color  ListPrice
-----------  --------------------------------  -----  ----------
775          Mountain-100 Black, 38            Black  3374,99
776          Mountain-100 Black, 42            Black  3374,99
749          Road-150 Red, 62                  Red    3578,27
750          Road-150 Red, 44                  Red    3578,27
```

As you can see, the first query does not return the correct values because the *ORDER BY* clause is executed *after* the *TOP* clause.

Tuning Query Performance

There are several ways to optimize queries. Optimization consists of tasks such as rewriting the query, de-normalizing or normalizing tables, adding indexes, removing indexes, or a combination of these tasks.

The Graphical Execution Plan

The graphical execution plan is a useful tool for optimizing queries. This chapter discusses several execution plans. Some of the items that you should look for in the execution plan are shown in Table 6-3.

TABLE 6-3 Items from the Graphical Execution Plan

ITEM TO WATCH FOR	POSSIBLE IMPLICATIONS
Thick arrows	A thick arrow represents a large number of rows moving from one operation in the execution plan to another. The greater the number of rows transferred from one operation to another, the thicker the arrow.
Hash operations Hash Match (Inner Join) Cost: 73 %	If a hash operation is used to handle clauses such as *GROUP BY* and *JOIN*, it often means that an appropriate index did not exist to optimize the query.
Sorts Sort Cost: 69 %	A sort isn't necessarily bad, but if it is a high percentage of the query cost, you should consider whether an index can be built to remove the need for the sort operation.

ITEM TO WATCH FOR	POSSIBLE IMPLICATIONS
Large plans	The plan with fewer operations is typically the better optimized plan.
Table or clustered index scans Table Scan [Customers] [c1] Cost: 100 % Clustered Index Scan (Clustered) [Customers].[Index1] [c1] Cost: 100 %	A clustered index scan and a table scan indicate that no appropriate index can be used to optimize the query.

Using Search Arguments

A *search argument (SARG)* is a filter expression that is used to limit the number of rows returned by a query and that can use an index seek operation that substantially improves the performance of the query. Typically, a filter expression is not a SARG if the column from the table is used in an expression (such as LEFT(Name, 1) = 'A'). If the filter is not a SARG and no other SARGs exist in the query, this results in an index or table scan, which iterates through the entire index or table. Instead of a scan, you want a seek operation to be performed. A *seek* implies the use of the index's balanced tree to find the values for which the query searched. The use of a balanced tree significantly decreases the work that SQL Server needs to perform to find a row. The difference between a *seek* and a *scan* can be orders of magnitude. For example, in the following query, SQL Server scans the *OrderDateIndex* index (rather than seeking through it). The execution plan for the following query, which you can view by pressing Ctrl+M in SQL Server Management Studio (SSMS), is shown in Figure 6-1:

```
USE AdventureWorks;

CREATE NONCLUSTERED INDEX OrderDateIndex
    ON Sales.SalesOrderHeader (OrderDate);

SELECT COUNT(*) FROM Sales.SalesOrderHeader
    WHERE YEAR(OrderDate) = 2004;
```

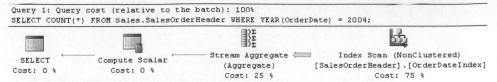

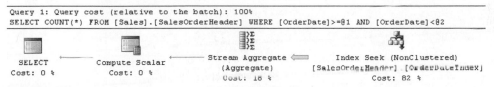

FIGURE 6-1 The actual execution plan from SSMS showing an index scan operation

If the query instead is rewritten so that the *OrderDate* column is not used in an expression, an index seek operation can be used instead of a scan. The execution plan for the following query is shown in Figure 6-2.

```
SELECT COUNT(*) FROM Sales.SalesOrderHeader
    WHERE OrderDate >= '20040101' AND OrderDate < '20050101';
```

FIGURE 6-2 The actual execution plan from SSMS showing an index seek operation

Note that the use of the *COLLATE* operator in a filter expression also invalidates the use of an index on that column. You learn about this in more detail in Lesson 2, "Creating Indexes."

Using Joins

To optimize queries, one of the first basic strategies is to minimize the number of join clauses used. Another consideration is that outer joins incur more cost than inner joins because of the extra work needed to find the unmatched rows. If only inner joins are used in a query, the behavior of the *ON* and *WHERE* clauses is the same; it does not matter if you put an expression in the *ON* or *WHERE* clause. Compare the following two queries, with the differences shown in bold type; they both return the same results and use identical execution plans:

```
-- Query 1
SELECT p.ProductID, p.Name, sod.SalesOrderID
FROM Production.Product AS p
INNER JOIN Sales.SalesOrderDetail AS sod
    ON sod.ProductID = p.ProductID
WHERE p.Color = 'Black';


-- Query 2
SELECT p.ProductID, p.Name, sod.SalesOrderID
FROM Production.Product AS p
INNER JOIN Sales.SalesOrderDetail AS sod
    ON sod.ProductID = p.ProductID
        AND p.Color = 'Black';
```

If these queries had been written with an outer join, they would not be syntactically equal and could have substantially different performance.

Subqueries Without Correlation to the Outer Query

As explained in Chapter 4, "Using Additional Query Techniques," an uncorrelated subquery is executed only once per query execution and returns only one value. These queries typically incur very little overhead. Note that this type of subquery cannot have any reference (correlation) to the outer query. The following example uses a subquery to return all products that are cheaper than the average product price. The subquery calculating the average product price is executed first (only once), and then the value returned by the subquery is used as a parameter in the outer query:

```
USE AdventureWorks;

SELECT
    p.ProductID
    ,p.Name
    ,p.ListPrice
FROM Production.Product AS p
WHERE p.ListPrice > (
    SELECT AVG(p2.ListPrice)
    FROM Production.Product AS p2
);
```

Correlated Subqueries

Correlated subqueries include a reference to the outer query. Typically, this reference is used to filter the correlated subquery. A correlated subquery is typically equal in performance compared to using a *JOIN* when used in combination with the *EXISTS* operator to filter the outer query. The following example query uses the *EXISTS* operator to return only products that have been sold:

```
USE AdventureWorks;

SELECT p.ProductID, p.Name
FROM Production.Product AS p
WHERE EXISTS (
    SELECT * FROM Sales.SalesOrderDetail AS sod
    WHERE sod.ProductID = p.ProductID
);
```

While this type of correlated subquery is typically a good implementation, the use of correlated subqueries in the *SELECT* clause often has a negative effect on performance compared to *JOIN*s. Of course, this depends on the number of rows returned by the outer query. If a large number of rows are returned, each query in the *SELECT* clause would be executed for each row, so that means a large number of query executions. The following query returns 6,224 rows and includes two correlated subqueries. Each of these queries is executed once per row, resulting in a total of 12,448 subquery executions:

```
USE AdventureWorks;

SELECT
    soh.SalesOrderID
    ,soh.OrderDate
    ,(
        SELECT TOP(1)
            sod1.UnitPrice
        FROM Sales.SalesOrderDetail AS sod1
        WHERE sod1.SalesOrderID = soh.SalesOrderID
        ORDER BY sod1.OrderQty DESC
    ) AS UnitPrice
    ,(
        SELECT TOP(1)
            sod2.OrderQty
        FROM Sales.SalesOrderDetail AS sod2
        WHERE sod2.SalesOrderID = soh.SalesOrderID
        ORDER BY sod2.OrderQty DESC
    ) AS OrderQty
FROM Sales.SalesOrderHeader AS soh
WHERE soh.TerritoryID = 4;
```

There is also a potential bug in this query. Because each subquery is executed separately, they might end up using different indexes. This means that these queries might not return values from the same row (which they are probably intended to) if the same value for *OrderQty* exists for multiple sales order details in any sales order.

There are several ways to rewrite this query; the most common one in SQL Server 2008 is probably to use the new *APPLY* clause. If the subquery is used in the *FROM, JOIN,* or *APPLY* clauses, it might also be referred to as a *derived table,* as explained in Chapter 4. The *APPLY* clause basically gives you the opportunity to combine two subqueries into one, cutting the number of subquery executions in half. For the new query to return the same results as the previous query, you must use an *OUTER APPLY.* (An *OUTER APPLY* works similarly to a left outer join, and its counterpart, the *CROSS APPLY* clause, behaves like an inner join.) This works in this example because, in the previous query, the outer query returns a row even if the subqueries return nothing. The new query could be written as follows:

```
USE AdventureWorks;

SELECT
    soh.SalesOrderID
    ,soh.OrderDate
    ,a.*
```

```
FROM Sales.SalesOrderHeader AS soh
OUTER APPLY (
        SELECT TOP(1)
            sod.UnitPrice
            ,sod.OrderQty
        FROM Sales.SalesOrderDetail AS sod
        WHERE sod.SalesOrderID = soh.SalesOrderID
        ORDER BY sod.OrderQty DESC
) AS a
WHERE soh.TerritoryID = 4;
```

This query has a cost of roughly 76, while the first query's cost was double that, about 151.

Another solution to this type of problem is to make use of the *ROW_NUMBER* function instead of a correlated subquery. By using the *ROW_NUMBER* function, you can find the specific number of rows that you need by filtering on the row number rather than using the *TOP* clause. To be able to filter on the result of the *ROW_NUMBER* function, the query needs to be placed inside a derived table or a common table expression (CTE). The larger the result set, the better this approach performs compared to the previous queries. The cost for the following query drops from 76 to about 3.6, an enormous reduction:

```
-- Common table expression.
WITH a AS (
    SELECT
        soh.SalesOrderID
        ,soh.OrderDate
        ,sod.UnitPrice
        ,sod.OrderQty
        ,ROW_NUMBER() OVER (
                            PARTITION BY soh.SalesOrderID
                            ORDER BY sod.OrderQty DESC
                    ) AS RowNo
    FROM Sales.SalesOrderDetail AS sod
    INNER JOIN Sales.SalesOrderHeader AS soh
        ON sod.SalesOrderID = soh.SalesOrderID
    WHERE soh.TerritoryID = 4
)
SELECT
    a.SalesOrderID
    ,a.OrderDate
    ,a.UnitPrice
    ,a.OrderQty
FROM a
WHERE a.RowNo = 1;
```

Scalar UDFs

A scalar UDF is a function that returns a single value (not a result set). This type of function is frequently used in queries and can significantly degrade performance. The reason for this is that these functions are not expanded and optimized into the main query plan by the optimizer; rather, they are just called from the execution plan without any optimization based on the context into which it is inserted in the plan. This also means that the cost of whatever is done inside the function is not included in the cost estimates found in the graphical execution plan for the query. This same problem occurs for the output of the *SET STATISTICS IO ON* statement, which contains no references to what is done inside the UDF. As an example, this section compares the performance of a query using a UDF and that of another query using a correlated subquery. The UDF and the subquery perform identical *SELECT* statements. Because the cost of the UDF is not reflected in the query cost metric, the more appropriate performance metric for these queries is the execution time, which is returned using the *SET STATISTICS TIME ON* statement.

> **BEST PRACTICES** **QUERY EXECUTION TIME**
>
> When using query execution times as a performance metric, it is typically a good idea to execute each query a few times and use either the lowest execution time or the median as the metric. Also, note that metrics in a test environment might not accurately reflect performance in a production environment. This depends on a number of factors, including how users actually interact with real-life data.

The following is a query using a UDF. The execution plan produced for the query is shown in Figure 6-3:

```
USE AdventureWorks;
GO

CREATE FUNCTION dbo.fnGetCustomerAccountNumber(@CustomerID INT)
RETURNS VARCHAR(10)
AS
BEGIN
    RETURN ISNULL(
      (
       SELECT
            AccountNumber
       FROM Sales.Customer
       WHERE CustomerID = @CustomerID
    ), 'NOT FOUND');
END
GO
```

```
SET STATISTICS IO ON;
SET STATISTICS TIME ON;

SELECT
    soh.SalesOrderID
    ,soh.OrderDate
    ,dbo.fnGetCustomerAccountNumber(soh.CustomerID)
FROM Sales.SalesOrderHeader AS soh;
```

```
Query 1: Query cost (relative to the batch): 100%
SELECT soh.SalesOrderID ,soh.OrderDate ,dbo.fnGetCustomerAccountNumber(soh.Cus
```

SELECT	Compute Scalar	Clustered Index Scan (Clustered)
Cost: 0 %	Cost: 1 %	[SalesOrderHeader].[PK_SalesOrderHe…
		Cost: 99 %

FIGURE 6-3 The actual execution plan from SSMS for the query using a UDF

The cost of this query is 0.56 and the number of page reads is 706 (neither metric is accurate and thus cannot be used to gauge performance), while the execution time on the test machine used in this example is 25 seconds. Examine the graphical execution plan and note that it contains no reference to the *Sales.Customer* table.

The following is an example query that uses a correlated subquery in place of the UDF. The query's execution plan is shown in Figure 6-4:

```
USE AdventureWorks;

SET STATISTICS IO ON;
SET STATISTICS TIME ON;

SELECT
    soh.SalesOrderID
    ,soh.OrderDate
    ,ISNULL(
      (
       SELECT
            AccountNumber
       FROM Sales.Customer
       WHERE CustomerID = soh.CustomerID
    ), 'NOT FOUND')
FROM Sales.SalesOrderHeader AS soh;
```

The cost of the query without the UDF goes up to 1.05 and the number of page reads to 742 (both of which are accurate values). At the same time, the execution time drops to about 1 second. As you can see, the first query using the UDF is about 25 times slower than the latter query because of the UDF use.

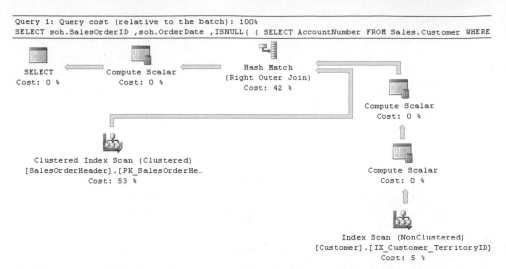

```
Query 1: Query cost (relative to the batch): 100%
SELECT soh.SalesOrderID ,soh.OrderDate ,ISNULL ( ( SELECT AccountNumber FROM Sales.Customer WHERE
```

FIGURE 6-4 The actual execution plan from SSMS for the query using a correlated subquery

Why was the inline table-valued UDF so much faster? The use of inline table-valued UDFs or views does not incur the same performance penalty as the use of scalar UDFs because both inline table-valued UDFs and views are optimized (expanded) into the query plan.

Table-Valued UDFs

There are three different types of table-valued UDFs. Two of them can be developed in T-SQL and the other one in a CLR language, such as C# or Microsoft Visual Basic .NET:

- T-SQL inline table-valued UDF
- T-SQL multistatement table-valued UDF
- CLR table-valued UDF

> **MORE INFO** **T-SQL AND CLR UDFs**
>
> Chapter 5, "Programming Microsoft SQL Server with T-SQL User-Defined Stored Procedures, Functions, Triggers, and Views," explains T-SQL UDFs in greater detail. Chapter 7, "Extending Microsoft SQL Server Functionality with XML, SQLCLR, and *Filestream*," gives more information about CLR UDFs.

These different types of functions behave differently. A T-SQL inline table-valued UDF is actually just a view that can accept parameters. It is optimized in the same way as a view or any *SELECT* statement would be. An advantage of using inline table-valued UDFs instead of views is that you can require the user that uses the function to supply parameters. In this way you can make sure that a filter is always used for the query inside the function (based on the parameters provided).

T-SQL multistatement table-valued UDFs, on the other hand, can be considered to work like a stored procedure that populates a temporary table that can be used by an outer query. If you include a multistatement table-valued UDF in a query (for example, in a join), the function has to be executed fully (that is, it must finish execution) before the query can use its results. This means that if a multistatement table-valued UDF needs to return 1,000,000 rows, the function must process all rows before the query can use the function's results.

The third type, CLR table-valued UDFs, stream their results. This means that while the CLR table-valued UDF is executing, its results become available to the calling query. This difference can help performance because the outer query does not have to wait for the entire result from the function to be available before it can start processing the returned rows. A CLR table-valued UDF consists of two CLR methods: one method that manages the overall execution of the function and one method that is called for every row that is returned by the function. The method that is run for each row returned by the function is not run until the method that manages the function execution starts executing *yield return* commands. This is important to remember because any processing before the start of the *yield return* commands has to be finished before any rows are returned from the function. CLR table-valued UDFs are typically useful for querying objects other than tables, such as strings (by using regular expressions) or the file system. Note that the processing done by a CLR function is not accurately included in the query cost or page read metrics of a query.

Cursors

You should generally avoid using cursors because of their negative effect on performance. They have such an effect partly because each execution of a *FETCH* statement in a cursor loop is similar in performance cost to executing a *SELECT* statement that returns one row. Another problem is that a data manipulation language (DML) statement is optimized as a single unit, while a cursor loop cannot be optimized in the same way (if at all). Instead, each item in the loop is optimized and executed separately for each iteration of the loop.

You should try to rewrite cursor logic into one or more set-based statements (*SELECT, INSERT, UPDATE, DELETE,* or *MERGE*). If you cannot convert the cursor logic to a set-based statement, consider implementing the logic using a CLR stored procedure or a table-valued UDF instead (depending on the functionality you need).

Finding Out Which Queries to Tune

As you have probably figured out, you can do a lot to improve query performance. The next problem is obviously finding which queries to tune. To do this effectively, you should use SQL Server Profiler, which is used to listen for events that occur on a SQL Server instance. There are several events that you can listen for, but for tuning, you typically want to use the *SQL:BatchCompleted* and *RPC:Completed* events. In addition to deciding which events to listen for, you also need to specify which columns to retrieve when the events are raised. The columns that are typically useful when determining whether an event contains something that needs to be tuned are as follows:

- **Duration**   Returns the number of milliseconds (or microseconds when writing the events to a file or table instead of using the graphical utility to view the events)
- **Reads**   Returns the total number of 8-kilobyte (KB) pages read during execution
- **Writes**   Returns the total number of 8-KB pages written during execution
- **CPU**   Returns the total CPU time used during execution

A higher-than-desired value for any of these columns should lead you to look into the query's performance.

Because SQL Server Profiler typically returns a lot of rows when used against a production server, you can consider letting SQL Server Profiler write the result to a file or table. Note that you can also start traces on the server without using the SQL Server Profiler graphical interface. SQL Server Profiler can be used to create the script necessary to start the trace on the server. To do so, just start the trace in SQL Server Profiler, and then, from the File menu, select Export, Script Trace Definition, For SQL Server 2005–2008. The server trace supports only tracing to a file. If you trace to a file, you can still query it from SQL Server by passing the name of the trace file as a parameter to the *fn_trace_gettable* table-valued UDF function.

Lesson Summary

- Understanding how queries are logically constructed is important to knowing that they correctly return the intended result.
- Understanding how queries are logically constructed helps you understand what physical constructs (like indexes) help the query execute faster.
- Make sure you understand your metrics when you measure performance.

PRACTICE   **Tuning Query Performance**

In this practice, you test the query performance of three different versions of one particular query that produces the same result set. The query that you use should return all customers in a specific territory, as well as the last order received for those customers. If a customer does not have any orders, it should still be returned.

EXERCISE 1   Test Using a Small Result Set

In this exercise, you execute the three queries mentioned in the practice preface and record each query's cost. In this case, the parameter supplied to all three queries (*TerritoryID*) yields a small result set of 64 rows.

1. Open SSMS and connect to the appropriate instance of SQL Server 2008.

2. In a new query window, type and execute the following SQL statements to create the *TestDB* database, the *Test* schema, and the two tables that are used in this exercise:

```
CREATE DATABASE TestDB;
GO


USE TestDB;
GO


CREATE SCHEMA Test;
GO


SELECT * INTO Test.SalesOrderHeader
FROM AdventureWorks.Sales.SalesOrderHeader;
GO


SELECT * INTO Test.Customer
FROM AdventureWorks.Sales.Customer;
GO


ALTER TABLE Test.SalesOrderHeader

    ADD CONSTRAINT PKSalesOrderHeader
     PRIMARY KEY(SalesOrderID);
GO


ALTER TABLE Test.Customer
    ADD CONSTRAINT PKCustomer
    PRIMARY KEY(CustomerID);
```

3. Turn on the Actual Execution Plan feature in SSMS by pressing Ctrl+M or by selecting Include Actual Execution Plan from the Query menu.

4. In the existing query window, type, highlight, and execute Query 1, shown here, to test the performance of a query that uses two correlated subqueries.

   Because of the use of two separate correlated subqueries in this query, it is not guaranteed that both these subqueries return data from the same row in the *Test.Customer* table:

```
-- Query 1
SELECT
    c.CustomerID
```

```
      ,c.AccountNumber
      ,(
          SELECT TOP(1) soh.SalesOrderID
          FROM Test.SalesOrderHeader AS soh
          WHERE soh.CustomerID = c.CustomerID
          ORDER BY OrderDate DESC
      ) AS SalesOrderID
      ,(
          SELECT TOP(1) soh.OrderDate
          FROM Test.SalesOrderHeader AS soh
          WHERE soh.CustomerID = c.CustomerID
          ORDER BY OrderDate DESC
      ) AS OrderDate
FROM Test.Customer AS c
WHERE c.TerritoryID = 2;
```

Record the total query cost of Query 1.

(You can find the value in the Execution Plan tab by moving the pointer over the *SELECT* operator and locating the value named Estimated Subtree Cost.)

5. In the existing query window, type, highlight, and execute Query 2, shown here, to test the performance of a query that uses an *OUTER APPLY*:

```
-- Query 2
SELECT
    c.CustomerID
    ,c.AccountNumber
    ,o.*
FROM Test.Customer AS c
OUTER APPLY (
    SELECT TOP(1) soh.SalesOrderID, soh.OrderDate
    FROM Test.SalesOrderHeader AS soh
    WHERE soh.CustomerID = c.CustomerID
    ORDER BY OrderDate DESC
) AS o
WHERE c.TerritoryID = 2;
```

Record the total cost of Query 2.

6. In the existing query window, type, highlight, and execute Query 3, shown here, to test the performance of a query that uses *ROW_NUMBER*:

```
-- Query 3
WITH a AS (
    SELECT
        c.CustomerID
```

```
        ,c.AccountNumber
        ,c.TerritoryID
        ,soh.SalesOrderID
        ,soh.OrderDate
        ,ROW_NUMBER() OVER (PARTITION BY c.CustomerID
                ORDER BY soh.OrderDate DESC) AS RowNo
    FROM Test.Customer AS c
    LEFT OUTER JOIN Test.SalesOrderHeader AS soh
        ON soh.CustomerID = c.CustomerID
)
SELECT
    a.CustomerID
    ,a.AccountNumber
    ,a.SalesOrderID
    ,a.OrderDate
FROM a
WHERE a.RowNo = 1 AND a.TerritoryID = 2;
```

Record the total cost of Query 3.

EXERCISE 2   Test Using a Large Result Set

In this exercise, you execute the three queries mentioned in the practice preface and record each query's cost. In this case, the parameter supplied to all three queries (*TerritoryID*, shown below in bold type) yields a larger result set of 3,433 rows (compared to 64 rows in Exercise 1).

1. Open SSMS, if necessary, and connect to the appropriate instance of SQL Server 2008.

2. In a new query window, type and execute the following SQL statement to connect to the *TestDB* database created in Exercise 1:

   ```
   USE TestDB;
   ```

3. Turn on the Actual Execution Plan feature in SSMS by pressing Ctrl+M or by selecting Include Actual Execution Plan from the Query menu.

4. In the existing query window, type, highlight, and execute Query 1, shown here, to test the performance of a query using two correlated subqueries and a large result set.

   Again, because of the use of two separate correlated subqueries in this query, it is not guaranteed that both these subqueries return data from the same row in the *Test.Customer* table:

   ```
   -- Query 1
   SELECT
       c.CustomerID
       ,c.AccountNumber
       ,(
           SELECT TOP(1) soh.SalesOrderID
           FROM Test.SalesOrderHeader AS soh
   ```

```
        WHERE soh.CustomerID = c.CustomerID
        ORDER BY OrderDate DESC
    ) AS SalesOrderID
    ,(
        SELECT TOP(1) soh.OrderDate
        FROM Test.SalesOrderHeader AS soh
        WHERE soh.CustomerID = c.CustomerID
        ORDER BY OrderDate DESC
    ) AS OrderDate
FROM Test.Customer AS c
WHERE c.TerritoryID = 1;
```

Record the total cost of Query 1.

(You can find the value in the Execution Plan tab by moving the pointer over the *SELECT* operator and locating the value named Estimated Subtree Cost.)

5. In the existing query window, type, highlight, and execute Query 2, shown here, to test the performance of a query using *OUTER APPLY* and a large result set:

```
-- Query 2
SELECT
    c.CustomerID
    ,c.AccountNumber
    ,o.*
FROM Test.Customer AS c
OUTER APPLY (
    SELECT TOP(1) soh.SalesOrderID, soh.OrderDate
    FROM Test.SalesOrderHeader AS soh
    WHERE soh.CustomerID = c.CustomerID
    ORDER BY OrderDate DESC
) AS o
WHERE c.TerritoryID = 1;
```

Record the total cost of Query 2.

6. In the existing query window, type, highlight, and execute Query 3, shown here, to test the performance of a query that uses *ROW_NUMBER* and a large result set:

```
-- Query 3
WITH a AS (
    SELECT
        c.CustomerID
        ,c.AccountNumber
        ,c.TerritoryID
        ,soh.SalesOrderID
        ,soh.OrderDate
```

```
      ,ROW_NUMBER() OVER (PARTITION BY c.CustomerID
              ORDER BY soh.OrderDate DESC) AS RowNo
    FROM Test.Customer AS c
    LEFT OUTER JOIN Test.SalesOrderHeader AS soh
        ON soh.CustomerID = c.CustomerID
)
SELECT
    a.CustomerID
    ,a.AccountNumber
    ,a.SalesOrderID
    ,a.OrderDate
FROM a
WHERE a.RowNo = 1 AND a.TerritoryID = 1;
```

What was the total cost of Query 3?

EXERCISE 3   Optimize Query 3

In this exercise, you make a small change to Query 3 to optimize it.

1. Open SSMS, if necessary, and connect to the appropriate instance of SQL Server 2008.

2. In a new query window, type and execute the following SQL statement to connect to the *TestDB* database created in Exercise 1:

```
USE TestDB;
```

3. Turn on the Actual Execution Plan feature in SSMS by pressing Ctrl+M or by selecting Include Actual Execution Plan from the Query menu.

4. In the existing query window, type, highlight, and execute the new version of Query 3, shown here, with the small result set (*TerritoryID = 2*). The changes from the previous version of the query are shown in bold type:

```
WITH a AS (
    SELECT
        c.CustomerID
        ,c.AccountNumber
        ,c.TerritoryID
        ,soh.SalesOrderID
        ,soh.OrderDate
        ,ROW_NUMBER() OVER (PARTITION BY c.CustomerID
                    ORDER BY soh.OrderDate DESC) AS RowNo
    FROM Test.Customer AS c
    LEFT OUTER JOIN Test.SalesOrderHeader AS soh
        ON soh.CustomerID = c.CustomerID
    WHERE c.TerritoryID = 2
)
```

```
SELECT
     a.CustomerID
    ,a.AccountNumber
    ,a.SalesOrderID
    ,a.OrderDate
FROM a
WHERE a.RowNo = 1;
```

Record the total cost of this version of Query 3.

5. In the existing query window, type, highlight, and execute the new version of Query 3, shown here, with the large result set (*TerritoryID = 1*). The difference from the previous version of the query is again shown in bold type:

```
WITH a AS (
    SELECT
         c.CustomerID
        ,c.AccountNumber
        ,c.TerritoryID
        ,soh.SalesOrderID
        ,soh.OrderDate
        ,ROW_NUMBER() OVER (PARTITION BY c.CustomerID
                       ORDER BY soh.OrderDate DESC) AS RowNo
    FROM Test.Customer AS c
    LEFT OUTER JOIN Test.SalesOrderHeader AS soh
        ON soh.CustomerID = c.CustomerID
    WHERE c.TerritoryID = 1
)
SELECT
     a.CustomerID
    ,a.AccountNumber
    ,a.SalesOrderID
    ,a.OrderDate
FROM a
WHERE a.RowNo = 1;
```

What was the total cost of this version of Query 3 for the large result set?

6. To clean up after this practice, close all open query windows in SSMS, open a new query window, and execute the following SQL statements:

```
USE master;
DROP DATABASE TestDB;
```

Lesson 2: Creating Indexes

SQL Server 2008 supports two basic types of indexes: clustered and nonclustered. Both indexes are implemented as a balanced tree, where the leaf level is the bottom level of the structure. The difference between these index types is that the clustered index is the actual table; that is, the bottom level of a clustered index contains the actual rows, including all columns, of the table. A nonclustered index, on the other hand, contains only the columns included in the index's key, plus a pointer pointing to the actual data row. If a table does not have a clustered index defined on it, it is called a *heap,* or an unsorted table. You could also say that a table can have one of two forms: It is either a heap (unsorted) or a clustered index (sorted).

> **After this lesson, you will be able to:**
> - Decide which type of index to implement.
> - Create indexes.
>
> **Estimated lesson time: 40 minutes**

Improving Performance with Covered Indexes

The notion of a covered index is that SQL Server doesn't need to use lookups between the nonclustered index and the table to return the query results. Because a clustered index is the actual table, clustered indexes always cover queries.

To consider the index covered, it must contain all columns referenced in the query (in any clause, *SELECT, JOIN, WHERE, GROUP BY, HAVING,* and so on). Consider the following SQL table and query.

TEST.TABLEA		
Column1	Column2	Column3

```
SELECT Column1 FROM Test.TableA
WHERE Column2 = 1;
```

For an index to cover this query, it must contain at least the columns *Column1* and *Column2.* You can do this in several ways. All the following indexes would cover this query:

```
CREATE NONCLUSTERED INDEX TestIndex ON Test.TableA (Col1, Col2);
CREATE NONCLUSTERED INDEX TestIndex ON Test.TableA (Col2, Col1);
CREATE NONCLUSTERED INDEX TestIndex ON Test.TableA (Col1) INCLUDE (Col2);
CREATE NONCLUSTERED INDEX TestIndex ON Test.TableA (Col2) INCLUDE (Col1);
CREATE NONCLUSTERED INDEX TestIndex ON Test.TableA (Col1, Col2, Col3);
CREATE NONCLUSTERED INDEX TestIndex ON Test.TableA (Col3) INCLUDE (Col1, Col2);
```

As you can see, the columns only need to be found in the index; their position and whether they are found in the index key or are included columns (discussed in detail in the section entitled "Using Included Columns and Reducing Index Depth" later in this lesson) does not matter. Of course, both the execution plan and the performance could differ greatly between these indexes; however, they all cover the query.

The performance benefit gained by using a covered index is typically great for queries that return a large number of rows (a nonselective query) and smaller for queries that return few rows (a selective query). Remember that a small number of rows is a relative term—it could mean 10 for a table with a couple of hundred rows and 1,000 for a table with millions of rows. This section presents a performance comparison of four queries. The table that the queries are executed against has the following schema and is populated with 1,000,000 rows:

```
CREATE TABLE Test.CoveredIndexTest (
    Col1 INT NOT NULL
    ,Col2 NVARCHAR(2047) NOT NULL
);
INSERT Test.CoveredIndexTest (Col1, Col2)
    VALUES (0, 'A lonely row...');
INSERT Test.CoveredIndexTest (Col1, Col2)
    SELECT TOP(999999) message_id, text FROM sys.messages AS sm
    CROSS JOIN (
        SELECT TOP(15) 1 AS Col FROM sys.messages
    ) AS x;
```

On the test machine in this example, the size of this table is 27,377 pages (roughly 213 megabytes). Also, note that the table is a heap; that is, it does not have a clustered index defined on it. The queries and indexes used in this test have the definitions shown in the following code. The performance metrics (measured in page reads) for the queries are shown in Table 6-4.

```
--Non-covered index:
CREATE NONCLUSTERED INDEX NonCovered ON Test.CoveredIndexTest (Col1);

--Covered index:
CREATE NONCLUSTERED INDEX Covered ON Test.CoveredIndexTest (Col1) INCLUDE (Col2);
-- Query 1:
-- Returns 1 row.
SELECT Col1, Col2 FROM Test.CoveredIndexTest
    WHERE Col1 = 0;

-- Query 2:
-- Returns roughly 0.1% of the rows found in the table.
-- (1,056 rows)
SELECT Col1, Col2 FROM Test.CoveredIndexTest
    WHERE Col1 BETWEEN 1205 AND 1225;
```

```
-- Query 3:
-- Returns roughly 0.5% of the rows found in the table.
-- (5,016 rows)
SELECT Col1, Col2 FROM Test.CoveredIndexTest
    WHERE Col1 BETWEEN 1205 AND 1426;


-- Query 4 (non-selective):
-- Returns roughly 5% of the rows found in the table.
-- (50,028 rows)
SELECT Col1, Col2 FROM Test.CoveredIndexTest
    WHERE Col1 BETWEEN 1205 AND 2298;
```

TABLE 6-4 Query Peformance Matrix for Logical Reads

	QUERY 1 (1 ROW)	QUERY 2 (SELECTIVE)	QUERY 3 (SOMEWHAT SELECTIVE)	QUERY 4 (NONSELECTIVE)
No index	29,141 pages	29,141 pages	29,141 pages	29,141 pages
Noncovered index	4 pages	1,703 pages	5,099 pages	46,647 pages
Covered index	3 pages	43 pages	142 pages	1,346 pages

The performance metric that is shown in this table is the number of data pages that SQL Server handled during the query execution (*SET STATISTICS IO ON*, logical reads).

Note that the so-called selective query (Query 2) returns 0.01 percent of the rows in the table. For a table of this size, that still amounts to 1,000 rows. If you are speaking to someone about the number of rows that are affected by a query, and he or she says that number is "only a small percentage of the table," this usually translates to a lot of rows.

Some conclusions you can draw from the test are given here. (This is only with regard to read performance; write performance is discussed later in this lesson.)

- A covered index always performs better than a noncovered index.

- For queries that return a very limited number of rows, a noncovered index also performs very well.

- For the somewhat-selective query (Query 3), the noncovered index reads more than 34 times more pages than the covered index. In this case, a query was considered selective by the optimizer when it matched less than roughly 0.77 percent of the table.

Using Included Columns and Reducing Index Depth

In versions of SQL Server prior to SQL Server 2005, creating covered nonclustered indexes could often be impossible because an index could contain no more than 16 columns or be more than 900 bytes wide. The new Included Column feature makes it possible to add columns to an index without adding them to the index's key. Included columns cannot be used for tasks such as filtering or sorting; their sole benefit is reducing page reads through covering queries by avoiding table lookups.

An index can have a maximum of 1,023 included columns, and a table can have a maximum of 1,024 columns, making it possible to create a nonclustered index that covers the entire table, which is almost like having a second clustered index! In addition, columns that use one of the large data types [VARCHAR(max), NVAR-CHAR(max), VARBINARY(max), XML, TEXT, NTEXT, and IMAGE] are allowed to be included in an index as an included column.

Only columns that are used for filtering, grouping, or sorting should be part of the index key; all other columns included in the index should be included columns. Besides allowing for more columns in the index, included columns have other benefits. In the following SQL script, a table with 1,000,000 rows is created with two indexes. One index has all columns in the index key, while the other index has only one column in the key (the one that would be filtered on), and the rest of the columns are included. The width of each row in the index is a little over 300 bytes. This might sound like a very wide index row, but having this kind of width is not uncommon. This also makes up for the fact that the test table contains only 1 million rows; for larger tables, the width of the index does not need to be this big to make a performance difference. The following script defines (and populates) objects and indexes used in subsequent examples:

```
CREATE TABLE Test.IncludedColumnsTest(
    PKCol UNIQUEIDENTIFIER NOT NULL DEFAULT NEWSEQUENTIALID()
        PRIMARY KEY CLUSTERED
    ,Col1 INT IDENTITY NOT NULL
    ,Col2 CHAR(20) NOT NULL
    ,Col3 CHAR(20) NOT NULL
    ,Col4 CHAR(20) NOT NULL
    ,Col5 CHAR(20) NOT NULL
    ,Col6 CHAR(20) NOT NULL
    ,Col7 CHAR(20) NOT NULL
    ,Col8 CHAR(20) NOT NULL
    ,Col9 CHAR(20) NOT NULL
    ,Col10 CHAR(20) NOT NULL
    ,Col11 CHAR(20) NOT NULL
    ,Col12 CHAR(20) NOT NULL
    ,Col13 CHAR(20) NOT NULL
    ,Col14 CHAR(20) NOT NULL
    ,Col15 CHAR(20) NOT NULL
    ,Col16 CHAR(20) NOT NULL
);
INSERT Test.IncludedColumnsTest (Col2, Col3, Col4, Col5, Col6, Col7, Col8,
        Col9, Col10, Col11, Col12, Col13, Col14, Col15, Col16)
SELECT TOP(1000000)
    CAST(message_id AS CHAR(20)) AS Col2
    ,CAST(message_id AS CHAR(20)) AS Col3
    ,CAST(message_id AS CHAR(20)) AS Col4
```

```
    ,CAST(message_id AS CHAR(20)) AS Col5
    ,CAST(message_id AS CHAR(20)) AS Col6
    ,CAST(message_id AS CHAR(20)) AS Col7
    ,CAST(message_id AS CHAR(20)) AS Col8
    ,CAST(message_id AS CHAR(20)) AS Col9
    ,CAST(message_id AS CHAR(20)) AS Col10
    ,CAST(message_id AS CHAR(20)) AS Col11
    ,CAST(message_id AS CHAR(20)) AS Col12
    ,CAST(message_id AS CHAR(20)) AS Col13
    ,CAST(message_id AS CHAR(20)) AS Col14
    ,CAST(message_id AS CHAR(20)) AS Col15
    ,CAST(message_id AS CHAR(20)) AS Col16
FROM sys.messages AS sm
CROSS JOIN (
    SELECT TOP(15) 1 AS Col FROM sys.messages
) AS x;


CREATE NONCLUSTERED INDEX IncludedColumns ON Test.IncludedColumnsTest (Col1)
    INCLUDE (Col2, Col3, Col4, Col5, Col6, Col7, Col8, Col9, Col10, Col11, Col12,
    Col13, Col14, Col15, Col16);


CREATE NONCLUSTERED INDEX NoIncludedColumns ON Test.IncludedColumnsTest
    (Col1, Col2, Col3, Col4, Col5, Col6, Col7, Col8, Col9, Col10, Col11,
    Col12, Col13, Col14, Col15, Col16);
```

Table 6-5 shows some of the interesting differences between indexes with and without included columns.

TABLE 6-5 Index Size Matrix

	INCLUDEDCOLUMN	NOINCLUDEDCOLUMN
Total size	40,147 pages	41,743 pages
Size of the nonleaf level of the index	146 pages	1,743 pages
Index depth	Three levels (a root page + one intermediate level + one leaf level)	Five levels (a root page + three intermediate levels + one leaf level)
Average size of rows in the nonleaf levels of the index	27 bytes	327 bytes
Average size of rows in the leaf level of the index	321 bytes	321 bytes

You can retrieve this information from the *sys.dm_db_index_physical_stats* dynamic management function by executing the following query:

```
SELECT
    *
FROM sys.dm_db_index_physical_stats(
    DB_ID()
    ,OBJECT_ID('Test.IncludedColumnsTest')
    ,NULL
    ,NULL
    ,'DETAILED'
) AS a;
```

The total size of the index is reduced by only about 4 percent because the leaf levels of both indexes contain the same data. However, the nonleaf levels of the index with included columns contain only the one column that is in the index's key (plus pointers to the next level), while, for the other index, all columns are part of the index key, making each row in the nonleaf level roughly the same size as that of the leaf level. Table 6-6 shows the layout of each level of a *NoIncludedColumns* index.

TABLE 6-6 Levels of the *NoIncludedColumns* Index

LEVEL	CONTENTS
Root	1 page with 4 rows pointing to the next level
First intermediate level	4 pages with a total of 72 rows pointing to the next level
Second intermediate level	70 pages with a total of 1,668 rows pointing to the next level
Third intermediate level	1,668 pages with a total of 40,000 rows pointing to the next level
Leaf level	40,000 pages containing all of the 1,000,000 rows of the index

Table 6-7 shows the layout of each level of an *IncludedColumns* index.

TABLE 6-7 Levels of the *IncludedColumns* Index

LEVEL	CONTENTS
Root	1 page with 145 rows pointing to the next level
Intermediate level	145 pages with a total of 40,003 rows pointing to the next level
Leaf level	40,003 pages containing all of the 1,000,000 rows of the index

Because the rows in the nonleaf level pages of the *NoIncludedColumns* index are substantially larger than those of the *IncludedColumns* index, more pages (and therefore more levels) are needed to create the balanced tree for the index. Because the *NoIncludedColumns* index is two levels (that is, 40 percent) deeper than the *IncludedColumns* index, each search through the *NoIncludedColumns* index needs two more page reads to get to the bottom of the index. This might not sound like much, but if the index is used for repeated searches, such as for joins or very frequent queries, the extra levels cause performance degradation.

In Table 6-8, three example queries are shown that join a table called *Test.OtherTable* with the *Test.IncludedColumnsTest* table using different indexes. Note that the index hints [*WITH(INDEX)*] are used only to force SQL Server to use the specified index instead of the optimal index (which would be the *IncludedColumns* index). A new index named *NotCovered* is added to show the performance of a nonclustered index that does not cover the query. The following script defines additional objects and indexes required by the example:

```
-- Create the NotCovered index.
CREATE NONCLUSTERED INDEX NotCovered ON Test.IncludedColumnsTest (Col1);

-- Create and populate the Test.OtherTable table.
CREATE TABLE Test.OtherTable (
    PKCol INT IDENTITY NOT NULL PRIMARY KEY
    ,Col1 INT NOT NULL
);


INSERT Test.OtherTable (Col1)
    SELECT Col1 FROM Test.IncludedColumnsTest;
```

TABLE 6-8 Performance Comparison Matrix

QUERY	DEFINITION	PAGE READS

Query 1
Index: *IncludedColumns*
 	
The execution plan is shown in Figure 6-5.
	SELECT o.PKCol, i.Col2
	FROM Test.OtherTable AS o
	INNER JOIN
	    Test.IncludedColumnsTest AS i
	    WITH(INDEX(**IncludedColumns**))
	    ON o.Col1 = i.Col1
	WHERE o.PKCol BETWEEN 1
	    AND 10000;
		32,726 pages

QUERY	DEFINITION	PAGE READS
Query 2 **Index:** *NoIncludedColumns* The execution plan is shown in Figure 6-6.	SELECT o.PKCol, i.Col2 FROM Test.OtherTable AS o INNER JOIN Test.IncludedColumnsTest AS i WITH(INDEX(**NoIncludedColumns**)) ON o.Col1 = i.Col1 WHERE o.PKCol BETWEEN 1 AND 10000;	53,994 pages
Query 3 **Index:** *NotCovered* The execution plan is shown in Figure 6-7.	SELECT o.PKCol, i.Col2 FROM Test.OtherTable AS o INNER JOIN Test.IncludedColumnsTest AS i WITH(INDEX(**NotCovered**)) ON o.Col1 = i.Col1 WHERE o.PKCol BETWEEN 1 AND 10000;	62,900 pages

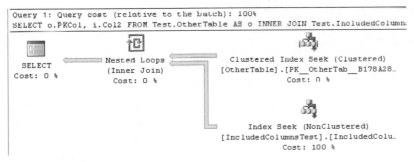

FIGURE 6-5 The actual execution plan of Query 1 in SSMS

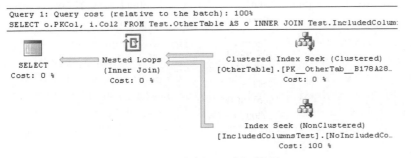

FIGURE 6-6 The actual execution plan of Query 2 in SSMS

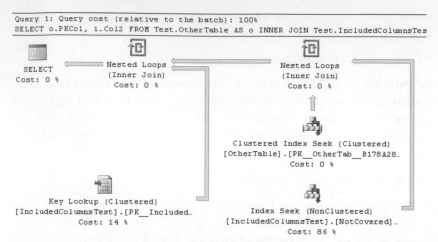

```
Query 1: Query cost (relative to the batch): 100%
SELECT o.PKCol, i.Col2 FROM Test.OtherTable AS o INNER JOIN Test.IncludedColumnsTes
```

SELECT
Cost: 0 %

Nested Loops
(Inner Join)
Cost: 0 %

Nested Loops
(Inner Join)
Cost: 0 %

Clustered Index Seek (Clustered)
[OtherTable].[PK__OtherTab__B178A28…
Cost: 0 %

Key Lookup (Clustered)
[IncludedColumnsTest].[PK__Included…
Cost: 14 %

Index Seek (NonClustered)
[IncludedColumnsTest].[NotCovered]…
Cost: 86 %

FIGURE 6-7 The actual execution plan of Query 3 in SSMS

Query 1, with the *IncludedColumns* index, is the best-performing query, with 32,726 page reads. Query 2, with the *NoIncludedColumns* index, used 53,994 page reads. As you can see, the difference in the number of page reads between the two indexes is roughly the same as the difference in index levels (40 percent). Query 3, with the *NotCovered* index, is the worst-performing query with 62,900 page reads because of the extra reads necessary to fetch the data that was not found in the index from the table. (Note the extra *Nested Loops Join* operator in the execution plan of Query 3.)

Using Clustered Indexes

Because a clustered index is the actual table, reading from the clustered index never results in lookups. Therefore, a clustered index should generally be defined on columns that are often queried and typically return a lot of data. Using a clustered index avoids the problem of lookups and fetching a large number of rows. Two good candidates for the clustered index are either the most frequently queried foreign key column of the table (a search on a foreign key typically returns many rows) or the most frequently searched date column. (Date searches typically return a large number of rows as well.)

Another important consideration when selecting the column or columns on which to create the clustered index is that the key size of the clustered index should be as small as possible. If a clustered index exists on a table, all nonclustered indexes on that table use the key of the clustered index as the row pointer from the nonclustered index to the table. If a clustered index does not exist, the row identifier is used, which takes up 8 bytes of storage in each row of each nonclustered index. This can significantly increase the index size for larger tables. Consider the following scenario:

- You have a table with 40,000,000 rows.
- The table has five nonclustered indexes.
- The clustered index key is 60 bytes wide. (This is not uncommon when you have clustered indexes that span a few columns.)

The total size of all row pointers from the nonclustered indexes on this table (only the pointers—nothing else) would be

*40,000,000 * 5 * 60 = 12,000,000,000 bytes (close to 12 gigabytes)*

If the clustered index key were changed to only one column with a smaller data type, such as an integer for a foreign key, each row pointer would be only 4 bytes. Because 4 bytes are added to all duplicates of the clustered index key to keep it unique internally, the clustered index key size that actually results would be 8 bytes. The total size of all row pointers would then be as follows:

*40,000,000 * 5 * 8 = 1,600,000,000 bytes (close to 1.5 GB)*

The reduction in storage needed is more than 10 GB.

Read Performance vs. Write Performance

The addition of indexes helps boost only the read performance. Write performance is typically degraded because the indexes must be kept up-to-date with the data in the table. If a table has five nonclustered indexes defined on it, an *INSERT* into that table is really six *INSERT*s: one for the table and one for each index. The same goes for *DELETE* statements. With *UPDATE* statements, only indexes that contain the columns that are updated by the statement must be touched.

When index keys are updated, the row in the index must be moved to the appropriate position in the index (unless the update modifies only data in included columns). The result is that the *UPDATE* is split into a *DELETE* followed by an *INSERT*. Depending on the internal fragmentation of the index pages, this might also cause page splits.

Consider the following simple performance test on the *Test.IndexInsertTest* table containing 1,000,000 rows. In each test, 10,000 rows are inserted. The table is recreated between tests. First, the *INSERT* is performed against the table without any nonclustered indexes, then it is performed with one nonclustered index, and finally, it is performed with five nonclustered indexes. The following code sets up the test:

```
CREATE TABLE Test.IndexInsertTest (
    PKCol UNIQUEIDENTIFIER NOT NULL DEFAULT NEWSEQUENTIALID()
        PRIMARY KEY CLUSTERED
    ,Col1 INT NOT NULL
);

INSERT Test.IndexInsertTest (Col1)
    SELECT TOP(1000000)
        ROW_NUMBER() OVER (ORDER BY message_id) AS Col1
    FROM sys.messages AS sm
    CROSS JOIN (
        SELECT TOP(15) 1 AS Col FROM sys.messages
    ) AS x;
```

```
-- Rebuild the table's clustered index.
ALTER INDEX ALL ON Test.OtherTable REBUILD;


-- Create table containing the rows used to perform the inserts.
CREATE TABLE Test.OtherTable (
    PKCol INT IDENTITY(100000,4) NOT NULL PRIMARY KEY
    ,OtherCol INT NOT NULL
);


INSERT Test.OtherTable (OtherCol)
    SELECT Col1 FROM Test.IncludedColumnsTest
    WHERE Col1 BETWEEN 1 AND 10000;
```

The following is the first test, without any nonclustered indexes defined on the table. The execution plan for this *INSERT* statement is shown in Figure 6-8:

```
INSERT Test.IndexInsertTest (Col1)
    SELECT PKCol FROM Test.OtherTable;
```

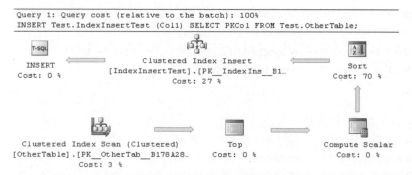

FIGURE 6-8 The actual execution plan from SSMS of the *INSERT* statement used in the first test

The estimated query cost for the *INSERT* statement in this test was 0.88, and SQL Server touched 32,085 pages in the *Test.IndexInsertTest* table while performing the *INSERT*s.

The following is the second test, with one nonclustered index defined on the table. The execution plan for this *INSERT* statement is shown in Figure 6-9:

```
-- 1. Drop and re-create the Test.IndexInsertTest table.
-- 2. Add one non-clustered index.
CREATE NONCLUSTERED INDEX NCIdx1 ON Test.IndexInsertTest (Col1);


-- 3. Execute the insert statement.
INSERT Test.IndexInsertTest (Col1)
    SELECT PKCol FROM Test.OtherTable;
```

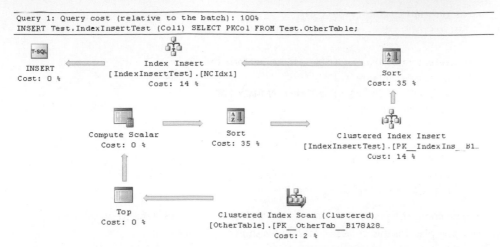

```
Query 1: Query cost (relative to the batch): 100%
INSERT Test.IndexInsertTest (Col1) SELECT PKCol FROM Test.OtherTable;
```

T-SQL
INSERT
Cost: 0 %

Index Insert
[IndexInsertTest].[NCIdx1]
Cost: 14 %

Sort
Cost: 35 %

Compute Scalar
Cost: 0 %

Sort
Cost: 35 %

Clustered Index Insert
[IndexInsertTest].[PK__IndexIns__B1...
Cost: 14 %

Top
Cost: 0 %

Clustered Index Scan (Clustered)
[OtherTable].[PK__OtherTab__B178A28...
Cost: 2 %

FIGURE 6-9 The actual execution plan from SSMS of the *INSERT* statement used in the second test

The estimated query cost for the *INSERT* statement in this test was 1.58, and SQL Server touched 64,902 pages in the *Test.IndexInsertTest* table while performing the *INSERT*s. This is roughly twice the cost and twice the number of pages compared with Test 1.

The following is the third test, with five nonclustered indexes defined on the table. The execution plan for this *INSERT* statement is shown in Figure 6-10:

```
-- 1. Drop and recreate the Test.IndexInsertTest table.
-- 2. Add five non-clustered indexes.
CREATE NONCLUSTERED INDEX NCIdx1 ON Test.IndexInsertTest (Col1);
CREATE NONCLUSTERED INDEX NCIdx2 ON Test.IndexInsertTest (Col1);
CREATE NONCLUSTERED INDEX NCIdx3 ON Test.IndexInsertTest (Col1);
CREATE NONCLUSTERED INDEX NCIdx4 ON Test.IndexInsertTest (Col1);
CREATE NONCLUSTERED INDEX NCIdx5 ON Test.IndexInsertTest (Col1);

-- 3. Execute the insert statement.
INSERT Test.IndexInsertTest (Col1)
    SELECT PKCol FROM Test.OtherTable;
```

This time, the estimated query cost for the *INSERT* statement was 5.04 and SQL Server handled a staggering 196,170 pages in the *Test.IndexInsertTest* table while performing the *INSERT*s. As you can see, the cost for performing the *INSERT*s is roughly doubled with each new nonclustered index. However, in this case, each nonclustered index is roughly the same width as the table itself. For typical tables, the nonclustered indexes are narrower than the table and do not hurt performance (percentage-wise) to the same degree as in this test.

Because the ratio between read and write operations varies greatly between systems (and even tables), it is typically a good idea to create indexes to optimize read performance and then test the effect that the created indexes have on write performance. So long as the write

```
Query 1: Query cost (relative to the batch): 100%
INSERT Test.IndexInsertTest (Col1) SELECT PKCol FROM Test.OtherTable;
```

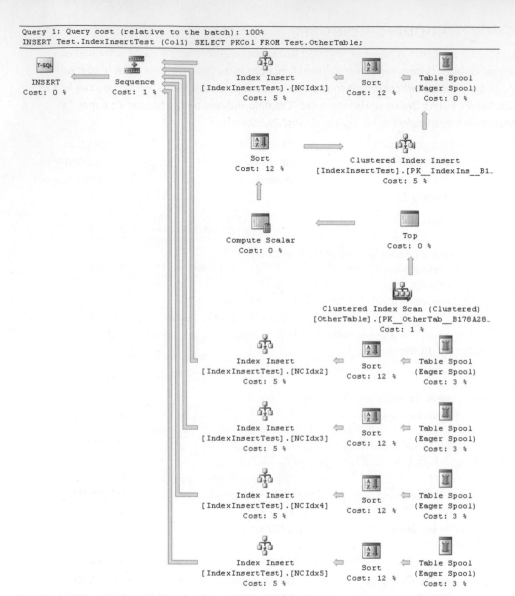

FIGURE 6-10 The actual execution plan from SSMS of the *INSERT* statement used in the third test

performance is acceptable (and you have enough disk space to manage the created indexes), you can keep the created indexes. It is typically also advisable to run such a test every so often to verify that the read versus write ratio for the table hasn't changed.

You should also note that both the *UPDATE* and *DELETE* statements benefit from certain indexes to locate the rows in the table that they need to update or delete.

Using Computed Columns

A computed column is generally derived from other columns in the same table and can reference both system- and user-defined functions in its definition. To be able to create an index on a computed column, it must adhere to a few requirements, which you can find in SQL Server Books Online under the topic "Creating Indexes on Computed Columns," at *http://msdn.microsoft.com/en-us/library/ms189292.aspx*.

By defining a computed column and indexing it, it is possible to make queries that would typically require an index or table scan to instead use a seek operation. Consider the following query for sales orders in the *AdventureWorks* database. The query's execution plan is shown in Figure 6-11:

```
USE AdventureWorks;

-- First create an index on the OrderDate column
-- to support this query.
CREATE NONCLUSTERED INDEX OrderDateIndex ON
    Sales.SalesOrderHeader (OrderDate);
GO

SET STATISTICS IO ON;

SELECT
    COUNT(*) FROM Sales.SalesOrderHeader
WHERE MONTH(OrderDate) = 5;
```

```
Query 1: Query cost (relative to the batch): 100%
SELECT COUNT(*) FROM Sales.SalesOrderHeader WHERE MONTH(OrderDate) = 5;
```

SELECT	Compute Scalar	Stream Aggregate (Aggregate)	Index Scan (NonClustered) [SalesOrderHeader].[OrderDateIndex]
Cost: 0 %	Cost: 0 %	Cost: 20 %	Cost: 80 %

FIGURE 6-11 The actual execution plan of the *SELECT* statement without a SARG

Because the query did not use a valid SARG (the column in the *WHERE* clause is used in an expression), the *OrderDateIndex* index can be used only for scanning and not for seeking. To be able to produce an index seek, SQL Server must maintain an index of the result of the function call, in this case, *MONTH(OrderDate)*. You can do this by adding a computed column to the table and indexing that column as follows (the query's execution plan is shown in Figure 6-12):

```
-- Add the column.
ALTER TABLE Sales.SalesOrderHeader
    ADD OrderMonth AS MONTH(OrderDate);
```

```
-- Create an index on the computed column.
CREATE NONCLUSTERED INDEX OrderMonthIndex
    ON Sales.SalesOrderHeader (OrderMonth);
GO


SET STATISTICS IO ON;


-- Run the query and reference the new column.
SELECT COUNT(*) FROM Sales.SalesOrderHeader
WHERE OrderMonth = 5;
```

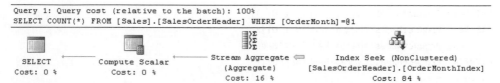

FIGURE 6-12 The actual execution plan of the SELECT statement using the computed column in the *WHERE* clause

This time, the query performs a seek operation on the index of the computed column, resulting in only eight page reads. Depending on the complexity of your query and computed column definition, the optimizer automatically uses the index of the computed column without the computed column being referenced in the query. The following query, for example, also generates the execution plan previously shown in Figure 6-12:

```
SET STATISTICS IO ON;


-- Run the query without referencing the computed column.
SELECT COUNT(*) FROM Sales.SalesOrderHeader
WHERE MONTH(OrderDate) = 5;
```

As you can see, SQL Server used the index of the computed column without having a reference to it in the query. This is a great feature because it makes it possible to add computed columns and index them without having to change the queries in applications or stored procedures to use the new index.

Besides using indexed computed columns with function calls, you can also use indexed computed columns to provide indexes in different collations. Consider that you have the table *Test.Person* with the column *Name* using the *Latin1_General_CI_AI* collation. Now you want to find all rows starting with the character Ö. In *Latin1_General*, the dots over the O are just considered accents, but in other languages, such as German and Swedish, Ö is a different character than O. Consider that the table is typically queried by English-speaking customers who expect to get both O and Ö back from a search such as *LIKE 'Ö%'* and occasionally by Swedish customers who expect to get only Ö back from that same search. Because the table is typically queried by English-speaking customers, it makes sense to keep the *Latin1_General_CI_AI* collation, and, when Swedish customers query the table, to use the *COLLATE* keyword to use the *Finnish_Swedish_CI_AI* collation explicitly. Review the following script and queries. The execution plans for the two queries in the following script are shown in Figures 6-13 and 6-14:

```
-- Create and populate the table
CREATE TABLE Test.ProductNames (
    Name NVARCHAR(50) COLLATE Latin1_General_CI_AI
);

INSERT Test.ProductNames (Name) VALUES ('Öl');
INSERT Test.ProductNames (Name) VALUES ('Olja');
INSERT Test.ProductNames (Name) VALUES ('Beer');
INSERT Test.ProductNames (Name) VALUES ('Oil');

CREATE CLUSTERED INDEX NameIndex ON Test.ProductNames
    (Name);
GO


-- Query 1
-- Query for all product names that begin with the letter Ö
-- using the default collation.
SELECT Name FROM Test.ProductNames
    WHERE Name LIKE 'Ö%';
```

Here is the result of Query 1:

```
Name
------------
Oil
Öl
Olja
```

Query 2 looks like this:

```
-- Query 2
-- Query for all product names that begin with the letter Ö
-- using the Finnish_Swedish_CI_AI collation.
SELECT Name FROM Test.ProductNames
    WHERE Name LIKE 'Ö%' COLLATE Finnish_Swedish_CI_AI;
```

Here is the result of Query 2:

```
Name
-------------
Öl
```

```
Query 1: Query cost (relative to the batch): 100%
SELECT Name FROM Test.ProductNames WHERE Name LIKE 'Ö%';
```

FIGURE 6-13 The actual execution plan of Query 1 in SSMS

```
Query 1: Query cost (relative to the batch): 100%
SELECT Name FROM Test.ProductNames WHERE Name LIKE 'Ö%' COLLATE Finnish_Swedish_CI_AI;
```

FIGURE 6-14 The actual execution plan of Query 2 in SSMS

Comparing the execution plans of Query 1 (Figure 6-13) and Query 2 (Figure 6-14), you can see that in Query 2, because the comparison needs to use a collation other than that of the column (and therefore, the index), a clustered index scan is used instead of an index seek, as in Query 1. By adding an indexed computed column to this table and specifying the *Finnish_Swedish_CI_AS* collation for this column (as shown in the next code example), SQL Server can automatically use that index instead. Note that the query itself need not change, and that this is a viable solution only if you are using a relatively low number of collations because these indexes need to be both stored and maintained, like all other indexes. The execution plan for the query in the following script is shown in Figure 6-15:

```
-- Add a computed column with another collation.
ALTER TABLE Test.ProductNames
    ADD Name_Finnish_Swedish_CI_AI
        AS Name COLLATE Finnish_Swedish_CI_AI;


-- Create an index on the computed column.
CREATE NONCLUSTERED INDEX NameIndex2 ON Test.ProductNames
    (Name_Finnish_Swedish_CI_AI);
GO


-- Query for all product names that begin with the letter Ö
-- using the Finnish_Swedish_CI_AI collation without specifying
-- the computed column.
SELECT Name FROM Test.ProductNames
    WHERE Name LIKE 'Ö%' COLLATE Finnish_Swedish_CI_AI;
```

Here is the result of this query:

```
Name
-------------
Öl
```

```
Query 1: Query cost (relative to the batch): 100%
SELECT Name FROM Test.ProductNames WHERE Name LIKE 'Ö%' COLLATE Finnish_Swedish_CI_AI;
```

```
    SELECT          ◄──────       Index Seek (NonClustered)
    Cost: 0 %                     [ProductNames].[NameIndex2]
                                          Cost: 100 %
```

FIGURE 6-15 The actual execution plan of the query using an alternate collation index in SSMS

Using Indexed Views

A *normal database view* is just a named *SELECT* statement that can be used from other *SELECT* statements. These views have no particular impact on performance. Beginning with SQL Server 2000, you could create one or more indexes on a view so long as the view satisfies certain requirements. These requirements are quite extensive and can be found in SQL Server Books Online in the article "Creating Indexed Views," at *http://msdn.microsoft.com/en-us/library/ms191432.aspx.* By creating an index on a view, the view is materialized. This means that, in the logical sense, it is still a view, but the view actually stores the data found in the view. (Materialized views are explained in detail in Chapter 5.) If the data is changed in the tables on which the view is based, the view is automatically updated to reflect those changes.

Creating indexed views can greatly improve the read performance of queries. An important aspect of indexed views is that, depending on your SQL Server edition, the optimizer can automatically detect and use an indexed view that satisfies a certain query, even if the indexed view is not referenced in the query. This, however, is true only for SQL Server 2008 Enterprise Edition and Developer Edition.

The following example shows a query and its execution plan (shown in Figure 6-16) without an indexed view:

```
USE AdventureWorks;

SELECT
    p.Name
    ,sod.OrderQty
    ,soh.OrderDate
FROM Production.Product AS p
INNER JOIN Sales.SalesOrderDetail AS sod
    ON sod.ProductID = p.ProductID
INNER JOIN Sales.SalesOrderHeader AS soh
    ON soh.SalesOrderID = sod.SalesOrderID
WHERE soh.TerritoryID = 1;
```

The cost of the previous query was 2.03. Next, an indexed view is created to optimize the query and then the same query is executed again. The execution plan for this query is shown in Figure 6-17. The first index created on a view must materialize the entire view, which means

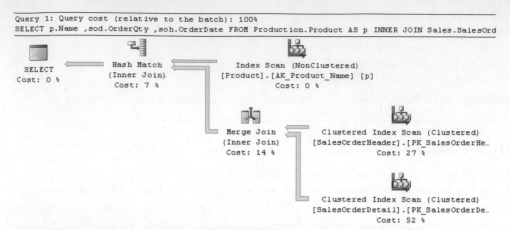

```
Query 1: Query cost (relative to the batch): 100%
SELECT p.Name ,sod.OrderQty ,soh.OrderDate FROM Production.Product AS p INNER JOIN Sales.SalesOrd
```

FIGURE 6-16 The actual execution plan of the query without an indexed view in SSMS

that the resulting index must be a clustered index. The first index also must be unique (which is why the column *SalesOrderDetailID* has been added to the example's indexed view):

```
CREATE VIEW Sales.ProductsSoldVw
WITH SCHEMABINDING
AS
SELECT
    soh.TerritoryID
    ,sod.SalesOrderDetailID
    ,p.Name
    ,sod.OrderQty
    ,soh.OrderDate
FROM Production.Product AS p
INNER JOIN Sales.SalesOrderDetail AS sod
    ON sod.ProductID = p.ProductID
INNER JOIN Sales.SalesOrderHeader AS soh
    ON soh.SalesOrderID = sod.SalesOrderID
GO

CREATE UNIQUE CLUSTERED INDEX ProductsSoldVwIdx
    ON Sales.ProductsSoldVw (TerritoryID, SalesOrderDetailID);

GO

SELECT
    p.Name
    ,sod.OrderQty
    ,soh.OrderDate
```

```
FROM Production.Product AS p
INNER JOIN Sales.SalesOrderDetail AS sod
    ON sod.ProductID = p.ProductID
INNER JOIN Sales.SalesOrderHeader AS soh
    ON soh.SalesOrderID = sod.SalesOrderID
WHERE soh.TerritoryID = 1;
```

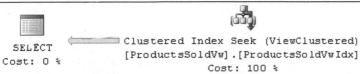

Query 1: Query cost (relative to the batch): 100%
SELECT p.Name ,sod.OrderQty ,soh.OrderDate FROM Product:

SELECT
Cost: 0 %

Clustered Index Seek (ViewClustered)
[ProductsSoldVw].[ProductsSoldVwIdx]
Cost: 100 %

FIGURE 6-17 The actual execution plan of the query with a materialized indexed view available in SSMS in SQL Server 2008 Enterprise Edition or Developer Edition

This time (if you are using SQL Server 2008 Enterprise Edition or Developer Edition), the query uses the indexed view, even though it is not referenced, and the query cost drops to 0.12.

After you have created the unique clustered index on the view, it is possible to create additional nonclustered indexes on the same view.

> **NOTE SQL SERVER EDITION**
>
> If you are using any edition of SQL Server other than Enterprise Edition or Developer Edition, your query must reference the view directly, and you must add the optimizer hint *WITH(NOEXPAND)* to the query:
>
> ```
> SELECT
>     Name
>     ,OrderQty
>     ,OrderDate
> FROM Sales.ProductsSoldVw WITH(NOEXPAND)
> WHERE TerritoryID = 1;
> ```

Analyzing Index Usage

Because indexes incur a cost (for storage space and for keeping them up-to-date when DML statements are executed), it is important to keep track of which indexes are actually being used in your applications. If an index is never used, it is likely that it can be dropped both to save storage space and to reduce the cost of write operations. However, keep in mind that some indexes are created for a specific purpose; for example, to optimize the monthly salary reports. Therefore, you should be careful when dropping unused or seldom-used indexes. When you drop an index that is seldom used, you should document your actions so that the dropped index can be re-created if it is needed later.

You can query the *sys.dm_db_index_usage_stats* dynamic management view (DMV) to find index-usage information. The columns from this view that are particularly interesting are shown in Table 6-9; you can find documentation of the whole table at SQL Server Books Online at *http://msdn.microsoft.com/en-us/library/ms188755.aspx*.

TABLE 6-9 Subset of the *sys.dm_db_index_usage_stats* DMV

COLUMN NAME	DATA TYPE	DESCRIPTION
database_id	*smallint*	ID of the database on which the table or view is defined
object_id	*int*	ID of the table or view on which the index is defined
index_id	*int*	ID of the index
user_seeks	*bigint*	Number of seeks by user queries
user_scans	*bigint*	Number of scans by user queries
user_lookups	*bigint*	Number of lookups by user queries
user_updates	*bigint*	Number of updates by user queries
last_user_seek	*datetime*	Time of last user seek
last_user_scan	*datetime*	Time of last user scan
last_user_lookup	*datetime*	Time of last user lookup

You should typically query this view for indexes that have low values in the *user_seeks* or *user_scans* column. All values in the *sys.dm_db_index_usage_stats* view are reset whenever the SQL Server service is restarted. The values for a specific database are removed if the database is either detached or shut down. Note that indexes that have not been used since the *sys.dm_db_index_usage_stats* view was reset are not included in the view.

Partitioning

Starting with SQL Server 2005, you can choose to partition tables and indexes horizontally (that is, by rows) into smaller chunks. The main use for this is improving import performance by reducing the work needed to be performed by SQL Server when importing data. Why would it reduce the work needed? As shown earlier in this lesson, it is quite a lot of work for SQL Server to maintain indexes when rows are inserted, updated, or deleted. Of course, this is also true when performing an import. If you don't use partitioning, you have the choice of either importing your new data into a table and letting SQL Server automatically update the indexes. As you have seen, this causes a lot of fragmentation. If it caused enough fragmentation, you are likely to want to rebuild your indexes after the import. Considering that this happens, it is faster to drop all the indexes, import the data, and then re-create all the indexes again. That way, SQL Server doesn't waste resources maintaining the indexes during the import. This is where partitioning really excels. What if, instead of re-creating your indexes for the entire table, you just did it for the data being inserted? The import performance would vastly improve. With partitioning, you could create a new table without any indexes on it, import the data into the table, create the indexes on this new table, and finally add it as a new partition to the main table.

Partitioning can also help query performance, but query performance is best helped using indexes rather than partitioning.

To be able to partition tables and indexes, you first need to create two objects: a partition function and a partition scheme. The partition function simply defines the points (or rather, values) where each partition ends. The partition scheme defines on which file group each partition goes; note that you can also define one file group to hold all partitions.

Partition Functions

Partition functions are created using the *CREATE PARTITION FUNCTION* statement. A partition function is simply a list of up to 999 values that define dividers between partitions. You can decide if the values that you supply are interpreted as "less than or equal to" (<=) or "less than" (<) by defining the partition function as either *LEFT* or *RIGHT*.

The following code creates a partition function defined as *LEFT*. The resulting partitions are shown in Table 6-10:

```
CREATE PARTITION FUNCTION PF(INT)
AS RANGE LEFT
FOR VALUES (10, 20, 30);
```

TABLE 6-10 Partitions Available with the *PF* Partition Function

PARTITION NUMBER	PARTITION RANGE
1	<= 10
2	> 10 AND <= 20
3	> 20 AND <= 30
4	> 30

Now consider the following code, which creates virtually the same partition function but defined as *RIGHT* instead of *LEFT*. The resulting partitions are shown in Table 6-11:

```
CREATE PARTITION FUNCTION pf (INT)
AS RANGE RIGHT
FOR VALUES (10, 20, 30);
```

TABLE 6-11 Partitions Available with the *PF* Partition Function

PARTITION NUMBER	PARTITION RANGE
1	< 10
2	>= 10 AND < 20
3	>= 20 AND < 30
4	>= 30

Partition Schemes

You define a partition function by using the *CREATE PARTITION SCHEME* statement. The partition scheme is a simple map between partitions for a particular partition and file groups. The reason for using different file groups for different partitions is typically to be able to store different parts of a table on different types of storage devices; you might want to store older data on slower but cheaper devices and new data on faster but more expensive devices.

The following example creates a partition scheme that maps each of the partitions defined in Table 6-11 to its own file group; as you can see, the same file group can be used for multiple partitions:

```
CREATE PARTITION SCHEME PS
AS PARTITION PF TO (FG1, FG2, FG1, FG2);
```

As another example, the statement shown here creates a partition scheme mapping all partitions to the primary file group:

```
CREATE PARTITION SCHEME PS
AS PARTITION PF ALL TO ([PRIMARY]);
```

Creating the Partitioned Table

After you have created the partition function and partition scheme, you can create tables and indexes on the partition scheme using the *ON* clause of the *CREATE TABLE* and *CREATE INDEX* statements. Even though you can have a table on one partition scheme and its indexes on different partition schemes (or one on a partition scheme and one not), it is recommended that they all be created on the same partition scheme to support adding and removing partitions as needed, without having to shut down any applications. A table with all indexes defined on the same partition scheme is said to have "aligned partitions." Nonunique, nonclustered indexes are aligned automatically with the table's partition scheme when created; that is, you don't even need to specify the *ON* clause for the *CREATE INDEX* statement. For unique indexes, however, you must include the partitioning column in the index key to make it aligned with the table. This typically defeats the purpose of having a unique index. For example, if you want to add a unique index on the *SSN* column in a table partitioned over the ID column, you have to make it a composite index over both *SSN* and *ID* to align it. You typically must have any unique index defined as nonaligned; and if you need to add or remove a partition, you must drop the nonaligned index, add or remove the partition, and then re-create the nonaligned index. Doesn't doing all this defeat the purpose of the partitioning? Not really—if you have five aligned indexes and one nonaligned, you need only re-create the nonaligned index, whereas without partitioning, you potentially have to re-create all six indexes.

Now let's look at an example of using partitioning to improve import performance. The following batch creates a partition function and partition scheme, as well as a table and a nonclustered index defined on the partition scheme. After the objects are created, an *INSERT* statement is used to populate the table with an initial 19,185 rows. Note that even though the *CREATE INDEX* statement doesn't use the *ON* clause to specify the partition scheme, the index is created on the partition scheme. The last part of the script is a query against the *sys.partitions* catalog view, which returns the 8 partitions created by the script: 4 for the table (*heap, index_id* = 0) and 4 for the nonclustered index (*index_id* = 2):

```
USE AdventureWorks;

CREATE PARTITION FUNCTION PFCustomerID (INT)
AS RANGE LEFT
FOR VALUES (5000, 10000, 15000);

CREATE PARTITION SCHEME PSCustomerID
AS PARTITION PFCustomerID ALL TO ([PRIMARY]);

CREATE TABLE Test.CustomersPartitioned (
    CustomerID INT IDENTITY NOT NULL
    ,AccountNumber VARCHAR(50) NOT NULL
    ,ModifiedDate DATETIME2 NOT NULL
) ON PSCustomerID (CustomerID);

CREATE NONCLUSTERED INDEX AccountNumberIdx
    ON Test.CustomersPartitioned (AccountNumber);

INSERT Test.CustomersPartitioned (AccountNumber, ModifiedDate)
    SELECT AccountNumber, ModifiedDate FROM Sales.Customer;

SELECT index_id, partition_number, rows FROM sys.partitions
    WHERE object_id = OBJECT_ID('Test.CustomersPartitioned')
    ORDER BY index_id, partition_number;
```

Here are the results of the query against the *sys.partitions* catalog view:

index_id	partition_number	rows
0	1	5000
0	2	5000
0	3	5000
0	4	4185
2	1	5000
2	2	5000
2	3	5000
2	4	4185

To import data into the *Test.CustomersPartitioned* table by adding a new partition, you need to define the new partition. To do that, you need to find the next divider value for the partition function and add it to the partition function. The following query finds the next divider for the *PFCustomerID* partition function:

```
SELECT MAX(CustomerID) AS MaxCustomerID FROM Test.CustomersPartitioned;
```

Here is the result, showing the divider value you need:

```
MaxCustomerID
-------------
19185
```

Now that you have the value 19185, you can define the next divider value as 19185. Because the partition function is defined as *LEFT,* the fourth partition now contains the *CustomerID* range 15001 to 19185 and the new partition contains all *CustomerID*s greater than 19185. The following script alters the partition function and displays the new list of partitions in the table:

```
ALTER PARTITION FUNCTION PFCustomerID()
    SPLIT RANGE (19185);

SELECT index_id, partition_number, rows FROM sys.partitions
    WHERE object_id = OBJECT_ID('Test.CustomersPartitioned')
    ORDER BY index_id, partition_number;
```

Here are the results of the query against the *sys.partitions* catalog view with the new partition:

index_id	partition_number	rows
0	1	5000
0	2	5000
0	3	5000
0	4	4185
0	5	0
2	1	5000
2	2	5000
2	3	5000
2	4	4185
2	5	0

The next step is to import the new data, which is done by creating a new table with exactly the same schema as the main table and then importing the new data into it. Note that if you use multiple file groups, this new table has to exist on the same file group as the partition that you want it to become. The following script creates the new table, imports the data, and creates the nonclustered index on the table. (If you had any constraints, such as a primary key, check constraint, or foreign key, these would also have to be added before you can add the new table to the partitioned table.) One caveat with the nonclustered index is that you must include the column that you are partitioning the table on in the nonclustered index definition to allow the new table to be added to the partitioned table. This is done automatically when the table is already partitioned, but not for the new table because it simply isn't partitioned—at this point, it is still just a normal table:

```
-- New empty table.
CREATE TABLE Test.NewCustomers (
    CustomerID INT IDENTITY(19186, 1) NOT NULL
    ,AccountNumber VARCHAR(50) NOT NULL
    ,ModifiedDate DATETIME2 NOT NULL
);

-- Import into the empty table, note that no indexes
-- that need to be maintained exist yet!
INSERT Test.NewCustomers (AccountNumber, ModifiedDate)
    SELECT TOP(3000) AccountNumber, ModifiedDate
    FROM Sales.Customer;

-- Now you create the index (and any constraints needed).
CREATE NONCLUSTERED INDEX AccountNumberIdx
    ON Test.NewCustomers (AccountNumber) INCLUDE (CustomerID);
```

To finally add the *Test.NewCustomers* table to the partitioned table as partition 5, you must define a check constraint on it that guarantees that it matches the values allowed for partition 5 (values greater than 19185). The following script adds the check constraint and then switches the new table with the current partition 5 (which is empty) in the partitioned table, and the current partition 5 now becomes the empty *Test.NewCustomers* table, which can then be dropped:

```
-- Add the check constraint.
ALTER TABLE Test.NewCustomers ADD CHECK(CustomerID > 19185);

-- Switch places between the new table and partition 5 in the partitioned table.
ALTER TABLE Test.NewCustomers SWITCH TO Test.CustomersPartitioned PARTITION 5;

-- Finally drop the Test.NewCustomers table.
DROP TABLE Test.NewCustomers;

-- Done:
SELECT index_id, partition_number, rows FROM sys.partitions
    WHERE object_id = OBJECT_ID('Test.CustomersPartitioned')
    ORDER BY index_id, partition_number;
```

Here are the results of the query against the *sys.partitions* catalog view, showing the number of rows that have been added to the new partition:

```
index_id    partition_number rows
----------- ---------------- --------------------
0           1                5000
0           2                5000
0           3                5000
0           4                4185
```

0	5	3000
2	1	5000
2	2	5000
2	3	5000
2	4	4185
2	5	3000

So why is this import so much better now than it was without the partitions? First, consider that only the imported rows needed to be handled during the operation—the existing rows were never touched. Also, the partitioned table was much more available to users; it was inaccessible only during the execution of the *ALTER TABLE...SWITCH...* statement. Because *ALTER TABLE...SWITCH...* changes only pointers in the system catalog, it is executed in virtually no time, no matter how many rows are being added.

So, you can potentially improve import performance a great deal by implementing partitioning. But what about query performance? Well, partitioning also can improve query performance, especially if the partitioned column is one that you often query over. If so, SQL Server can do partition elimination during optimization so that it needs to do seek or scan operations on only certain partitions instead of on the entire table. However, comparing the query performance of a partitioned table without an appropriate index with a nonpartitioned table with an appropriate index, you see that the index performs much better than the partitioning (without an index). The following query is run against the schema and the rows (the original 19,185 rows) defined in the previous example on partitioning, and the results are shown in Table 6-12. The query is designed so that it needs to scan only two of the partitions in the table:

```
SET STATISTICS IO ON;

SELECT COUNT(*) FROM Test.CustomersPartitioned
    WHERE CustomerID BETWEEN 1000 AND 10000;
```

TABLE 6-12 Performance Comparison

DESCRIPTION	LOGICAL READS (I/O)	COST
Nonpartitioned table without an index on *CustomerID*	85 pages	0.095
Partitioned table without an index on *CustomerID*	44 pages	0.049
Nonpartitioned table with an index on *CustomerID*	20 pages	0.030
Partitioned table with an index on *CustomerID*	23 pages	0.031

Note that when no index is available, the query against the partitioned table performs best. But when an index is available, the query against the nonpartitioned table performs best. Why does the query against the nonpartitioned table with an index perform better than the query against the partitioned table with an index? Because in the partitioned table, the query performs a seek operation against two indexes (one for each partition), whereas the query against the nonpartitioned table performs a seek operation against only one index.

Tuning Indexes Automatically

Besides tuning indexes manually, SQL Server provides other ways that help you choose the right indexing solution for a specific query. When viewing the graphical execution plan, you may see a note about a "Missing Index." In this case, you can right-click the missing index note, which lets you retrieve the script needed to create the missing index. An aggregation of missing indexes that the optimizer has needed can be found in the *sys.dm_db_missing_index_details,* *sys.dm_db_missing_index_groups,* and *sys.dm_db_missing_index_group_stats* database management views (DMVs).

You can also use the Database Engine Tuning Advisor graphical utility to retrieve information on indexes, indexed views, and even partitioning solutions that may help query performance. The Database Engine Tuning Advisor can either be run against a script containing queries that need tuning or against a SQL Server Profiler trace file containing a workload of queries that need tuning.

Note that neither the graphical execution plan missing index help, the missing index DMVs, nor the Database Engine Tuning Advisor can replace manually tuning both the query itself and the indexes. Remember that these utilities are not going to know if you really need that last join to retrieve that extra column to enhance the look of that special executive report—only you can make that decision.

Lesson Summary

- Indexes typically help read performance but can hurt write performance.
- Indexed views can increase performance even more than indexes, but they are restrictive and typically cannot be created for the entire query.
- Deciding which columns to put in the index key and which should be implemented as included columns is important.
- Analyze which indexes are actually being used and drop the ones that aren't. This saves storage space and minimizes the resources used to maintain indexes for write operations.

PRACTICE Indexing to Support Queries

In this practice, you use two different indexing techniques to optimize a specific query. The query returns the customer IDs and the total amount for all purchases in a specific territory for all customers who have made purchases. This practice considers read performance only; it does not take write performance into account.

You are optimizing the following query:

```
-- Query that will be optimized:
USE AdventureWorks;

SELECT
    soh.CustomerID
    ,SUM(sod.OrderQty * sod.UnitPrice) AS TotalPurchases
FROM Test.SalesOrderHeader AS soh
INNER JOIN Test.SalesOrderDetail AS sod
    ON sod.SalesOrderID = soh.SalesOrderID
WHERE soh.TerritoryID = 1
GROUP BY soh.CustomerID;
```

EXERCISE 1   **Set a Performance Base Line for the Query**

In this exercise, you create the base line for the query that needs to be optimized by executing it without adding any indexes.

1. Open SSMS and connect to the appropriate instance of SQL Server 2008.

2. In a new query window, type and execute the following SQL statements to create the *TestDB* database, the *Test* schema, and the two tables that are used in this exercise:

```
CREATE DATABASE TestDB;
GO

USE TestDB;
GO

CREATE SCHEMA Test;
GO

SELECT * INTO Test.SalesOrderHeader
FROM AdventureWorks.Sales.SalesOrderHeader;
GO

SELECT * INTO Test.SalesOrderDetail
FROM AdventureWorks.Sales.SalesOrderDetail;
GO

ALTER TABLE Test.SalesOrderHeader
    ADD CONSTRAINT PKSalesOrderHeader
    PRIMARY KEY(SalesOrderID);
GO
```

```
ALTER TABLE Test.SalesOrderDetail
    ADD CONSTRAINT PKSalesOrderDetail
    PRIMARY KEY(SalesOrderDetailID);
```

3. Turn on the Actual Execution Plan feature in SSMS by pressing Ctrl+M or by selecting Include Actual Execution Plan from the Query menu.

4. In the existing query window, type, highlight, and execute the following SQL statement to turn on the reporting of page reads:

```
SET STATISTICS IO ON;
```

5. In the existing query window, type, highlight, and execute the following SQL statement:

```
SELECT
    soh.CustomerID
    ,SUM(sod.OrderQty * sod.UnitPrice) AS TotalPurchases
FROM Test.SalesOrderHeader AS soh
INNER JOIN Test.SalesOrderDetail AS sod ON sod.SalesOrderID = soh.SalesOrderID
WHERE soh.TerritoryID = 1
GROUP BY soh.CustomerID;
```

Record the total cost of the query. A table for this purpose is provided in Exercise 5.

(You can find the value in the Execution Plan tab by moving the pointer over the *SELECT* operator and locating the value named Estimated Subtree Cost.)

Record the total number of page reads for the query.

(You can find this value by scrolling to the bottom of the Messages tab and summing the values for logical reads.)

6. In the existing query window, type, highlight, and execute the following SQL statement to clean up after this exercise:

```
USE master;
DROP DATABASE TestDB;
```

EXERCISE 2 Tune the Query by Using Clustered Indexes

In this exercise, you optimize the query by modifying the primary key constraints to be nonclustered indexes and then creating appropriate clustered indexes.

1. Open SSMS, if necessary, and connect to the appropriate instance of SQL Server 2008.

2. In a new query window, type and execute the following SQL statements to create the *TestDB* database, the *Test* schema, and the two tables that are used in this exercise:

```
CREATE DATABASE TestDB;
GO

USE TestDB;
GO
```

```
CREATE SCHEMA Test;
GO

SELECT * INTO Test.SalesOrderHeader
FROM AdventureWorks.Sales.SalesOrderHeader;
GO

SELECT * INTO Test.SalesOrderDetail
FROM AdventureWorks.Sales.SalesOrderDetail;
GO

ALTER TABLE Test.SalesOrderHeader
    ADD CONSTRAINT PKSalesOrderHeader
    PRIMARY KEY(SalesOrderID);
GO

ALTER TABLE Test.SalesOrderDetail
    ADD CONSTRAINT PKSalesOrderDetail
    PRIMARY KEY(SalesOrderDetailID);
```

3. In the existing query window, type, highlight, and execute the following SQL statements to modify the primary key constraint on the *Test.SalesOrderHeader* table to become a nonclustered index and then create an appropriate clustered index for the query:

```
-- Modify the PK to be a non-clustered index.
ALTER TABLE Test.SalesOrderHeader
    DROP CONSTRAINT PKSalesOrderHeader;

ALTER TABLE Test.SalesOrderHeader
    ADD CONSTRAINT PKSalesOrderHeader
    PRIMARY KEY NONCLUSTERED (SalesOrderID);

-- Create the clustered index.
CREATE CLUSTERED INDEX CluIdx ON Test.SalesOrderHeader
    (TerritoryID, CustomerID);
```

4. In the existing query window, type, highlight, and execute the following SQL statements to modify the primary key constraint on the *Test.SalesOrderDetail* table to become a nonclustered index and then create an appropriate clustered index for the query:

```
-- Modify the PK to be a non-clustered index.
ALTER TABLE Test.SalesOrderDetail
    DROP CONSTRAINT PKSalesOrderDetail;
```

```
ALTER TABLE Test.SalesOrderDetail
    ADD CONSTRAINT PKSalesOrderDetail
    PRIMARY KEY NONCLUSTERED (SalesOrderDetailID);

-- Create the clustered index.
CREATE CLUSTERED INDEX CluIdx ON Test.SalesOrderDetail
    (SalesOrderID);
```

5. Turn on the Actual Execution Plan feature in SSMS by pressing Ctrl+M or by selecting Include Actual Execution Plan from the Query menu.

6. In the existing query window, type, highlight, and execute the following SQL statement to turn on the reporting of page reads:

```
SET STATISTICS IO ON;
```

7. In the existing query window, type, highlight, and execute the following SQL statement:

```
SELECT
    soh.CustomerID
    ,SUM(sod.OrderQty * sod.UnitPrice) AS TotalPurchases
FROM Test.SalesOrderHeader AS soh
INNER JOIN Test.SalesOrderDetail AS sod ON sod.SalesOrderID = soh.SalesOrderID
WHERE soh.TerritoryID = 1
GROUP BY soh.CustomerID;
```

Record the total cost of the query.

Record the total number of page reads for the query.

8. In the existing query window, type, highlight, and execute the following SQL statement to clean up after this exercise:

```
USE master;
DROP DATABASE TestDB;
```

EXERCISE 3   Tune the Query by Using Covered Nonclustered Indexes

In this exercise, you optimize the query by creating covered nonclustered indexes.

1. Open SSMS, if necessary, and connect to the instance of SQL Server 2008 running on your machine.

2. In a new query window, type and execute the following SQL statements to create the *TestDB* database, the *Test* schema, and the two tables that are used in this exercise:

```
CREATE DATABASE TestDB;
GO

USE TestDB;
GO
```

```
CREATE SCHEMA Test;
GO


SELECT * INTO Test.SalesOrderHeader
FROM AdventureWorks.Sales.SalesOrderHeader;
GO


SELECT * INTO Test.SalesOrderDetail
FROM AdventureWorks.Sales.SalesOrderDetail;
GO


ALTER TABLE Test.SalesOrderHeader
    ADD CONSTRAINT PKSalesOrderHeader
    PRIMARY KEY(SalesOrderID);
GO


ALTER TABLE Test.SalesOrderDetail
    ADD CONSTRAINT PKSalesOrderDetail
    PRIMARY KEY(SalesOrderDetailID);
```

3. In the existing query window, type, highlight, and execute the following SQL statement to create the covered nonclustered index that will be used by the query when accessing the *Test.SalesOrderHeader* table:

```
CREATE NONCLUSTERED INDEX TestIndex
    ON Test.SalesOrderHeader (TerritoryID, SalesOrderID)
        INCLUDE (CustomerID);
```

4. In the existing query window, type, highlight, and execute the following SQL statement to create the covered nonclustered index that will be used by the query when accessing the *Test.SalesOrderDetail* table:

```
CREATE NONCLUSTERED INDEX TestIndex
    ON Test.SalesOrderDetail (SalesOrderID)
        INCLUDE (OrderQty, UnitPrice);
```

5. Turn on the Actual Execution Plan feature in SSMS by pressing Ctrl+M or by selecting Include Actual Execution Plan from the Query menu.

6. In the existing query window, type, highlight, and execute the following SQL statement to turn on the reporting of page reads:

```
SET STATISTICS IO ON;
```

7. In the existing query window, type, highlight, and execute the following SQL statement:

```
SELECT
    soh.CustomerID
    ,SUM(sod.OrderQty * sod.UnitPrice) AS TotalPurchases
```

```
FROM Test.SalesOrderHeader AS soh
INNER JOIN Test.SalesOrderDetail AS sod ON sod.SalesOrderID = soh.SalesOrderID
WHERE soh.TerritoryID = 1
GROUP BY soh.CustomerID;
```

Record the total cost of the query.

Record the total number of page reads for the query.

8. In the existing query window, type, highlight, and execute the following SQL statement to clean up after this exercise:

```
USE master;
DROP DATABASE TestDB;
```

EXERCISE 4   Tune the Query by Implementing an Indexed View

In this exercise, you optimize the query by creating an indexed view to cover the query.

1. Open SSMS, if necessary, and connect to the appropriate instance of SQL Server 2008.

2. In a new query window, type and execute the following SQL statements to create the *TestDB* database, the *Test* schema, and the two tables that are used in this exercise:

```
CREATE DATABASE TestDB;
GO


USE TestDB;
GO


CREATE SCHEMA Test;
GO


SELECT * INTO Test.SalesOrderHeader
FROM AdventureWorks.Sales.SalesOrderHeader;
GO


SELECT * INTO Test.SalesOrderDetail
FROM AdventureWorks.Sales.SalesOrderDetail;
GO


ALTER TABLE Test.SalesOrderHeader
    ADD CONSTRAINT PKSalesOrderHeader
    PRIMARY KEY(SalesOrderID);
GO


ALTER TABLE Test.SalesOrderDetail
    ADD CONSTRAINT PKSalesOrderDetail
    PRIMARY KEY(SalesOrderDetailID);
```

3. In the existing query window, type, highlight, and execute the following SQL statement to create the view:

```sql
CREATE VIEW Test.SalesByCustomerVw
WITH SCHEMABINDING
AS
SELECT
    soh.TerritoryID
    ,soh.CustomerID
    ,SUM(sod.OrderQty * sod.UnitPrice) AS TotalPurchases
    ,COUNT_BIG(*) AS NumberOfRows
FROM Test.SalesOrderHeader AS soh
INNER JOIN Test.SalesOrderDetail AS sod
    ON sod.SalesOrderID = soh.SalesOrderID
GROUP BY soh.TerritoryID, soh.CustomerID;
```

4. In the existing query window, type, highlight, and execute the following SQL statement to index the view:

```sql
CREATE UNIQUE CLUSTERED INDEX SalesByCustomerVwIdx
    ON Test.SalesByCustomerVw (TerritoryID, CustomerID);
```

5. Turn on the Actual Execution Plan feature in SSMS by pressing Ctrl+M or by selecting Include Actual Execution Plan from the Query menu.

6. In the existing query window, type, highlight, and execute the following SQL statement to turn on the reporting of page reads:

```sql
SET STATISTICS IO ON;
```

7. In the existing query window, type, highlight, and execute the following SQL statement:

```sql
SELECT
    soh.CustomerID
    ,SUM(sod.OrderQty * sod.UnitPrice) AS TotalPurchases
FROM Test.SalesOrderHeader AS soh
INNER JOIN Test.SalesOrderDetail AS sod ON sod.SalesOrderID = soh.SalesOrderID
WHERE soh.TerritoryID = 1
GROUP BY soh.CustomerID;
```

Verify that the indexed view is used to execute the query by examining the query execution plan. If the indexed view is not used (which would be the case if you are not running the Developer Edition or the Enterprise Edition of SQL Server 2008), instead execute the following query to force the use of the indexed view:

```sql
SELECT CustomerID, TotalPurchases
FROM Test.SalesByCustomerVw WITH(NOEXPAND)
WHERE TerritoryID = 1;
```

Record the total cost of the query.

Record the total number of page reads for the query.

8. In the existing query window, type and execute the following SQL statement to clean up after this exercise:

```
USE master;
DROP DATABASE TestDB;
```

EXERCISE 5 Compare Your Test Results

In this exercise, you compare the results from the earlier exercises.

1. Enter the cost and page read count for each index technique in the following table.

INDEX TECHNIQUE	COST	PAGES
Base line		
Clustered indexes		
Covered nonclustered indexes		
Indexed view		

Which of these techniques provided the lowest (best) cost?

Which of these techniques provided the lowest (best) page count?

Your results should show that the indexed view is the best performing option, followed by the covered nonclustered index, and finally by the clustered index.

Chapter Review

To practice and reinforce the skills you learned in this chapter further, you can do any or all of the following:

- Review the chapter summary.
- Review the list of key terms introduced in this chapter.
- Complete the case scenario. This scenario sets up a real-world situation involving the topics of this chapter and asks you to create solutions.
- Complete the suggested practices.
- Take a practice test.

Chapter Summary

- Always evaluate different ways of implementing costly queries.
- Because indexes take up space (if not disabled) and are maintained for write operations, try to drop unused indexes.
- When measuring query performance, always include the query execution time as a metric; don't just rely on cost and page reads.
- Create covered indexes for the most frequently executed queries.
- Evaluate creating indexed views to cover entire queries or parts of queries.

Key Terms

Do you know what these key terms mean? You can check your answers by looking up the terms in the glossary at the end of the book.

- Cost
- Page
- Index
- Heap
- Clustered index
- Nonclustered index
- Partition function
- Partition scheme

Case Scenario

In the following case scenario, you apply what you have learned about in this chapter. You can find answers to these questions in the "Answers" section at the end of this book.

Case Scenario: Tune Query Performance

In this scenario, you are a database developer in your company. You have been assigned the task of optimizing the database used by the company Web site. Because of heavy user activity on the company Web site, there are two performance problems. First, the user response time for the online chat forums is very poor. The Web site developers have narrowed this problem down to slow response times from the forum stored procedures in the SQL Server instance hosting the forums. You need to optimize these stored procedures. Second, employees in the finance department use database queries from Microsoft Office Excel 2007 to retrieve usage statistics for the Web site. These queries currently take up to 10 minutes to execute, depending on what statistics are being retrieved. The CFO has stated that the execution time for these queries must be reduced to a couple of seconds.

Answer the following question for your manager:

- What steps should you take to solve these problems?

Suggested Practices

To help you master the exam objectives presented in this chapter, do all the following practices:

Create and Alter Indexes

- **Practice 1**   Create a simple table without indexes, insert 1,000,000 rows into the table, and write down the query cost and execution time for the insertion. Add one nonclustered index to the table, truncate the table, reinsert the 1,000,000 rows, and write down the query cost and execution time again. Add a few more nonclustered indexes and review the performance difference of populating the table after each index has been added.

- **Practice 2**   Create a simple table (with a row width of at least 50 bytes) without indexes and insert 1,000,000 rows into the table. Execute queries that retrieve 10, 100, 1,000, 10,000, and 100,000 rows (for example, using a *BETWEEN* filter on an identity column in the table) against the table without indexes and write down the query cost and number of page reads for each query. Create a clustered index on the column being searched, reexecute the queries, and write down the performance metrics again. Do the same thing for a covered and uncovered nonclustered index.

Take a Practice Test

The practice tests on this book's companion CD offer many options. For example, you can test yourself on just one exam objective, or you can test yourself on all the 70-433 certification exam content. You can set up the test so that it closely simulates the experience of taking a certification exam, or you can set it up in study mode so that you can look at the correct answers and explanations after you answer each question.

> **MORE INFO** **PRACTICE TESTS**
>
> For details about all the practice test options available, see the section entitled "How to Use the Practice Tests" in the Introduction to this book.

Extending Microsoft SQL Server Functionality with XML, SQLCLR, and *Filestream*

Microsoft SQL Server 2008 comes loaded with a host of capabilities that widely extend the notion of the typical relational database management system (RDBMS). In this version of the software, support has been added for managing large binary data portions without them being stored inside the database files, while still allowing for transactional consistency and consistent backup and restore operations. Microsoft also made enhancements to SQL Server's support for Extensible Markup Language (XML) data and Common Language Runtime (CLR) code within the database. In this chapter, you learn what you need to get started using these new and enhanced capabilities.

Exam objectives in this chapter:
- Create and deploy CLR-based objects.
- Retrieve relational data as XML.
- Transform XML data into relational data.
- Query XML data.
- Manage XML data.

Lessons in this chapter:

Before You Begin

To complete the lessons in this chapter, you must have:

- A basic understanding of Transact-SQL (T-SQL).
- A basic understanding of XML.

- Microsoft SQL Server 2008 Developer Edition, Enterprise Edition, or Enterprise Evaluation Edition, and the *AdventureWorks* sample database installed.
- It also helps if you have experience developing applications in either C# or Microsoft Visual Basic .NET.

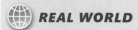 **REAL WORLD**

Tobias Thernström

I once came across a customer who had big problems with a very business-logic-oriented stored procedure. The procedure in question required more than 100 parameters to be passed to it and was a nightmare to call. Some of the parameters were actually lists of values that had to be split into a table variable using a user-defined function (UDF) before being used within the procedure. I suggested replacing all these parameters with a single parameter of the *XML* data type and an XML schema applied to it. They were resistant at first, but after making the change to the procedure, they found it much easier to call from the calling application because it used just one parameter, required fewer "plumbing" changes because everything was passed in the XML parameter, and used less code in the stored procedure. In addition, it executed more quickly because the routines that they used to split the strings into table variables were less efficient than using the *nodes*-method of the *XML* data type.

Lesson 1: Working with XML

XML is a hierarchical text markup language, easily readable by human beings, that is typically used for data exchange within and between systems. Because XML itself is such a big topic, it can't be covered within the scope of this book. A basic understanding of XML is a prerequisite for this lesson.

> **NOTE** **DATABASE**
>
> Unless otherwise stated, all examples shown in this lesson use the *AdventureWorks* sample database for SQL Server 2008.

For reference, a simple example of an XML document containing two customers (denoted by the *<Customer>* tag), each with a few orders (denoted by the *<Order>* tag), is shown here:

```
<?xml version="1.0"?>
<Customers>
  <Customer Id="1" AccountNumber="AW00000001" Type="S">
    <Orders>
        <Order Id="43860" OrderDate="2001-08-01T00:00:00" ShipDate="2001-08-08T00:00:00" />
        <Order Id="44501" OrderDate="2001-11-01T00:00:00" ShipDate="2001-11-08T00:00:00" />
        <Order Id="45283" OrderDate="2002-02-01T00:00:00" ShipDate="2002-02-08T00:00:00" />
        <Order Id="46042" OrderDate="2002-05-01T00:00:00" ShipDate="2002-05-08T00:00:00" />
    </Orders>
  </Customer>
  <Customer Id="2" AccountNumber="AW00000002" Type="S">
    <Orders>
        <Order Id="46976" OrderDate="2002-08-01T00:00:00" ShipDate="2002-08-08T00:00:00" />
        <Order Id="47997" OrderDate="2002-11-01T00:00:00" ShipDate="2002-11-08T00:00:00" />
        <Order Id="49054" OrderDate="2003-02-01T00:00:00" ShipDate="2003-02-08T00:00:00" />
        <Order Id="50216" OrderDate="2003-05-01T00:00:00" ShipDate="2003-05-08T00:00:00" />
        <Order Id="51728" OrderDate="2003-08-01T00:00:00" ShipDate="2003-08-08T00:00:00" />
        <Order Id="57044" OrderDate="2003-11-01T00:00:00" ShipDate="2003-11-08T00:00:00" />
        <Order Id="63198" OrderDate="2004-02-01T00:00:00" ShipDate="2004-02-08T00:00:00" />
        <Order Id="69488" OrderDate="2004-05-01T00:00:00" ShipDate="2004-05-08T00:00:00" />
    </Orders>
  </Customer>
</Customers>
```

As mentioned, the previous code sample is an *XML document*. In this lesson, XML fragments also are discussed. *XML fragments* are similar to XML documents; the difference is that they are not in themselves a document. Sound strange? The thought is just that an XML fragment is supposed to be part of an XML document, that is, it has been taken out of the context of the document. This means that an XML fragment lacks the XML declaration (*<?xml...>*) and does not have to have a root element (such as *<Customers>* in the previous example). Here is an example of an XML fragment:

```
<Order Id="43860" OrderDate="2001-08-01T00:00:00" ShipDate="2001-08-08T00:00:00" />
<Order Id="44501" OrderDate="2001-11-01T00:00:00" ShipDate="2001-11-08T00:00:00" />
<Order Id="45283" OrderDate="2002-02-01T00:00:00" ShipDate="2002-02-08T00:00:00" />
```

Whether or not to use XML within a relational database system is often debated. As with most features, when and where to use it depends on the problem that you are trying to solve. XML can be used for several actions related to a database. The major uses are listed here:

- **Retrieving relational data as XML**   Instead of retrieving a tabular result set from the database, you retrieve an XML document.

- **Passing data as XML to the database**   Instead of passing scalar values to the database by issuing multiple data manipulation language (DML) statements or running a stored procedure multiple times, an XML document or fragment can be passed directly to the database.

- **Storing and querying an actual XML document or fragment in the database**   This is one of the more controversial topics. Why would you store XML directly in a table? There are several reasons, which are covered later in this lesson.

After this lesson, you will be able to:

- Use *FOR XML* to retrieve relational data as XML from SQL Server.
- Use the *XML* data type and its methods to work with XML inside SQL Server.

Estimated lesson time: 60 minutes

Retrieving Tabular Data as XML

To start with, why would you want to retrieve an XML document or fragment from the database instead of a tabular result set? One reason might simply be that the person for whom you are retrieving this data wants it as XML. Another reason might simply be that the data you are fetching lends itself better to being described using XML than using a table. This is true for hierarchical data, like the first example in this chapter with customers and their respective orders. If you think about it, it is probably very common for an application to fetch a hierarchy of data like this. If you can't use XML as the data for the format, you have two other options in SQL Server.

The first option is to execute two separate *SELECT* statements and combine the customers with their respective orders in the client application. Note that you need to include the *CustomerID* in both queries to allow for combining the results in the client:

```
SELECT
    c.CustomerID
    ,c.AccountNumber
    ,c.CustomerType
FROM Sales.Customer AS c
WHERE c.CustomerID IN (1, 2);
```

```
SELECT
    soh.CustomerID
    ,soh.SalesOrderID
    ,soh.OrderDate
    ,soh.ShipDate
FROM Sales.SalesOrderHeader AS soh
WHERE soh.CustomerID IN (1, 2);
```

Here are the results:

```
CustomerID  AccountNumber CustomerType
----------- ------------- ------------
1           AW00000001    S
2           AW00000002    S


CustomerID  SalesOrderID OrderDate               ShipDate
----------- ------------ ----------------------- -----------------------
1           43860        2001-08-01 00:00:00.000 2001-08-08 00:00:00.000
1           44501        2001-11-01 00:00:00.000 2001-11-08 00:00:00.000
1           45283        2002-02-01 00:00:00.000 2002-02-08 00:00:00.000
1           46042        2002-05-01 00:00:00.000 2002-05-08 00:00:00.000
2           46976        2002-08-01 00:00:00.000 2002-08-08 00:00:00.000
2           47997        2002-11-01 00:00:00.000 2002-11-08 00:00:00.000
2           49054        2003-02-01 00:00:00.000 2003-02-08 00:00:00.000
2           50216        2003-05-01 00:00:00.000 2003-05-08 00:00:00.000
2           51728        2003-08-01 00:00:00.000 2003-08-08 00:00:00.000
2           57044        2003-11-01 00:00:00.000 2003-11-08 00:00:00.000
2           63198        2004-02-01 00:00:00.000 2004-02-08 00:00:00.000
2           69488        2004-05-01 00:00:00.000 2004-05-08 00:00:00.000
```

The second option is to execute one *SELECT* and retrieve the desired columns from each table using a join. This option still relies on the client application determining what data belongs to the customer and what data belongs to the order. Of course, this can be made easier by applying appropriate column aliases, but you probably agree that it can be a bit of a mess handling this result in the client application. Two observations are worth nothing about this query. First, you must use a *LEFT OUTER JOIN* to combine the two tables to allow customers without orders to be returned. Second, the *ORDER BY* clause is useful (but not required) to simplify managing the results in the client application because all orders for a specific customer are guaranteed to be returned sequentially. The join query looks like this:

```
SELECT
    c.CustomerID AS Customer_CustomerID
    ,c.AccountNumber AS Customer_AccountNumber
    ,c.CustomerType AS Customer_CustomerType
    ,soh.SalesOrderID AS Order_SalesOrderID
    ,soh.OrderDate AS Order_OrderDate
    ,soh.ShipDate AS Order_ShipDate
FROM Sales.Customer AS c
```

```
LEFT OUTER JOIN Sales.SalesOrderHeader AS soh
    ON soh.CustomerID = c.CustomerID
WHERE c.CustomerID IN (1, 2)
ORDER BY Customer_CustomerID;
```

Here is the result (some columns have been omitted to save space):

```
Customer_CustomerID Customer_AccountNumber Order_SalesOrderID
------------------- ---------------------- ------------------
1                   AW00000001             43860
1                   AW00000001             44501
1                   AW00000001             45283
1                   AW00000001             46042
2                   AW00000002             46976
2                   AW00000002             47997
2                   AW00000002             49054
2                   AW00000002             50216
2                   AW00000002             51728
2                   AW00000002             57044
2                   AW00000002             63198
2                   AW00000002             69488
```

Both of the previous tabular solutions create a fair amount of work for the client application.

So why would the XML solution be desirable? Because the result that you want from the database is a hierarchy (customers having orders); therefore, retrieving the result as XML, which is hierarchical by definition, can simplify matters for the application.

For reference, look at the *SELECT* statement shown here, which returns an XML result. You examine this query in detail later in this lesson:

```
SELECT
    c.CustomerID AS "@Id"
    ,c.AccountNumber AS "@AccountNumber"
    ,c.CustomerType AS "@Type"
    ,(
        SELECT
            soh.SalesOrderID AS "@Id"
            ,soh.OrderDate AS "@OrderDate"
            ,soh.ShipDate AS "@ShipDate"
        FROM Sales.SalesOrderHeader AS soh
        WHERE soh.CustomerID = c.CustomerID
        FOR XML PATH('Order'), TYPE
    ) AS "Orders"
FROM Sales.Customer AS c
WHERE c.CustomerID IN (1, 2)
FOR XML PATH('Customer'), ROOT('Customers');
```

Here is the result:

```
<Customers>
  <Customer Id="1" AccountNumber="AW00000001" Type="S">
   <Orders>
      <Order Id="43860" OrderDate="2001-08-01T00:00:00" ShipDate="2001-08-08T00:00:00" />
      <Order Id="44501" OrderDate="2001-11-01T00:00:00" ShipDate="2001-11-08T00:00:00" />
      <Order Id="45283" OrderDate="2002-02-01T00:00:00" ShipDate="2002-02-08T00:00:00" />
      <Order Id="46042" OrderDate="2002-05-01T00:00:00" ShipDate="2002-05-08T00:00:00" />
    </Orders>
  </Customer>
  <Customer Id="2" AccountNumber="AW00000002" Type="S">
   <Orders>
      <Order Id="46976" OrderDate="2002-08-01T00:00:00" ShipDate="2002-08-08T00:00:00" />
      <Order Id="47997" OrderDate="2002-11-01T00:00:00" ShipDate="2002-11-08T00:00:00" />
      <Order Id="49054" OrderDate="2003-02-01T00:00:00" ShipDate="2003-02-08T00:00:00" />
      <Order Id="50216" OrderDate="2003-05-01T00:00:00" ShipDate="2003-05-08T00:00:00" />
      <Order Id="51728" OrderDate="2003-08-01T00:00:00" ShipDate="2003-08-08T00:00:00" />
      <Order Id="57044" OrderDate="2003-11-01T00:00:00" ShipDate="2003-11-08T00:00:00" />
      <Order Id="63198" OrderDate="2004-02-01T00:00:00" ShipDate="2004-02-08T00:00:00" />
      <Order Id="69488" OrderDate="2004-05-01T00:00:00" ShipDate="2004-05-08T00:00:00" />
    </Orders>
  </Customer>
</Customers>
```

Now let's take a quick look at how you can execute this query from a .NET application, retrieve the XML into memory, and easily loop through the customers and their respective orders. For simplicity, a console application is used in the example:

```vb
'VB:
Imports System
Imports System.Xml
Imports System.Data.SqlClient


Module TK433
Sub Main()
    Using conn As SqlConnection = New SqlConnection( _
        "server=.;database=AdventureWorks;trusted_connection=yes")
        Dim cmd As SqlCommand = conn.CreateCommand()
        cmd.CommandText = _
        "SELECT " & vbCrLf & _
        "    c.CustomerID AS ""@Id""" & vbCrLf & _
        "    ,c.AccountNumber AS ""@AccountNumber""" & vbCrLf & _
        "    ,c.CustomerType AS ""@Type""" & vbCrLf & _
        "    ,(" & vbCrLf & _
        "        SELECT" & vbCrLf & _
        "            soh.SalesOrderID AS ""@Id""" & vbCrLf & _
```

```
"                    ,soh.OrderDate AS ""@OrderDate""" & vbCrLf & _
"                    ,soh.ShipDate AS ""@ShipDate""" & vbCrLf & _
"           FROM Sales.SalesOrderHeader AS soh" & vbCrLf & _
"          WHERE(soh.CustomerID = c.CustomerID)" & vbCrLf & _
"           FOR XML PATH('Order'), TYPE" & vbCrLf & _
"        ) AS Orders" & vbCrLf & _
"      FROM Sales.Customer AS c" & vbCrLf & _
"WHERE c.CustomerID IN (1, 2)" & vbCrLf & _
"FOR XML PATH('Customer'), ROOT('Customers')"

        conn.Open()

        ' Execute the query using an XML reader.
        Dim reader As XmlReader = cmd.ExecuteXmlReader()

        ' Use the XML reader to populate an XML document.
        Dim doc As XmlDocument = New XmlDocument()
        doc.Load(reader)

        ' Loop through the customers.
        For Each customer As XmlElement In doc.SelectNodes("/Customers/Customer")
            Console.WriteLine("Customer: {0}", customer.Attributes("Id").Value)
            For Each order As XmlElement In customer.SelectNodes("Orders/Order")
                Console.WriteLine(vbTab & "Order: {0}", order.Attributes("Id").Value)
            Next
        Next
    End Using
    Console.WriteLine("Press [ENTER] to exit...")
    Console.ReadLine()
End Sub
End Module

//C#:
using System;
using System.Xml;
using System.Data.SqlClient;

class TK433Demo
{
    static void Main()
    {
        using (SqlConnection conn = new SqlConnection(
            "server=.;database=AdventureWorks;trusted_connection=yes;"))
        {
            SqlCommand cmd = conn.CreateCommand();
            cmd.CommandText = @"
```

```
            SELECT
                c.CustomerID AS ""@Id""
                ,c.AccountNumber AS ""@AccountNumber""
                ,c.CustomerType AS ""@Type""
                ,(
                    SELECT
                        soh.SalesOrderID AS ""@Id""
                        ,soh.OrderDate AS ""@OrderDate""
                        ,soh.ShipDate AS ""@ShipDate""
                    FROM Sales.SalesOrderHeader AS soh
                    WHERE soh.CustomerID = c.CustomerID
                    FOR XML PATH('Order'), TYPE
                ) AS Orders
            FROM Sales.Customer AS c
            WHERE c.CustomerID IN (1, 2)
            FOR XML PATH('Customer'), ROOT('Customers');";
            conn.Open();

            // Execute the query using an XML reader to retrieve the results.
            XmlReader reader = cmd.ExecuteXmlReader();

            // Use the XML reader to populate an XML document.
            XmlDocument doc = new XmlDocument();
            doc.Load(reader);

            // Loop through the customers.
            foreach (XmlElement customer in doc.SelectNodes("/Customers/Customer"))
            {
                Console.WriteLine("Customer: {0}", customer.Attributes["Id"].Value);
                foreach (XmlElement order in customer.SelectNodes("Orders/Order"))
                {
                    Console.WriteLine("\tOrder: {0}", order.Attributes["Id"].Value);
                }
            }
        }
        Console.WriteLine("Press [ENTER] to exit...");
        Console.ReadLine();
    }
}
```

The simplicity can be seen specifically in the following code, which loops through the customers and orders:

'VB:
```
For Each customer As XmlElement In doc.SelectNodes("/Customers/Customer")
    Console.WriteLine("Customer: {0}", customer.Attributes("Id").Value)
    For Each order As XmlElement In customer.SelectNodes("Orders/Order")
```

```
        Console.WriteLine(vbTab & "Order: {0}", order.Attributes("Id").Value)
    Next
Next

//C#:
foreach (XmlElement customer in doc.SelectNodes("/Customers/Customer"))
{
    Console.WriteLine("Customer: {0}", customer.Attributes["Id"].Value);
    foreach (XmlElement order in customer.SelectNodes("Orders/Order"))
    {
        Console.WriteLine("\tOrder: {0}", order.Attributes["Id"].Value);
    }
}
```

As you can see, because XML is hierarchical in nature, you don't need to keep track of which customer or order you are currently iterating over. Instead, this is managed by the hierarchy in your XML document.

FOR XML *<mode>*

As you saw in the previous example, an additional clause, *FOR XML*, is added to the end of the *SELECT* statement to produce an XML result. In SQL Server 2008, there are four flavors (or modes) of the *FOR XML* clause: *RAW, AUTO, EXPLICIT*, and *PATH*. In the previous example, the *PATH* mode is used. This is both the recommended mode and the most powerful mode. For completeness, and because you might run into them, this chapter covers the other three variations as well. Because it is the simplest one, we start with the *RAW* mode.

FOR XML RAW

The *SELECT...FOR XML RAW* statement is the simplest implementation of *FOR XML*, but it can still be useful. Consider the query shown here:

```
SELECT
    c.CustomerID
    ,c.AccountNumber
FROM Sales.Customer AS c
WHERE c.CustomerID IN (1,2)
FOR XML RAW;
```

You can see from the results shown here that in its default usage (just specifying *FOR XML RAW*), the *FOR XML RAW* query basically returns each row as an XML element and each column as an XML attribute (*<row Column1="…" Column2="…" />*):

```
<row CustomerID="1" AccountNumber="AW00000001" />
<row CustomerID="2" AccountNumber="AW00000002" />
```

Some enhancements were made in SQL Server 2005 to allow you to add and name a root element, as well as name the elements created for each row. An example of this is shown in the next block of code that uses the *ROOT* directive, as well as adds a parameter to the *RAW* mode specifying the element name (the changes are shown in bold type). Also note that by changing the name of the column by using an alias, you are also changing the attribute's name (this was also supported in SQL Server 2000):

```
SELECT
    c.CustomerID AS Id
    ,c.AccountNumber
FROM Sales.Customer AS c
WHERE c.CustomerID IN (1,2)
FOR XML RAW('Customer'), ROOT('Customers');
```

Here is the result:

```
<Customers>
  <Customer Id="1" AccountNumber="AW00000001" />
  <Customer Id="2" AccountNumber="AW00000002" />
</Customers>
```

A question you might ask yourself is how *NULLs* are handled in XML results. The default implementation is to simply remove the attribute if the value is *NULL*. This is good for most applications, but some applications might differentiate between a missing value and *NULL*. How can they be differentiated? Consider the following example:

A customer's XML element describes a customer in the database that needs to be updated. The customer has 10 attributes that can possibly exist in the XML element, but only 2 of them exist in this particular XML element. When passing this XML element to the database to perform an update of the customer, the database can take one of two actions:

- Update all 10 attributes, setting 8 of them to *NULL* because they are missing and 2 of them to their new values.
- Update only the 2 attributes that exist in the XML element being passed to the database and skip the remaining 8, letting them keep their current values.

If you choose the second option, just leaving the attributes out of the XML element if they are actually *NULL* won't work. You must somehow define explicitly that they are actually *NULL* (or should be set to *NULL*). This is supported through an element in XML called *NIL*. *NIL* in XML is equal to what the database refers to as *NULL*. If a value should be defined as *NIL*, it cannot be stored in an attribute. Rather, it must be stored as its own element because it needs an attribute that defines it as *NIL* if necessary. Look at the following example, where the first element representing a product has *Color* set to *NULL*. The previously used *FOR XML RAW* query was used as a reference. Note that the *Color* attribute is missing for the first product:

```
SELECT
    p.ProductID AS Id
    ,p.ListPrice
    ,p.Color
FROM Production.Product AS p
WHERE p.ProductID IN (514, 707)
FOR XML RAW('Product'), ROOT('Products');
```

The query returns this result:

```
<Products>
  <Product Id="514" ListPrice="133.3400" />
  <Product Id="707" ListPrice="34.9900" Color="Red" />
</Products>
```

Now consider the next example, where you add the *ELEMENTS* directive to make each column an XML element instead of an attribute. Note that the *Color* element is still missing for the first product:

```
SELECT
    p.ProductID AS Id
    ,p.ListPrice
    ,p.Color
FROM Production.Product AS p
WHERE p.ProductID IN (514, 707)
FOR XML RAW('Product'), ROOT('Products'), ELEMENTS;
```

Here is the result:

```
<Products>
  <Product>
    <Id>514</Id>
    <ListPrice>133.3400</ListPrice>
  </Product>
  <Product>
    <Id>707</Id>
    <ListPrice>34.9900</ListPrice>
    <Color>Red</Color>
  </Product>
</Products>
```

Finally, you add the *XSINIL* directive to the *ELEMENTS* directive to tell SQL Server to handle *NULL*s by keeping the XML element for the missing value and setting its *NIL* attribute to *True*. In this case, you can see that *Color* is actually *NULL* (or *NIL*) and not just "missing":

```
SELECT
    p.ProductID AS Id
    ,p.ListPrice
    ,p.Color
FROM Production.Product AS p
WHERE p.ProductID IN (514, 707)
FOR XML RAW('Product'), ROOT('Products'), ELEMENTS XSINIL;
```

Here is the result, with the *NULL* color shown in bold type:

```
<Products xmlns:xsi="http://www.w3.org/2001/XMLSchema-instance">
  <Product>
    <Id>514</Id>
```

```
   <ListPrice>133.3400</ListPrice>
   <Color xsi:nil="true" />
 </Product>
 <Product>
   <Id>707</Id>
   <ListPrice>34.9900</ListPrice>
   <Color>Red</Color>
 </Product>
</Products>
```

In the last example, you can also see that an XML namespace reference called *xsi* that references *http://www.w3.org/2001/XMLSchema-instance* has been added to the root element. This is because the *NIL* attribute is defined in this namespace. The namespace reference is always added if you use the *XSINIL* directive. Before moving on to the next *FOR XML* mode, *AUTO*, you should know that both the *ELEMENTS* and *XSINIL* directives exist for the *AUTO* mode but not for the two other modes, *EXPLICIT* and *PATH*.

FOR XML AUTO

The *AUTO* mode differs from *RAW* in that it natively supports hierarchies. However, the hierarchies have to be simple because *AUTO* doesn't support more than one path of branches. For example, the following hierarchy works:

Customer

　Order

　　Order row

But the following does not work because it has multiple paths:

Customer

　Order

　　Order row

　Contacts

In *AUTO* mode, each table included in the query gets its own element in the hierarchy and the name of the element is derived from the table alias used in the query. The hierarchy is created from the order of the columns returned by the query, not the order of the tables. Look at the query in the next example that returns customers with orders using *FOR XML AUTO*. Note that the join is performed from order to customer, but the customer is still above the order in the hierarchy. This is because the customer columns are listed before the order columns in the column list of the *SELECT* clause. Also note that each customer element is repeated a few times in the XML result. This is because the hierarchy is also built from the order of the rows in the result. That means you must make sure that the *ORDER BY* clause is used correctly to group each order under its customer (in this example, you sort the rows by a unique identifier/GUID column in the table to get a random-looking sorting):

```
SELECT
    Customer.CustomerID AS Id
    ,Customer.AccountNumber
    ,"Order".SalesOrderID
    ,"Order".rowguid AS RowGuid
FROM Sales.SalesOrderHeader AS "Order"
RIGHT OUTER JOIN Sales.Customer AS Customer ON Customer.CustomerID = "Order".CustomerID
WHERE Customer.CustomerID IN (1,2)
ORDER BY "Order".rowguid
FOR XML AUTO, ROOT('Customers');
```

Here is the XML result:

```
<Customers>
  <Customer Id="2" AccountNumber="AW00000002">
    <Order SalesOrderID="49054" RowGuid="01C5EFDE-5C6E-47C9-B1AE-077937989297" />
    <Order SalesOrderID="51728" RowGuid="C2B5D4CC-113E-4102-884B-22A6DACEEDE6" />
  </Customer>
  <Customer Id="1" AccountNumber="AW00000001">
    <Order SalesOrderID="46042" RowGuid="62991BDA-C42D-494F-9EF1-2754BEC25FAE" />
    <Order SalesOrderID="43860" RowGuid="D2745233-B05B-409C-93BB-4451569F4253" />
    <Order SalesOrderID="44501" RowGuid="1A116F86-71E4-40A2-A32C-4938D8977D26" />
  </Customer>
  <Customer Id="2" AccountNumber="AW00000002">
    <Order SalesOrderID="63198" RowGuid="C6C5306D-F416-433C-92CC-4DB4747DC133" />
    <Order SalesOrderID="46976" RowGuid="8A533BE6-0669-470A-B361-796DD1CD0ED4" />
  </Customer>
  <Customer Id="1" AccountNumber="AW00000001">
    <Order SalesOrderID="45283" RowGuid="F57AB920-675E-4B1D-B43C-8EA091CF6F38" />
  </Customer>
  <Customer Id="2" AccountNumber="AW00000002">
    <Order SalesOrderID="47997" RowGuid="1FAAD98B-1DE0-4B80-A804-9FBBB6F289EB" />
    <Order SalesOrderID="69488" RowGuid="50144563-A6B4-4857-9451-B229D21C7ED5" />
    <Order SalesOrderID="50216" RowGuid="00A755D8-7BD9-4B12-AF58-E4EF22D39AA1" />
    <Order SalesOrderID="57044" RowGuid="1841BF49-544C-4A8F-8ACE-F63DADA00314" />
  </Customer>
</Customers>
```

Here is the tabular result (created by omitting the *FOR XML* part of the query):

```
Id           AccountNumber SalesOrderID RowGuid
-----------  ------------- ------------ ------------------------------------
2            AW00000002    49054        01C5EFDE-5C6E-47C9-B1AE-077937989297
2            AW00000002    51728        C2B5D4CC-113E-4102-884B-22A6DACEEDE6
1            AW00000001    46042        62991BDA-C42D-494F-9EF1-2754BEC25FAE
1            AW00000001    43860        D2745233-B05B-409C-93BB-4451569F4253
```

1	AW00000001	44501	1A116F86-71E4-40A2-A32C-4938D8977D26
2	AW00000002	63198	C6C5306D-F416-433C-92CC-4DB4747DC133
2	AW00000002	46976	8A533BE6-0669-470A-B361-796DD1CD0ED4
1	AW00000001	45283	F57AB920-675E-4B1D-B43C-8EA091CF6F38
2	AW00000002	47997	1FAAD98B-1DE0-4B80-A804-9FBBB6F289EB
2	AW00000002	69488	50144563-A6B4-4857-9451-B229D21C7ED5
2	AW00000002	50216	00A755D8-7BD9-4B12-AF58-E4EF22D39AA1
2	AW00000002	57044	1841BF49-544C-4A8F-8ACE-F63DADA00314

To fix the problem shown in the previous example, you obviously just need to sort the result correctly. This might sound simple, but it is a really insidious, easy-to-miss bug that can sneak into your code if you're not careful. In the next example, you solve the problem by sorting by *CustomerID* to group all orders together that belong to a specific customer. Here, a little trick using a derived table called *Orders* to create an XML element between the *Customer* and *Order* elements is employed:

```
SELECT
    Customer.CustomerID AS Id
    ,Customer.AccountNumber
    ,Orders.X
    ,"Order".SalesOrderID
    ,"Order".rowguid AS RowGuid
FROM Sales.SalesOrderHeader AS "Order"
RIGHT OUTER JOIN Sales.Customer AS Customer ON Customer.CustomerID = "Order".CustomerID
CROSS JOIN (SELECT NULL AS X) AS Orders
WHERE Customer.CustomerID IN (1,2)
ORDER BY Customer.CustomerID
FOR XML AUTO, ROOT('Customers');
```

Here is the XML result:

```
<Customers>
  <Customer Id="1" AccountNumber="AW00000001">
    <Orders>
      <Order SalesOrderID="43860" RowGuid="D2745233-B05B-409C-93BB-4451569F4253" />
      <Order SalesOrderID="44501" RowGuid="1A116F86-71E4-40A2-A32C-4938D8977D26" />
      <Order SalesOrderID="45283" RowGuid="F57AB920-675E-4B1D-B43C-8EA091CF6F38" />
      <Order SalesOrderID="46042" RowGuid="62991BDA-C42D-494F-9EF1-2754BEC25FAE" />
    </Orders>
  </Customer>
  <Customer Id="2" AccountNumber="AW00000002">
    <Orders>
      <Order SalesOrderID="46976" RowGuid="8A533BE6-0669-470A-B361-796DD1CD0ED4" />
      <Order SalesOrderID="47997" RowGuid="1FAAD98B-1DE0-4B80-A804-9FBBB6F289EB" />
      <Order SalesOrderID="49054" RowGuid="01C5EFDE-5C6E-47C9-B1AE-077937989297" />
      <Order SalesOrderID="50216" RowGuid="00A755D8-7BD9-4B12-AF58-E4EF22D39AA1" />
      <Order SalesOrderID="51728" RowGuid="C2B5D4CC-113E-4102-884B-22A6DACEEDE6" />
      <Order SalesOrderID="57044" RowGuid="1841BF49-544C-4A8F-8ACE-F63DADA00314" />
```

```
            <Order SalesOrderID="63198" RowGuid="C6C5306D-F416-433C-92CC-4DB4747DC133" />
            <Order SalesOrderID="69488" RowGuid="50144563-A6B4-4857-9451-B229D21C7ED5" />
        </Orders>
      </Customer>
</Customers>
```

Here is the tabular result (created by omitting the *FOR XML* part of the query):

```
Id          AccountNumber X           SalesOrderID RowGuid
----------- ------------- ----------- ------------ -----------------------------------
1           AW00000001    NULL        43860        D2745233-B05B-409C-93BB-4451569F4253
1           AW00000001    NULL        44501        1A116F86-71E4-40A2-A32C-4938D8977D26
1           AW00000001    NULL        45283        F57AB920-675E-4B1D-B43C-8EA091CF6F38
1           AW00000001    NULL        46042        62991BDA-C42D-494F-9EF1-2754BEC25FAE
2           AW00000002    NULL        46976        8A533BE6-0669-470A-B361-796DD1CD0ED4
2           AW00000002    NULL        47997        1FAAD98B-1DE0-4B80-A804-9FBBB6F289EB
2           AW00000002    NULL        49054        01C5EFDE-5C6E-47C9-B1AE-077937989297
2           AW00000002    NULL        50216        00A755D8-7BD9-4B12-AF58-E4EF22D39AA1
2           AW00000002    NULL        51728        C2B5D4CC-113E-4102-884B-22A6DACEEDE6
2           AW00000002    NULL        57044        1841BF49-544C-4A8F-8ACE-F63DADA00314
2           AW00000002    NULL        63198        C6C5306D-F416-433C-92CC-4DB4747DC133
2           AW00000002    NULL        69488        50144563-A6B4-4857-9451-B229D21C7ED5
```

FOR XML EXPLICIT

The third *FOR XML* mode is *EXPLICIT,* which is awkward to write and even more awkward to maintain. The interesting fact about the *EXPLICIT* mode is that you can create virtually any XML structure, even some not supported by the *PATH* mode that you learn about later in this lesson. In essence, to create an XML document using *FOR XML EXPLICIT,* you must return a specific result set; that is, you must name your columns in a specific way. Much like the *AUTO* mode, you must also sort the results appropriately to reach the desired result. The *EXPLCIIT* mode result set must contain two columns called *Tag* and *Parent.* In the *Tag* column, you add an integer identifier for each XML element that you want to return, and in the *Parent* column, you specify the *Tag* identifier of the XML element that is the element's parent. If the element doesn't have a parent, you specify *NULL* in the *Parent* column. The rest of the columns in the result set are used to define both the names and values of the elements and attributes that should be returned. The following example shows how you can create the customer and order example using *EXPLICIT* mode:

```
SELECT
    1 AS Tag
    ,NULL AS Parent
    ,NULL AS "Customers!1!!element"
    ,NULL AS "Customer!2!Id"
    ,NULL AS "Customer!2!AccountNumber"
    ,NULL AS "Order!3!Id"
    ,NULL AS "Order!3!OrderDate"
UNION ALL
```

```
SELECT
    2 AS Tag
    ,1 AS Parent
    ,NULL AS "Customers!1!!element"
    ,c.CustomerID AS "Customer!2!Id"
    ,c.AccountNumber AS "Customer!2!AccountNumber"
    ,NULL AS "Order!3!Id"
    ,NULL AS "Order!3!OrderDate"
FROM Sales.Customer AS c
WHERE c.CustomerID IN (1,2)
UNION ALL
SELECT
    3 AS Tag
    ,2 AS Parent
    ,NULL AS "Customers!1!!element"
    ,soh.CustomerID AS "Customer!2!Id"
    ,NULL AS "Customer!2!AccountNumber"
    ,soh.SalesOrderID AS "Order!3!Id"
    ,soh.OrderDate AS "Order!3!OrderDate"
FROM Sales.SalesOrderHeader AS soh
WHERE soh.CustomerID IN (1,2)
ORDER BY "Customer!2!Id", Tag
FOR XML EXPLICIT;
```

Here is the result:

```
<Customers>
  <Customer Id="1" AccountNumber="AW00000001">
    <Order Id="43860" OrderDate="2001-08-01T00:00:00" />
    <Order Id="44501" OrderDate="2001-11-01T00:00:00" />
    <Order Id="45283" OrderDate="2002-02-01T00:00:00" />
    <Order Id="46042" OrderDate="2002-05-01T00:00:00" />
  </Customer>
  <Customer Id="2" AccountNumber="AW00000002">
    <Order Id="46976" OrderDate="2002-08-01T00:00:00" />
    <Order Id="47997" OrderDate="2002-11-01T00:00:00" />
    <Order Id="49054" OrderDate="2003-02-01T00:00:00" />
    <Order Id="50216" OrderDate="2003-05-01T00:00:00" />
    <Order Id="51728" OrderDate="2003-08-01T00:00:00" />
    <Order Id="57044" OrderDate="2003-11-01T00:00:00" />
    <Order Id="63198" OrderDate="2004-02-01T00:00:00" />
    <Order Id="69488" OrderDate="2004-05-01T00:00:00" />
  </Customer>
</Customers>
```

FOR XML PATH

FOR XML PATH mode is the best choice of the different *FOR XML* modes for most solutions. *PATH* mode allows for the easy creation of different XML structures by simply interpreting column names specified using an XPath-like expression when generating the XML result. Consider the following query:

```
SELECT
    c.CustomerID AS "@Id"
    ,c.AccountNumber AS "@AccountNumber"
    ,c.RowGuid AS "comment()"
    ,CAST('<Test/>' AS XML) AS "node()"
    ,c.CustomerType AS "AdditionalInfo/@Type"
    ,c.ModifiedDate AS "AdditionalInfo/text()"
    ,c.rowguid AS "node()"
FROM Sales.Customer AS c
WHERE c.CustomerID IN (1, 2)
FOR XML PATH('Customer'), ROOT('Customers');
```

Here is the result:

```
<Customers>
  <Customer Id="1" AccountNumber="AW00000001">
    <!--3F5AE95E-B87D-4AED-95B4-C3797AFCB74F-->
    <Test />
    <AdditionalInfo Type="S">2004-10-13T11:15:07.263</AdditionalInfo>
  </Customer>
  <Customer Id="2" AccountNumber="AW00000002">
    <!--E552F657-A9AF-4A7D-A645-C429D6E02491-->
    <Test />
    <AdditionalInfo Type="S">2004-10-13T11:15:07.263</AdditionalInfo>
  </Customer>
</Customers>
```

In the XML result, you can see the following:

- The *@Id* column resulted in the attribute *Id* in the *Customer* element.

- The *@AccountNumber* column resulted in the attribute *AccountNumber* in the *Customer* element.

- The *comment()* column resulted in the value of the *RowGuid* column being returned as an XML comment.

- The *node()* column resulted in the XML constant in the query being placed directly into the XML result without ending up in a subelement.

- The *AdditionalInfo/@Type* column resulted in the attribute *Type* in the subelement *AdditionalInfo*.

- The *AdditionalInfo/text()* column resulted in the text of the subelement *AdditionalInfo* being set.

This mode is far more powerful than both the *RAW* and *AUTO* modes because it allows you to add both attributes and subelements to the output, as well as including other types of XML constructs. The *PATH* mode is also far simpler to use and easier to read than a query that uses *EXPLICIT* mode.

Nesting *FOR XML* Queries

All *FOR XML* mode queries can be nested to produce a hierarchy. This means that you can place a *FOR XML* query as a subquery in another *FOR XML* query to produce a complete XML document:

Consider the following query and result:

```
SELECT
    c.CustomerID AS "@Id"
    ,c.AccountNumber AS "@AccountNumber"
    ,c.CustomerType AS "@Type"
    ,(
        SELECT TOP(2) -- Included to limit the size of the XML result.
            soh.SalesOrderID AS "@Id"
            ,soh.OrderDate AS "@OrderDate"
            ,soh.ShipDate AS "@ShipDate"
            ,(
                SELECT TOP(2) -- Included to limit the size of the XML result.
                    sod.ProductID AS "@ProductId"
                    ,sod.OrderQty AS "@Quantity"
                FROM Sales.SalesOrderDetail AS sod
                WHERE sod.SalesOrderID = soh.SalesOrderID
                FOR XML PATH('OrderDetail'), TYPE
            )
        FROM Sales.SalesOrderHeader AS soh
        WHERE soh.CustomerID = c.CustomerID
        FOR XML PATH('Order'), TYPE
    ) AS "Orders"
FROM Sales.Customer AS c
WHERE c.CustomerID = 1
FOR XML PATH('Customer');
```

Here is the result:

```
<Customer Id="1" AccountNumber="AW00000001" Type="S">
  <Orders>
    <Order Id="43860" OrderDate="2001-08-01T00:00:00" ShipDate="2001-08-08T00:00:00">
      <OrderDetail ProductId="761" Quantity="2" />
      <OrderDetail ProductId="770" Quantity="1" />
    </Order>
```

```
  <Order Id="44501" OrderDate="2001-11-01T00:00:00" ShipDate="2001-11-08T00:00:00">
    <OrderDetail ProductId="761" Quantity="1" />
    <OrderDetail ProductId="768" Quantity="3" />
  </Order>
 </Orders>
</Customer>
```

Note that the *TYPE* option is required in each subquery. Without the *TYPE* option, SQL Server interprets the result of the subquery as an XML-encoded string. The following XML would be returned if the *TYPE* option were removed from the subqueries in the previous example:

```
<Customer Id="1" AccountNumber="AW00000001" Type="S">
  <Orders>
    &lt;Order Id="43860" OrderDate="2001-08-01T00:00:00" ShipDate="2001-08-08T00:
00:00"&gt;&amp;lt;OrderDetail ProductId="761" Quantity="2"/&amp;gt;&amp;lt;OrderD
etail ProductId="770" Quantity="1"/&amp;gt;&lt;/Order&gt;&lt;Order Id="44501" Ord
erDate="2001-11-01T00:00:00" ShipDate="2001-11-08T00:00:00"&gt;&amp;lt;OrderDetail
ProductId="761" Quantity="1"/&amp;gt;&amp;lt;OrderDetail ProductId="768" Quantity=
"3"/&amp;gt;&lt;/Order&gt;
  </Orders>
</Customer>
```

Finally, it is possible to add an XML namespace to the result by including the *WITH XMLNAMESPACES* clause in the query. In the following example, the namespace *http://www.contoso.com/CustomerSchema* is added as the default namespace for the XML document, and the namespace *http://www.contoso.com/CustomerSchemaV2* is added under the alias *v2* (the *AdditionalInfo* subelement is the only element that uses the *v2* alias):

```
WITH XMLNAMESPACES(
    DEFAULT 'http://www.contoso.com/CustomerSchema'
    ,'http://www.contoso.com/CustomerSchemaV2' AS v2
)
SELECT
    c.CustomerID AS "@Id"
    ,c.AccountNumber AS "@AccountNumber"
    ,c.CustomerType AS "@Type"
    ,c.ModifiedDate AS "v2:AdditionalInfo/@ModifiedDate"
FROM Sales.Customer AS c
WHERE c.CustomerID IN (1, 2)
FOR XML PATH('Customer'), ROOT('Customers');
```

Here is the result:

```
<Customers xmlns:v2="http://www.contoso.com/CustomerSchemaV2"
           xmlns="http://www.contoso.com/CustomerSchema">
  <Customer Id="1" AccountNumber="AW00000001" Type="S">
    <v2:AdditionalInfo ModifiedDate="2004-10-13T11:15:07.263" />
  </Customer>
```

```
    <Customer Id="2" AccountNumber="AW00000002" Type="S">
      <v2:AdditionalInfo ModifiedDate="2004-10-13T11:15:07.263" />
    </Customer>
</Customers>
```

Using the *XML* Data Type

SQL Server 2008 includes the *XML* data type, which can be used to store both XML fragments and documents. Internally, the *XML* data type is stored using the *varbinary(max)* data type; that is, the XML is not stored as a text string but rather as a binary representation of an XML document or fragment.

The *XML* data type can be either typed or untyped. *Typed* simply means that an XML schema collection is assigned to the type to verify its contents.

The following example shows the creation of an XML schema collection and a table with both untyped and typed XML columns. Note that the typed XML column includes the use of the *DOCUMENT* option to force the column to support only XML documents (and not fragments).

```
CREATE XML SCHEMA COLLECTION BooksSchemaCollection
AS
N'<?xml version="1.0"?>
<xs:schema xmlns:xs="http://www.w3.org/2001/XMLSchema"
    targetNamespace="http://www.contoso.com/BooksSchema"
    xmlns="http://www.contoso.com/BooksSchema"
    elementFormDefault="qualified">
    <xs:element name="Book">
        <xs:complexType>
          <xs:attribute name="Title" type="xs:string"/>
          <xs:attribute name="Price" type="xs:decimal"/>
        </xs:complexType>
    </xs:element>
</xs:schema>';
GO

CREATE TABLE Test.Person
(
    PersonID INT IDENTITY PRIMARY KEY
    ,Name NVARCHAR(50) NOT NULL
    ,FavoriteBookUntypedXml XML NULL
    ,FavoriteBookTypedXml XML(DOCUMENT BooksSchemaCollection) NULL
);
```

Now let's look at the following DML statements. Note that updating a typed column with invalid data (in this case, a book with an invalid price of *FortyFive* instead of *45*) receives an XML validation error message, but the same invalid data is allowed in the untyped XML column:

```
INSERT Test.Person (Name) VALUES ('Jane Dow');

-- Will succeed:
UPDATE Test.Person SET
    FavoriteBookUntypedXml =
        '<Book xmlns="http://www.contoso.com/BooksSchema"
            Title="The Best Book" Price="FortyFive"/>'
WHERE PersonID = 1;

-- Will not succeed:
UPDATE Test.Person SET
    FavoriteBookTypedXml =
        '<Book xmlns="http://www.contoso.com/BooksSchema"
            Title="The Best Book" Price="FortyFive"/>'
WHERE PersonID = 1;

-- Will succeed:
UPDATE Test.Person SET
    FavoriteBookTypedXml =
        '<Book xmlns="http://www.contoso.com/BooksSchema"
            Title="The BestBook" Price="45"/>'
WHERE PersonID = 1;
```

Here are the results:

```
(1 row(s) affected)

(1 row(s) affected)

Msg 6926, Level 16, State 1, Line 3
XML Validation: Invalid simple type value: 'FortyFive'. Location: /*:Book[1]/@*:Price

(1 row(s) affected)
```

One last important note is that there is a problem with using typed XML columns, and that is the fact that the data structure might change. If you need to change the schema (such as by adding more attributes to an element), you must first alter all columns that uses the schema to instead use untyped XML. Then, you must drop the schema collection, re-create it with the added attributes, and finally alter the columns again to use the schema. The problem isn't just that it's a lot of work to create the scripts to perform this change (though that's bad enough). It also creates a lot of work for SQL Server because untyped and typed XML code have different structures internally (for example, all data in untyped XML is stored as strings, whereas in typed XML, the data is stored using the actual data type selected in the schema) and SQL Server must then convert all data from typed to untyped and then back again each time you want to change the XML schema.

Here is an example that removes the schema from the column and then reattaches it:

```
ALTER TABLE Test.Person
    ALTER COLUMN FavoriteBookTypedXml XML NULL;
GO

ALTER TABLE Test.Person
    ALTER COLUMN FavoriteBookTypedXml XML(DOCUMENT BooksSchemaCollection) NULL;
```

Working with XML Stored in an XML Variable or Column

When you have data stored using an *XML* data type, you want to both query and modify it. This is performed using a few methods provided by the *XML* data type.

THE *EXIST* METHOD

The *exist* method returns a bit value and is used to verify if an XPath expression is found within an XML instance. The following example shows a simple query against the *Demographics* column that uses the *exist* method to find all surveys with a value for *TotalPurchaseYTD* greater than 5,000. It also uses the *xs:decimal* XPath function to convert the element to a decimal value. (Note that this conversion is not necessary when using typed XML because SQL Server derives from the *XML* schema that the element is in fact a decimal.)

```
WITH XMLNAMESPACES(DEFAULT
    'http://schemas.microsoft.com/sqlserver/2004/07/adventure-works/IndividualSurvey')
SELECT
    COUNT(*)
FROM Sales.Individual
WHERE Demographics.exist(
    '/IndividualSurvey/TotalPurchaseYTD[xs:decimal(.) > 5000]') = 1;
```

THE *VALUE* METHOD

The *value* method is used to perform an XQuery against the XML instance to fetch a single scalar value from it. In this example, the XPath aggregate function *count* is used to calculate the number of *IndividualSurvey* elements in the XML column *Demographics*, and then the SQL aggregate function *SUM* is used to summarize the counts returned by the *value* method:

```
WITH XMLNAMESPACES(DEFAULT
    'http://schemas.microsoft.com/sqlserver/2004/07/adventure-works/IndividualSurvey')
SELECT
    SUM(Demographics.value('count(/IndividualSurvey)', 'INT')) AS NumberOfIndividualSurveys
FROM Sales.Individual;
```

Here is the result:

```
NumberOfIndividualSurveys
---------------------------
18484
```

Note that the second argument of the *value* method indicates which SQL data type the value retrieved from the XML document should be converted to in the result.

THE *NODES* METHOD

The *nodes* method is used to shred the XML into a tabular form. In the following example, each *Order* element found is returned as a separate row in the query result. In addition to using the *nodes* method, the code also uses the *value* method to retrieve specific values from the XML document into the resulting columns. Note that this method can be used with an *INSERT…SELECT* or an *UPDATE* statement to pass multiple values to SQL Server in a single parameter:

```
DECLARE @Orders XML;
SET @Orders = N'
<Orders>
    <Order Product="Bike" Quantity="1"/>
    <Order Product="Bike" Quantity="2"/>
    <Order Product="Car" Quantity="4"/>
</Orders>';

SELECT
    tab.col.value('@Product', 'NVARCHAR(50)') AS Product
    ,tab.col.value('@Quantity', 'INT') AS Quantity
    ,tab.col.value('count(../Order)', 'INT') AS TotalNumberOfOrders
FROM @Orders.nodes('/Orders/Order[xs:integer(@Quantity) > 1]') AS tab(col);
```

Here is the result:

```
Product   Quantity    TotalNumberOfOrders
--------  ----------- --------------------
Bike      2           3
Car       4           3
```

Notice the use of the *count* function and the parent path (..) used to create the *TotalNumberOfOrders* column. This can be very useful, but be aware that using parent paths in a *value* method call on a *nodes* method result can degrade performance significantly.

THE *QUERY* METHOD

The *query* method is used to perform an XQuery against the XML instance to retrieve an XML fragment rather than a scalar value or a tabular result. In the query method, you use the XQuery language's FLWOR expressions to retrieve the parts of the XML document that you need and present it in the way you want. XQuery FLWOR expressions can actually be used in other XML data type methods as well, but it is typically used in the context of the *query* method. A FLWOR expression consists of the *for, let, return, order by,* and *where* keywords, where *for* is roughly equal to *FROM* in SQL, *let* is roughly equal to a common table expression (CTE) declaration, *return* is roughly equal to *SELECT* in SQL, and *order by* and *where* are equal to their SQL namesakes.

The following example uses a FLWOR expression to return all orders of a quantity of two or more from the XML document, sorted with the greatest quantity being returned first and the actual XML elements being translated to Swedish:

```
DECLARE @Orders XML;
SET @Orders = N'
<Orders>
    <Order Product="Bike" Quantity="1"/>
    <Order Product="Bike" Quantity="2"/>
    <Order Product="Car" Quantity="4"/>
</Orders>';

SELECT @Orders.query('
<Beställningar>
{
    for $o in /Orders/Order
    where xs:decimal($o/@Quantity) >= 2
    order by xs:decimal($o/@Quantity) descending
    return <Beställning Produkt="{data($o/@Product)}" Antal="{data($o/@Quantity)}"/>
}
</Beställningar>
');
```

Here is the result:

```
<Beställningar>
  <Beställning Produkt="Car" Antal="4" />
  <Beställning Produkt="Bike" Antal="2" />
</Beställningar>
```

Lesson Summary

- XML can be generated using a *SELECT* statement in four different modes: *FOR XML RAW*, *FOR XML AUTO*, *FOR XML PATH*, and *FOR XML EXPLICIT*.
- *FOR XML PATH* is typically the preferred mode used to generate XML.
- The *XML* data type can be either typed (validated by an XML schema collection) or untyped.
- In an untyped *XML* data type, all values are always interpreted as strings.
- You can use the *value*, *query*, *exist*, *nodes*, and *modify* methods to query and alter instances of the *XML* data type.

PRACTICE   **Using XML**

In this practice, you use both a *FOR XML PATH* mode query to return an XML result set from SQL Server and a combination of the *nodes* and *value* methods to insert rows into a table based on an *XML* parameter passed to a stored procedure.

EXERCISE 1   Use *FOR XML PATH*

In this exercise, you query the *Production.Product, Sales.SalesOrderHeader,* and *Sales.SalesOrderDetail* tables to create an XML document.

1. Open Microsoft SQL Server Management Studio (SSMS) and connect to the appropriate instance of SQL Server 2008.

2. In a new query window, execute a SQL query against the *AdventureWorks* database that produces the following XML document for *ProductID* = 707:

```
<Product Id="707">
  <Info Name="Sport-100 Helmet, Red" ListPrice="34.9900" />
  <Order Id="43665" Date="2001-07-01T00:00:00" CustomerId="146" />
  <Order Id="43668" Date="2001-07-01T00:00:00" CustomerId="514" />
  <Order Id="43673" Date="2001-07-01T00:00:00" CustomerId="618" />
  <Order Id="43677" Date="2001-07-01T00:00:00" CustomerId="679" />
  . . .
</Product>
```

Here are the correct statements—but don't look at them before you have tried to create the query yourself. Type, highlight, and execute the following:

```
USE AdventureWorks;
GO

SELECT
    p.ProductID AS "@Id"
    ,p.Name AS "Info/@Name"
    ,p.ListPrice AS "Info/@ListPrice"
    ,(
        SELECT DISTINCT
            soh.SalesOrderID AS "@Id"
            ,soh.OrderDate AS "@Date"
            ,soh.CustomerID AS "@CustomerId"
        FROM Sales.SalesOrderHeader AS soh
        INNER JOIN Sales.SalesOrderDetail AS sod
            ON sod.SalesOrderID = soh.SalesOrderID
        WHERE sod.ProductID = p.ProductID
        FOR XML PATH('Order'), TYPE
    )
FROM Production.Product AS p
WHERE p.ProductID = 707
FOR XML PATH('Product');
```

EXERCISE 2   Use the *nodes* and *value* Methods

In this exercise, you create a stored procedure that accepts an *XML* data type as its parameter. The stored procedure shreds the XML document into tabular form using the *nodes* and *value* methods and then inserts the results into a table.

1. If necessary, open SSMS and connect to the appropriate instance of SQL Server 2008.

2. In the query window, type, highlight, and execute the following SQL statements to create a new table and schema in the *AdventureWorks* database:

```
USE AdventureWorks;
GO

CREATE SCHEMA TestXml;
GO

CREATE TABLE TestXml.Messages
(
    MessageId INT IDENTITY PRIMARY KEY
    ,FromUser NVARCHAR(50) NOT NULL
    ,Message NVARCHAR(max) NOT NULL
    ,CreatedDateTime DATETIME2 NOT NULL DEFAULT SYSDATETIME()
);
```

3. In the existing query window, type, highlight, and execute the following SQL statements to create the stored procedure that populates the *TestXml.Messages* table from an XML document:

```
CREATE PROCEDURE TestXml.spMessageInsertMultiple
@Messages XML
AS
BEGIN
    SET NOCOUNT ON;

    INSERT TestXml.Messages (FromUser, Message)
        SELECT
            tab.col.value('@FromUser', 'NVARCHAR(50)')
            ,tab.col.value('text()[1]', 'NVARCHAR(max)')
        FROM @Messages.nodes('/Messages/Message') AS tab(col);
END
```

4. Finally, in the existing query window, type, highlight, and execute the following SQL statements to run the stored procedure (adding two messages to the table) and then query the table to see the results:

```
EXEC TestXml.spMessageInsertMultiple @Messages = N'
<Messages>
    <Message FromUser="Jeff Low">Hi, how are you?</Message>
    <Message FromUser="Jane Dow">Not bad, and yourself?</Message>
</Messages>';

SELECT * FROM TestXml.Messages;
```

The result returned by the query should look like this:

```
MessageId   FromUser   Message                CreatedDateTime
---------   --------   --------------------   ----------------------
1           Jeff Low   Hi, how are you?       2008-11-05 12:40:56.14
2           Jane Dow   Not bad, and yourself?  2008-11-05 12:40:56.14
```

Lesson 2: Using SQLCLR and *Filestream*

Let's begin this lesson by discussing what SQLCLR is. *SQLCLR* refers to the use of CLR execution within the SQL Server Database Engine. CLR is also often referred to as the *.NET Framework,* just *.NET,* or by the name of the programming language that might be used, such as Visual Basic .NET or C#. The use of CLR within SQL Server is an important aspect of making SQL Server more extensible, allowing developers to do more than what is possible with just the T-SQL language and its system functions. In this lesson, we start by exploring the basics of using CLR within SQL Server, and then cover why you might want to build certain database objects using CLR. Next, we look at how stored procedures, triggers, functions, types, and aggregates can be created using CLR. At the end of this lesson, we look at how you can use *Filestream* objects to store binary large objects (BLOBs) in SQL Server 2008.

> **After this lesson, you will be able to:**
> - Create stored procedures using SQLCLR.
> - Create scalar user-defined functions (UDFs) using SQLCLR.
> - Create table-valued UDFs using SQLCLR.
> - Create triggers using SQLCLR.
> - Create user-defined types using SQLCLR.
> - Create user-defined aggregates using SQLCLR.
> - Store BLOBs in SQL Server using a *Filestream* object.
>
> **Estimated lesson time: 60 minutes**

The Basics of Using SQLCLR

To use CLR within the database, you must perform the following steps:

1. You must set the SQL Server instance to allow CLR code to run.
2. You must write the code that the object uses with a .NET language (in this chapter, we include C# and Visual Basic .NET code examples for reference).
3. You must compile the code to an assembly (a CLR executable).
4. You must load the assembly into SQL Server.
5. Finally, you must create the database object and point it to the assembly using Data Definition Language (DDL).

We now follow each of these steps to create a very simple CLR stored procedure that should simply execute the SQL statement SELECT * FROM Sales.Customer WHERE CustomerID = @CustomerID. Even though you would never use the CLR for this particular stored procedure, it is a good example because it allows you to see clearly the difference between creating a stored procedure using T-SQL to run a parameterized query and using SQLCLR to run a parameterized query. For reference, the T-SQL version of the stored procedure is shown here:

```
CREATE PROCEDURE Sales.spCustomerGet
@CustomerID INT
AS
BEGIN
    SELECT * FROM Sales.Customer
    WHERE CustomerID = @CustomerID;
END
```

To run the same query using SQLCLR, first we allow SQLCLR code to be executed within this SQL Server instance by executing the T-SQL code shown here. Note that system types and functions that use SQLCLR (such as the spatial types *geography* and *geometry*) do not require the CLR to be enabled; it is required only for user code:

```
EXEC sp_configure 'clr enabled', 1;
RECONFIGURE;
```

The first line of code changes the 'CLR enabled' setting to 1 (true) and the second line of code tells SQL Server to start using any changed configuration settings.

Now it is time to write the .NET code (C# or Visual Basic .NET) for the stored procedure. In this example, we create a single file containing the .NET code and then compile it using the command prompt.

> **TIP** **USING VISUAL STUDIO TO CREATE FILES**
>
> If you have Microsoft Visual Studio handy, you can use it to create the files. Use the SQL Server Project template, which can be found under the Database project type heading, to create your CLR database objects. Visual Studio can even deploy CLR database objects directly to SQL Server (meaning that Visual Studio performs for you the rest of the steps that we describe here).

We create a file called CLRStoredProc.cs (if you are using C#) or CLRStoredProc.vb (if you are using Visual Basic .NET) and add the following code to it:

```
'VB:
Imports System
Imports System.Data.SqlTypes
Imports System.Data.SqlClient
Imports Microsoft.SqlServer.Server

Namespace TK433.Clr
    Public Class Demo
        Public Shared Sub CustomerGetProcedure(ByVal customerId As SqlInt32)
            Using conn As SqlConnection = New SqlConnection("context connection=true")
                Dim cmd As SqlCommand = conn.CreateCommand()
```

```
                 cmd.CommandText = "SELECT * FROM Sales.Customer " & vbCrLf & _
                              "WHERE CustomerID = @CustomerID;"
                 cmd.Parameters.AddWithValue("@CustomerID", customerId)
                 conn.Open()

                 ' Execute the command and send the results to the caller.
                 SqlContext.Pipe.ExecuteAndSend(cmd)
             End Using
        End Sub
    End Class
End Namespace

//C#:
using System;
using System.Data.SqlTypes;
using System.Data.SqlClient;
using Microsoft.SqlServer.Server;

namespace TK433.Clr
{
    public class Demo
    {
        static public void CustomerGetProcedure(SqlInt32 customerId)
        {
            using (SqlConnection conn = new SqlConnection("context connection=true"))
            {
                SqlCommand cmd = conn.CreateCommand();
                cmd.CommandText = @"SELECT * FROM Sales.Customer
                                WHERE CustomerID = @CustomerID";
                cmd.Parameters.AddWithValue("@CustomerID", customerId);
                conn.Open();

                // Execute the command and send the results to the caller.
                SqlContext.Pipe.ExecuteAndSend(cmd);
            }
        }
    }
}
```

Note the following points in this example:

■ The connection string "context connection=true" tells the *SqlConnection* object to connect to the SQL Server instance within which you are already executing. Note that you are still in the same session as you were in outside the CLR code. This means that you are not blocked by any locks that are held by the session that executed this CLR code.

- The additional namespaces used are the following:
  - The *System.Data.SqlClient* namespace contains the *SqlConnection* and *SqlCommand* classes used in the example. These classes are used to connect to SQL Server and execute the query. Note that these classes are the same ones that you use when connecting from an application.
  - The *System.Data.SqlTypes* namespace contains the *SqlInt32* type used in the example. This type mimics the behavior of an *INTEGER* in SQL Server. You can use the *Value* property of the *SqlInt32* type to retrieve a CLR integer.
  - The *Microsoft.SqlServer.Server* namespace contains the *SqlContext* and *SqlPipe* classes (needed for the *SqlContext.Pipe* call) used in the example. These classes are specific to the SQLCLR implementation and are used to communicate to the SQL Server session within which you are executing.
- The code is very similar to any code that accesses SQL Server from an application.
- This seems pretty cumbersome for executing only this simple *SELECT* statement. As you can clearly see, you won't want to use SQLCLR for simple stored procedures like the one in this example.

The next step is to compile the code to a CLR assembly. This is accomplished by executing the C# compiler (csc.exe) or the Visual Basic .NET compiler (vbc.exe). Both these compilers can typically be found in the directory C:\Windows\Microsoft.NET\Framework\v3.5. To compile the code from a command prompt, execute the following command within the directory where you store the source code. (Note that you must have your path set up so that it points to the directory containing the compiler.)

```
'VB:
vbc.exe /target:library /out:CLRStoredProc.dll CLRStoredProc.vb
```

```
//C#:
csc.exe /target:library /out:CLRStoredProc.dll CLRStoredProc.cs
```

The */target:library* switch tells the compiler that you are compiling an assembly without a starting point; that is, the assembly can't be executed directly. It is simply a type library, and therefore, it should use the .dll extension. The */out* switch simply tells the compiler what it should name the created assembly.

Now it is time to load the created assembly into your database. This is accomplished by using the *CREATE ASSEMBLY* statement. When the statement is executed, the assembly is copied physically into the database to which you are attached. Therefore, you can delete the .dll assembly file after it has been loaded because SQL Server doesn't need it. Having the assembly stored within the database is very useful when you are moving a database to another instance because all assemblies within the database are moved with the database. To see which assemblies exist within a database, you can query the *sys.assemblies* catalog view.

The following T-SQL code loads the assembly into the *AdventureWorks* database and displays its properties by querying the *sys.assemblies* catalog view:

```
USE AdventureWorks;

CREATE ASSEMBLY TK433ClrDemo
    FROM 'C:\TK433Clr\CLRStoredProc.dll';


SELECT assembly_id, name
FROM sys.assemblies
WHERE name = 'TK433ClrDemo';
```

The result should look like this:

```
assembly_id    name
-------------  ------------------------
65544          TK433ClrDemo
```

It is finally time for the last step: creating the stored procedure so that it can be executed by users. The following T-SQL code creates a stored procedure named *Sales.spCustomerGetClr* that points to the CLR method named *CustomerGetProcedure* in the class *TK433.Clr.Demo* in the assembly *TK433ClrDemo*. After creating the stored procedure in the next example, we also query the *sys.assembly_modules* catalog view for information regarding this CLR stored procedure. T-SQL modules can be found in the *sys.sql_modules* catalog view:

```
CREATE PROCEDURE Sales.spCustomerGetClr
@CustomerID INT
AS
EXTERNAL NAME TK433ClrDemo."TK433.Clr.Demo".CustomerGetProcedure;
GO


SELECT assembly_id, assembly_class, assembly_method
FROM sys.assembly_modules
WHERE object_id = OBJECT_ID('Sales.spCustomerGetClr');
```

The result should look like this:

```
assembly_id    assembly_class     assembly_method
-------------  -----------------  ----------------------
65544          TK433.Clr.Demo     CustomerGetProcedure
```

After the stored procedure has been created, we can execute it. Note that executing the stored procedure looks exactly like executing a T-SQL stored procedure:

```
EXEC Sales.spCustomerGetClr @CustomerID = 1;
```

Here is the result (which has been truncated for clarity):

```
CustomerID     TerritoryID    AccountNumber    CustomerType...
-------------  -------------  ---------------  ------------...
1              1              AW00000001       S          ...
```

Before we continue looking at more details of creating the different types of SQLCLR objects, it is worth noting that you can also store the CLR source code in the database. SQL Server does not use the source code, but it is handy to store the code in the database because it is then possible to retrieve it from the database later (you may have lost the actual source code by then...). To add a source code file to the database, execute the following statement:

```
ALTER ASSEMBLY TK433ClrDemo
    ADD FILE FROM 'C:\TK433Clr\CLRStoredProc.cs'; -- Or .vb...
```

To see which files have been added to an assembly, you can query the *sys.assembly_files* catalog view. Note that the actual assembly (.dll file) can also be found through this view.

Objects That Can Be Created Using SQLCLR

The following types of objects can be created using SQLCLR:

- Stored procedures (as shown in the previous example)
- Scalar UDFs that return a single value
- Table-valued UDFs that return a table and can be called from the *FROM, JOIN*, or *APPLY* clauses
- Triggers (DML, DDL, and logon triggers)
- User-defined aggregates
- User-defined types (UDTs)

It is worth noting that the last two objects, user-defined aggregates and UDTs, can be created only using SQLCLR; they cannot be created using T-SQL.

Because we have already covered how to create a CLR stored procedure, we start by looking at how to create a scalar UDF.

Creating a Scalar UDF

Much like the CLR stored procedure, a scalar UDF consists of a single method. The difference is that for the UDF, the method needs to return a value, whereas for the stored procedure, the method should return *void* (for C#) or be a *Sub* (for Visual Basic .NET). UDFs are where SQLCLR really excels because you can easily create UDFs that let you use basically anything within the .NET Framework. You should typically use a CLR UDF only to perform computations, that is, not to access any tables. Your functions are then typically used in an SQL DML statement. In this example, we create a UDF that allows you to use regular expressions in SQL Server. Using regular expressions is an often-needed feature that does not exist natively in SQL Server but that you can easily "steal" from the .NET Framework using SQLCLR. In the following examples, we do not cover compiling or loading the assembly because those steps were covered earlier in this lesson.

To create the new UDF, the following CLR code is used. For abbreviation, only the method itself and the imported namespaces are included:

```vb
'VB:
Imports System
Imports System.Data.SqlTypes
Imports System.Text.RegularExpressions
Imports Microsoft.SqlServer.Server
...
<SqlFunction(IsPrecise:=True, Isdeterministic:=True)> _
Public Shared Function IsRegExMatch(ByVal input As SqlString, ByVal pattern As
    SqlString) _
        As SqlBoolean
    If input.IsNull Or pattern.IsNull Then
        Return SqlBoolean.Null ' Return NULL if either parameter is NULL.
    End If
    Return CType(Regex.IsMatch(input.Value, pattern.Value), SqlBoolean)
End Function
...
```

```csharp
//C#:
using System;
using System.Data.SqlTypes;
using System.Text.RegularExpressions;
using Microsoft.SqlServer.Server;
...
[SqlFunction(IsDeterministic = true, IsPrecise = true)]
static public SqlBoolean IsRegExMatch(SqlString input, SqlString pattern)
{
    if (input.IsNull || pattern.IsNull)
        return SqlBoolean.Null; // Return NULL if either parameter is NULL.
    return (SqlBoolean)Regex.IsMatch(input.Value, pattern.Value);
}
...
```

Notice the *SqlFunction* attribute that is used to define the function. This attribute tells SQL Server that the function is both precise (that is, doesn't use floating point calculations that affect its return value) and deterministic (that is, doesn't return different values when called multiple times with the same input values). Because of this, the result of the function can be both persisted in a computed column and indexed.

After compiling and loading the assembly into SQL Server, the following T-SQL code is executed to create the function:

```sql
CREATE FUNCTION dbo.fnIsRegExMatch
(
    @Input NVARCHAR(MAX)
    ,@Pattern NVARCHAR(100)
)
```

```
RETURNS BIT
AS
EXTERNAL NAME TK433ClrDemo."TK433.Clr.Demo".IsRegExMatch;
```

Now this function can be used when you want to apply a regular expression in a query. In the following T-SQL example, the query returns the number of rows in the *Sales.CreditCard* table that do not have a credit card number with exactly 14 numbers. This is done using the regular expression ^[0-9]{14}$:

```
SELECT
    COUNT(*) AS InvalidCreditCardNumbers
FROM Sales.CreditCard
WHERE dbo.fnIsRegExMatch(CardNumber, N'^[0-9]{14}$') = 0;
```

Here is the result:

```
InvalidCreditCardNumbers
--------------------------

0
```

Another interesting aspect of CLR (and T-SQL) UDFs is that they can be used in constraints. The following example shows how we can add a check constraint to the *Sales.CreditCards* table so that it allows only credit card numbers that are *NULL* or that match the regular expression from the previous example:

```
ALTER TABLE Sales.CreditCard
    ADD CONSTRAINT CKCreditCardNumber
    CHECK(dbo.fnIsRegExMatch(CardNumber, N'^[0-9]{14}$') = 1 OR CardNumber IS NULL);


-- Test the constraint by trying to insert an invalid card number.
UPDATE Sales.CreditCard SET CardNumber = '1234' WHERE CreditCardID = 1;
```

Here is the error that results:

```
Msg 547, Level 16, State 0, Line 1
The UPDATE statement conflicted with the CHECK constraint "CKCreditCardNumber". The
  conflict occurred in database "AdventureWorks", table "Sales.CreditCard", column
  'CardNumber'.
```

Because we marked the function as both precise (*IsPrecise*) and deterministic (*IsDeterministic*) in the CLR code, we can both persist and index a computed column that uses the function. Although the result in this particular example isn't really useful for indexing or persisting, we look at how to go about doing it because it is useful in other cases. To index the result of the function, it must first be placed in the expression of a computed column. In the following T-SQL example, a computed column using the function is added to the table and marked with the persisted attribute. The persisted attribute tells SQL Server to calculate the result of the function only whenever it writes to the underlying column or columns and to store the result of the function physically in the table row. After we add the column, we also create an index on top of it. Note that the computed column does not need to be marked as persisted for you to be able to index it. The query that is executed against the new column at the end of the example uses the newly created index:

```
ALTER TABLE Sales.CreditCard
    ADD IsValidCardNumber AS dbo.fnIsRegExMatch(CardNumber, N'^[0-9]{14}$')
    PERSISTED;
GO

CREATE NONCLUSTERED INDEX IsValidCardNumberIdx
    ON Sales.CreditCard (IsValidCardNumber);
GO

-- This query makes use of the IsValidCardNumberIdx index and performs
-- an index seek operation against it.
SELECT
    COUNT(*)
FROM Sales.CreditCard
WHERE IsValidCardNumber = 1;
```

Creating a Table-Valued CLR UDF

Because a table-valued UDF returns multiple values (or rather, multiple rows), it is a bit more complex than a scalar UDF. While a scalar UDF consists of a single method, a table-valued UDF consists of two methods:

- A method that acts as the iterator or state machine, looping over the values that should be returned as rows
- A method that is executed for every row and populates the actual row being returned to the SQL Server execution engine

Consider the following CLR code, which defines these two methods for a table-valued UDF. This particular function can be used to split comma-delimited strings.

Why No Visual Basic .NET Example?

This example uses the *yield* keyword in C# to create an iterator. The *yield* keyword doesn't exist in Visual Basic .NET, so a Visual Basic .NET code sample is not included. You can create table-valued functions using Visual Basic .NET, but this requires that you create a class that acts as the iterator and handles looping over the values (that is, what *yield* in C# does for you).

```
//C#:
using System;
using System.Collections;
using System.Collections.Generic;
```

```
using System.Data.SqlTypes;
using Microsoft.SqlServer.Server;

...
[SqlFunction(FillRowMethodName = "SplitStringFillRow",
    TableDefinition = "ValueIndex INT, Value NVARCHAR(100)")]
static public IEnumerator SplitString(SqlString stringToSplit)
{
    // Exit if the string to split is NULL.
    if (stringToSplit.IsNull)
        yield break;

    int valueIndex = 0;
    foreach (string s in stringToSplit.Value.Split(new char[] { ',' },
        StringSplitOptions.RemoveEmptyEntries))
    {
        yield return new KeyValuePair<int, string>(valueIndex++, s.Trim());
    }
}

static public void SplitStringFillRow(object oKeyValuePair,
    out SqlInt32 valueIndex, out SqlString value)
{
    // Fetch the key value pair from the first parameter.
    KeyValuePair<int, string> keyValuePair = (KeyValuePair<int, string>)oKeyValuePair;

    // Set each output parameter's value.
    valueIndex = keyValuePair.Key;
    value = keyValuePair.Value;
}
...
```

In the previous example, you can see that we created the two methods *SplitString* and *SplitStringFillRow*. When you execute the UDF from SQL Server, the *SplitString* method is executed first. Each *yield return* statement that is executed within this method calls the *SplitStringFillRow* method (that is, the fill row method specified in the *SqlFunction* attribute). As you can see, the result set that is returned by the *SplitString* function is defined using the *TableDefinition* parameter of the *SqlFunction* attribute.

The fill row method always takes one parameter of type *System.Object* that contains a reference to whatever you called *yield return* for, as well as one *out* parameter for each column that should be returned by the function according to the *TableDefinition* parameter. In the following example, you can see the T-SQL code used to create and query the table-valued UDF:

```
CREATE FUNCTION dbo.fnSplitString
(
    @StringToSplit NVARCHAR(max)
)
```

```
RETURNS TABLE (ValueIndex INT, Value NVARCHAR(100))
AS
EXTERNAL NAME TK433ClrDemo."TK433.Clr.Demo".SplitString;
GO

SELECT
    ValueIndex
    ,Value
FROM dbo.fnSplitString('Hi,how,are,you?') AS a;
```

Here is the result:

```
ValueIndex   Value
-----------  ---------
0            Hi
1            how
2            are
3            you?
```

Creating a CLR Trigger

Creating a CLR trigger is very similar to creating a CLR stored procedure. The CLR code
consists of a single method or *Sub* that performs the actions that you want the trigger to
perform. Just like a T-SQL trigger, a CLR trigger has access to the trigger-specific *inserted* and
deleted tables. In the following example of a CLR trigger, the transaction is rolled back if the
statement that triggered the trigger deleted more than one row:

```
'VB:
Imports System.Data.SqlClient
Imports System.Text.RegularExpressions
Imports Microsoft.SqlServer.Server

...
Public Shared Sub ClrTrigger()
    ' If this wasn't a delete statement, just exit.
    If SqlContext.TriggerContext.TriggerAction <> TriggerAction.Delete Then
        Return
    End If

    Using conn As SqlConnection = New SqlConnection("context connection=true")
        Dim cmd As SqlCommand = conn.CreateCommand()
        cmd.CommandText = "SELECT COUNT(*) FROM deleted"
        conn.Open()
```

```
        ' Check the number of rows that were found in the deleted table.
        If (CType(cmd.ExecuteScalar(), Integer)) > 1 Then
            cmd.CommandText = _
                "RAISERROR('Too many rows deleted, rolling back " & _
                    "transaction.', 16, 1);" & vbCrLf & _
                "ROLLBACK TRAN;"

            ' This try/catch is needed in order to skip the error that is
            ' caused by the RAISERROR being executed.
            Try
                SqlContext.Pipe.ExecuteAndSend(cmd)
            Catch
            End Try
        End If
    End Using
End Sub
...


//C#:
using System;
using System.Data.SqlClient;
using Microsoft.SqlServer.Server;

...
static public void ClrTrigger()
{
    // If this wasn't a delete statement, just exit.
    if (SqlContext.TriggerContext.TriggerAction != TriggerAction.Delete)
        return;

    using (SqlConnection conn = new SqlConnection("context connection=true"))
    {
        SqlCommand cmd = conn.CreateCommand();
        cmd.CommandText = "SELECT COUNT(*) FROM deleted;";
        conn.Open();

        // Check the number of rows that were found in the deleted table.
        if (((int)cmd.ExecuteScalar()) > 1)
        {
            cmd.CommandText = @"RAISERROR('Too many rows deleted, " +
                            "rolling back transaction.', 16, 1);" +
                        "ROLLBACK TRAN;";

            // This try/catch is needed in order to skip the error that is
            // caused by the RAISERROR being executed.
            try
```

```
        {
            SqlContext.Pipe.ExecuteAndSend(cmd);
        }
        catch { }
    }
}
}
```

The following code would be used to create the trigger:

```
CREATE TRIGGER dbo.ClrTrigger
ON dbo.MyTable
AFTER DELETE
AS
EXTERNAL NAME TK433ClrDemo."TK433.Clr.Demo".ClrTrigger;
GO
```

Just as with CLR stored procedures, creating this otherwise simple trigger becomes very cumbersome compared to creating a T-SQL trigger because you need to use a *SqlConnection* and *SqlCommand* object every time that you want to execute an SQL statement. As you can see, there is a property of the *SqlContext* class called *TriggerContext* (of type *SqlTriggerContext*), which can be used to perform trigger-specific checks from the CLR code.

CLR triggers should be used only when you need to perform tasks that cannot be performed using regular T-SQL triggers, or when the tasks are heavily calculation-intensive and the CLR trigger outperforms the T-SQL trigger.

Creating a CLR User-Defined Aggregate

The possibility of creating custom aggregation functions can be very useful when you want to create an aggregate that isn't included with SQL Server (such as a product aggregate) or to create an aggregate function that can handle a custom CLR UDT.

When creating a CLR user-defined aggregate, you must create an entire CLR type (either *class* or *struct*) rather than just one or two methods as with the previous CLR objects. This is because the aggregate needs to be able to do a few things, including the following:

- **Initialize itself**   This is performed using the *Init* method of the aggregate CLR type.
- **Add another value to the calculation**   For each value that needs to be added to the calculation, the *Accumulate* method is called.
- **Combine itself with another instance of the same aggregate function**   This is performed by calling the *Merge* method.
- **Return its result**   This is performed by calling the *Terminate* method.

Before we explore more details of user-defined aggregates, take a few moments to read through the following example of CLR code, which defines a mathematical product aggregate. The result of this aggregate is all inputs multiplied together (such as 5 * 10 * 15 = 750). To add some extra functionality to this aggregate, we have included a second parameter that tells the aggregate whether or not to include zeros in the calculation (because the inclusion of a zero would always result in an aggregate of zero). The possibility of having multiple parameters in user-defined aggregates was added in SQL Server 2008. There are quite a few observations to make about this code:

- In this example, the *SqlUserDefinedAggregate* attribute tells SQL Server that we will manually manage serializing the aggregate (if necessary) by specifying the format to be user-defined (*Format.UserDefined*). The attribute also tells SQL Server that it should return *NULL* if no values are included in the aggregation (*IsNullIfEmpty = True*), that the aggregate cares about duplicates (*IsInvariantToDuplicates = False*), doesn't care about *NULL* values (*IsInvariantToNulls = True*), and doesn't care about the order of the input (*IsInvariantToOrder = True*). Finally, the attribute tells SQL Server that the maximum storage space used when serializing this aggregate is 19 bytes (16 bytes for the decimal value and 1 byte each for three Boolean values).

- The *SqlFacet* attribute is used a few times throughout the code to specify the precision and scale of the *SqlDecimal* type.

- The *IBinarySerialize* interface must be implemented because we used the user-defined format when defining the aggregate. You can also choose to use the native format; however, that does not work in this example because the decimal data type here is not supported by native serialization.

- The *IBinarySerialize.Write* method is called by SQL Server to serialize the instance during execution, if needed.

- The *IBinarySerialize.Read* method is called by SQL Server to deserialize the instance during execution, if needed.

```vb
'VB:
Imports System
Imports System.Data.SqlTypes
Imports System.Runtime.InteropServices
Imports Microsoft.SqlServer.Server

...
<SqlUserDefinedAggregate(Format.UserDefined, IsNullIfEmpty:=True, _
IsInvariantToDuplicates:=False, IsInvariantToNulls:=True, _
IsInvariantToOrder:=True, MaxByteSize:=19)> _
Public Structure DecimalProductAggregate
    Implements IBinarySerialize

    Private m_Value As Decimal ' 16 bytes storage.
    Private m_ValueIsNull As Boolean ' 1 byte storage.
    Private m_SkipZeros As Boolean ' 1 byte storage.
    Private m_SkipZerosIsNull As Boolean ' 1 byte storage.
```

```
Public Sub Init()
    Me.m_ValueIsNull = True
    Me.m_SkipZerosIsNull = True
End Sub

Public Sub Accumulate(<SqlFacet(Precision:=38, Scale:=5)> ByVal value _
    As SqlDecimal, ByVal skipZeros As SqlBoolean)
    If skipZeros.IsNull Then
        Throw New InvalidOperationException( _
            "The @SkipZeros parameter cannot be null.")
    End If


    If value.IsNull Then
        Return
    End If


    ' Init skip zeros flag if it hasn't' been set.
    If (Me.m_SkipZerosIsNull) Then
        Me.m_SkipZeros = skipZeros.Value
        Me.m_SkipZerosIsNull = False
    ElseIf Me.m_SkipZeros <> skipZeros.Value Then
        ' Don't allow the skip zeros setting to change during execution.
        Throw New InvalidOperationException( _
            "The @SkipZeros parameter cannot be changed.")
    End If


    ' Skip zero values if the settings tells us to
    ' and the current value is zero.
    If Me.m_SkipZeros And value.Value = 0 Then
        Return
    End If


    ' If this is the first value, just set it.
    If Me.m_ValueIsNull Then
        Me.m_Value = value.Value
        Me.m_ValueIsNull = False
        Return
    End If


    Me.m_Value *= value.Value
End Sub

Public Sub Merge(ByVal other As DecimalProductAggregate)
    Dim skipZeros As SqlBoolean
    If other.m_SkipZerosIsNull Then
        skipZeros = SqlBoolean.Null
```

```vb
        Else
            skipZeros = other.m_SkipZeros
        End If
        Dim otherValue As SqlDecimal = other.Terminate()


        Me.Accumulate(otherValue, skipZeros)
    End Sub


    Public Function Terminate() As <SqlFacet(Precision:=38, Scale:=5)> SqlDecimal
        If Me.m_ValueIsNull Then
            Return SqlDecimal.Null
        End If
        Return Me.m_Value
    End Function


    ' Read the aggregate from SQL Server.
    Sub Read(ByVal r As System.IO.BinaryReader) Implements IBinarySerialize.Read
        Me.m_ValueIsNull = r.ReadBoolean()
        Me.m_Value = r.ReadDecimal()
        Me.m_SkipZerosIsNull = r.ReadBoolean()
        Me.m_SkipZeros = r.ReadBoolean()
    End Sub


    ' Write the aggregate to SQL Server.
    Sub Write(ByVal w As System.IO.BinaryWriter) Implements IBinarySerialize.Write
        w.Write(Me.m_ValueIsNull)
        w.Write(Me.m_Value)
        w.Write(Me.m_SkipZerosIsNull)
        w.Write(Me.m_SkipZeros)
    End Sub
End Structure
...


//C#:
using System;
using System.Data.SqlTypes;
using System.Runtime.InteropServices;
using Microsoft.SqlServer.Server;


...

[SqlUserDefinedAggregate(Format.UserDefined, IsNullIfEmpty=true,
IsInvariantToDuplicates=false, IsInvariantToNulls=true,
IsInvariantToOrder=true, MaxByteSize=19)]
public struct DecimalProductAggregate : IBinarySerialize
```

```
{
        private decimal m_Value; // 16 bytes storage.
        private bool m_ValueIsNull; // 1 byte storage.
        private bool m_SkipZeros; // 1 byte storage.
        private bool m_SkipZerosIsNull; // 1 byte storage.

        public void Init()
        {
            this.m_ValueIsNull = true;
            this.m_SkipZerosIsNull = true;
        }

        public void Accumulate([SqlFacet(Precision = 38, Scale = 5)]SqlDecimal value,
            SqlBoolean skipZeros)
        {
            if (skipZeros.IsNull)
            {
                throw new InvalidOperationException(
                    "The @SkipZeros parameter cannot be null.");
            }
            if (value.IsNull)
                return;

            // Init skip zeros flag if it hasn't been set.
            if (this.m_SkipZerosIsNull)
            {
                this.m_SkipZeros = skipZeros.Value;
                this.m_SkipZerosIsNull = false;
            }
            // Don't allow the skip zeros setting to change during execution.
            else if (this.m_SkipZeros != skipZeros.Value)
            {
                throw new InvalidOperationException(
                    "The @SkipZeros parameter cannot be changed.");
            }

            // Skip zero values if the settings tells us to
            // and the current value is zero.
            if (this.m_SkipZeros && value.Value == 0M)
            {
                return;
            }

            // If this is the first value, just set it.
            if (this.m_ValueIsNull)
```

```
        {
            this.m_Value = value.Value;
            this.m_ValueIsNull = false;
            return;
        }

        this.m_Value *= value.Value;
    }


    public void Merge(DecimalProductAggregate other)
    {
        SqlBoolean skipZeros = other.m_SkipZerosIsNull ? SqlBoolean.Null
                              : other.m_SkipZeros;
        SqlDecimal otherValue = other.Terminate();

        this.Accumulate(otherValue, skipZeros);
    }


    [return: SqlFacet(Precision = 38, Scale = 5)]
    public SqlDecimal Terminate()
    {
        if (this.m_ValueIsNull)
        {
            return SqlDecimal.Null;
        }
        return this.m_Value;
    }


    // Read the aggregate from SQL Server.
    void IBinarySerialize.Read(System.IO.BinaryReader r)
    {
        this.m_ValueIsNull = r.ReadBoolean();
        this.m_Value = r.ReadDecimal();
        this.m_SkipZerosIsNull = r.ReadBoolean();
        this.m_SkipZeros = r.ReadBoolean();
    }


    // Write the aggregate to SQL Server.
    void IBinarySerialize.Write(System.IO.BinaryWriter w)
    {
        w.Write(this.m_ValueIsNull);
        w.Write(this.m_Value);
        w.Write(this.m_SkipZerosIsNull);
        w.Write(this.m_SkipZeros);
    }
}
...
```

After loading the assembly into SQL Server, you can execute the following T-SQL code to create the user-defined aggregate:

```
CREATE AGGREGATE dbo.PRODUCT_DECIMAL_38_5
(
    @Input DECIMAL(38,5)
    ,@SkipZeros BIT
)
RETURNS DECIMAL(38,5)
EXTERNAL NAME TK433ClrDemo."TK433.Clr.DecimalProductAggregate";
```

In this case, we named the aggregate *PRODUCT_DECMIAL_38_5* so that it reflects the actual type for which it can calculate the product. You can see how we can use the user-defined aggregate in an SQL query in the following T-SQL code:

```
WITH Numbers AS (
    SELECT * FROM (VALUES
        (0)
        ,(5.5)
        ,(10.5)
        ,(15.5)
    ) AS a(Number)
)
SELECT
    dbo.PRODUCT_DECIMAL_38_5(Number, 1) AS ProductExcludingZeros
    ,dbo.PRODUCT_DECIMAL_38_5(Number, 0) AS ProductIncludingZeros
FROM Numbers;
```

Here is the result:

```
ProductExcludingZeros   ProductIncludingZeros
---------------------   ---------------------
895.12500               0.00000
```

In this example, the query is executed against a CTE, but the user-defined aggregate can be used against tables as well.

Creating a CLR UDT

The final CLR object that is supported by SQL Server is a UDT. Creating custom UDTs is similar to creating user-defined aggregates. The type consists of a CLR type (*class* or *struct*) that uses the *SqlUserDefinedType* attribute to inform SQL Server of its various behaviors. In the following example, you can see the CLR code that is used to define a CLR UDT. This type, called *CURRENCY_VALUE*, can be used to store a monetary value (a decimal) and its currency code (a string). (Note that this example has not been rigorously tested and should not be used in production code.)

As with user-defined aggregates, there are a few observations to make about this code:

- In this example, the *SqlUserDefinedType* attribute tells SQL Server that we will manually manage serializing the type by specifying the format to be user-defined (*Format .UserDefined*). The attribute also tells SQL Server that a method named *Validate* should be run to verify the integrity of the type whenever a binary value is cast to this type (*ValidationMethodName*) and that the type is not byte-ordered (*IsByteOrdered = False*). Because the only sorting of UDTs supported by SQL Server is byte sorting, you should be very careful how you implement it. Remember that an integer value of –1 is larger than 1 when comparing the byte structures because the most significant bit in the integer is set to 1 if it is negative and to zero if it is positive. The other two options that are set are *IsFixedLength,* which tells SQL Server whether this type always uses the same number of bytes for storage, and *MaxByteSize*, which, as for a user-defined aggregate, tells SQL Server the maximum number of bytes needed to store a serialized instance of this type.

- The *SqlFacet* attribute is used a few times throughout the code to specify the precision and scale of the *SqlDecimal* type, as well as the maximum length of the *SqlString* type.

- The *SqlMethod* attribute is used in two places to specify that both the *CurrencyCode* and the *Value* properties are deterministic and precise; therefore, it can be indexed and persisted.

- The *Parse* method is used to convert from a string to the UDT. It is automatically called by SQL Server both when implicitly and explicitly converting a string to this type.

- The *ToString* method is used by SQL Server when converting from the UDT to a string. Note that it is typically a very good idea for the *Parse* and *ToString* methods to use the same string representation of the type.

- The *IBinarySerialize* interface must be implemented because we used the user-defined format when defining the type. You can also choose to use the native format; however, it will not work in this example because neither the decimal nor the string data types that are used in this example are supported for native serialization.

- The *IBinarySerialize.Write* method is called by SQL Server to serialize the type.

- The *IBinarySerialize.Read* method is called by SQL Server to deserialize the type.

```
'VB:
Imports System
Imports System.Data.SqlTypes
Imports System.Runtime.InteropServices
Imports Microsoft.SqlServer.Server

...
<SqlUserDefinedType(Format.UserDefined, ValidationMethodName:="Validate", _
IsByteOrdered:=False, IsFixedLength:=True, MaxByteSize:=20)> _
Public Structure CurrencyValueType
    Implements IBinarySerialize, INullable

    Private m_Value As Decimal ' 16 bytes storage.
```

```
Private m_CurrencyCode As String ' 4 bytes storage.
Private m_IsNull As Boolean

Public Sub New(ByVal value As Decimal, ByVal currencyCode As String)
    Me.m_Value = value
    Me.m_CurrencyCode = currencyCode.ToUpper()
    Me.m_IsNull = False
End Sub

' Get a null instance of the CurrencyValueType type.
Public Shared ReadOnly Property Null() As CurrencyValueType
    Get
        Dim currValue As CurrencyValueType = New CurrencyValueType()
        currValue.m_IsNull = True
        Return currValue
    End Get
End Property

<SqlFacet(MaxSize:=3)> _
Public Property CurrencyCode() As SqlString
    <SqlMethod(IsPrecise:=True, IsDeterministic:=True)> _
    Get
        If Me.m_IsNull Then
            Return SqlString.Null
        End If
        Return Me.m_CurrencyCode
    End Get
    Set(ByVal value As SqlString)
        Me.m_CurrencyCode = value.Value.ToUpper()
        If Me.Validate() = False Then
            Throw New InvalidOperationException( _
                "The currency code is invalid.")
        End If
    End Set
End Property

<SqlFacet(Precision:=38, Scale:=5)> _
Public Property Value() As SqlDecimal
    <SqlMethod(IsPrecise:=True, IsDeterministic:=True)> _
    Get
        If Me.m_IsNull Then
            Return SqlDecimal.Null
        End If
        Return Me.m_Value
    End Get
```

```vb
        Set(ByVal value As SqlDecimal)
            Me.m_Value = value.Value
        End Set
    End Property


    ' Called by SQL Server to validate the currency value.
    Public Function Validate() As Boolean
        Return System.Text.RegularExpressions.Regex.IsMatch( _
            Me.m_CurrencyCode, "^[A-Z]{3}$")
    End Function


    ' Convert a string to a currency value.
    Public Shared Function Parse(ByVal input As SqlString) As CurrencyValueType
        If input.IsNull Then
            Return CurrencyValueType.Null
        End If

        Dim space As Integer = input.Value.IndexOf(" ")
        If space <> 3 Then
            Throw New InvalidOperationException( _
                "The input string cannot be converted to a currency value.")
        End If

        Dim currencyCode As String = input.Value.Substring(0, 3)
        Dim value As Decimal = SqlDecimal.Parse(input.Value.Substring( _
            4, input.Value.Length - 4)).Value

        Return New CurrencyValueType(value, currencyCode)
    End Function


    ' Convert a currency value to a string.
    Public Overrides Function ToString() As String
        If Me.m_IsNull Then
            Return Nothing
        End If
        Return String.Format("{0} {1}", Me.CurrencyCode.Value, _
            Me.Value.ToString())
    End Function


    ' Read the type from SQL Server.
    Public Sub Read(ByVal r As System.IO.BinaryReader) _
        Implements IBinarySerialize.Read
        Me.m_Value = r.ReadDecimal()
        Me.m_CurrencyCode = r.ReadString()
        Me.m_IsNull = False
    End Sub
```

```vb
' Write the type to SQL Server.
Public Sub Write(ByVal w As System.IO.BinaryWriter) _
    Implements IBinarySerialize.Write
    w.Write(Me.m_Value)
    w.Write(Me.m_CurrencyCode)
End Sub

Public ReadOnly Property IsNull() As Boolean Implements INullable.IsNull
    Get
        Return Me.m_IsNull
    End Get
End Property
End Structure
...
```

```csharp
//C#:
using System;
using System.Data.SqlTypes;
using System.Runtime.InteropServices;
using Microsoft.SqlServer.Server;

...
[SqlUserDefinedType(Format.UserDefined, ValidationMethodName="Validate",
IsByteOrdered=false, IsFixedLength=true, MaxByteSize=20)]
public struct CurrencyValueType : IBinarySerialize, INullable
{

    private decimal m_Value; // 16 bytes storage.
    private string m_CurrencyCode; // 4 bytes storage.
    private bool m_IsNull; // Not stored...

    public CurrencyValueType(decimal value, string currencyCode)
    {
        this.m_Value = value;
        this.m_CurrencyCode = currencyCode.ToUpper();
        this.m_IsNull = false;
    }

    // Get a null instance of the CurrencyValueType type.
    static public CurrencyValueType Null
    {
        get
        {
            return new CurrencyValueType() { m_IsNull = true };
        }
    }
}
```

```csharp
[SqlFacet(MaxSize = 3)]
public SqlString CurrencyCode
{
    [SqlMethod(IsPrecise = true, IsDeterministic = true)]
    get
    {
        if (this.m_IsNull)
            return SqlString.Null;
        return this.m_CurrencyCode;
    }
    set
    {
        this.m_CurrencyCode = value.Value.ToUpper();
        if (!this.Validate())
        {
            throw new InvalidOperationException("The currency code is invalid.");
        }
    }
}


[SqlFacet(Precision = 38, Scale = 5)]
public SqlDecimal Value
{
    [SqlMethod(IsPrecise=true, IsDeterministic=true)]
    get
    {
        if (this.m_IsNull)
            return SqlDecimal.Null;
        return this.m_Value;
    }
    set
    {
        this.m_Value = value.Value;
    }
}

// Called by SQL Server to validate the currency value.
private bool Validate()
{
    return System.Text.RegularExpressions.Regex.IsMatch(
        this.m_CurrencyCode, "^[A-Z]{3}$");
}
```

```csharp
// Convert a string to a currency value.
static public CurrencyValueType Parse(SqlString input)
{
    if (input.IsNull)
        return CurrencyValueType.Null;

    int space = input.Value.IndexOf(' ');
    if (space != 3)
        throw new InvalidOperationException(
            "The input string cannot be converted to a currency value.");

    string currencyCode = input.Value.Substring(0, 3);
    decimal value = SqlDecimal.Parse(input.Value.Substring(
        4, input.Value.Length - 4)).Value;

    return new CurrencyValueType(value, currencyCode);
}


// Convert a currency value to a string.
override public string ToString()
{
    if (this.m_IsNull)
        return null;
    return string.Format("{0} {1}", this.CurrencyCode.Value,
        this.Value.ToString());
}


// Read the type from SQL Server.
void IBinarySerialize.Read(System.IO.BinaryReader r)
{
    this.m_Value = r.ReadDecimal();
    this.m_CurrencyCode = r.ReadString();
    this.m_IsNull = false;
}


// Write the type to SQL Server.
void IBinarySerialize.Write(System.IO.BinaryWriter w)
{
    w.Write(this.m_Value);
    w.Write(this.m_CurrencyCode);
}
```

```
    bool INullable.IsNull
    {
        get
        {
            return this.m_IsNull;
        }
    }
}
...
```

After loading the assembly into SQL Server, you can execute the following T-SQL code to create the UDT:

```
CREATE TYPE dbo.CURRENCY_VALUE
EXTERNAL NAME TK433ClrDemo."TK433.Clr.CurrencyValueType";
```

In the T-SQL example shown here, a new table is created and populated with rows from the *Production.Product* table. Note that we convert the prices from the *Product* table to *CURRENCY_VALUE* when we insert them into the new table. Also note that we can use the public properties of the type to read and write data:

```
CREATE TABLE Production.TestProducts
(
    Name NVARCHAR(100) NULL
    ,Price dbo.CURRENCY_VALUE NULL
);

INSERT Production.TestProducts (Name, Price)
    SELECT
        Name
        ,CAST('SEK ' + CAST(ListPrice AS NVARCHAR(100)) AS dbo.CURRENCY_VALUE)
    FROM Production.Product;

UPDATE Production.TestProducts SET
    Price.CurrencyCode = 'USD'
WHERE Price.Value = 3578.27000;

SELECT
    Name
    ,Price.CurrencyCode
    ,Price.Value
    ,Price
FROM Production.TestProducts
WHERE Price.CurrencyCode = 'USD';
```

Here is the result:

```
        Price
---- ------------  -----------------------------------------
USD  3578.27000    0xC3750500000000000000000000020003555344
USD  3578.27000    0xC3750500000000000000000000020003555344
USD  3578.27000    0xC3750500000000000000000000020003555344
USD  3578.27000    0xC3750500000000000000000000020003555344
USD  3578.27000    0xC3750500000000000000000000020003555344
```

As you can see, when you query the UDT without calling a property, you see the raw byte form of the type. For the value 0x**C375050000000000000000000002**0003555344, the first 16 bytes shown in bold type represent the decimal value. It is placed before the string simply because we wrote it out before the string in the *Write* method. Of course, it is very important to read the data in the same order that you write it in the *Read* method; otherwise, you will end up with some really nasty bugs. If you were to use the native format instead, you wouldn't need to worry about this. However, because the native format is very limited as to which data types can be used, you typically will need to use the user-defined format. The last 4 bytes of the type are the string that represents the currency code 03555344 (03 = three characters in the string, followed by the hexadecimal representation of each character: 55H/85D = U, 53H/83D = S, and 44H/68D = D).

As with UDFs, the result of a UDT's method can be persisted and indexed (in this case, it must be persisted to be indexed) using a computed column. Consider the following T-SQL example, where we create a persisted computed column to index the currency code of the price in the *Production.TestProducts* table and then query the column for the number of prices that are noted in Swedish kronor (SEK):

```
ALTER TABLE Production.TestProducts
    ADD ComputedCurrencyCode AS Price.CurrencyCode
    PERSISTED; -- Must be persisted in order to index.

CREATE NONCLUSTERED INDEX ComputedCurrencyCodeIdx
    ON Production.TestProducts (ComputedCurrencyCode );
GO

SELECT COUNT(*)
FROM Production.TestProducts
WHERE ComputedCurrencyCode = 'SEK';
-- SQL Server performs an index seek operation using the
-- ComputedCurrencyCodeIdx index.
```

An interesting note is that the optimizer notices that the *ComputedCurrencyCodeIdx* exists for the expression used in the last query and uses the index even if we do not query the computed column directly, as in this example (the change is shown in bold type):

```
SELECT COUNT(*)
FROM Production.TestProducts
WHERE Price.CurrencyCode = 'SEK';
-- SQL Server still performs an index seek operation using the
-- ComputedCurrencyCodeIdx index.
```

What Is My CLR Code Allowed to Do?

The CLR code that is used within your database can be placed in one of three different "permission sets": *SAFE, EXTERNALACCESS,* and *UNSAFE*. The default permission set is *SAFE*. *SAFE* is the permission set that has been used for all examples in this lesson, and it is also the permission set that you should try to use at all times to minimize both security problems as well as the potential impact of bugs. The meaning of each permission set is explained here:

- **SAFE**   A *SAFE* assembly is not allowed to access any resources outside the database to which it is deployed; it can only perform calculations and access the local database.

- **EXTERNAL ACCESS**   An *EXTERNAL ACCESS* assembly is allowed to access resources outside the local SQL Server instance to which it is deployed, such as another SQL Server instance, the file system, or even a network resource such as a Web service.

- **UNSAFE**   An *UNSAFE* assembly is allowed to go even further than *EXTERNAL ACCESS*. It is allowed to execute non-CLR (also called *unmanaged*) code such as a Win32 API or a COM component.

Using *Filestream*

Filestream is an option that can be specified for columns of the *varbinary(max)* data type. In essence, it makes SQL Server store the data in these columns in separate files in the file system instead of inside the actual database files. The use of *Filestream* can greatly enhance both the read and the write performance of this type of data.

Filestream is typically recommended if the data that you store in the column is at least 1 megabyte (MB) in size. *Filestream* can hurt performance if you have very frequent inserts of small BLOB data.

To be able to use *Filestream*, you need to enable it in SQL Server by setting the *sp_configure* option to 1, 2, or 3. Setting the configuration option to 1 allows only T-SQL access to the *Filestream* data, and setting the option to 2 also allows direct file access to the data through the file system. Finally, setting the option to 3 allows access to the *Filestream* data through a file (network) share. To use *Filestream*, you must also create a filegroup that contains a *Filestream* database file. The *Filestream* database file isn't really a file; it is a directory where the *Filestream* data files are stored. A *Filestream* filegroup can have only one "database file."

The following code example shows how to add a *Filestream* filegroup to the *AdventureWorks* database (the *FILENAME* string has been formatted to fit on the printed page):

```
ALTER DATABASE AdventureWorks
    ADD FILEGROUP FileStreamPhotosFG
        CONTAINS FILESTREAM;

ALTER DATABASE AdventureWorks
    ADD FILE
    (
        NAME = 'FileStreamPhotosDF'
        ,FILENAME = 'C:\Program Files\Microsoft SQL Server\
                    MSSQL10.MSSQLSERVER\MSSQL\DATA\FileStreamPhotosDF'
    )
    TO FILEGROUP FileStreamPhotosFG;
```

When the filegroup has been added, *varbinary(max) Filestream* columns can be created. For a table to contain *Filestream* columns, it must have a *uniqueidentifier* column marked with the property *ROWGUIDCOL* and having a unique constraint defined on it. The following code sample shows how to add a *ROWGUIDCOL* to the *Production.ProductPhoto* table:

```
ALTER TABLE Production.ProductPhoto
    ADD RowGuid UNIQUEIDENTIFIER NOT NULL
        ROWGUIDCOL
        CONSTRAINT DFProductPhotoRowGuid DEFAULT NEWSEQUENTIALID()
        CONSTRAINT UQProductPhotoRowGuid UNIQUE;
```

Now we can add a *varbinary(max) Filestream* column and copy data into it using regular T-SQL:

```
ALTER TABLE Production.ProductPhoto
    ADD ThumbNailPhotoAsFileStream VARBINARY(MAX) FILESTREAM NULL;
GO

UPDATE Production.ProductPhoto SET
    ThumbNailPhotoAsFileStream = ThumbNailPhoto;
```

If we examine the C:\Program Files\Microsoft SQL Server\MSSQL10.MSSQLSERVER\MSSQL\DATA\FileStreamPhotosDF folder, we find the following items in it:

- The $FSLOG directory acts as the *Filestream* data's transaction log.
- The Filestream.hdr file stores metadata about the *Filestream* filegroup.
- All other directories with GUID names, such as 09A42544-450A-4932-B25F-5E33F117C179, are the directories that store the actual data.

When you delete *Filestream* data (either by using an *UPDATE* or a *DELETE* statement), SQL Server doesn't immediately delete the file. Instead, the files are deleted when the *Filestream* garbage collection process is run. This process in turn is run when the database checkpoint process is executed.

Lesson Summary

- To use user-defined objects based on SQLCLR, SQLCLR must be enabled on the SQL Server instance.
- The objects most suitable for development using SQLCLR are UDFs and user-defined aggregates.
- If you create UDTs based on SQLCLR, make sure that you test them thoroughly.
- Consider using *Filestream* if the relevant data mostly involves storing streams larger than 1 MB.

PRACTICE SQLCLR

In this practice, you create and use both a scalar and table-valued CLR UDF in the *AdventureWorks* database.

EXERCISE 1 Create a Scalar UDF

In this exercise, you create a scalar UDF that allows a *datetime2* value to be converted to a string by applying a *format* string (such as *yyyy-MM-dd*).

1. Create a new directory in the root of your hard drive called TK433SQLCLR (the path would be C:\TK433SQLCLR).

2. Create a new file in the C:\TK433SQLCLR directory called ScalarUDF.cs (if you want to use C# to create the function) or ScalarUDF.vb (if you want to use Visual Basic .NET).

3. Type the following code block into the file using a text editor such as Notepad.exe, and then save and close the file:

```
'VB:
Imports System
Imports System.Data.SqlTypes

Namespace TK433.ClrLab
    Public Class ScalarUdf
        Public Shared Function DateTimeToString( _
            ByVal dateTime As SqlDateTime, ByVal format As SqlString) _
            As SqlString

            If dateTime.IsNull Or format.IsNull Then
                Return SqlString.Null
            End If

            Return dateTime.Value.ToString(format.Value)
        End Function
    End Class
End Namespace
```

```csharp
//C#:
using System;
using System.Data.SqlTypes;

namespace TK433.ClrLab
{
    public class ScalarUdf
    {
        static public SqlString DateTimeToString(SqlDateTime dateTime, SqlString
          format)
        {
            if(dateTime.IsNull || format.IsNull)
                return SqlString.Null;

            return dateTime.Value.ToString(format.Value);
        }
    }
}
```

4. Open a new command prompt and enter the following commands to set the path environment variable to point to the directory that contains the CLR compilers and to change the folder in which you saved your source code:

```
PATH "C:\Windows\Microsoft.NET\Framework\v3.5"
C:
CD \TK433SQLCLR
```

5. In the same command prompt, enter the following command to compile the assembly:

```csharp
//C#:
csc /target:library /out:ScalarUDF.dll ScalarUDF.cs
```

```vbnet
'VB:
vbc /target:library /out:ScalarUDF.dll ScalarUDF.vb
```

6. If necessary, open SSMS and connect to the appropriate instance of SQL Server 2008.

7. In a new query window, type and execute the following SQL statements to create the *ScalarUDF* assembly in the *AdventureWorks* database:

```sql
USE AdventureWorks;
GO

CREATE ASSEMBLY ScalarUDF
    FROM 'C:\TK433SQLCLR\ScalarUDF.dll';
```

8. In the existing query window, type, highlight, and execute the following SQL statements to create the *fnDateTimeToString* UDF.

```
CREATE FUNCTION dbo.fnDateTimeToString
(
    @DateTime DATETIME
    ,@Format NVARCHAR(50)
)
RETURNS NVARCHAR(50)
AS
EXTERNAL NAME ScalarUDF."TK433.ClrLab.ScalarUdf".DateTimeToString;
```

9. In the same query window, type, highlight, and execute the following *SELECT* statement to execute the *fnDateTimeToString* UDF:

```
SELECT TOP(5)
    CustomerID
    ,dbo.fnDateTimeToString(OrderDate, N'yyyy_MM_dd')
FROM Sales.SalesOrderHeader;
```

The result should look like this:

```
CustomerID
------------- -----------
676           2001_07_01
117           2001_07_01
442           2001_07_01
227           2001_07_01
510           2001_07_01
```

EXERCISE 2   Create a Table-Valued UDF

In this exercise, you create a table-valued UDF that returns a numbers table. Because of the extra code involved with using Visual Basic .NET, only a C# solution is provided.

1. In the C:\TK433SQLCLR directory created in Exercise 1, create a new file called TableValuedUDF.cs.

2. Type the following code block into the file using a text editor such as Notepad.exe, and then save and close the file:

```
//C#
using System;
using System.Collections;
using System.Data.SqlTypes;
using Microsoft.SqlServer.Server;

namespace TK433.ClrLab
{
    public class TableValuedUdf
```

```
        {
            [SqlFunction(FillRowMethodName = "GetNumbersTableFillRow",
            TableDefinition = "Number INT")]
            static public IEnumerable GetNumbersTable(
                SqlInt32 startNumber, SqlInt32 endNumber)
            {
                for (int number = startNumber.Value; number <= endNumber.Value;
                    ++number)
                {
                    yield return number;
                }
            ]

            static private void GetNumbersTableFillRow(
                object value, out SqlInt32 number)
            {
                number = (int)value;
            }
        }
    }
```

3. Open a command prompt and enter the following commands to set the path environment variable to point to the directory that contains the CLR compilers and change to the folder in which you saved the source code:

```
PATH "C:\Windows\Microsoft.NET\Framework\v3.5"
C:
CD \TK433SQLCLR
```

4. In the same command window, enter the following command to compile the assembly.

```
csc /target:library /out:TableValuedUDF.dll TableValuedUDF.cs
```

5. If necessary, open SSMS and connect to the appropriate instance of SQL Server 2008.

6. In a new query window, type and execute the following SQL statements to create the *TableValuedUDF* assembly in the *AdventureWorks* database:

```
USE AdventureWorks;
GO

CREATE ASSEMBLY TableValuedUDF
    FROM 'C:\TK433SQLCLR\TableValuedUDF.dll';
```

7. In the existing query window, type, highlight, and execute the following SQL statements to create the *fnGetNumbersTable* UDF.

```
CREATE FUNCTION dbo.fnGetNumbersTable
(
    @StartNumber INT
    ,@EndNumber INT
)
```

```
RETURNS TABLE (Number INT)
AS
EXTERNAL NAME TableValuedUDF."TK433.ClrLab.TableValuedUdf".GetNumbersTable;
```

8. In the existing query window, type, highlight, and execute the following *SELECT* statement to execute the *fnGetNumbersTable* UDF.

```
SELECT *
FROM dbo.fnGetNumbersTable(501, 505) AS n;
```

The result should look like this:

```
Number
-----------
501
502
503
504
505
```

Chapter Review

To practice and reinforce the skills you learned in this chapter further, you can do any or all of the following:

- Review the chapter summary.
- Review the list of key terms introduced in this chapter.
- Complete the case scenario. This scenario sets up a real-world situation involving the topics of this chapter and asks you to create solutions.
- Complete the suggested practices.
- Take a practice test.

Chapter Summary

- Consider whether using XML as a transport protocol between your application (or parts of your application) and SQL Server is the right solution for your business needs.
- Think twice about storing data in the database as XML; only do so if storing these values in tabular form either is not possible or is very cumbersome.
- Consider the pros and cons of using XML schema collections to validate your XML. Remember that schema validation isn't always beneficial.
- Before using SQLCLR, make sure that it is allowed on the SQL Server instance that your application is using.
- Think twice about using SQLCLR. As with XML, only do so if it is clearly the right way to meet your business needs; for instance, if the performance is a lot better than T-SQL or perhaps because it makes the code much easier to write and maintain.
- Remember that there is extra work associated with deploying SQLCLR objects (installing assemblies and so forth).

Key Terms

- XML
- XML document
- XML fragment
- *FOR XML*
- *XML* data type
- SQLCLR
- *Filestream*

Case Scenario

In the following case scenario, you apply what you have learned in this chapter. You can find answers to these questions in the "Answers" section at the end of this book.

Case Scenario: How Should You Store Data?

You are a database developer for Contoso News Corporation. You have been given the responsibility to design the storage of news articles produced by the organization's reporters. An article always has a title, but its content may consist of several paragraphs, tables, headings, and lists. An article must always be assigned to a predefined category.

Answer the following question for your manager:

- How would you design the storage of this data? That is, which tables do you need and which columns do you need in each table?

Suggested Practices

To help you master the exam objectives presented in this chapter, do all of the following practices:

Create and Deploy CLR-Based Objects

- **Practice 1**   Create the tables suggested in the answer of the case scenario and populate them with at least five articles.

Retrieve Relational Data as XML

- **Practice 2**   Create an XML schema collection that validates the content XML column from Practice 1.

- **Practice 3**   Apply the XML schema collection from Practice 2 to the content column.

Transform XML Data into Relational Data

- **Practice 4**   Modify the schema used by the XML schema collection in Practice 3 by, for example, changing the name of one of the defined elements.

Query XML Data

- **Practice 5**   Using SQLCLR, create a UDT that can store information about a customer, including name, phone number, and address.

- **Practice 6**   Use the data type that you created in Practice 5 to create a column in a table, and then populate it with a few customers.

Manage XML Data

- **Practice 7**   Change the definition of your customer UDT by creating a column in the table to store the address. Instead of using a UDT, move the address from the UDT to the new column, remove the *address* property from the UDT, and redeploy the UDT to the SQL Server instance.

Take a Practice Test

The practice tests on this book's companion CD offer many options. For example, you can test yourself on just the content covered in this chapter, or you can test yourself on all the 70-433 certification exam content. You can set up the test so that it closely simulates the experience of taking a certification exam, or you can set it up in study mode so that you can look at the correct answers and explanations after you answer each question.

> **MORE INFO   PRACTICE TESTS**
>
> For details about all the practice test options available, see the section entitled "How to Use the Practice Tests" in the Introduction to this book.

Extending Microsoft SQL Server Functionality with the Spatial, Full-Text Search, and Service Broker

With the new spatial data types provided in Microsoft SQL Server 2008, you can store location data that allows you to work with location and geospatial information. You can use the *geography* and *geometry* data types to track standard geometric *x, y,* and *z* coordinates, as well as ellipsoidal (round-earth) representations such as latitude and longitude. Companies might use this data to track sales regions, determine routes from a warehouse to a store, or determine the location of a particular classroom in a school and find the distance to the nearest fire escape.

As a database developer, your databases can contain special function data types such as *varchar(max)*, *XML*, *geometry*, or *geography*. SQL Server 2008 provides you with the tools you need to use this data efficiently. The full-text search capabilities allow you to perform advanced linguistic based searches that are well beyond the capabilities of the *LIKE* clause. In addtion, these searches can be completed on columns with data types such as *varbinary(max)* that cannot be listed as key columns in standard indexes.

In addition, SQL Server Service Broker allows you to build applications that take advantage of the guaranteed asynchronous message delivery between local or remote services. Service Broker uses a combination of objects such as queues, dialogs, contracts, services, and message types to develop asynchronous messaging solutions. A company might use Service Broker to design a series of applications that automate the reimbursement of travel expenses for company employees. When employees fill out expense reports, the information is sent to a queue where it is stored until the nightly batch processing of the reports. Expense reports with the appropriate information are then sent to an application to be paid. Incomplete expense reports are flagged and then forwarded through another service to a queue to await manual processing by a manager.

Exam objectives in this chapter:

- Implement data types.
- Implement full-text search.
- Implement Service Broker solutions.

Lessons in this chapter:

Before You Begin

To complete the lessons in this chapter, you must have:

- A basic understanding of SQL Server data types
- A general understanding of Common Language Runtime (CLR) data types
- An understanding of basic data manipulation language (DML) constructs, such as *INSERT*, *UPDATE*, and *DELETE*
- A general understanding of *SELECT* statement syntax
- A basic understanding of data definition language (DDL) code structure
- Knowledge about how to open and execute queries in SQL Server Management Studio (SSMS)
- SQL Server 2008 Developer Edition, Enterprise Edition, or Enterprise Evaluation Edition, with the *AdventureWorks2008* sample database installed

 REAL WORLD

Michael Hotek

A customer of mine who runs a very large retail Web site had a large business problem when processing credit cards. Their Web site required the customer's credit card to be charged before checkout could be completed. Once the order was completed, the available inventory could be debited.

Credit card processing is a complicated process with many components. Credit cards are received on the Web site, encrypted, and securely submitted to a payment gateway. The payment gateway forwards the request to your merchant processor. The merchant processor might forward the request to a payment aggregator or intermediary bank. The request is then forwarded to the credit card company. The credit card company looks up the account, performs fraud and account balance checks, and returns an approval or rejection.

If any system is unavailable between the Web site and credit card company, payments cannot be processed. The payment system also has a timing mechanism that attempts to defeat hacking and other third-party fraud activity such that if a response is not received within a specific amount of time, the charge is automatically rejected. If any system between the merchant and credit card company is overwhelmed with requests and too busy to respond in a timely manner, payments cannot be processed.

One or more systems between the company's Web site and the credit card company were frequently unavailable, thereby causing a significant number of outages. While each outage was usually less than one hour, any problems cost the company a significant amount of revenue. Solving the outages could be accomplished very easily by taking all the payment processing offline and allowing the orders to be completed. Unfortunately, this customer was dealing with very limited inventory where the demand almost always exceeded the supply, hence the requirement to receive payment before an order was allowed to complete and inventory debited.

We solved their outage problems, which were costing the company millions of dollars in lost revenue, by implementing a Service Broker solution. Service Broker allowed us to move the payment processing to a background task when necessary. Orders would first be processed using the normal methods, but if the credit card could not be processed due to an outage, the order would be placed onto a Service Broker queue and the customer would be allowed to complete their order, subject to payment acceptance. The Service Broker application would then retry the payment system until the payment could be processed. To preserve the integrity of the inventory, once an order was placed on the Service Broker queue, all orders would be sent to the queue to ensure a first-come, first-served access to available inventory. Only when the queue was empty would the order processing revert to directly processing payments.

The implementation of Service Broker saved the company hundreds of thousands of dollars of custom development and third-party applications. The Service Broker implementation also eliminated all the outages caused by the payment system, thereby adding over $20 million in net profit.

Lesson 1: Implementing Spatial Data Types

SQL Server 2008 includes a variety of new data types, including two spatial data types that allow you to manage geographical and geometric data. By using these data types, you can store location information such as latitude and longitude, which can be used in conjunction with Microsoft Virtual Earth to provide a visual representation of your geospatial data.

> **After this lesson, you will be able to:**
> - Describe the functionality of the *geometry* and *geography* data types.
> - Instantiate spatial data types.
>
> **Estimated lesson time: 60 minutes**

> **MORE INFO   ADDITIONAL DATA TYPES**
>
> For more information about SQL Server data types and how they function, see Chapter 3, "Tables, Data Types, and Declarative Data Integrity."

Understanding Spatial Data Types

SQL Server 2008 includes two new data types to help you work with spatial data. The *geometry* and *geography* data types offer this support and are implemented as .NET CLR data types in SQL Server 2008. Both the *geometry* and *geography* types are predefined and available in each database on your server as system objects and do not require any additional configuration before they can be used.

> **REAL WORLD**
>
> Michael Hotek
>
> One of our customers, a large engineering firm specializing in custom machinery, needed to streamline its supply chain and be able to return quotes to its customers. New machinery requests were first sent to a drafting department, where an engineering team created detailed specifications of each component. Once the detailed specifications were created, a research team would search through hundreds of electronic catalogs to locate any components that could be purchased off the shelf. Any components that could not be located would be sent out for a quote to custom fabricators. The entire process could take as long as three months to compile a quote for the customer, and more than 60 percent of the components required custom fabrication. By reducing the number of components requiring custom fabrication, the firm could reduce the overall cost to the customer as well as reducing the delivery time.

To improve the offerings to their customers, a new system was designed that used the *geometry* data type. The drafting department created detailed specifications for each component in a machine. Once created, the CAD system generated two-dimensional slices of the three-dimensional components at each 1 millimeter of height. The catalogs of all their suppliers were also imported into a SQL Server database. All components were also modeled with two-dimensional slices taken at each 1 millimeter of height. After the detailed design specifications were created by the drafting department, a spatial query could be executed that located all stock components that matched the dimensions. The query was designed with a 10 percent error factor, which would allow the drafting team to decide if small changes to a component could be made such that it matched a stock component, thereby eliminating a custom component.

Once implemented, the system increased the match rate and the firm was able to purchase more than 70 percent of the necessary components off the shelf. The response to customers for a quote was reduced to an average of six weeks. However, the biggest impact was in the cost savings. By being able to match a higher percentage of off-the-shelf components, the firm was able to reduce the overall cost of a machine by more than 40 percent and is projecting a reduction in the assembly time of almost 50 percent, thereby saving their customers an average of $6 million per machine.

Understanding Spatial Data Terminology

When you are working with spatial data, you need to be familiar with the following terms:

- *geography* **data type**   A data type used to store ellipsoidal data, such as latitude and longitude coordinates. Virtual Earth, many mapping products, and census results typically feature ellipsoidal measurements.

- *geometry* **data type**   A data type used to store two and three dimensional data coordinates. For example, you can use the *geometry* data type to track locations where different products are stored within a warehouse.

> **MORE INFO**   **COMPARING TYPES OF SPATIAL DATA**
>
> For more information about differences between the two spatial data types as well as how measurements and orientation are affected with each data type, see the article "Types of Spatial Data" in SQL Server Books Online.

- **Open Geospatial Consortium (OGC)**   An international, nonprofit organization that develops standards for geospatial- and location-based services.

MORE INFO OGC STANDARDS ORGANIZATION

For more information about the Open Geospatial Consortium (OGC) and the associated standards, see *http://www.opengeospatial.org/.*

- **Well-known text (WKT)** A standard created by the OGC used to represent text-based descriptions of geospatial objects.

- **Well-known binary (WKB)** The binary equivalent to WKT, which is sometimes used to transfer and store spatial data.

- **Methods** Actions an object can perform.

- **OGC and Extended Methods** Methods designed to work with *geometry* and *geography* data types.

- **Object** A collection of properties and methods that provide a defined functionality.

- **Instantiation** The process of producing a particular instance of an object based on the object's properties and methods.

- **Spatial Reference Identifier (SRID***)* A reference ID associated with a specific model of the earth. These IDs reference the European Petroleum Survey Group (EPSG) standard identification system. For example, SRID 4326, the default geography SRID, maps to the WGS 84 standard. Since *geometry* data types can exist in undefined planar space, the default geometry SRID is 0, representing undefined planar space.

MORE INFO WGS 84

For more information about the WGS 84 system and additional geodetic standards, see *http://www.ngs.noaa.gov/faq.shtml#WGS84.*

- **Instance types (or spatial data objects)** A group of 11 spatial data objects designed to allow you to work with geometrical or geographical data. Only seven of these objects are instantiable in a database. The spatial instance types are part of the *GeometryCollection* and are built in a hierarchy. Each object receives properties from its parent object in the class hierarchy, as shown in Figure 8-1.

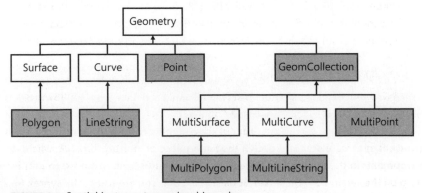

FIGURE 8-1 Spatial instance types class hierarchy

Both the *geometry* and *geography* data types support these spatial instance types (data objects). As indicated by the gray boxes in Figure 8-1, the *Point*, *LineString*, *Polygon*, *MultiPolygon*, *MultiLineString*, *MultiPoint*, and *GeomCollection* instance types can be instantiated in your SQL Server databases. The white boxes represent spatial instance types that are used to define general properties that are inherited by objects below them but are not complete enough to be instantiated on their own.

Restrictions When Using the *geography* Data Type

When you use the *geography* data type, each *geography* instance must fit inside a single hemisphere. You cannot store objects larger than a hemisphere. We typically think of hemispheres as the Northern, Southern, Eastern, and Western Hemispheres, but this is not the case with the *geography* data type. For the *geography* data type, a hemisphere simply represents one half of the globe. In addition, if you use a *geography* data type that requires the input of two or more *geography* instances, and the results from the methods do not fit inside a single hemisphere, the output returns *NULL*. Finally, when you use a WKT or WKB representation, the results must fit inside a single hemisphere or the system throws an *ArgumentException*.

Instantiating Spatial Data Types

Before you can instantiate spatial data types, you must create a table that includes a column defined with the *geometry* or *geography* data type. For our examples in this chapter, we use the *geography* data type.

The following sample code creates a table named *Museum*. The *Location* column holds geospatial data for the museum location:

```
CREATE TABLE Museum
(MuseumID int IDENTITY PRIMARY KEY,
 MuseumName nchar(50),
 MuseumAddress nvarchar(200),
 Location geography);
```

Once you have created the table with a *geography* column, you can instantiate the spatial data type by inserting geodetic data, such as latitude and longitude, into the table.

There are a large number of methods available to allow you to enter information of different formats into the *geography* column. The *Point* extended static *geography* method constructs an instance representing a point that includes information on the longitude, latitude, and SRID.

IMPORTANT **ORDER OF ARGUMENTS**

It is important to remember that geospatial data is frequently referred to in terms of latitude followed by longitude. If you used a Community Technology Preview (CTP) release of SQL Server 2008 prior to CTP 6, the order of the commands was also latitude followed by longitude. Beginning with CTP 6 and in the final release of SQL Server 2008, Microsoft put the arguments in the order of longitude followed by latitude, in response to user input. Depending on the version of SQL Server Books Online that you are using, the syntax for the spatial methods might have the longitude and latitude values reversed.

The *Parse* extended static *geography* method returns a *geography* instance when the input is expressed in the OGC WKT representation. The *Parse* method has a single input parameter that defines the WKT representation of the *geometry* instance to be returned.

The following code adds a row for the COSI museum in Columbus, Ohio, to the *Museum* table. This code uses the *Parse* and *Point* methods to create an instance of a point based on a WKT description. The default SRID of 4326 is used:

```
INSERT INTO Museum
 (MuseumName, MuseumAddress, Location)
 VALUES
 ('COSI Columbus',
   '333 West Broad Street, Columbus, OH 43215',
   geography::Parse('POINT(-83.0086 39.95954)'));
```

Figure 8-2 shows a *SELECT* command and result set displaying the text output for the COSI museum row entered previously.

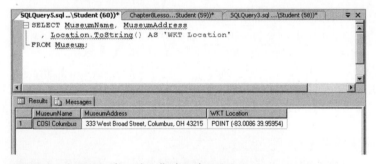

FIGURE 8-2 A *geography* point displayed as text

The *ToString* function displays the *geography* value as readable text in the same WKT representation that you used when you added the row. Figure 8-3 shows location information without converting the location to a string for readability.

Notice in Figure 8-3, that an additional tab named Spatial Results appears next to the Results tab. This tab can be used to view a graphical representation of your spatial data.

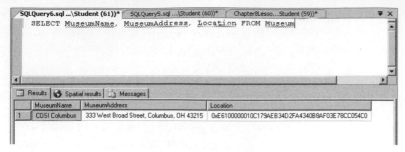

FIGURE 8-3 A *geography* point returned as a hexadecimal value, which is difficult to read

Before creating Figure 8-4, a new row for the Columbus Art Museum is added to the table. You can use the following code to add the second row to the *Museum* table:

```
INSERT INTO Museum
 (MuseumName, MuseumAddress, Location)
VALUES
('Columbus Art Museum',
  '480 East Broad Street, Columbus, OH 43215',
  geography::Parse('POINT(-82.98775 39.963775)'));
```

Figure 8-4 represents two points of data in the museum table. Unfortunately, it is difficult to see these individual points in the screen capture. A description of the point appears when you place the pointer over the location, as shown in Figure 8-4.

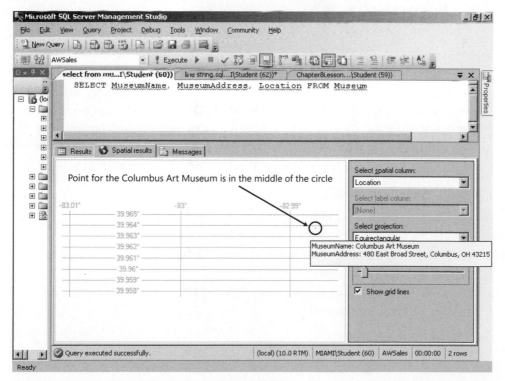

FIGURE 8-4 Sample of two points in the Spatial Results tab

To better demonstrate the Spatial Results tab, you can create a line using the *STLineFromText* and *LINESTRING* methods. The following code defines a *geography* type variable and sets the variable to a line between two points. Figure 8-5 shows the line displayed in the Spatial Results tab.

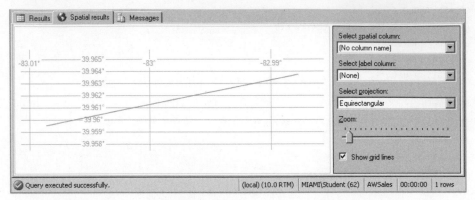

FIGURE 8-5 Example of the *LINESTRING* method

> **MORE INFO** **SQL SERVER SPATIAL DATA**
>
> For more information about working with spatial data in SQL Server 2008, see "Spatial Ed" at *http://blogs.msdn.com/edkatibah/*.

PRACTICE Instantiating Spatial Data Types

In this practice, you create a new table named *Airports* to store location data for airports used by customers of your travel agency. You then use several methods to add the geodetic coordinates for each location. You also create a *Sales* table to track the sales regions in which your travel agents are assigned customers. You use the Spatial Results tab in SSMS to view a sales region.

EXERCISE 1 Work with Points

In this exercise, you instantiate spatial data points and use the Spatial Results tab to view the points that you entered.

1. Start SSMS (if it's not already started), connect to the appropriate SQL Server instance, and open a new query window.

2. In the new query window, type and execute the following command to create a new database for your travel agency:

```
CREATE DATABASE Travel;
GO
```

3. Below the existing text, type, highlight, and execute the following code to create the *Airports* and *Sales* tables:

```
USE Travel;

CREATE TABLE Airports
(AirportID int IDENTITY PRIMARY KEY
, AirportName nchar(50)
, AirportCode nchar(3)
, Location geography);

 CREATE TABLE Sales
(SalesPersonID int IDENTITY PRIMARY KEY
, FirstName nchar(50)
, LastName nchar(50)
, SalesRegionName Nchar(50)
, SalesRegionDesc nvarchar(200)
, SalesRegion geography);
```

4. Below the existing text, type, highlight, and execute the following code to add rows for the Los Angeles International Airport (LAX) and London Heathrow Airport (LHR) to the *Airports* table:

```
INSERT INTO Airports
    (AirportName, AirportCode, Location)
    VALUES ('Los Angeles International Airport'
    , 'LAX'
    , geography::STGeomFromText('POINT( -118.4071611 33.9425222)', 4326));

INSERT INTO Airports
    (AirportName, AirportCode, Location)
    VALUES ('London Heathrow Airport'
    , 'LHR'
    , geography::Parse('POINT(-0.45277777 51.47138888)'));
```

5. Practice using various methods to add rows for the remaining airports in the Airport.xls file, which you can find in the Chapter08\Lesson 1 folder in the samples installed from the companion CD.

6. Below the existing text, type, highlight, and execute the following command to view the data that you have entered into the *Airports* table:

```
SELECT * FROM Airports;
```

7. Switch to the Spatial Results tab. Place the pointer over each of the dots representing the airports to view their properties. If necessary, use *WHERE* clauses to limit the result set to make it easier to read.

8. Leave SSMS open for the next exercise.

EXERCISE 2   Work with a Polygon

In this exercise, you instantiate spatial data as a polygon and use the Spatial Results tab to view the polygon that you created.

1. Open a new query window.

2. In the query window, type and execute the following code to add Kim Abercrombie to the *Sales* table:

```
USE Travel;


INSERT INTO Sales
 (FirstName, LastName, SalesRegionName, SalesRegionDesc, SalesRegion)
 VALUES
 ('Kim',
  ' Abercrombie ',
  'Southeast US',
  'Florida, Georgia, Alabama',
  geography::STGeomFromText('POLYGON(( -88.34609167 30.286825,
       -86.28281667 30.43045278,
       -85.10322222 29.63877222,
       -84.04541389 30.06674722,
       -82.78871389 29.10671389,
       -82.80399722 28.12101667,
       -82.63304722 27.47348611,
       -82.12766111 26.46439722,
       -81.65219167 25.88982778,
       -81.06721944 25.18627222,
       -80.41878333 25.15618611,
       -80.01395278 26.75898889,
       -80.55964722 28.29220833,
       -80.53146667 28.59193056,
       -81.41381944 30.69794444,
       -80.90161944 31.97196944,
       -83.19839167 34.92200556,
       -88.13663611 34.96236944,
       -88.34609167 30.286825 ))', 4326));
```

3. Below the existing text, type and execute the following text to view the row that you entered into the *Sales* table.

```
SELECT * FROM Sales;
```

4. In the query window, review the results of the query, click the Spatial Results tab, and review the shape of the Southeast US region.

5. Save your script, and close SSMS.

Lesson Summary

- The *geography* and *geometry* data types provide you with the ability to work with spatial data with system-defined data types rather than having to define your own CLR data types.

- You can instantiate spatial data by using any of the spatial methods included with SQL Server 2008.

Lesson 2: Implementing Full-Text Search

SQL Server 2008 includes a fully integrated full-text search engine. Full-text search allows you to build advanced queries that go beyond the capabilities of the traditional *SELECT* command with the *LIKE* argument. By using the *CONTAINS* and *FREETEXT* predicates as well as the *CONTAINSTABLE* and *FREETEXTTABLE* functions, you can write queries that return the following:

- Inflectional forms of a verb that you input
- Matched results from data stored as a PDF file in a *varbinary(max)* column
- Synonyms of the search term located through a thesaurus search

This lesson provides you with an overview of the full-text search architecture and an overview of how to configure full-text search in SQL Server 2008. You also learn about and practice writing full-text search queries.

After this lesson, you will be able to:

- Describe the full-text search capabilities in SQL Server 2008.
- Configure full-text indexes.
- Write full-text queries by using *CONTAINS, CONTAINSTABLE, FREETEXT,* and *FREETEXTTABLE*.

Estimated lesson time: 60 minutes

Overview of Full-Text Search

Full-text search capabilities were introduced in SQL Server 7.0 and continue to progress and improve through each new release. In SQL Server 2008, the full-text search service is fully integrated with the Database Engine and no longer requires an external search service. In addition, full-text indexes can exist as a part of the database structure rather than in a separate file in the file system.

Full-Text Search Architecture

To be able to troubleshoot improperly functioning full-text queries, you should be familiar with the general architecture and configuration of full-text search.

The following processes make up the full-text search architecture:

- **SQL Server process (Sqlservr.exe)** Contains the Full-Text Engine, which manages full-text indexing and queries. Because of this complete integration with the Database Engine, the optimizer recognizes and enhances performance on full-text queries.

- **Filter daemon host process (Fdhost.exe)**   Runs as an isolated process to host third-party components, thus protecting the SQL Server process from those components.
- **SQL Full-Text Filter Daemon Launcher (Fdlauncher.exe)**   Starts Fdhost.exe processes when required.

Full-Text Terminology

In learning about full-text search, you might encounter a large number of new concepts and terminology. These concepts and terms include the following:

- **Term**   The word, phrase, or character string included as input in the full-text query.
- **Full-text catalog**   A virtual object that represents a group of full-text indexes. When you create a full-text catalog in a SQL Server 2008 environment, the full-text catalog does not belong to any filegroups.
- **Full-text index**   An object that contains significant words and their locations within the columns included in the index. When you define the full-text index, you specify a unique index that identifies the rows in the table, what columns are to be included in the index, the catalog to which the index belongs, the filegroup on which the index is created, and additional options.
- **Word breaker**   A process that finds word boundaries (that is, tokenizes words) based on the linguistic rules for the data language defined. You can define the language of the data in the column when creating a full-text index on a table.
- **Token**   A word or character string defined by a word breaker.
- **Stemmer**   A process that conjugates verbs based on the linguistic rules of the data language defined.
- **Thesaurus**   Extensible Markup Language (XML) files that define the synonyms for a term in a specific language. You must define thesaurus mappings for a given language before full-text queries can look for synonyms in that language. The thesaurus files are empty by default.
- **Stopword**   A word that is commonly used and adds no meaning to a search, such as *a, an,* and *the.* Stopwords in SQL Server 2008 provide similar functionality to noise words in SQL Server 2005.

- **Stoplist**   A database object that is used to manage stopwords. There is a system-defined stoplist and you can also create your own stoplists. A stoplist can be associated with a full-text index.

- **Filter**   A component that processes a document to extract the textual information from documents stored in a *varbinary(max)* or *image* column and then sends that information to the word breaker. Each file type (such as .doc, .xls, and .pdf) must have its own filter. When you define a full-text index on a *varbinary(max)* or *image* column containing documents, you must also define a type column that contains the file extension associated with the file type contained in the same row.

- **Population (crawl)**   The process of adding data to (populating) an index either during creation or when the index is rebuilt. This can be initiated automatically or manually.

- **Full-Text Engine**   An integral component of the SQL Server Service process that manages full-text administrative tasks, handles full-text query execution, and manages the filter daemon host process.

- **Filter daemon host process (Fdhost.exe)**   A process that manages third-party components such as filters, word breakers, and stemmers separated from the SQL Server process.

- **SQL Full-Text Filter Daemon Launcher (Fdlauncher.exe***)   A service that starts Fdhost.exe processes when the Full-Text Engine requires them. This is the only function of this service.

> **MORE INFO   STOPLISTS AND THESAURUS FILES**
>
> For more information about stoplists and thesaurus files, including how to create and edit them, see "CREATE FULL-TEXT STOPLIST (Transact-SQL)," "Thesaurus Configuration," and "How to: Edit a Thesaurus File (Full-Text Search)" in SQL Server Books Online. Another resource is Chapter 5, "Managing Full Text Indexes," in *MCTS Self-Paced Training Kit (Exam 70-432): Microsoft SQL Server 2008—Implementation and Maintenance* by Michael Hotek (Microsoft Press, 2009).

Configuring Full-Text Searches

Although a database administrator typically configures and manages full-text indexes, as a database developer, you should have a basic understanding of how to enable and configure full-text searches. You can perform all the required steps with either Transact-SQL (T-SQL) code or through SSMS. In this section, you use T-SQL code.

> **MORE INFO   HOW TO CONFIGURE FULL-TEXT SEARCHES WITH SSMS**
>
> For more information about how to configure full-text indexes and catalogs by using SSMS, see the article "Full-Text Catalog and Index How-to Topics (Full-Text Search)" in SQL Server Books Online.

By default, when you install the SQL Server 2008 Database Engine, full-text search is included in the installation. If you choose not to install the full-text search components during SQL Server installation, you can use the SQL Server Installation Center to add this feature. In addition, in SQL Server 2008, all databases are enabled automatically to support full-text search. You can locate the SQL Server Installation Center by clicking Start, All Programs, Microsoft SQL Server 2008, and Configuration Tools.

To enable full-text search capabilities, you must create a full-text catalog and a full-text index, as explained in the next sections.

Creating Full-Text Catalogs

The first step in configuring full-text indexing on a database is to create a full-text catalog on the database where you want to query data by using full-text search capabilities. You cannot create full-text catalogs in the *master*, *model*, or *tempdb* databases. You can use the *CREATE FULLTEXT CATALOG* command to create the full-text catalog.

The *CREATE FULLTEXT CATALOG* command includes the following arguments:

- **Catalog_name** Specifies the name that the catalog will be given.
- **ON FILEGROUP filegroup** Included for backward compatibility and has no effect in SQL Server 2008.
- **IN PATH 'rootpath'** Included for backward compatibility and has no effect in SQL Server 2008.
- **ACCENT_SENSITIVITY ON/OFF** Specifies whether searches are accent-sensitive. If you do not specify this option, the accent sensitivity from the database collation is used.
- **AS DEFAULT** Specifies the catalog you are creating as the default catalog for the database. (If you create a full-text index in the same database without specifying a catalog, the default catalog is used.)
- **AUTHORIZATION owner_name** Sets the owner of the full-text catalog.

The following code creates a catalog named *ftCatalog* as the default full-text catalog on the *AdventureWorks2008* database:

```
USE AdventureWorks2008;
CREATE FULLTEXT CATALOG ftCatalog AS DEFAULT
```

Creating Full-Text Indexes

Before you can create a full-text index by using the *CREATE FULLTEXT INDEX* command, you must satisfy the following requirements:

- A full-text index cannot already exist on the table. You can create only one full-text index per table.
- A unique key index must exist on the table. This key index must be based on a unique, single-key column that does not allow *NULL* values.
- A full-text catalog must exist in the respective database. If a default catalog does not exist in the table's database, you must specify a catalog name in your *CREATE FULLTEXT INDEX* command.

The *CREATE FULLTEXT INDEX* command includes the following arguments:

- **Table_name** Specifies the table or indexed view on which the full-text index is created.

- **Column_name** Specifies the columns to be included in the full-text index. If you do not specify any columns, the command completes successfully to create the full-text index, but no columns are included in the index. Before you can populate or query the full-text index, you must add columns.

- **TYPE COLUMN type_column_name** Defines the column that contains the extension representing the file type of information included in a *varbinary, varbinary(max),* or *image* column. If you specify this option but you do not include a binary column with data in the full-text index, an error is generated.

- **LANGUAGE language_term** Defines the string, integer, or hexadecimal value that represents the locale identifier. If a language is not specified, the default language of the SQL Server instance is used.

- **KEY INDEX index_name** Defines the name of the unique index required by the full-text index to identify each row in the table. This value is required.

- **fulltext_catalog_name** Defines the logical full-text catalog where the index is created. If a default catalog does not exist, you must specify a valid full-text catalog name in the table's database.

- **FILEGROUP filegroup_name** Defines the valid name of an existing filegroup on which the full-text index is stored. If you do not specify a filegroup, the full-text index is stored on the same filegroup as the specified table or view. If the table is partitioned, the full-text index is stored on the primary filegroup for the partitioned table.

- **CHANGE_TRACKING** Specifies how changes to the table are propagated to the full-text index. The settings for this argument are as follows:

  - *AUTO* Specifies that the propagation of changes happens automatically. Changes still might not be reflected immediately in the full-text index. This is the default setting.

  - *MANUAL* Specifies that the *ALTER FULLTEXT INDEX...START UPDATE POPULATION* statement must be run either manually or by using SQL Server Agent jobs to propagate changes to the full-text index.

  - *OFF* Specifies that SQL Server does not track changes to the table. A full population must be performed for any changes to be propagated to the full-text index. Unless the *NO POPULATION* option is specified, an initial population of the full-text index will occur automatically after the full-text index is created.

- *OFF, NO POPULATION* Specifies that the initial population of the full-text index does not occur after the full-text index is created. The *NO POPULATION* option is valid only with the *OFF* change tracking option.

> **NOTE MODIFICATIONS MADE BY USING THE *WRITETEXT* AND *UPDATETEXT* COMMANDS**
>
> Modifications made by using the *WRITETEXT* and *UPDATETEXT* commands are not reflected in the full-text index and are not tracked through change tracking.

- **STOPLIST** Specifies a stoplist to be associated with the full-text index. If this option is not specified, the default full-text system stoplist is used. The options for this argument are as follows:
  - *OFF* Specifies that a stoplist is not associated with this full-text index.
  - *SYSTEM* Specifies that the default system stoplist is associated with this full-text index.
  - *Stoplist_name* Specifies the valid name of an existing stoplist to be associated with this full-text index.

The following code creates a full-text index on the *Description* column in the Production.ProductDescription table. The full-text index uses the *AW2008FullTextCatalog* and uses the system stoplist:

```
CREATE FULLTEXT INDEX ON Production.ProductDescription (Description)
  KEY INDEX PK_ProductDescription_ProductDescriptionID
  ON AW2008FullTextCatalog
  WITH STOPLIST = SYSTEM;
```

Writing Full-Text Queries

When you write full-text queries, you can choose between the *CONTAINS* and *FREETEXT* predicates and the *CONTAINSTABLE* and *FREETEXTTABLE* functions. These commands provide you with a variety of query terms that allow you to return different forms of data. In this section, you learn the functionality of these predicates and functions and examine samples of each type of query.

Troubleshooting Full-Text Searches

As you are learning about and practicing full-text queries, you should understand the tools available to help you troubleshoot and understand the query results being returned.

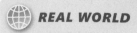
When you execute a full-text query before the full-text population has completed, the query might return only a portion of the matching rows. You can use the *FULLTEXTCATALOGPROPERTY* function to determine the population status of the full-text catalog. If a population is in progress, a value of 1 is typically returned.

You would execute the following command to verify the population status of the *AdvWksDocFTCat* catalog:

```
SELECT FULLTEXTCATALOGPROPERTY('AdvWksDocFTCat', 'PopulateStatus');
```

In addition, the *sys.dm_fts_index_population* dynamic management object returns current population status. Figure 8-6 displays the *sys.dm_fts_index_population* function in its simplest form.

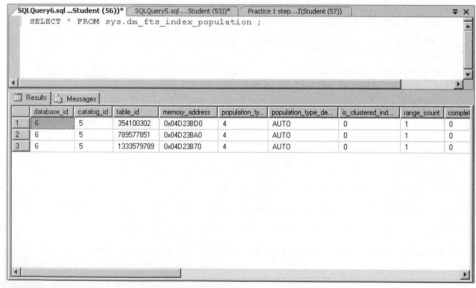

FIGURE 8-6 Basic *sys.dm_fts_index_population* syntax and sample results

To make the results more readable, you can create stored procedures that return a more user-friendly output. The code shown here uses aliases and system functions to improve the readability of the *sys.dm_fts_index_population* dynamic management view (DMV). Figure 8-7 shows the results of this query:

```
SELECT DB_NAME(database_id) AS 'Database Name'
        , database_id AS 'DB_ID'
        , OBJECT_NAME(table_id) AS 'Table Name'
        , table_id
        , population_type_description AS 'Population Desc.'
        , status_description AS 'Status Desc.'
        , completion_type_description AS 'Completion Desc.'
        , start_time
FROM sys.dm_fts_index_population;
```

	Database Name	DB_ID	Table Name	table_id	Population Desc.	Status Desc.	Completion Desc	start_time
1	AdventureWorks2008	6	ProductReview	354100302	AUTO	Starting	NONE	2008-11-24 05:03:07.330
2	AdventureWorks2008	6	Document	789577851	AUTO	Starting	NONE	2008-11-24 05:03:08.610
3	AdventureWorks2008	6	JobCandidate	1333579789	AUTO	Starting	NONE	2008-11-24 05:03:00.610

FIGURE 8-7 Example of a more user-friendly output for the *sys.dm_fts_index_population* DMV

To view what columns are included in a full-text index, you can use the *sys.fulltext_index_columns* catalog view, as shown in the following command.

```
SELECT OBJECT_NAME (object_id) AS TableName
        , object_id
        , COL_NAME(object_id, column_id) AS ColumnName
        , column_id
        , COL_NAME(object_id, type_column_id) AS TypeColumn
        , language_id
FROM sys.fulltext_index_columns;
```

Figure 8-8 shows the names of the tables and columns where a full-text index has been defined.

	TableName	object_id	ColumnName	column_id	TypeColumn	language_id
1	ProductReview	354100302	Comments	7	NULL	1033
2	Document	789577851	DocumentSummary	11	NULL	1033
3	Document	789577851	Document	12	FileExtension	1033
4	JobCandidate	1333579789	Resume	3	NULL	1033

FIGURE 8-8 Sample syntax and output from the *sys.fulltext_index_columns* catalog view

If a full-text query does not return the expected result set, you can use the *sys.dm_fts_parser* DMF to view the final tokenization result from the query. The tokenization result is based on the input term and conditions, such as the word breaker, thesaurus, and stoplists used.

The syntax for the *sys.dm_fts_parser* function is as follows:

```
sys.dm_fts_parser('query_string', lcid, stoplist_id, accent_sensitivity)
```

The following arguments are used with this function:

- **query_string** Defines the string for which you would like to view the word breaker output. This string can include any valid options from the *CONTAINS* predicate, including *INFLECTIONAL, THESAURUS,* and Boolean operators.

- **lcid** Defines the location identifier that defines the word breaker to be used.

> **NOTE** **VIEWING AVAILABLE LANGUAGES**
>
> You can view the available languages for a particular SQL Server instance by executing the following query:
>
> ```
> SELECT * FROM sys.full-text_languages ORDER BY lcid
> ```

- **stoplist** Defines the identifier number (ID) of the stoplist associated with the query. A value of 0 specifies that the system-supplied stoplist is to be used, and a value of *NULL* specifies that no stoplist is to be used.

- **accent_sensitivity** Specifies the accent sensitivity to be used. Set this argument to 1 for accent-sensitive queries and 0 for accent-insensitive queries. When a language such as French includes an accent, this option determines whether or not a word such as *ou* matches *où* . With accent sensitivity set to 1, these two words would not be considered a match.

Figure 8-9 shows a sample of the *sys.dm_fts_parser* DMF. The result set includes matches for inflectional forms of the verb *read*.

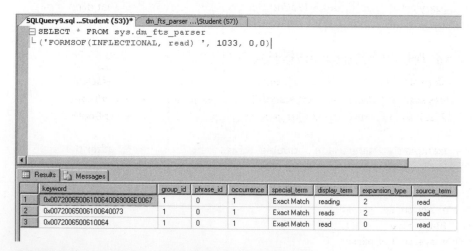

FIGURE 8-9 The syntax and result set for forms of the verb *read*

When your search data includes special characters such as an ampersand or a forward slash, you might not receive the result set that you expect. These characters and a few others have special meaning to the Full-Text Engine. Figure 8-10 displays the results from the following queries on the term *n/a*:

```
SELECT * FROM sys.dm_fts_parser
  ('n/a', 1033, 0, 0);
SELECT * FROM sys.dm_fts_parser
  ('n/a', 1033, NULL, 0);
SELECT * FROM sys.dm_fts_parser
  ('"n/a"', 1033, 0, 0);
```

	keyword	group...	phrase...	occurren...	special_te...	display_te...	expansion_ty...	source_te...
1	0x006E	1	0	1	Noise Word	n	0	n/a
2	0x0061	1	0	2	Noise Word	a	0	n/a

	keyword	group...	phrase...	occurren...	special_term	display_te...	expansion_ty.	source_te...
1	0x006E	1	0	1	Exact Match	n	0	n/a
2	0x0061	1	0	2	Exact Match	a	0	n/a

	keyword	group...	phrase...	occurren...	special_te...	display_te...	expansion_ty...	source_te...
1	0x006E	1	0	1	Noise Word	n	0	n/a
2	0x0061	1	0	2	Noise Word	a	0	n/a

FIGURE 8-10 Sample syntax and results from a variety of searches on the term *n/a*

The first query uses the system noise list. The parser views the input (*query_string*) as two separate terms, *n* and *a*. Single letters are flagged as noise words, and in an actual query against your data, no rows would be returned because noise words are ignored in the result set.

The second query uses the *NULL* option to tell the parser to ignore all stoplists. Because of this, an actual query against your data using these options would return all rows with the letter *n* by itself and all rows that include the letter *a* by itself.

The final query adds double quotes around the term and demonstrates that even though the input is now seen as *n/a*, the parser still resolves it to *n* and *a*.

> **MORE INFO FULL-TEXT SEARCH AND SPECIAL CHARACTERS**
>
> For more information about full-text search and how it behaves with special characters, including how special characters affect thesaurus files, see *http://support.microsoft.com/default .aspx/kb/923317* and the article "sys.dm_fts_parser (Transact-SQL)" in SQL Server Books Online.

The final example shows the usage of double quotes to define a phrase rather than a single term. The second query also shows the usage of Boolean operators within the query. The results are displayed in Figure 8-11.

```
SELECT * FROM sys.dm_fts_parser
('"Backyard Playground"', 1033,0,0)
SELECT * FROM sys.dm_fts_parser
('"Backyard Playground" OR "Swing Set" ', 1033,0,0)
```

	keyword	group_id	phrase_id	occurrence	special_term	display_term	expansion_type	source_term
1	0x006200610063006B00790...	1	0	1	Exact Match	backyard	0	Backyard Playground
2	0x0070006C0061007900670...	1	0	2	Exact Match	playground	0	Backyard Playground

	keyword	group_id	phrase_id	occurrence	special_term	display_term	expansion_type	source_term
1	0x006200610063006B00790...	1	0	1	Exact Match	backyard	0	Backyard Playground
2	0x0070006C0061007900670...	1	0	2	Exact Match	playground	0	Backyard Playground
3	0x007300770069006E0067	2	0	1	Exact Match	swing	0	Swing Set
4	0x007300650074	2	0	2	Exact Match	set	0	Swing Set

FIGURE 8-11 Sample syntax and output with double quotes and Boolean operators

CONTAINS and CONTAINSTABLE

The *CONTAINS* predicate allows you to write queries to return exact matches to your input as well as fuzzy (less precise) matches to the input term. The *CONTAINSTABLE* function has the same search conditions as the *CONTAINS* predicate, but it also allows you to return a relevance value (*RANK*) and the full-text key (*KEY*) for each row in the result set. With these commands, you can search for the following:

- Exact matches of a word or phrase.

- A synonym (thesaurus match) for a word or phrase. For example, you can create a custom thesaurus that returns "teacher," "educator," and "professor" when you query on the term *teacher*.

- The conjugated verb forms (inflectional forms) of a word. For example, if you query on the term *write*, an inflectional query also returns such matches as "wrote," "written," and "writes."

- A series of characters that appear at the beginning of a word or at the beginning of any word within a phrase. For example, you can define a prefix term as the phrase "local school." Full-text search on such a term returns "local schools" and "locally schooled."

- A word that is located near another word.

The *CONTAINS* predicate has two arguments, an *InludedColumns* argument and a *SearchCondition* argument. The *IncludedColumns* argument can contain any of the following components:

- **Column_name**   Set this to the name of the column if you want to search only a single column.

- **Column_list**   Set this to the names of the columns to be included in the search if you want to search multiple columns.

- *****   An asterisk (*) signifies that all full-text-enabled columns in the table in the *FROM* clause are to be included in the search. If more than one table is listed in the *FROM* clause, you must specify the table name (for example, *production.productreview.**).

- **Language** Set this to the language of the query. This value can be set to the name of a language in the *syslanguages* table (enclosed in single quotes), to an integer-based locale identifier (LCID) number, or to the hexadecimal value of an LCID.

The *SearchCondition* argument can contain the following components:

- **Simple Term** Set this to a word (a string of characters without punctuation or spaces) or phrase (one or more words, typically with a space between each word). Phrases should be contained within double quotes ("").

- **Prefix Term** Set this to a word or phrase when you want to match words or phrases that start with your input prefix term. All prefix terms should be followed by an asterisk, and the full term including the asterisk should be contained within double quotes. If you use single quotes, SQL Server interprets the query as a simple term, not a prefix term. For a prefix term, the asterisk is interpreted as 0 or more characters. For example, if your *contains_search_condition_* is "text*", rows with the values of "text" and "textbook" are both returned.

- **Generation Term** Set this to *INFLECTIONAL* or *THESAURUS* to define a language-dependent lookup. The *INFLECTIONAL* term uses the stemmer for a given language to find forms of nouns or verbs. The *THESAURUS* term uses the thesaurus for the corresponding language to match the longest pattern or patterns from the word or phrase provided in *contains_Search_Condition* to the thesaurus file. If a match is not found in the thesaurus file, the *Generation Term* is ignored, and a simple term lookup is performed.

- **Proximity Term** Set this to *NEAR* or a tilde (~) to specify that the term to the left of the proximity operator should be close to the term on the right. When you link more than two terms with proximity operators, all the terms should be close to each other. The word *NEAR* and the tilde (~) function identically.

- **Weighted Term** Set this to *ISABOUT* to identify the use of a weighted term. Also, it uses the *WEIGHT* keyword and a number between 0.0 and 1.0 to specify the relative weight for each component in the weighted term. It has meaning only when used with the *CONTAINSTABLE* function.

- **Logical Operators** Set this to *AND* (or &), to *AND NOT* (or &!), or to *OR* (or |). The keywords and symbols can be used interchangeably. *AND* indicates that both conditions must be met, while *AND NOT* indicates that the first condition must be true and the second condition must be false. *OR* indicates that either one or both of the conditions must be met.

> **NOTE** **ORDER OF OPERATIONS**
>
> When multiple logical operators are included, parenthesized groups are evaluated first, followed by *NOT*, then *AND*, then *OR*. *NOT* must follow an *AND*, as in *AND NOT*. The order of multiple uses of the same operator is not important (for example, 1 OR 2 OR 3 evaluates the same as 2 OR 3 OR 1) because Boolean operators are associative.

The *CONTAINSTABLE* function includes the following additional arguments:

- **Table** Specifies the name of a table for which full-text search is enabled.
- **Top_n_by_rank** Specifies that only the specified number of rows with the highest rankings should be returned. You can improve query performance by using this option to limit the results to only the most relevant rows.

CONTAINS and *CONTAINSTABLE* Samples

The following query returns rows from the *ProductReview* table where the word *quality* is found near the word *comfort*. To show the product name rather than the product ID, the sample includes a join to the *Product* table. Because the *CONTAINS* predicate can query only one full-text index, you must specify from which table you want to query columns in the *WHERE* clause, as shown in bold type in this query:

```
SELECT ProductReviewID, Production.Product.Name AS 'Product Name'
, Rating, Comments, Production.ProductReview.ModifiedDate
FROM Production.Product
JOIN Production.ProductReview
ON Production.Product.ProductID = Production.ProductReview.ProductID
WHERE CONTAINS(Production.ProductReview.*,'Quality NEAR comfort')
```

The following query returns rows in the *ProductReview* table that include forms of the word *bike*, such as *biking*:

```
SELECT ProductReviewID, Production.Product.Name AS 'Product Name'
, Rating, Comments, Production.ProductReview.ModifiedDate
FROM Production.Product
JOIN Production.ProductReview
ON Production.Product.ProductID = Production.ProductReview.ProductID
WHERE CONTAINS(Production.ProductReview.*,'FORMSOF(INFLECTIONAL , bike)')
```

> **NOTE BOOST PERFORMANCE**
>
> If you use a variable to set the simple term of the query, use a variable of data type *nvarchar*, not of data type *varchar*. If you use the *varchar* data type, SQL Server must perform an implicit conversion. Conversions limit query optimization techniques.

The following code returns rows from the *ProductDescription* table that include the words *safety*, *performance*, or *comfort*. Each word is given a relative weight value, and the results are ordered from the highest-ranking match to the lowest:

```
USE AdventureWorks2008
GO
SELECT FT_Table.ProductDescriptionID, FT_Table.[Description]
  , KEY_TBL.RANK
```

```
    FROM Production.ProductDescription AS FT_Table
      INNER JOIN CONTAINSTABLE(production.ProductDescription, Description,
      'ISABOUT (comfort weight (.8)
      , Safety weight (.5)
      , Performance weight(.2) )' ) AS KEY_TBL
        ON FT_Table.ProductDescriptionID = KEY_TBL.[KEY]
ORDER BY KEY_TBL.RANK DESC;
```

FREETEXT and FREETEXTTABLE

The *FREETEXT* predicate allows you to write queries that return values that match the meaning of the search condition, not simply the exact words or synonyms of the search condition. The full-text query engine performs the following tasks when you execute a full-text query by using the *FREETEXT* predicate:

- Uses the word breaker to split the value of the string entered for the search condition into words.
- Uses stemming to create inflectional forms of the words created by the word breaker.
- Uses the thesaurus to locate additional expansions or replacements for the search terms.

The *FREETEXT* command has the following arguments:

- **Column** An individual column name, a list of columns separated by commas and enclosed within parentheses, or an asterisk (*) to designate all full-text columns.
- **Free-text string** Inputs the string to search for in the listed columns. If you enclose the string in double quotes, a phrase search is performed. With a phrase search, stemming and thesaurus lookups are not performed.
- **Language** The language that is used for word breaking, stemming, stoplists, and thesaurus lookups.

The *FREETEXTTABLE* command includes a combination of arguments from both the *FREETEXT* and *CONTAINSTABLE* commands. The *FREETEXTTABLE* command includes the *Table*, *Column*, *Free-text string*, *Language*, and *Top-n-by-rank* arguments as defined previously.

FREETEXT and FREETEXTTABLE Samples

The following command uses the *FREETEXT* predicate to return rows with descriptions that match the general meaning of the phrase "provides a light stiff ride." The result set for this command returns 34 of the 762 rows in the *ProductDescription* table when a full-text index is built on the description column:

```
SELECT * FROM Production.ProductDescription
WHERE FREETEXT(*,'provides a light stiff ride')
```

In contrast, if you execute the following command, only one row is returned:

```
SELECT * FROM Production.ProductDescription
WHERE CONTAINS(*,'"provides a light stiff ride"')
```

The following code uses the *FREETEXTTABLE* command to return rows with a meaning close to the input text. The full-text search engine assigns a rank based on how close the match is to the input phrase. The results are returned with the highest ranking rows listed first:

```
SELECT FT_TBL.ProductDescriptionID, FT_TBL.Description, KEY_TBL.RANK
FROM Production.ProductDescription AS FT_TBL
INNER JOIN FREETEXTTABLE (Production.ProductDescription, description,
        'light stiff ride') AS KEY_TBL
    ON FT_TBL.ProductDescriptionID = KEY_TBL.[KEY]
 ORDER BY KEY_TBL.RANK DESC
```

> ✔ **Quick Check**
>
> - You need to write a query that returns all tenses of the verb *write*. Which generational term should you include in your query?
>
> **Quick Check Answer**
>
> - *INFLECTIONAL*

 **Writing Full-Text Queries**

In this practice, you execute queries against tables and columns in the *AdventureWorks2008* database that have been enabled for full-text indexing.

EXERCISE 1   Review Full-Text Indexed Tables

In this exercise, you review the existing full-text indexes in the *AdventureWorks2008* database.

1. Start SSMS (if it's not already started), connect to your SQL Server instance, and open a new query window.

2. In the new query window, type and execute the following command to view the tables with populated full-text indexes:

    ```
    USE AdventureWorks2008;
    GO

    SELECT db_name(database_id) AS 'Database Name'
    , OBJECT_NAME(table_id) AS 'Table Name'
    FROM sys.dm_fts_index_population;
    ```

3. Review the result set and notice that full-text indexing has been enabled on the *ProductReview*, *Document*, and *JobCandidate* tables.

4. If necessary, open Object Explorer by selecting Object Explorer from the View menu.

5. In Object Explorer, expand the Databases node, expand AdventureWorks2008, expand Tables, right-click *Production.ProductReview*, select Full-Text Index, and then select Properties.

6. In the Full-Text Index Properties window, in the Select A Page pane, click Columns.

7. On the Columns page, note the columns that have been enabled for full-text indexing.

8. Repeat steps 5–7 for the *Production.Document* and *HumanResources.JobCandidate* tables. Notice that the *Document* column of the *Production.Document* table has a *Type Column* value of *FileExtension*. This is because the document column has a *varbinary(max)* data type and the data must be interpreted by the appropriate filter defined by the file name extension included in the *FileExtension* column. All the files in the sample have the .doc extension and will be interpreted by the Microsoft Office Word filter.

9. Leave SSMS open for the next exercise.

EXERCISE 2   Use the *CONTAINS* Command

In this exercise, you use the *CONTAINS* command to query the *ProductionDocument* table. You also use the *sys.dm_fts_parser* function to view how the word breaker interprets a term.

1. Open a new query window, and type and execute the following command to retrieve rows from the *Production.Document* table that contain any verb form of the word *lubricate* in any full-text indexed column:

```
USE AdventureWorks2008;
GO

SELECT Title, Filename, FileExtension, DocumentSummary
FROM Production.Document
WHERE CONTAINS(*, 'FORMSOF(INFLECTIONAL, lubricate) ');
```

2. Notice that the *DocumentSummary* column includes the word "lubricating." Because the *Document* column is returned as a binary data type, you cannot read the words included in the file, but you can verify that the document actually contains a verb form of this word by searching on only the *Document* column, rather than both the *Document* and *DocumentSummary* columns, as in the prior command. To do this, in the current query window, copy and paste the *SELECT* statement from step 1 just below the existing query. In the query that you just pasted, change the * to *Document*, highlight this new query, and execute it.

Notice that your result set is the same, verifying that forms of the word "lubricate" exist in both the *Document* and *DocumentSummary* columns.

3. Open a new query window. In the new query window, type and execute the following command to view the output generated by the *FORMSOF* option, which is used by the Full-Text Engine as a comparison to locate matching rows. This command uses the English word breaker with an ID of 1033, the system stoplist, and no accent sensitivity:

```
SELECT * FROM sys.dm_fts_parser
('FORMSOF(INFLECTIONAL, lubricate) ', 1033, 0,0)
```

4. Review the *display_term* column in the result set, and notice that the noun "lubrication" is not returned as a match for the verb "lubricate."

5. Leave SSMS open for the next exercise.

EXERCISE 3   Use the *FREETEXTTABLE* Command to Rank Results

In this exercise, you use the *FREETEXTTABLE* command to rank the results of your query. The rows best matching the term *quality bike* are returned at the top of the result set.

1. Open a new query window, and type and execute the following command to return matching rows along with their relative ranking:

```
SELECT FT_TBL.ProductReviewID, FT_TBL.COMMENTS, KEY_TBL.RANK
FROM Production.ProductReview AS FT_TBL
INNER JOIN FREETEXTTABLE (Production.ProductReview, comments,
        'quality bike') AS KEY_TBL
        ON FT_TBL.ProductReviewID = KEY_TBL.[KEY]
ORDER BY KEY_TBL.RANK DESC
```

2. Review the result set.

3. Save your scripts and exit SSMS.

Lesson Summary

- SQL Server 2008 provides fully integrated full-text search capabilities.
- Full-text indexes are created and maintained inside the database and are organized into virtual full-text catalogs.
- The *CONTAINS* and *FREETEXT* predicates, as well as the *CONTAINSTABLE* and *FREETEXTTABLE* functions, allow you to fully query text, XML, and certain forms of binary data.

Lesson 3: Implementing Service Broker Solutions

Service Broker was introduced in SQL Server 2005 to provide a reliable, scalable, and asynchronous message queuing system for local or distributed applications. Service Broker solutions can range from a simple application existing in a single database to a complex application reaching across several remote SQL Server instances.

This lesson provides you with an overview of the components you work with to create a Service Broker solution. You also learn how to configure a simple Service Broker application within a single SQL Server instance.

> **After this lesson, you will be able to:**
> - Describe the components of Service Broker.
> - Determine an activation method.
> - Configure Service Broker.
> - Start a dialog and send and receive messages.
>
> **Estimated lesson time: 60 minutes**

Service Broker Overview

To be able to work with Service Broker, you must first understand the components that work together to provide a Service Broker solution. As in SQL Server 2005, a Service Broker solution is made of queues, services, messages, message types, and contracts.

> **NOTE** **SERVICE BROKER PREREQUISITES**
>
> Before enabling Service Broker on a database, you must create a database master key for that database. If you do not, processes appear to work, but messages are never delivered to the queue.

New Features in SQL Server 2008

In addition to the components listed previously, SQL Server 2008 provides the following new Service Broker features:

- **Broker Priorities** Allow you to give one conversation precedence over another. Broker priorities are created by using the *CREATE BROKER PRIORITY* statement.
- **Ssbdiagnose utility** Used to analyze conversations and Service Broker services.
- **System Monitor Object and Counters** Provides added analysis capabilities with the *Broker TO Statistics* object and five new counters added to the *Broker Statistics* object.

MORE INFO   GATHERING SERVICE BROKER STATISTICS

For more information about Service Broker statistics, see the articles "SQL Server, Broker Statistics Object" and "SQL Server, Broker TO Statistics Object" in SQL Server Books Online.

Service Broker Components

The SQL Server 2008 Service Broker components can be divided into the following three major categories:

- **Conversation components**   These components are created at run time and function according to the rules defined with the service definition and network and security components. A conversation exists between an initiator and a target. *Conversations* are long-termed, asynchronous, and reliable. Conversations are made of messages. A *message* can belong to one and only one conversation and is made of a specific message type. A conversation between two specific Service Broker services is called a *dialog*. Dialogs provide exactly once-in-order (EOIO) message delivery by managing the flow of messages between the services. Each dialog belongs to a *conversation group* and follows the rules specified in a contract. *Conversation priorities* set the relative precedence for conversations.

- **Service definition components**   You define these components as you design your Service Broker solution:

  - Queues   These are tables where messages are stored until they are processed. Each row in the table represents a message. When a new message is added to the queue, a row is appended to the bottom of the table. When messages are received and the *RETENTION* option is not specified, the messages are removed from the top of the table.

  - Services   This is the name given to the group of tasks that require messages to be sent. When a service is created, the queue that holds incoming messages is defined as part of the service definition. Contracts are associated with services to manage incoming conversations. More than one contract can be associated with a target service. If you create a service that initiates conversations but never is the target for any new conversations, you do not need to include a contract in the service definition. If a service can receive messages on the *DEFAULT* contract, you must specify the *DEFAULT* contract when you define the service.

  - Contracts   This is an agreement between two services that defines the message types the services send to accomplish certain tasks. It also defines what participants can send which message types. A contract exists in the database where it is created. If you are developing a solution that involves multiple databases, you must create an identical contract in each database that participates in the solution. The *DEFAULT* contract contains the *DEFAULT* message type. When you initiate a dialog and do not specify a contract, the *DEFAULT* contract is used.

- Message types   This is the object that defines the name and contents of a message. Every database contains a message type named *DEFAULT* that uses a validation of *NONE*. Be careful not to confuse the *DEFAULT* message type with the system *DEFAULT* contract. In addition, you should be aware that *DEFAULT* is a delimited object name, not a keyword, when used to define a contract or a message type.

- **Network and security components**   These components are used to define the infrastructure that allows the messages to be delivered. They are as follows:

  - Routes   These are used to determine where to deliver messages. By default, every database contains a route to which all messages without a specific route definition should be delivered within the current SQL Server instance. This route is named *AutoCreatedLocal* and matches a service name and broker instance. When you define a route, you define the service name associated with the route; the broker instance identifier, which identifies a specific database where the messages should be sent; and the *Network* address, which contains the actual machine address or a keyword that identifies the machine that hosts the service.

  - Remote service bindings   These are used to provide security to dialogs with remote databases.

> **MORE INFO**   **DIALOG SECURITY**
>
> Dialog security lets your Service Broker solution use authorization, authentication, and encryption. Some of these settings can be controlled with the *BEGIN DIALOG CONVERSATION* statement. Additional specifications are controlled through remote service bindings. For more information about dialog security and encryption see the article "Service Broker Dialog Security" in SQL Server Books Online.

> **MORE INFO**   **CREATING REMOTE SERVICE BINDINGS**
>
> For more information about creating remote service bindings, see the article "CREATE REMOTE SERVICE BINDING (Transact-SQL)" in the SQL Server Books Online.

- Service Broker endpoints   These are used to configure SQL Server to send and receive messages over TCP/IP connections. Endpoints can be used to control connections to the endpoint and provide transport security. By default, Service Broker cannot communicate on the network because there are no Service Broker endpoints unless you configure them.

Creating Service Broker Applications

Several applications function together to provide a Service Broker solution. To start a conversation and send messages, an application for the initiating service issues the *BEGIN DIALOG* statement, which includes all the required information about the initiating and target services, contracts, and so on. Once messages have been sent to a queue, the target application must be started to receive and process messages. You can configure one or more of the four startup options for the Server Broker applications in your solution.

Applications where there is a continuous stream of messages and applications that require a large number of resources to start up can be configured to start when SQL Server starts, as part of the Microsoft Windows startup group or as a service. Because these applications are always running, they continually hold on to their resources, but they are also available immediately to process messages without the time lag required to start a new application.

The second startup option that you can configure uses the SQL Server agent to schedule the application to run at specific times. Using scheduled tasks to start applications is common for target applications that might be performed as a batch. For example, employees can submit travel reimbursement forms throughout the day. The reimbursement messages can be stored in the queue throughout the day. Overnight, the target application receives all the messages and either processes the reimbursement check or flags the message for manual review and uses another application to send the form on to another queue to await processing by another target application. Figure 8-12 shows the information flow for the expense reimbursement example.

In the expense reimbursement scenario, weeks may pass without any messages being sent to the manual review queue. In such a situation it would be inefficient to process this queue on a scheduled basis. Also, because it is important for the company to handle expense reimbursements quickly and efficiently, you need an activation method to support these requirements. The internal and event-based activation processes meet these requirements.

Service Broker Activation

You can configure Service Broker activation to allow your solutions to start automatically when there is work for the program to do. The two automatic activation methods are *internal activation* and *event-based activation*.

Internal activation is managed by using stored procedures and requires the application to be written as stored procedures. Event-based activation is managed by an external application and is activated by a SQL Server queue activation event sent to the external application.

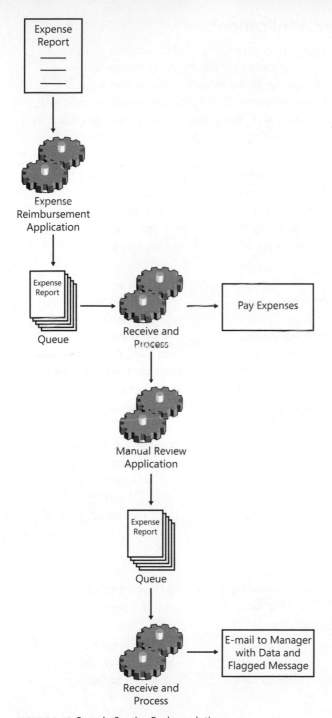

FIGURE 8-12 Sample Service Broker solution

These Service Broker activations are ideal for applications that can start quickly and for applications where the frequency or number of messages varies over time. In addition to starting an application where messages are received infrequently, you can also use Service Broker activation to allow applications to add queue reader processes automatically when messages start to accumulate in a queue.

MORE INFO **CONFIGURING SERVICE BROKER ACTIVATION**

For more information about selecting a startup method for your Service Broker applications, as well as information on Service Broker activation and how to implement, see the following articles in SQL Server Books Online:

- "Choosing a Startup Strategy "
- "Service Broker Activation"
- "Implementing Internal Activation"
- "Understanding When Activation Occurs"

Enabling Service Broker

New in SQL Server 2008, Service Broker is enabled by default in all user databases as well as the *msdb* database. By using Object Explorer in SSMS, you can view and modify the Service Broker–related properties on the Options page of the Properties window of a particular database, as shown in Figure 8-13.

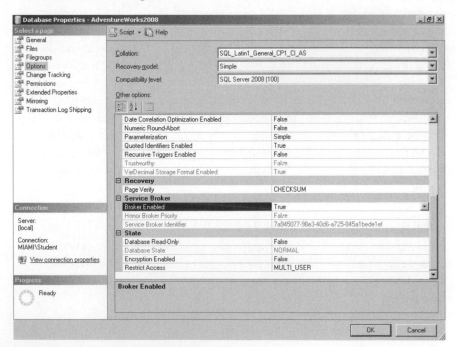

FIGURE 8-13 Service Broker–related database options

Alternatively, the following query displays the Service Broker properties for the *AdventureWorks2008* database:

```
SELECT name, service_broker_guid
   , is_broker_enabled, is_honor_broker_priority_on
   FROM sys.databases
   WHERE name = 'AdventureWorks2008'
```

You can also use the *ALTER DATABASE* command to modify the database options related to Service Broker.

You use the following syntax with the *ALTER DATABASE* command to modify Service Broker options:

```
ALTER DATABASE database_name
SET {
    ENABLE_BROKER
  | DISABLE_BROKER
  | NEW_BROKER
  | ERROR_BROKER_CONVERSATIONS
  | HONOR_BROKER_PRIORITY { ON | OFF}
}
```

The *DISABLE_BROKER* option disables the Service Broker in the current database and stops messages from being delivered, but it maintains the current Service Broker identifier. When you use the *ENABLE_BROKER* option to reenable Service Broker, the current Service Broker identifier is also maintained. The *NEW_BROKER* option creates a new Service Broker identifier and immediately removes all existing conversations without cleanly ending conversations or sending end dialog messages. All conversations that were started with the old Service Broker identifier must be restarted to be valid. The *ERROR_BROKER_CONVERSATIONS* option can be used if two databases involved in conversations become out of sync due to a failure or error on one of the databases. When you use this option, Service Broker remains enabled and the Service Broker identifier is maintained, but all conversations are ended with an error message. This option can also be used to tell an application to perform regular cleanup of existing conversations. The final option, *HONOR_BROKER_PRIORITY,* is set to *ON* or *OFF* to specify whether the system gives a preference to messages that come from conversations with a high priority value.

> **NOTE TIMING OF *HONOR_BROKER_PRIORITY* CHANGES**
>
> Changes to the *HONOR_BROKER_PRIORITY* option do not take effect for dialogs with existing messages until the current messages have been sent. This means that there might be a significant delay between when you set the option and when all dialogs have started using the new setting.

Configuring Service Broker Components

Before you can build your Service Broker solution applications, you need to be able to create and configure the individual components. The components that you configure include queues, services, message types, contracts, and conversation priorities.

Creating Message Types

When you create a message type, you define the name for the message. You also define whether Service Broker performs validation on the messages with that name. Before you start conversations, you must define the same message types for both sides of the conversation.

You can see the full syntax for the *CREATE MESSAGE TYPE* command here:

```
CREATE MESSAGE TYPE message_type_name
    [ AUTHORIZATION owner_name ]
    [ VALIDATION = {   NONE
                     | EMPTY
                     | WELL_FORMED_XML
                     | VALID_XML WITH SCHEMA COLLECTION
                                                   schema_collection_name
                 } ]
[ ; ]
```

The *CREATE MESSAGE TYPE* command includes the following arguments:

- **message_type_name**   Defines the name of the message type that you reference when you create the contract(s) that use this message type. When you create a message type, it is created in the current database and you must specify a one-part name (not including server, database, or schema).

- **AUTHORIZATION**   Defines the owner for the message type. If you are logged on with an account that does not have *sa*, *dbo* permissions when you create the message type, you must define your own user account, a role that you belong to, or a user account to which you have the *impersonate* permission. If you do not specify this clause, it defaults to your current user account.

- **VALIDATION**   Set to *NONE, EMPTY, WELL_FORMED_XML,* or *VALID_XML WITH SCHEMA COLLECTION schema_collection_name* to define the type of validation that Service Broker should perform on messages of this type. The default validation setting of *NONE* specifies that no validation is performed. The *EMPTY* validation setting specifies that the message body must be *NULL*. The *WELL_FORMED_XML* setting specifies that the message body must contain well-formed XML. The final option, *VALID_XML WITH SCHEMA COLLECTION* specifies the name of an existing XML schema collection to which the message body must conform.

The following code creates a message type named *[///Adventure-Works.com/SampleType]*:

```
CREATE MESSAGE TYPE [//Adventure-Works.com/SampleType]
   AUTHORIZATION dbo
   VALIDATION = WELL_FORMED_XML
```

Creating Queues

When you create a Service Broker solution, you must create at least one queue. Service Broker uses queues to hold messages. You associate queues with services when you create the service.

You can see the full syntax for the *CREATE QUEUE* command here:

```
CREATE QUEUE <object>
    [ WITH
       [ STATUS = { ON | OFF }  [ , ] ]
       [ RETENTION = { ON | OFF } [ , ] ]
       [ ACTIVATION (
           [ STATUS = { ON | OFF } , ]
             PROCEDURE_NAME = <procedure> ,
             MAX_QUEUE_READERS = max_readers ,
             EXECUTE AS { SELF | 'user_name' | OWNER }
              ) ]
    ]
      [ ON { filegroup | [ DEFAULT ] } ]
[ ; ]


<object> ::=
{
    [ database_name. [ schema_name ] . | schema_name. ]
        queue_name
}


<procedure> ::=
{
    [ database_name. [ schema_name ] . | schema_name. ]
        stored_procedure_name
}
```

The only required option is the queue name. This command creates a queue named *TestQueue*:

```
CREATE QUEUE TestQueue
```

The *CREATE QUEUE* command includes the following arguments:

- **object**   Set this to the name of the queue to be created. The object name is expressed as a complete three-part name (*database_name.schema_name.queue_name*) or a partial name. If you do not specify a database name, the current database is used. If a schema is not specified, the default schema for the user that is executing the *CREATE QUEUE* statement is used.

- **STATUS**   Set this to *ON* if the queue is available or *OFF* when the queue is unavailable and no messages can be added to or removed from the queue. The default setting is *ON*.

- **RETENTION**   Set this to *ON* if you want sent and received messages from conversations that use this queue to remain in the queue until the associated conversation has ended. The default setting of *OFF* removes messages from the queue when the *RECEIVE* command is issued against the message.

- **ACTIVATION**   Specifies information about the stored procedure to start to process messages in the queue and includes the following arguments:

  - *STATUS*   Set this to *ON* if Service Broker should start the stored procedure.

  - *PROCEDURE_NAME*   Set this to the name of the required stored procedure. Like the queue name, the procedure name can be expressed as a full or partial three-part name in the format *database_name.schema_name.queue_name*.

  - *MAX_QUEUE_READERS*   Set this to the maximum number of instances of the stored procedure that can be started simultaneously.

  - *EXECUTE AS*   Specifies the user account to be used for the execution context of the stored procedure. This value can be set to *SELF, OWNER,* or a database *user_name*.

- **ON**   Specifies the filegroup on which the queue should be created.

Creating Contracts

Contracts specify the message types that can be used in a particular conversation. The contract also specifies by whom (initiator, target, or both) each particular message type can be sent.

You can see the full syntax for the *CREATE CONTRACT* command here:

```
CREATE CONTRACT contract_name
   [ AUTHORIZATION owner_name ]
      ( {   { message_type_name | [ DEFAULT ] }
```

```
        SENT BY { INITIATOR | TARGET | ANY }
      } [ ,...n] )
[ ; ]
```

The *CREATE CONTRACT* command includes the following arguments:

- **contract_name**   Defines the name of the contract that you reference when you start a conversation. When you create a contract, it is created in the current database. You cannot specify server, database, or schema names in the definition.

- **AUTHORIZATION**   Defines the owner for the contract. If you are logged on as an account that does not have *sa, dbo* permissions when you create the message type, you must define your own user account, a role that you belong to, or a user account to which you have the *impersonate* permission. If you do not specify this clause, it defaults to your current user account.

- **message_type_name**   Defines the names of the message types that are included in conversations specifying this contract. You can add multiple message types to a contract.

- **SENT BY**   Set to *INITIATOR, TARGET,* or *ANY* to specify which services can send the message type specified in the corresponding *message_type_name. ANY* specifies that both initiator and target services can use the corresponding message type.

Each database includes a contract named *DEFAULT* that specifies the *DEFAULT* message type, which uses a *VALIDATION* of *NONE*:

```
CREATE CONTRACT SampleContract
  AUTHORIZATION dbo
   (SampleType1 SENT BY INITIATOR,
    SampleType2 SENT BY ANY)
```

Creating Services

Once you have created a queue, the next step in the process is to create the services that define the queue and the contract to which the service is linked. The service represents the business task or group of tasks required by the application. Although many services can point to a single queue, each service typically uses a dedicated queue to facilitate receiving and processing messages.

You can see the full syntax for the *CREATE SERVICE* command here:

```
CREATE SERVICE service_name
  [ AUTHORIZATION owner_name ]
  ON QUEUE [ schema_name. ]queue_name
  [ ( contract_name | [DEFAULT] [ ,...n ] ) ]
[ ; ]
```

Unlike queues, where you can define the database and schema in which they are to be created, services are created in the current database and you cannot specify a schema for the service.

The *AUTHORIZATION* option defines the owner for the service. You must define the name of the queue where messages for this service will be stored in the *ON QUEUE* option.

> **BEST PRACTICES**   **SPECIFY A SCHEMA NAME**
>
> Although it is not required to specify a schema name as part of the queue name if the queue resides in the default schema for the user executing the command, including the schema name in your scripts improves readability and eliminates possible problems if the script is executed in the future in a different user context.

If a contract is not defined in the *CREATE SERVICE* command, the service might only initiate conversations and not be a target. If the *DEFAULT* contract is specified, the service may be a target for conversations that use the *DEFAULT* contract. The word *DEFAULT* in this query context is being used as a delimited name of a contract and not as a keyword as in some other commands such as *CREATE TABLE*.

Configuring Conversation Priorities

You can use the *CREATE BROKER PRIORITY COMMAND* to set a priority level for conversations that are associated with particular contracts and services. When you define the broker priority, you define the name for the conversation priority, the contract name, local and remote service names, and the priority level given to the combination of the contract and services defined. The priority level can be set to any value between 0 and 10. The default value of 5 is assigned if the *PRIORITY_LEVEL* is not specified or is set to *DEFAULT*.

The complete syntax for the *CREATE BROKER PRIORITY* command is here:

```
CREATE BROKER PRIORITY ConversationPriorityName
FOR CONVERSATION
[ SET ( [ CONTRACT_NAME = {ContractName | ANY } ]
        [ [ , ] LOCAL_SERVICE_NAME = {LocalServiceName | ANY } ]
        [ [ , ] REMOTE_SERVICE_NAME = {'RemoteServiceName' | ANY } ]
        [ [ , ] PRIORITY_LEVEL = {PriorityValue | DEFAULT } ]
      )
]
[;]
```

> **MORE INFO**   **CONVERSATION PRIORITY LEVELS**
>
> For more information about the criteria that Service Broker uses to assign a priority level to a conversation, see the article "CREATE BROKER PRIORITY (Transact-SQL)" in SQL Server Books Online.

Sending and Receiving Messages

Once you have configured the service definition components and the network and security components, you need to configure your applications to initiate dialogs, send messages, and handle receiving messages.

Creating a Dialog Conversation

You can use the *BEGIN DIALOG* statement to initiate a dialog conversation from one service to another. A dialog exists between two services and provides message delivery, guaranteeing that each message is received only once and in order.

The complete syntax for the *BEGIN DIALOG* command is here:

```
BEGIN DIALOG [ CONVERSATION ] @dialog_handle
    FROM SERVICE initiator_service_name
    TO SERVICE 'target_service_name'
        [ , { 'service_broker_guid' | 'CURRENT DATABASE' } ]
    [ ON CONTRACT contract_name ]
    [ WITH
    [ { RELATED_CONVERSATION = related_conversation_handle
      | RELATED_CONVERSATION_GROUP = related_conversation_group_id } ]
    [ [ , ] LIFETIME = dialog_lifetime ]
    [ [ , ] ENCRYPTION = { ON | OFF } ] ]
[ ; ]
```

Before the *BEGIN DIALOG* command is executed, you need to define the *@dialog_handle* variable as a *uniqueidentifier*. Once you have defined the *@dialog_handle* variable, you must include the following arguments as part of the *BEGIN DIALOG* command:

- **FROM SERVICE** Defines the name of the service initiating the dialog. This service must exist in the current database. The queue linked to this service is used to store messages returned by the target service.

- **TO SERVICE** Defines the name of the target service to which the messages are sent. This service name is case-sensitive even if the database uses a case-insensitive collation.

The following optional arguments can also be defined as part of the *BEGIN DIALOG* command:

- *service_broker_guid* Set to the globally unique identifier (GUID) of the Service Broker in a particular database. This argument can be used if your target service is hosted on multiple databases and you want to direct the dialog to the Service Broker of a particular database.

- *'CURRENT DATABASE'* Specifies that the Service Broker ID of the current database is used.

- **ON CONTRACT** Specifies the contract that is enforced for this dialog. If a contract is not specified, the contract named *DEFAULT* is used for this dialog.

- **RELATED_CONVERSATION or RELATED_CONVERSATION_GROUP** Defines the *related_conversation_handle* to add a single related conversation or the *related_conversation_groupid* for the group to which this new dialog should be added.

- **LIFETIME** Specifies the maximum amount of time that the conversation can remain open.

- **ENCRYPTION** Set to *OFF* or *ON* to define the encryption status of messages included in this dialog. The default setting, *ON*, requires messages between services on different SQL Server instances to be encrypted, but messages between services on the same SQL Server instance are never encrypted. However, a database master key and the appropriate certificates must be configured if the initiator and target services are in separate databases, even when on the same instance. This facilitates moving a database to a separate instance in the future.

In its simplest form, the *BEGIN DIALOG* command is similar to the following code:

```
DECLARE @dialog_handle uniqueidentifier
BEGIN DIALOG @dialog_handle
FROM SERVICE AW_Initiate
TO SERVICE AW_Target
```

Sending Messages

Once you have created a dialog, you use the *SEND* command to send messages on the conversation created in the *BEGIN DIALOG* command.

The *SEND* command is fairly straightforward and uses the following syntax:

```
SEND
   ON CONVERSATION conversation_handle
   [ MESSAGE TYPE message_type_name ]
   [ ( message_body_expression ) ]
[ ; ]
```

Once the initiator sends the message, the message is stored in the queue linked to the target service. The message type parameter is optional and typically is not included as part of the *SEND* command. Rather, it is defined as part of the contract specification. Although the message body expression is optional, if it is not specified, the message body is empty. Typically, the message body provides information pertinent to the target service.

Receiving Messages

Once messages are added to the queue, you can use a simple *SELECT* statement to view the messages included in the queue. To process the messages, you use the *RECEIVE* command to retrieve one or more messages from the queue. Messages are read from the top of the queue. If the *RETENTION* option for the queue is set to *OFF*, messages are removed from the queue when the *RECEIVE* command retrieves them. Here is the syntax of the *RECEIVE* command:

```
[ WAITFOR ( ]
    RECEIVE [ TOP ( n ) ]
        <column_specifier> [ ,...n ]
        FROM <queue>
        [ INTO table_variable ]
        [ WHERE { conversation_handle = conversation_handle
                | conversation_group_id = conversation_group_id } ]
[ ) ] [ , TIMEOUT timeout ]
[ ; ]

<column_specifier> ::=
{    *
  | { column_name | [ ] expression } [ [ AS ] column_alias ]
  | column_alias = expression
}    [ ,...n ]

<queue> ::=
{
    [ database_name . [ schema_name ] . | schema_name . ]
        queue_name
}
```

The *RECEIVE* command accepts the following arguments:

- **WAITFOR** Specifies that the *RECEIVE* command waits for a new message to be received. This argument is used only if the queue is currently empty.

- **TOP** Specifies the maximum number of messages to be retrieved from the queue. If the *TOP* option is not included in the command, all messages that meet the criteria defined in the *RECEIVE* statement are returned.

- **column Specifier** Lists a column name, an alias to a column expression.

- **FROM** Specifies the name of the queue from which you want to retrieve messages.

- **INTO** Optionally specifies a table variable name into which the results are returned to be processed. Alternatively, the result set can be processed directly. Most environments use the *INTO* option.

- **WHERE** Limits the rows retrieved by specifying a conversation or a conversation group on which the messages were received.

- **TIMEOUT** Limits the amount of time the *RECEIVE* command will wait for a new message when the *WAITFOR* option is also specified. The default wait time of -1 specifies that the *RECEIVE* command waits an unlimited amount of time for a new message to be received.

IMPORTANT COMMAND TERMINATOR

Although it is always good programming practice to put a semicolon (;) at the end of each T-SQL statement, it is required in the statement preceding a *RECEIVE* statement in a batch.

In this practice, you create the components required for a simple Service Broker solution. You also create a dialog, send messages on the dialog, and receive messages from the queue.

EXERCISE 1   Create Service Definition Components

In this exercise, you create the service definition components required to initiate a Service Broker conversation.

1. Start SSMS (if it's not already started), connect to your SQL Server instance, and open a new query window.

2. In the new query window, type and execute the following command to create a master key in the *AdventureWorks2008* database:

```
USE AdventureWorks2008;
CREATE MASTER KEY ENCRYPTION BY PASSWORD = 'dyfnds65;sdf%h457!;'
```

3. Open a new query window, and type and execute the following script to create the message types and contract to be used by the initiator and target services:

```
CREATE Message Type
  AWNewNotice
  VALIDATION = NONE;

CREATE Message Type
  AWAck
  VALIDATION = NONE;

CREATE CONTRACT
  NewNoticeContract
  AUTHORIZATION dbo
  (AWNewNotice SENT BY ANY,
   AWAck SENT BY ANY );
```

3. In the current query window, below the existing text, type, highlight, and execute the following script to create the queues and services for your solution:

```
CREATE QUEUE AWNewNoticeQueue;

CREATE QUEUE AWAckQueue;

CREATE SERVICE AWNewNoticeService
ON QUEUE AWNewNoticeQueue;

CREATE SERVICE AWAckService
ON QUEUE AWAckQueue;
```

4. Leave SSMS open for the next exercise.

EXERCISE 2   Send and Receive Messages

In this exercise, you initiate a dialog conversation and send and receive messages on the dialog conversation.

1. Open a new query window. Type, but do not execute, the following commands to define a dialog conversation between *AWNewNoticeService* and *AWAckService*:

```
DECLARE @dialog_handle uniqueidentifier
  , @XMLdata XML;

SET @XMLdata = (SELECT * FROM sys.tables FOR XML AUTO);

BEGIN DIALOG @dialog_handle
FROM SERVICE AWNewNoticeService
TO SERVICE 'AWAckService'
ON CONTRACT NewNoticeContract;
```

2. In the current query window, below the existing text, type the following command and execute the entire script to start the conversation and send a message on the conversation:

```
SEND ON CONVERSATION @dialog_handle
MESSAGE TYPE AWNewNotice;
```

3. Open a new query window, and type and execute the following command to view the *AWNewNoticeQueue* queue:

```
SELECT * FROM AWNewNoticeQueue;
```

4. In the current query window, below the existing text, type, highlight, and execute the following command to receive the message and view the XML data:

```
SELECT * FROM AWNewNoticeQueue;

DECLARE @dialog_handle UNIQUEIDENTIFIER
  , @XMLdata XML;

SET @XMLdata = (SELECT * FROM sys.tables FOR XML AUTO);

RECEIVE TOP (1) @dialog_handle = conversation_handle
  FROM AWNewNoticeQueue;

END CONVERSATION @dialog_handle;

SELECT @XMLData;
```

5. Execute the *SELECT * FROM AWNewNoticeQueue* statement again to verify that the row is no longer in the queue.

6. Save your scripts and exit SSMS.

Lesson Summary

- Service Broker provides reliable asynchronous messaging capabilities for your SQL Server instance.

- You need to configure the Service Broker components for your solution. These components might include message types, contracts, services, queues, dialogs, and conversation priorities.

- You use the *BEGIN DIALOG, SEND,* and *RECEIVE* commands to control individual conversations between two services.

Chapter Review

To practice and reinforce the skills you learned in this chapter further, you can do any or all of the following:

- Review the chapter summary.
- Review the list of key terms introduced in this chapter.
- Complete the case scenarios. These scenarios set up real-world situations involving the topics of this chapter and ask you to create solutions.
- Complete the suggested practices.
- Take a practice test.

Chapter Summary

- SQL Server 2008 provides two new spatial data types. The *geometry* and *geography* data types can be used to manage spatial data, such as the coordinate location of a classroom in a school or the longitude and latitude of the school's location.
- The fully integrated full-text search feature allows you to write advanced linguistic searches to locate matching rows with a variety of data types.
- Service Broker provides you with a reliable, asynchronous messaging system that can provide solutions ranging from within a single database to across multiple instances and servers.

Key Terms

- *geography* data type
- *geometry* data type
- Open Geospatial Consortium (OGC)
- Well-known text (WKT)
- Well-known binary (WKB)
- Methods
- OGC Extended Methods
- Object
- Instantiation
- Spatial reference identifier (SRID)
- Full-Text Engine
- Filter daemon host process (Fdhost.exe)
- SQL Full-Text Filter Daemon Launcher (Fdlauncher.exe)

- Population (crawl)
- Term
- Filter
- Stoplist
- Stopword
- Thesaurus
- Stemmer
- Token
- Word breaker
- Full-text index
- Full-text catalog
- Conversation
- Dialog
- Conversation group
- Conversation priority
- Message
- Queue
- Service
- Contract
- Message type
- Route
- Remote service binding
- Service Broker endpoint

Case Scenarios

In the following case scenarios, you apply what you have learned in this chapter. You can find answers to these questions in the "Answers" section at the end of this book.

Case Scenario 1: Initiating Spatial Data

You are a database developer for Wide World Importers. Your company has recently upgraded to SQL Server 2008, and management would like to take advantage of the new spatial data types to manage the import business better.

Management sees two separate functions that it wants to implement. The first function would allow them to design a two-dimensional model of the company's warehouses. They would like to track the location of specific categories of goods within the warehouse. The location would be represented by *x* and *y* coordinates and a unit of measure that defines the distance from the axis.

The second function includes tracking the physical location of each warehouse, as well as the region that each warehouse supplies. You want to use a mapping program to show the locations of the warehouses and to shade in the region that the warehouse serves.

Answer the following question for your manager:

- What data type and instantiation method should you use for each requested functionality?

Case Scenario 2: Querying a Full-Text Index

You are a database developer for Litware, Inc. Litware has scanned a large number of documents and is now storing them in *varbinary(max)* columns in the *LitwareDoc* database. The documents are Microsoft Office Word and Microsoft Office Excel documents. The database administrator has configured full-text indexes on the appropriate tables and has included the appropriate columns for each table. You need to define queries that retrieve the name and location of documents that include general phrases. You need to be able to query on a word such as *author* and also receive rows that include the words *writer* and *contributor*. You need to match rows with a similar meaning rather than exact terms. You do not want to match the word *Litware* even if it is entered as a search term; you want it to be ignored because it is in almost every document. You also need to return the rows with the most relevant rows at the top of the result set.

Answer the following questions for your manager:

1. What, if any, additional configuration needs to occur for your queries to work properly?
2. What command provides you with the required functionality?

Suggested Practices

To help you master the exam objectives presented in this chapter, do all the following practices:

Implement Data Types

- **Practice 1** Add *geometry* and *geography* data types to a test database. Practice instantiating spatial instances by using a variety of spatial methods.

Implement Full-Text Search

- **Practice 2** Write and execute a variety of *CONTAINS*, *CONTAINSTABLE*, *FREETEXT*, and *FREETEXTTABLE* commands. Review the result sets carefully.
- **Practice 3** Modify a thesaurus file and create a custom stoplist. Reexecute the commands you wrote for Practice 2 and review how these modifications affect your data. Also, try executing a command with a common word such as *to*, both with and without a stoplist.

Implement Service Broker Solutions

- **Practice 4** Create the components required to start a Service Broker dialog conversation, start a dialog, send messages, and receive messages.

- **Practice 5** Add to the solution that you completed in Lesson 3 to send an acknowledgment message from *AWAckService* to *AWNewNoticeService*.

Take a Practice Test

The practice tests on this book's companion CD offer many options. For example, you can test yourself on just the content covered in this chapter, or you can test yourself on all the 70-433 certification exam content. You can set up the test so that it closely simulates the experience of taking a certification exam, or you can set it up in study mode so that you can look at the correct answers and explanations after you answer each question.

> **MORE INFO** **PRACTICE TESTS**
>
> For details about all the practice test options available, see the section entitled "How to Use the Practice Tests" in the Introduction to this book.

An Introduction to Microsoft SQL Server Manageability Features

As a database developer, you might need to extend your database solutions beyond simply returning queried data to a front-end application. For example, you might need to e-mail reports to users or query metadata from the system. This chapter discusses several features in Microsoft SQL Server 2008 that allow you to disseminate and manage the data in your database efficiently. Features discussed include Database Mail, Windows PowerShell, and data change tracking. SQL Server 2005 introduced Database Mail, and SQL Server 2008 continues support for Database Mail to allow you to send e-mail messages to and from your server running SQL Server. In SQL Server 2008, Microsoft introduced Windows PowerShell to manage technologies supported by the SQL Server Management Objects (SMOs). In addition, database developers have new tools to track data changes more easily.

Exam objectives in this chapter:
- Integrate Database Mail.
- Implement scripts by using Windows PowerShell and SQL Server Management Objects (SMOs).
- Track data changes.

Lessons in this chapter:

Before You Begin

To complete the lessons in this chapter, you must have:

- An understanding of basic data manipulation language (DML) constructs such as *INSERT*, *UPDATE*, and *DELETE*

- A basic understanding of views, stored procedures, and functions used in SQL Server

- Knowledge about how to open and execute queries in SQL Server Management Studio (SSMS)

- SQL Server 2008 Developer Edition, Enterprise Edition, or Enterprise Evaluation Edition, with the *AdventureWorks2008* and the *AdventureWorksDW2008* sample databases installed

- A Simple Mail Transfer Protocol (SMTP) server with two valid e-mail addresses, one for the SQL Server Service account and one for receiving test e-mails

Lesson 1: Integrating Database Mail

With SQL Server 2005, Microsoft introduced Database Mail to allow the SQL Server service to send e-mail messages. By using Database Mail, you can develop database applications that send query results and file attachments to users. This lesson provides you with a short overview and explanation about configuring Database Mail followed by an in-depth discussion of how to use the *sp_send_dbmail* system stored procedure.

> **After this lesson, you will be able to:**
> - Understand the Database Mail configuration process.
> - Send e-mail messages by using *sp_send_dbmail.*
> - Understand the basics of managing Database Mail.
>
> **Estimated lesson time: 45 minutes**

 REAL WORLD

Ann Weber

Recently, a client and I were discussing the options to send very basic weekly reports to his database users automatically. The reports did not need special formatting, but they needed to be created and delivered to the users before the start of each business day. We were able to use the SQL Server Agent with Database Mail to meet the needs of the client successfully.

We created a job for each report set that needed to be sent. We then created a job step that used the *sp_send_dbmail* system stored procedure to execute a database query and send the results to the intended group. Because the queries were already built and used the *datetime* function to retrieve the current date, configuring Database Mail and the SQL Server Agent was quick and painless.

Overview of Database Mail

Database Mail allows administrators and developers to send e-mail messages generated by the SQL Server service. In SQL Server 2005, Database Mail was introduced to replace SQLMail. SQLMail is included in SQL Server 2008 only for backward compatibility. One of the primary benefits of Database Mail is that it communicates by using the SMTP protocol and does not require an Extended MAPI–compliant e-mail application, such as Microsoft Office Outlook, on the server running SQL Server. In addition, Database Mail provides fault tolerance by supporting multiple SMTP servers and multiple SMTP user accounts and profiles.

Configuring Database Mail

Although configuring Database Mail is traditionally a function of the database administrator role, a brief overview is provided here as general background information. You can use SSMS to start the Database Mail Configuration Wizard.

> **NOTE ENABLING DATABASE MAIL**
>
> To minimize the security footprint of your server, Database Mail is disabled by default. If you define Database Mail by using the Database Mail Configuration Manager, Database Mail is enabled as part of the configuration process. In addition, you can use the Surface Area Configuration Policy-Based Management facet or the *sp_configure* system stored procedure to enable Database Mail on one or more servers.

To configure Database Mail, you should perform the following steps:

1. Open SSMS and connect to the SQL Server instance that you want to configure.

2. In Object Explorer, expand the Management folder, right-click Database Mail, and select Configure Database Mail, as shown in Figure 9-1.

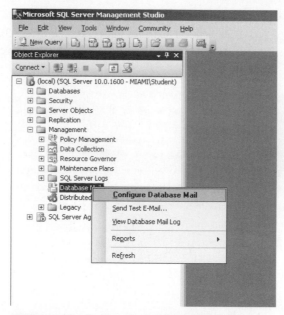

FIGURE 9-1 Configuring the Database Mail option

3. On the Database Mail Configuration Wizard Welcome page, review the information, and click Next.

4. On the Select Configuration Task page, verify that the Set up Database Mail by performing the Following Tasks option is selected, and then click Next.

5. If an SSMS warning message notifies you that the Database Mail feature is not available, click Yes to enable this feature.

6. On the New Profile page, type in a descriptive profile name and description in the appropriate fields.

7. In the SMTP Accounts section, click Add to create a new Database Mail account.

8. In the New Database Mail Account window, add the information that corresponds to the SMTP account that the SQL Server service will use, and then click OK. Figure 9-2 shows sample input. Replace this information with valid account information for your server.

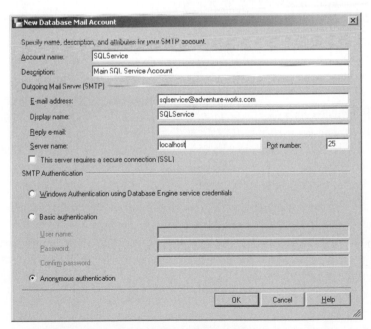

FIGURE 9-2 Sample input for the New Database Mail Account page

9. On the New Profile page, verify your configuration information, and then click Next.

10. On the Manage Profile Security page, configure the appropriate public or private profiles, and then click Next.

> **MORE INFO** **UNDERSTANDING PROFILE SECURITY SETTINGS**
>
> For more information about determining the appropriate profile security settings, see the articles "Manage Profile Security, Public Tab (Database Mail)" and "Manage Profile Security, Private Tab (Database Mail)," in SQL Server Books Online.

11. On the Configure System Parameters page, review the default system parameters, make any necessary changes, and click Next.

12. On the Complete the Wizard page, click Finish.

13. Verify the success of the configuration, and then click Close.

> **MORE INFO** **CONFIGURING DATABASE MAIL**
>
> For more information about enabling and configuring Database Mail, see the article "Database Mail Configuration Wizard" in SQL Server Books Online.

Sending Database Mail Messages

You can use the features of Database Mail to integrate e-mail messages into your applications. For example, you can add the *sp_send_dbmail* system stored procedure at the end of the stored procedure that your application calls to add a new customer to the credit database to send an e-mail message to the credit supervisor with the information added for the new customer.

The *sp_send_dbmail* system stored procedure is used to send e-mail messages from the SQL Server service to e-mail recipients. This command has options that allow you to define the standard e-mail message fields, such as To:, CC:, BCC:, and Subject:, along with more SQL Server–specific options (such as the query to be run) to provide flexibility when building SQL Server applications that need to send e-mail messages. The *sp_send_dbmail* system stored procedure includes the following arguments:

- *@profile_name* Specifies the name of the mail profile from which the message is sent. If no default mail profiles exist, you must include *@profile_name*. If no profile is listed, the system first attempts to use the default private profile for the current user. If the current user does not have a default private profile, the system uses the default public profile for the *msdb* database.

- *@recipients* Specifies the recipients of the e-mail message. The entire list of e-mail addresses should be enclosed in single quotes, and semicolons should separate the addresses. This field is optional, but if *@recipients*, *@copy_recipients*, and *@blind_copy_recipients* are all left blank, the command fails.

- **@copy_recipients** Specifies the e-mail addresses of recipients to be included in the CC: field. The entire list of e-mail addresses should be enclosed in single quotes, and semicolons should separate the addresses. This field is optional, but if *@recipients*, *@copy_recipients*, and *@blind_copy_recipients* are all left blank, the command fails.

- **@blind_copy_recipients** Specifies the e-mail addresses of recipients to be included in the BCC: field. The entire list of e-mail addresses should be enclosed in single quotes, and semicolons should separate the addresses. This field is optional, but if *@recipients*, *@copy_recipients*, and *@blind_copy_recipients* are all left blank, the command fails.

- **@subject** Specifies the value to be included in the Subject: heading of the e-mail. If no subject is specified, the subject will be 'SQL Server Message'. The subject heading should be enclosed in single quotes.

- **@body** Specifies the content of the message; should be enclosed in single quotes.

- **@body_format** Specifies whether the body of the message is 'TEXT' or 'HTML'. The default format type is TEXT.

- **@importance** Sets the importance level of the message to 'Low', 'Normal', or 'High'. If not listed, the default importance is 'Normal'.

- **@sensitivity** Sets the sensitivity level of the message to 'Normal', 'Personal', 'Private', or 'Confidential'. The default value is 'Normal'.

- **@file_attachments** Specifies a list of file names separated by semicolons that you want to attach to the message. The entire list should be enclosed in single quotes.

- **@query** Defines a query that the system executes. You can include the results of the query in the e-mail message body or as an attachment. The entire query is contained within single quotes.

- **@execute_query_database** Specifies the database context for the query. This argument is ignored if you do not specify *@query*.

- **@attach_query_result_as_file** Specifies whether the query results are included as an attachment or within the body of the mail message. A value of 1 specifies a file attachment will be used. A value of 0 specifies the query results will follow the content specified in the *@body* argument. This argument is ignored if you do not specify *@query*. If you do not include this option, the query results are returned in the body of the e-mail message.

- **@query_attachment_filename** Specifies the file name assigned to the query results attachment. This option requires single quotes if the file name includes a file name extension (such as .txt) or other disallowed characters. If *@attach_query_result_as_file* is set to 1 and this parameter is not included, Database Mail sets the default file name. The *@query_attachment_filename* is ignored if the *@attach_query_result_as_file* argument is not specified or set to 0 or *@query* is not defined.

- **@query_result_header** Set to 1 or 0 to specify whether or not column headers are included in the result set. The default value is 1, which specifies to include column headers. This argument is ignored if you do not specify *@query*.

- **@query_result_width** Specifies the number of characters to be included in a single line when formatting the result set. The default is 256 characters, but you can set this option to anything between 10 and 32767. This argument is ignored if you do not specify *@query*.

- **@query_result_separator** Specifies the character to be used to separate columns in the result set. The default value is a space.

- **@exclude_query_output** Is set to 0 or 1 to specify whether query error messages such as the one shown in Figure 9-3 are displayed on the monitor. A value of 0 includes the query error message on the monitor, and a value of 1 reports on the monitor only that the command completed successfully, even if the query within the stored procedure fails.

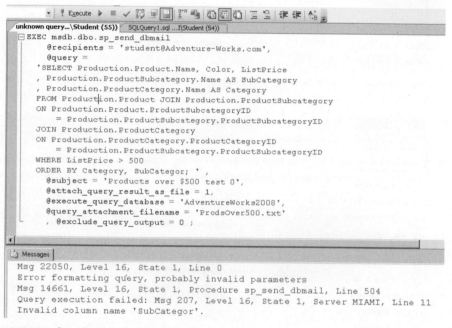

FIGURE 9-3 Sample query error message

- **@append_query_error** Specifies whether an e-mail message is still sent when a query error occurs. The default setting of 0 signifies that Database Mail does not send the e-mail message when the query fails. When the value is set to 1, Database Mail sends the e-mail message and appends the error message to the e-mail as displayed in Figure 9-4. This setting also affects the behavior of the *@exclude_query_output* argument.

- **@query_no_truncate** Is set to 0 or 1 to specify whether large variable-length columns in the result set are truncated. The default value of 0 truncates columns to 256 characters. If the value is set to 1, it does not truncate large variable-length columns, column headers are not included, and additional resources are required to run the query. Figures 9-5 and 9-6 show the difference in row length when the *Resume* column defined as an *XML* data type is sent as an attached text file. Figure 9-5 was executed with the *@query_no_truncate* argument set to 0. Figure 9-6 was executed with this option set to 1.

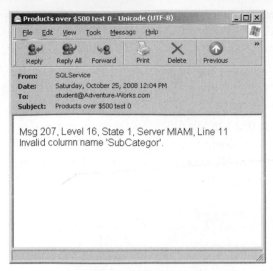

FIGURE 9-4 Sample of appended error message

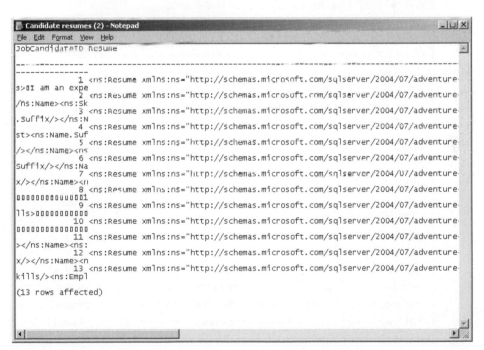

FIGURE 9-5 *Resume* column truncated

- **@mailitem_id [OUTPUT]**   Sets an optional output variable to return the *mailitem_id* of the message.

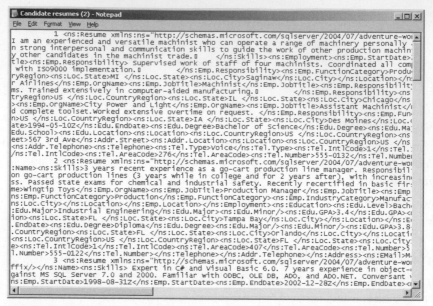

FIGURE 9-6 *Resume* column not truncated

The following query sends an e-mail message to student@Adventure-Works.com that has the subject heading of Job Candidate Resumes. The message includes an attachment named Candidate_resumes.txt. This attachment includes the results of a query returning the *JobCandidateID* and *Resume* columns from the *HumanResources.JobCandidate* table in the *AdventureWorks2008* database. The XML data retrieved from the *Resume* column is not truncated. The text file generated is shown in Figure 9-6:

```
EXEC msdb.dbo.sp_send_dbmail
    @recipients = 'student@Adventure-Works.com',
    @query =
 'SELECT JobCandidateID
    , Resume from HumanResources.JobCandidate' ,
    @subject = 'Job Candidate Resumes',
    @execute_query_database = 'AdventureWorks2008',
    @attach_query_result_as_file = 1,
    @query_attachment_filename = 'Candidate_resumes.txt',
    @query_no_truncate = 1;
```

> **IMPORTANT** **DEPRECATED COMMANDS**
>
> SQL Server 2008 includes *xp_sendmail* as well as a number of additional deprecated stored procedures to support SQLMail and backward compatibility. You should not use SQLMail in new development because support will be removed in a future version of SQL Server. You should implement Database Mail in any new projects. In addition, you should begin to convert your existing code to Database Mail.

Managing Database Mail

Although typically the configuration of Database Mail falls into the Database Administrator role, you can use the following system stored procedures to modify or troubleshoot configuration settings that affect the messages you are sending from your applications:

- **sysmail_configure_sp**   Configures parameters such as the maximum file size allowed for attachments, prohibited file name extensions that cannot be sent as attachments, and retry settings.

- **sysmail_help_configure_sp**   Displays the current settings for Database Mail.

- **sysmail_help_queue_sp**   Displays information about the status and mail queues. You can use this stored procedure to troubleshoot messages that were not received.

- **sysmail_delete_mailitems_sp**   Deletes e-mail messages permanently from Database Mail tables in the *msdb* database. These messages can be deleted based on their status or the date on which the message was sent. Attachments of deleted messages are also deleted, but associated logged events must be deleted independently by using *sysmail_delete_log_sp*.

- **sysmail_delete_log_sp**   Deletes entries permanently from the Database Mail logs. These entries can be deleted based on their status or the date on which the associated message was sent. The e-mail messages associated with the deleted log entries must be deleted independently by using *sysmail_delete_mailitems_sp*.

- **sysmail_start_sp**   Starts Database Mail by starting the associated Service Broker objects.

- **sysmail_stop_sp**   Stops Database Mail by stopping the associated Service Broker objects. You can use this stored procedure to troubleshoot Database Mail by temporarily pausing the processing of messages in the Database Mail queues. The *sp_send_dbmail* stored procedure still functions while the Service Broker objects are stopped.

PRACTICE   **Using Database Mail to Send Messages**

In this practice, you configure Database Mail on your SQL Server instance. You then configure mail settings and send a Database Mail message from SQL Server.

EXERCISE 1   Configure Database Mail

If Database Mail is not configured on your system, use the following steps to configure Database Mail:

1. Open SSMS.

2. In Object Explorer, expand the Management folder, right-click Database Mail, and click Configure Database Mail.

3. On the Database Mail Configuration Wizard Welcome page, review the information, and click Next.

4. On the Select Configuration Task page, verify that the Set up Database Mail by Performing the Following Tasks option is selected, and then click Next.

5. If an SSMS warning message notifies you that the Database Mail feature is not available, click Yes to enable this feature.

6. On the New Profile page, type a descriptive profile name and description in the appropriate fields.

7. In the SMTP Accounts section, click Add to create a new Database Mail account.

8. In the New Database Mail Account window, add the information that corresponds to the SMTP account that the SQL Server service will use, and then click OK. For the account to function, you must provide an account name, e-mail address, and proper server name and port number for your mail messages to be sent.

9. On the New Profile page, verify your configuration information, and then click Next.

10. On the Manage Profile Security page, in the Public Profiles tab, select the Public check box next to your profile name, select Yes in the drop-down list in the Default Profile column, and then click Next.

11. On the Configure System Parameters page, review the default system parameters, and click Next.

12. On the Complete the Wizard page, click Finish.

13. Verify the success of the configuration, and click Close.

14. Leave SSMS open for the next exercise.

EXERCISE 2   Verify Database Mail Configuration

In this exercise, you verify the Database Mail configuration by sending a test e-mail message.

1. In Object Explorer, expand the Management folder, right-click Database Mail, and click Send Test E-Mail.

2. In the Send Test E-Mail From *<server name>* window, select your Database Mail Profile, enter the e-mail address to which you want to send the test message in the To: box, review the Subject: and Body: information, and click Send Test E-mail. The Database Mail Test E-mail dialog box appears and provides you with verification that the e-mail has been queued.

3. Wait a few minutes, and then check your e-mail messages. If you receive the e-mail message, click OK to close the dialog box, or click Troubleshoot to open troubleshooting tips in SQL Server Books Online.

4. Leave SSMS open for the next exercise.

EXERCISE 3   Write Database Mail Messages

In this exercise, you send a variety of e-mail messages by using the different options of the *sp_send_dbmail* command.

1. To send a test message to your mail account by using the *sp_send_dbmail* command, replace the *@recipients* option with your e-mail address, and execute the following code in a new query window:

```
EXEC msdb.dbo.sp_send_dbmail
    @recipients = 'student@Adventure-Works.com'
    , @body = 'The command completed successfully.'
    , @subject = 'Test Automated Success Message' ;
```

2. Open a new query window.

3. In the new query window, type and execute the following command to send a mail message to your e-mail account with the results of a query included as an attachment. Remember to replace the *@recipients* option with your e-mail address.

```
EXEC msdb.dbo.sp_send_dbmail
   @recipients = 'student@Adventure-Works.com'
  ,@query =
   'USE AdventureWorks2008;
   Go
   SELECT Production.Product.Name, Color, ListPrice
     , Production.ProductSubcategory.Name AS SubCategory
     , Production.ProductCategory.Name AS Category
   FROM Production.Product JOIN Production.ProductSubcategory
   ON Production.Product.ProductSubcategoryID =
      Production.ProductSubcategory.ProductSubcategoryID
   JOIN Production.ProductCategory
   ON Production.ProductCategory.ProductCategoryID =
      Production.ProductSubcategory.ProductSubcategoryID
   WHERE ListPrice > 500
   ORDER BY Category, SubCategory; '
  ,@subject = 'Products over $500'
  ,@attach_query_result_as_file = 1 ;
```

4. Switch to your mail program and verify that the message was received with an attachment. Open and review the attachment. Notice the database context change information in the result set. To avoid this, you would use the *@execute_query_database* argument to specify the *AdventureWorks2008* database.

5. Switch to SSMS and modify the query from step 3 to set *@attach_query_result_as_file* to 0, which includes the results as a part of the message rather than as an attachment. Also, configure *@execute_query_database* to '*AdventureWorks2008*', and remove the *USE* database and *go* commands from the query to eliminate the database context change from the query results. The query you execute should look similar to the following code:

```
EXEC msdb.dbo.sp_send_dbmail
   @recipients = 'student@Adventure-Works.com'
  ,@query =
```

```
'SELECT Production.Product.Name, Color, ListPrice
, Production.ProductSubcategory.Name AS SubCategory
, Production.ProductCategory.Name AS Category
FROM Production.Product JOIN Production.ProductSubcategory
ON Production.Product.ProductSubcategoryID =
    Production.ProductSubcategory.ProductSubcategoryID
JOIN Production.ProductCategory
ON Production.ProductCategory.ProductCategoryID =
    Production.ProductSubcategory.ProductSubcategoryID
WHERE ListPrice > 500
ORDER BY Category, SubCategory; '
,@subject = 'Products over $500'
,@attach_query_result_as_file = 0
,@execute_query_database = 'AdventureWorks2008';
```

6. Switch to your mail program and verify that the message was received and includes the query result set.

7. Switch to SSMS and modify and execute the query from steps 3 and 5 to send an attachment using the file name ProdsOver500.txt. To achieve this, set the *@attach_query_result_as_file* option to 1 and include the following code after the last line of code, but before the semicolon:

```
, @query_attachment_filename = 'ProdsOver500.txt'
```

8. Switch to your mail program and verify that the message was received and includes the query result set.

Lesson Summary

- Database Mail was introduced in SQL Server 2005 and should be used in place of SQL Mail.

- Database Mail is disabled by default to minimize the surface area of the server.

- You should use the *sp_send_dbmail* system stored procedure to integrate Database Mail with your applications.

- A wide variety of arguments allows you to customize the e-mail messages and attachments sent from the database server.

Lesson 2: Implementing Scripts by Using Windows PowerShell

As a developer, you can use PowerShell in SQL Server 2008 to automate the process of deploying your applications. You can also use SQL Server PowerShell to automate the enumeration of database objects and the object properties. Additionally, you can invoke Sqlcmd through SQL Server PowerShell, allowing you to execute any valid SQL commands from within the Windows PowerShell environment.

> **After this lesson, you will be able to:**
> - Understand the capabilities of SQL Server PowerShell.
> - Navigate the SQL Server PowerShell hierarchy.
> - Use SQL Server PowerShell to enumerate objects.
>
> **Estimated lesson time: 45 minutes**

What Is Windows PowerShell?

Windows PowerShell is a command-line shell and scripting environment that allows you to automate administrative and development tasks by creating robust scripts. Because Windows PowerShell functions across many Microsoft applications, once you learn this common scripting language, you can use it to manage multiple servers and products.

When you install SQL Server 2008, the installation program installs Windows PowerShell 1.0 (if not already installed), the SQL Server PowerShell provider, a set of SQL Server PowerShell cmdlets, and the *sqlps* utility to enable SQL Server functionality within the PowerShell environment. With SQL Server PowerShell, you can create scripts that you can run as scheduled SQL Server Agent jobs, by using the Start PowerShell option in SSMS, or by executing a SQL Server PowerShell environment application such as *sqlps* or a custom application.

> **NOTE** **WINDOWS POWERSHELL SUPPORT**
>
> In SQL Server 2008, Windows PowerShell support is limited to the SMOs relating to the Database Engine and Service Broker. A Windows PowerShell provider for SQL Server Analysis Services (SSAS) is available on the CodePlex Web site at *http://www.codeplex.com/ powerSSAS*.

Navigating the SQL Server PowerShell Hierarchy

SQL Server uses a hierarchy to represent how objects are related to each other within a server. For example, a table exists in a schema, which exists within a database, which exists within a SQL Server instance, which resides on a server. SQL Server PowerShell uses a drive-and-path representation of this hierarchy. The drive-and-path structure used by SQL Server PowerShell is constructed using similar terminology and commands to the ones you use in a file system.

The root node for SQL Server is the SQLSERVER: drive. Under the SQLSERVER: drive, the SQL Server PowerShell provider implements the following three folders:

- **SQLSERVER:\SQL** Contains database objects, such as databases, tables, views, and stored procedures
- **SQLSERVER:\SQLPolicy** Contains policy-based management objects, such as policies and facets
- **SQLSERVER:\SQLRegistration** Contains registered server objects, such as server groups and registered servers

Within each engine and folder, you can define the path to the object you want to create, view, or manage. The folders, subfolders, and objects that you can access are defined by the SMO model included in SQL Server 2008.

When you use Object Explorer in SSMS to start a SQL Server PowerShell session, the path is set to the object from which you began the session, as shown in Figures 9-7 and 9-8.

The SQL Server PowerShell path starts with the drive, followed by one of the three supported folders. For the SQL folder, the server name and instance name follow the folder. If you are referring to the default instance, you must specify the word **DEFAULT**. After the instance name, the path alternates between the object type and the name of the object to which you are referring.

For example, SQLSERVER:\SQL\MIAMI\DEFAULT\Databases\AdventureWorks2008\Tables\Person.Address refers to the *Address* table in the *Person* schema in the *AdventureWorks2008* database on the default instance of a server named MIAMI.

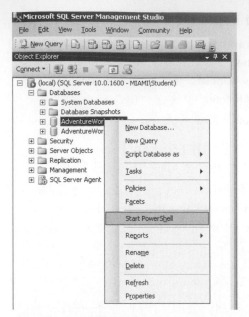

FIGURE 9-7 Using Object Explorer to start a SQL Server PowerShell session

FIGURE 9-8 A path set to the location where the SQL Server PowerShell session was initiated

---

✔️ **Quick Check**

- Which folder would you specify if you wanted to determine what objects existed in a particular schema?

Quick Check Answer

- You would specify the SQLSERVER:\SQL folder.

Using SQL Server PowerShell to Enumerate Objects

Once you set the path to the correct object, you can list child items, move items, rename items, and perform many other actions as well. PowerShell cmdlets can be referred to with their full names or with any of a number of aliases. A list of the cmdlets, their functions, and their alias implemented in SQL Server 2008 are as follows:

- **Get-Location**   Returns the current node name. Aliases: *gl, pwd*.
- **Set-Location**   Changes the current node. Aliases: *sl, cd, chdir*.
- **Get-ChildItem**   Lists the objects stored at the current node. Aliases: *gci, dir, ls*.
- **Get-Item**   Returns the properties of the current item. Alias: *gu*.
- **Move-Item**   Moves an item. Aliases: *mi, move, mv*.
- **Rename-Item**   Renames an object. Aliases: *rni, rn, ren,*
- **Remove-Item**   Deletes an object. Aliases: *ri, del, rd, rm, rmdir*.

> **BEST PRACTICES   USING ALIASES**
>
> Although it is usually easier to use aliases when working interactively, using the full cmdlet name will make stored scripts easier to read and maintain.

When you are working interactively in the SQL Server PowerShell session, you can use the following tips:

- Use the up and down arrow keys to scroll through commands that have been run previously.
- Use the right and left arrow keys to move through and edit a command that has been returned by using the up and down arrow keys, or one that you have just typed.
- Use aliases to minimize typing.
- Use the full or relative path depending on the current and desired paths, as shown in the following examples:
  - If your current path is SQLSERVER:\SQL\MIAMI\DEFAULT\Databases\ AdventureWorks2008\Tables\Person.Address and you want to move to the Tables subfolder directly above the current path, you can type **cd ..** to move up one level in the path.
  - If your current path is SQLSERVER:\SQL\MIAMI\DEFAULT\Databases\ AdventureWorks2008\Tables\Person.Address and you want to move to the SQL Policy folder, the easiest option is probably to type **cd \SQLPolicy**.
- Use *cls* to clear the screen to make your result set easier to read.
- Use the *–force* parameter to view system objects such as the *sys* schema and the objects in it.
- Use tab-completion to allow you to type a partial path or cmdlet name and press Tab to receive a list of objects whose names match what you have typed.

Additional SQL Server PowerShell Cmdlets

In addition to the cmdlets listed previously, the SQL Server PowerShell provider includes other built-in cmdlets to provide greater functionality. The following cmdlets might be beneficial to developers:

- ■ **Get-Help**   Provides help information about each cmdlet. The *–Full* parameter provides the full technical help, including the samples. Figure 9-9 shows the results of the Help screen for the *Invoke-Sqlcmd* cmdlet.

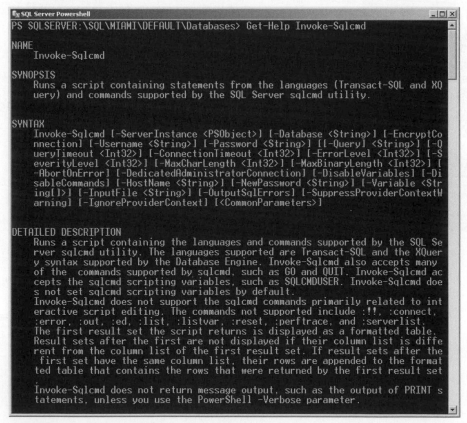

FIGURE 9-9 Sample Help screen

- ***Invoke-Sqlcmd*** Runs a Transact-SQL (T-SQL) or XQuery script.

- ***Encode-SqlName*** Encodes a SQL Server identifier (object name) to reformat any characters not supported by the SQL Server PowerShell language.

- ***Decode-SqlName*** Returns the original SQL identifier when provided with an encoded SQL identifier.

- ***Convert-UrnToPath*** Converts an SMO Uniform Resource Name (URN) to the path structure used by SQL Server PowerShell. Both the path and URN contain the same information, but the format is different.

For example, you can use the following command to retrieve the current date and time as shown in Figure 9-10:

```
Invoke-Sqlcmd –Query "SELECT GETDATE() AS 'Date';"
```

FIGURE 9-10 Sample of the *Invoke-Sqlcmd* cmdlet

Using SQL Server PowerShell—Examples

The following examples are provided to help you become more familiar with some of the cmdlets and options available when using SQL Server PowerShell with SQL Server 2008.

This first example uses the *Get-Item* option and evaluates and displays the current status of the SQL Server Login Mode policy on a server named MIAMI. This policy is one of the Best Practices policies included with SQL Server 2008, which you can import into your server's policies. If your server is set to Integrated-only authentication, the result returned is *True*. If your security settings allow both SQL- and Windows-integrated logins, the result returned is *False*, as shown in Figure 9-11.

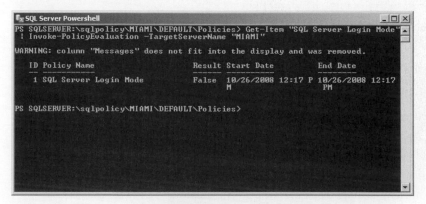

FIGURE 9-11 Sample of the *Get-Item* cmdlet

NOTE **COMMAND REQUIREMENTS**

Before executing the sample in Figure 9-11, you need to change to the appropriate path and verify that the RPC server is available.

The second sample, in Figure 9-12, shows the list of subfolders available under the DEFAULT instance on the MIAMI server in the SQL folder. Notice that the sample uses the *ls* alias rather than spelling out the complete *Get-ChildItem* cmdlet.

The final example, in Figure 9-13, demonstrates using the *Get-ChildItem* cmdlet to list the parameters defined on the *HumanResources.uspUpdateEmployeeLogin* user-defined stored procedure in the *AdventureWorks2008* database on the DEFAULT instance of the server MIAMI.

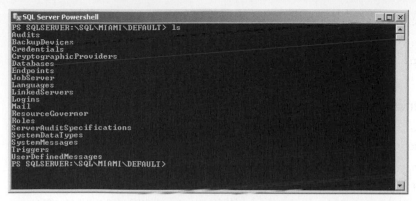

FIGURE 9-12 Sample of the *Get-ChildItem* cmdlet to list the subfolders available under the DEFAULT instance

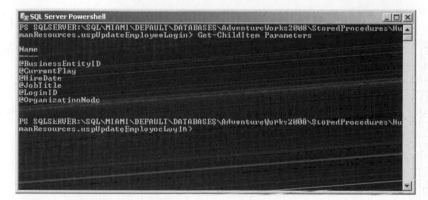

FIGURE 9-13 Sample of the *Get-ChildItem* cmdlet to list the parameters defined on a stored procedure

PRACTICE   **Using the SQL Server PowerShell Provider**

In this practice, you use SQL Server PowerShell to browse within the SQLSERVER context.

EXERCISE   Browse the SQL Server PowerShell Hierarchy

In this exercise, you browse through various paths and view objects by using the SQL Server PowerShell utility.

1. Open SSMS, if it is not already open.

2. In Object Explorer, expand the Databases folder, right-click the *AdventureWorks2008* database, and select Start PowerShell.

3. In the SQL Server PowerShell window, note that the active path is as follows:
   PS SQLSERVER:\SQL\MIAMI\DEFAULT\Databases\AdventureWorks2008.

4. Right-click within the SQL Server PowerShell window, and select Mark. Use the arrow keys to move the cursor three spaces to the right, to the first letter of your path. Use the Shift key in conjunction with the arrow keys to highlight the current path. Do not highlight the PS prompt before the path or the > at the end of the path. Press Enter before pressing any other keys. Your cursor should return to the end of the current command line.

5. On the current command line, type **Set-Location**, followed by a space, and then right-click within the SQL Server PowerShell window, and select Paste. Immediately following the pasted path, type **\Tables**, and press Enter. Verify that the path has changed to the Tables object level.

6. In the SQL Server PowerShell window, on the current command line, type **Get-ChildItem** and press Enter. Review the data that is returned. Notice that the schema, table name, and creation date for each user-defined table in the current database are returned.

7. In the SQL Server PowerShell window, on the current command line, type **Set-Location ..** to move up one level in the path.

8. In the SQL Server PowerShell window, on the current command line, type **cd Views** to change to the Views object level. Use the *Get-ChildItem* command from step 6 to list the user-defined views in the *AdventureWorks2008* database. Review the list of views returned.

9. While the current path is set to the Views subfolder, use the *Get-ChildItem –force* option to list all views, including system views. Notice the difference from the results that you obtained in step 8.

10. In the SQL Server PowerShell window, on the current command line, type **Set-Location HumanResources.vEmployee** and press Enter.

11. To view the columns defined in the *HumanResources.vEmployee* view, type **Get-ChildItem Columns** and press Enter. Review the columns defined in the *HumanResources.vEmployee* view.

Lesson Summary

- SQL Server PowerShell is a command-line shell and scripting environment, based on Windows PowerShell.
- SQL Server PowerShell uses a hierarchy to represent how objects are related to each other.
- The three folders that exist in the SQL Server PowerShell provider are SQLSERVER:\SQL, SQLSERVER:\SQLPolicy, and SQLSERVER\SQLRegistration.
- You can browse the hierarchy by using either the cmdlet names or their aliases.

Lesson 3: Tracking Data Changes

If you worked on previous versions of SQL Server, you may have built complex solutions that included adding timestamp columns, adding triggers, and possibly even configuring replication to track changes in your database. In SQL Server 2008, Microsoft introduced change tracking and change data capture (CDC) to help answer questions about data that changes in a database. In addition, SQL Server 2008 Enterprise Edition includes SQL Server Audit, which provides automatic auditing of a SQL Server instance. In addition to being able to audit server and database level events, SQL Server Audit provides you with a tool to log not only when a table is modified (*INSERT, UPDATE, DELETE*), but also when data is read from a table (*SELECT*).

> **After this lesson, you will be able to:**
> - Describe and compare the change tracking and CDC features and differences.
> - Enable change tracking on databases and tables.
> - Query for information about changed data when using change tracking.
> - Enable CDC on databases and tables.
> - Query for information about changed data when using CDC.
>
> **Estimated lesson time: 60 minutes**

Comparing Change Tracking to CDC

When implementing a method to track changes in your database, you need to decide between the change tracking and CDC methods. Each of these methods allows you to determine whether a change has occurred to the data. The following sections compare the benefits of each method and describe how each method operates.

Change Tracking

Change tracking has the following functions:

- Provides functionality with DML statements.
- Can answer questions such as:
  - What rows in the table have changed?
  - What columns have changed?
  - Has a particular row been updated?
  - Did an *INSERT, UPDATE,* or *DELETE* occur?
- Operates synchronously to provide change information immediately.
- Provides a lower storage overhead than CDC.

- Provides a built-in cleanup mechanism.
- Uses the transaction commit time to determine the order of the changes.
- Works without requiring schema changes to the table or additional triggers.
- Must be enabled at the database level by using *ALTER DATABASE*.

Change Data Capture

Change data capture has the following functions:

- Provides functionality with DML statements.
- Can answer the same questions as change tracking, as well as the following ones:
    - What were the intermediate changes made to the data since the last synchronization?
    - How many times has a row been updated since the last synchronization?
- Uses *change tables* to record modified column data and metadata that is required to apply changes to a target environment. The column structure of the change table mirrors the structure of the source table.
- Uses the transaction log as input for the information added to the change tables.
- Operates asynchronously and changes are available only after the DML statement has completed.
- Provides table-valued functions to allow access to the data in the change tables.
- Requires the database to be enabled by using *sys.sp_cdc_enable_db*.
- Requires SQL Server 2008 Enterprise, Developer, or Evaluation Edition.

 REAL WORLD

Ann Weber

A few weeks ago, I was working with a large retail company in the Chicago area. They currently use SQL Server 2005 OLTP databases along with Analysis Services. Their sales managers change territories on a regular basis. When a change occurs in the staging database for the OLAP data warehouse, a special program needs to be run before the cubes can be processed. We were talking about different ways to accomplish this in SQL Server 2005, and although it can be done, they need to add additional columns and triggers to their tables, which can slow input into this staging base and add complexity.

We also discussed SQL Server 2008 and change tracking. They only need to know if a row was updated and what the current data in the table is, so the lower performance overhead of change tracking is ideal for them. We also discussed the added functionality of CDC, but they did not need that functionality at this time.

Configuring Change Tracking

Before you can configure change tracking on your tables, you must enable change tracking on the database. You can use either SSMS or *ALTER DATABASE* to enable change tracking on your database.

> **IMPORTANT DATABASE COMPATIBILITY LEVEL**
>
> Before you can configure change tracking for a given database, you must set the database compatibility level to SQL Server 2005 (90) or higher for that database.

Enabling Change Tracking for a Database

When you enable change tracking for a database, you can configure the following options:

- **Change Tracking**   Set to *True* or *False* (the default) to enable or disable change tracking.
- **Retention Period**   Set to a numeric value that represents the minimum amount of time that changes are maintained. The default retention period is 2.
- **Retention Period Units**   Set to *Days* (the default), *Hours*, or *Minutes*.
- **Auto CleanUp**   Set to *ON* (the default) or *OFF* to enable or disable the process that removes outdated change tracking information.

> **WARNING ENABLING AUTO CLEAN-UP RESETS DEFAULTS**
>
> Each time the Auto Clean-Up option is set to *ON*, the Retention Period and Retention Period Units are reset to the default value of 2 and 2 days, respectively.

To enable change tracking by using SSMS, you should perform the following steps:

1. In Object Explorer, expand the Databases folder, right-click the database where you want to use change tracking, and select Properties.
2. In the select a page pane of the Database Properties window, click Change Tracking.
3. On the Change Tracking page, configure the appropriate options, and then click OK.

Figure 9-14 shows change tracking settings for the *AdventureWorks2008* database. The retention period is set to seven days. If the *Analysis Services* staging database is synchronized with the *AdventureWorks2008* database once every three days, the configured retention period allows a synchronization to be missed and repaired before the data is removed from the change tables. In this scenario, more space is required in the change tables than if you configure a shorter retention period.

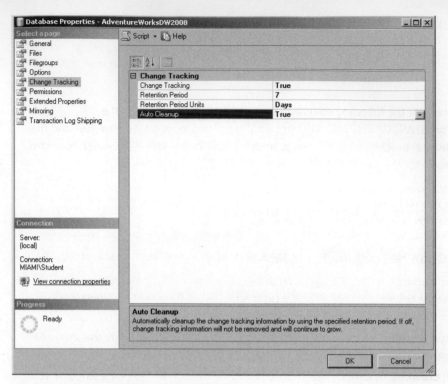

FIGURE 9-14 Change tracking database settings

You can enable change tracking by executing the *ALTER DATABASE* command. The following code includes the full syntax for the *ALTER DATABASE* command for the options related to change tracking:

```
ALTER DATABASE database_name
SET
{
<change_tracking_option> ::=
{
  CHANGE_TRACKING {
        = ON [ <change_tracking_option_list > ] |
    <change_tracking_option_list> |
        = OFF
  }
}
<change_tracking_option_list> ::=
{
    ( <change_tracking_option> | <change_tracking_option_list> ,
    <change_tracking_option> )
}
  <change_tracking_option> ::=
```

```
{
  AUTO_CLEANUP = { ON | OFF }
  | CHANGE_RETENTION = { retention_period { DAYS | HOURS | MINUTES } ]
}
}
```

You can execute the following command to enable change tracking on the *AdventureWorksDW2008* database. Changes are maintained for at least seven days and the automatic cleanup process removes change tracking information that was created more than seven days ago:

```
ALTER DATABASE AdventureWorksDW2008
SET CHANGE TRACKING = ON
(CHANGE_RETENTION = 7 DAYS, AUTO_CLEANUP = ON)
```

Enabling Change Tracking for a Table

Once change tracking has been enabled on the database, the *ALTER TABLE* command is used to enable change tracking on individual tables that you want to track. There are only two arguments in the *ALTER TABLE* command that affect change tracking:

- **Change_Tracking** Set to *ENABLE* (the default) or *DISABLE* to identify the status of change tracking on the table.
- **Track_Columns_Updated** Set to *ON* or *OFF* (the default) to designate whether you want to maintain a list of which columns are updated when the *UPDATE* command is executed against the table.

To configure change tracking by using SSMS, select the Change Tracking page of the Table Properties window for the table on which you want to track changes.

You can execute the following code to enable change tracking, including information about changes to individual columns that are modified on the *DimEmployee* table in the *AdventureWorksDW2008* database:

```
ALTER TABLE DimEmployee
ENABLE CHANGE_TRACKING
WITH (TRACK_COLUMNS_UPDATED = ON);
```

Disabling Change Tracking

You must disable change tracking on each table by using either SSMS or *ALTER TABLE* before you can disable change tracking on the database.

To determine which tables in the *AdventureWorksDW2008* database have change tracking enabled, you can query the *sys.change_tracking_tables* catalog view as shown in Figure 9-15.

To disable change tracking on the *FactInternetSales* table, execute the following code:

```
ALTER TABLE FactInternetSales
DISABLE CHANGE_TRACKING;
```

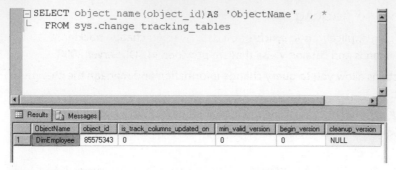

```
SELECT object_name(object_id) AS 'ObjectName' , *
  FROM sys.change_tracking_tables
```

	ObjectName	object_id	is_track_columns_updated_on	min_valid_version	begin_version	cleanup_version
1	DimEmployee	85575343	0	0	0	NULL

FIGURE 9-15 Viewing tables with change tracking enabled

Once you have disabled change tracking on all the tables in the database, you can disable change tracking on the database by using SSMS or the *ALTER DATABASE* command.

The following command disables change tracking on the *AdventureWorksDW2008* database:

```
ALTER DATABASE AdventureWorksDW2008
SET CHANGE_TRACKING = OFF
```

Understanding Additional Change Tracking Effects

The following commands may behave differently when change tracking is enabled:

- **TRUNCATE TABLE** Succeeds, but deleted rows are not tracked and the minimum valid version is updated, which requires applications to reinitialize before they can resume synchronization.

- **DROP INDEX or ALTER INDEX DISABLE** Fails only if referencing the index that enforces the *PRIMARY KEY* constraint.

- **DROP TABLE** Succeeds and removes all change tracking information pertaining to the dropped table.

- **ALTER TABLE DROP CONSTRAINT** Fails if you try to drop the *PRIMARY KEY* constraint. You must disable change tracking before you can drop the *PRIMARY KEY* constraint on the table.

- **ALTER TABLE DROP COLUMN** Succeeds so long as the column is not part of the *PRIMARY KEY* constraint. Unless the application is programmed to handle the dropped column, data from the dropped column might still be returned as part of the change tracking information.

- **ALTER TABLE ADD COLUMN** Succeeds and begins tracking changes that are made to the new column.

- **ALTER TABLE ALTER COLUMN** Succeeds, but data type changes on non–primary key columns are not tracked.

- **ALTER TABLE SWITCH** Fails if one or both of the tables has change tracking enabled.

Working with Change Tracking

When you are developing applications to synchronize data by using change tracking, you can use several T-SQL commands and catalog views that are provided in SQL Server 2008.

The following functions allow you to query change information and manage the change tracking environment:

- **CHANGETABLE**   Used to return all change information for a table by using the *CHANGES* option, or change information for a specific row by using the *VERSION* option.

- **CHANGE_TRACKING_MIN_VALID_VERSION**   Returns the minimum version that is valid for use in obtaining change tracking when you execute the *CHANGETABLE* function. You must specify the table object ID for the tracked table as an argument to the command.

- **CHANGE_TRACKING_CURRENT_VERSION**   Obtains the version that is associated with the last committed transaction. You can use this version information when you execute the *CHANGETABLE* function.

- **CHANGE_TRACKING_IS_COLUMN_IN_MASK**   Interprets the *SYS_CHANGE_COLUMNS* value returned by the *CHANGETABLE (CHANGES . . .)* function allowing your application to determine whether the column listed in the argument is included in the values returned for *SYS_CHANGE_COLUMNS*.

- **WITH CHANGE_TRACKING_CONTEXT**   Allows you to set context information to a *varbinary(128)* field in the change tracking information when updates occur. This allows you to determine what application initiated an update.

> **MORE INFO**   **CHANGE TRACKING FUNCTIONS SYNTAX**
>
> For detailed information about the syntax for the change tracking functions, see the article "Change Tracking Functions (Transact-SQL)" in SQL Server Books Online.

CHANGETABLE Function Output and Samples

The *CHANGETABLE(CHANGES)* function displays the following columns when queried:

- **SYS_CHANGE_VERSION**   Displays the version of the most recent change to the row.

- **SYS_CHANGE_CREATION_VERSION**   Displays the version value of the last *INSERT* operation.

- **SYS_CHANGE_OPERATION**   Displays U for *UPDATE*, D for *DELETE*, or I for *INSERT*.

- **SYS_CHANGE_COLUMNS**   Displays the columns that have changed since the baseline version. This column contains *NULL* under the following circumstances:

  - The *Track_Columns_Updated* argument is set to *OFF*.

  - The operation is an *INSERT* or *DELETE*.

  - All non–primary key columns were updated in the same operation.

- **SYS_CHANGE_CONTEXT**   Displays a context for the update if defined. You configure the context as part of the *INSERT*, *UPDATE*, or *DELETE* statement by using the *WITH* clause.

- **<primary key column value>**   Displays the primary key value for the row.

For the following sample queries, change tracking was enabled on the *AdventureWorksDW2008* database and the *DimEmployee* table in the *AdventureWorksDW2008* database. To start with, the *Track_Columns_Updated* argument is set to *OFF*.

A new row is inserted into the *DimEmployee* table for an employee named Jonathan Haas. His employee key is 299. Figure 9-16 displays the change by using the *CHANGETABLE* function. Notice that the *SYS_CHANGE_VERSION* is 1 and the *SYS_CHANGE_OPERATION* is I for *INSERT*.

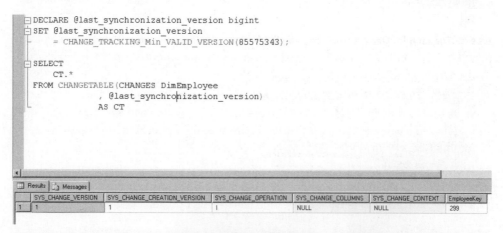

FIGURE 9-16 Sample output from a change table query with *Track_Columns_Updated* off

For the next sample, two rows are updated in the *DimEmployee* table. Jonathan Haas, Employee 299, became a salesperson (the *SalesPersonFlag* column was set to 1). Syed Abbas, Employee 294, is no longer a salesperson; therefore, the *SalesPersonFlag* column was set to 0. Figure 9-17 shows the results of the *CHANGETABLE(CHANGES)* function showing all updates from the first capture to this point. Notice that the *SYS_CHANGE_VERSION* has been incremented to 2 for the *EmployeeKey* 299, but the operation is still I. The row has not been synchronized since the initial *INSERT*, so an *INSERT* still needs to occur when the table is synchronized, but the new current data with a *SalesPersonFlag* of 1 is included in the synchronization. For Employee 294, the *SYS_CHANGE_VERSION* is now set to 3 (each update to the table increments this count), the *SYS_CHANGE_OPERATION* is U for *UPDATE*, but the *SYS_CHANGE_CREATION_VERSION* is set to *NULL* because this row was inserted before change tracking was enabled.

The final sample for this scenario includes the deletion of the new user, Jonathan Haas. Notice in Figure 9-18 that for the row with *EmployeeKey* 299, the *SYS_CHANGE_VERSION* has incremented to 4 and the *SYS_CHANGE_OPERATION* is now D for *DELETE*.

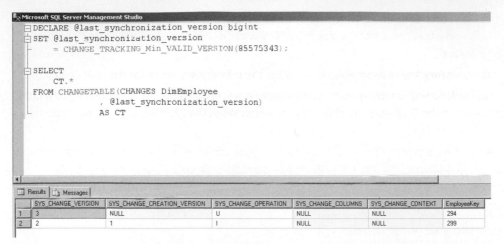

```
DECLARE @last_synchronization_version bigint
SET @last_synchronization_version
    = CHANGE_TRACKING_Min_VALID_VERSION(85575343);


SELECT
    CT.*
FROM CHANGETABLE(CHANGES DimEmployee
            , @last_synchronization_version)
            AS CT
```

	SYS_CHANGE_VERSION	SYS_CHANGE_CREATION_VERSION	SYS_CHANGE_OPERATION	SYS_CHANGE_COLUMNS	SYS_CHANGE_CONTEXT	EmployeeKey
1	3	NULL	U	NULL	NULL	294
2	2	1	I	NULL	NULL	299

FIGURE 9-17 The sample after the row from sample 1 and an additional row are updated

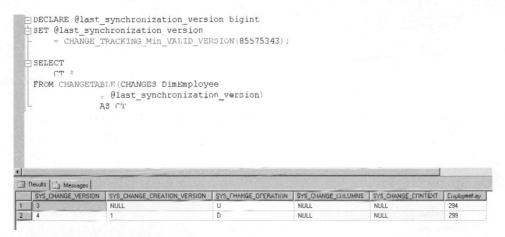

```
DECLARE @last_synchronization_version bigint
SET @last_synchronization_version
    = CHANGE_TRACKING_Min_VALID_VERSION(85575343);


SELECT
    CT.*
FROM CHANGETABLE(CHANGES DimEmployee
            , @last_synchronization_version)
            AS CT
```

	SYS_CHANGE_VERSION	SYS_CHANGE_CREATION_VERSION	SYS_CHANGE_OPERATION	SYS_CHANGE_COLUMNS	SYS_CHANGE_CONTEXT	EmployeeKey
1	3	NULL	U	NULL	NULL	294
2	4	1	D	NULL	NULL	299

FIGURE 9-18 The sample after the new row is deleted

In the second set of screenshots, a clean server is used and change tracking is enabled on the database once again. When change tracking is enabled on the *DimEmployee* table, the *TRACK_COLUMNS_UPDATED* argument is set to *ON*. Once again, a row for Jonathan Haas, now with an *EmployeeKey* of 297, is inserted into the database, and the query in Figure 9-19 is executed. Notice that the results are the same as with the first set of queries.

Once again, for the next query, two rows are updated in the *DimEmployee* table. Jonathan Haas, Employee 299, became a salesperson (the *SalesPersonFlag* column was set to 1). Syed Abbas, Employee 294, is no longer a salesperson; therefore, the *SalesPersonFlag* column was set to 0. Figure 9-20 shows the results of the *CHANGETABLE(CHANGES)* function showing all updates from

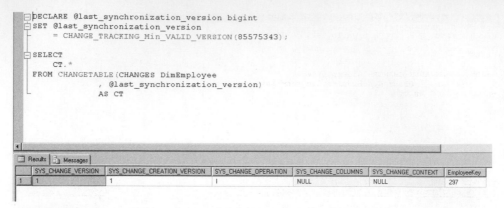

```
DECLARE @last_synchronization_version bigint
SET @last_synchronization_version
    = CHANGE_TRACKING_Min_VALID_VERSION(85575343);

SELECT
    CT.*
FROM CHANGETABLE(CHANGES DimEmployee
            , @last_synchronization_version)
            AS CT
```

	SYS_CHANGE_VERSION	SYS_CHANGE_CREATION_VERSION	SYS_CHANGE_OPERATION	SYS_CHANGE_COLUMNS	SYS_CHANGE_CONTEXT	EmployeeKey
1	1	1	I	NULL	NULL	297

FIGURE 9-19 A sample after the first insert with *TRACK_COLUMNS_UPDATED* on

the first capture to this point. Notice this time that the *SYS_CHANGE_COLUMNS* includes a binary value representing the column that was changed. You should use the *CHANGE_TRACKING_IS_COLUMN_IN_MASK* function when you need to interpret this information.

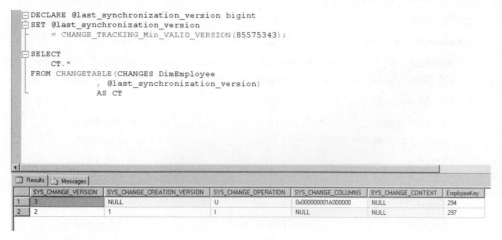

```
DECLARE @last_synchronization_version bigint
SET @last_synchronization_version
    = CHANGE_TRACKING_Min_VALID_VERSION(85575343);

SELECT
    CT.*
FROM CHANGETABLE(CHANGES DimEmployee
            , @last_synchronization_version)
            AS CT
```

	SYS_CHANGE_VERSION	SYS_CHANGE_CREATION_VERSION	SYS_CHANGE_OPERATION	SYS_CHANGE_COLUMNS	SYS_CHANGE_CONTEXT	EmployeeKey
1	3	NULL	U	0x000000001A000000	NULL	294
2	2	1	I	NULL	NULL	297

FIGURE 9-20 The sample after the columns are updated

For the final example, shown in Figure 9-21, we see once again that the *TRACK_COLUMNS_UPDATED* columns argument has no effect on the *DELETE* statement.

The *CHANGETABLE(VERSION)* function displays the following columns when queried:

- **SYS_CHANGE_VERSION**   Displays the version of the most recent change to the row.
- **SYS_CHANGE_CONTEXT**   Displays a context for the update if defined. You configure the context as part of the *INSERT*, *UPDATE*, or *DELETE* statement by using the *WITH* clause.
- **<primary key column value>**   Displays the primary key value for the row.

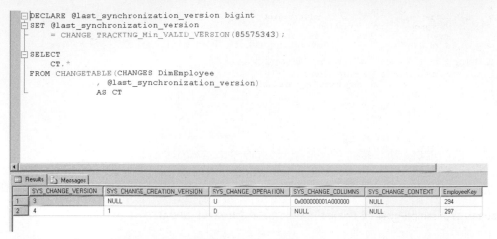

```
DECLARE @last_synchronization_version bigint
SET @last_synchronization_version
    = CHANGE_TRACKING_Min_VALID_VERSION(85575343);

SELECT
    CT.*
FROM CHANGETABLE(CHANGES DimEmployee
            , @last_synchronization_version)
            AS CT
```

	SYS_CHANGE_VERSION	SYS_CHANGE_CREATION_VERSION	SYS_CHANGE_OPERATION	SYS_CHANGE_COLUMNS	SYS_CHANGE_CONTEXT	EmployeeKey
1	3	NULL	U	0x000000001A000000	NULL	294
2	4	1	D	NULL	NULL	297

FIGURE 9-21 The sample after the newly added row is deleted

Managing Change Tracking

The following catalog views display change tracking configuration information:

- **sys.change_tracking_databases** Displays the following information:
  - *Database_id* An integer field that represents the unique database ID within the SQL Server instance for databases where change tracking has been enabled.
  - *Is_auto_cleanup_on* A bit field set to 0 for off and 1 for on.
  - *Retention_period* An integer field representing the minimum amount of time that tracked changes are saved before they are removed from the auto-cleanup process.
  - *Retention_period_units_desc* An *nvarchar* field specifying Minutes, Hours, or Days.
  - *Retention_period_unit* A *tinyint* field set to 1 for minutes, 2 for hours, or 3 for days.
- **sys.change_tracking_tables** Displays the following information:
  - *Object_id* An integer field that represents the unique table ID for tables in the database that have a change journal. A table where change tracking is currently disabled can still have a change journal.
  - *Is_track_columns_updated_on* A bit field set to 0 for off and 1 for on.
  - *Begin_version* A *bigint* field that contains the version of the database when change tracking began for the table.
  - *Cleanup_version* A *bigint* field that contains the version number where, prior to this version, data may have been removed by the auto-cleanup process.
  - *Min_valid_version* A *bigint* field that contains the minimum valid version number for change tracking information for each table.

Configuring CDC

Configuring CDC is a multistep process. Before you can enable CDC on your tables, you must enable CDC on the database that contains the tables that you want to track.

Enabling CDC on Your Database

To enable CDC on a database, you execute the *sys.sp_cdc_enable_db* system stored procedure.

The following command enables CDC on the *AdventureWorksDW2008* database:

```
USE AdventureWorksDW2008;
GO
EXECUTE sys.sp_cdc_enable_db;
GO
```

When you enable CDC for a database, the system sets the *is_cdc_enabled* column in the *sys.databases* catalog view to 1 and creates the system objects that CDC requires. These objects include the *cdc* schema, the *cdc* database user account, and the tables, jobs, stored procedures, and functions that the CDC process requires.

Enabling CDC on Your Tables

Once you have enabled CDC on your database, you can enable it for the tables in the database. When you enable CDC on a table by using the *sys.sp_cdc_enable_table* system stored procedure, you create a capture instance for the source table.

The *sys.sp_cdc_enable_table* system stored procedure includes the following arguments:

- **source_schema**   Defines the schema to which the source table belongs.
- **source_name**   Defines the name of the source table. This name must exist in the current database and cannot exist in the *cdc* schema.

- **role_name**   Defines the database role that is used to provide access to the captured data. If the role does not exist, SQL Server tries to create it. If the user executing the command does not have sufficient permissions to create a role, the whole stored procedure operation fails.

- **capture_Instance**   Defines a name given to the instance that is used for the naming of instance-specific objects. A source table can have up to two capture instances defined. If you do not specify *capture_instance*, the default name is *schemaname_sourcename*. The *capture_instance* name cannot exceed 100 characters.
- **supports_net_changes**   Set to 1 or 0 to define whether or not support for querying net changes is enabled. The default of 0 allows the functions to query only for all changes. A value of 1 allows you to query for net changes.

- **index_name**   Defines the name of a valid unique index on the source table.
- **captured_column_list**   Identifies the source columns that will be captured. If this field is *NULL*, all columns are included in the change table.

- ***filegroup_name*** Defines the name of the filegroup on which the change table will be created. If this value is *NULL*, the change table is created on the default filegroup. If *filegroup_name* is specified, the filegroup name must exist in the current database.

- ***partition_switch*** Set to *TRUE* or *FALSE* (the default) to indicate whether the *SWITCH PARTITION* command of *ALTER DATABASE* can be executed against the source table when CDC is enabled.

> **IMPORTANT** **HOW *SWITCH PARTITION* AND CDC INTERACT**
>
> Data changes that are caused by a *SWITCH PARTITION* command are not captured in the change table. For instance, if rows are switched out of the source table, and into another table, the *DELETE* operation is not captured.

You can use the following code sample to enable CDC on the *FactInternetSales* table in the *AdventureWorksDW2008* database. This sample allows you to query for net changes made to the data:

```
USE AdventureWorksDW2008;
GO
EXEC sys.sp_cdc_enable_table
    @source_schema = N'dbo'
  , @source_name = N'FactInternetSales'
  , @role_name = N'cdc_admin'
  , @capture_instance = N'InternetSales'
  , @supports_net_changes = 1
    GO
```

You can use the *cdc.fn_cdc_get_net_changes* function to verify the CDC configuration settings.

Understanding CDC Permissions

By default, the *sysadmin* and *db_owner* roles have full permissions to the data in the change tables.

When the *role_name* option is set to *NULL*, CDC is enabled without using a gating role. The gating role controls access to the data in the change table. When you configure your CDC system this way, any user with SELECT permission on the source table can access the information in the change table.

When you specify a specific built-in or user-defined role in the *role_name* argument, you define a *gating role* for the change table, thus forcing all users who need access to the captured data to have SELECT permission on the captured columns in the source table as well as membership in the gating role for that capture instance.

Querying for Changes

You use either the *cdc.fn_cdc_get_all_changes_<capture_instance>* or the *cdc.fn_cdc_get_net_changes_<capture_instance>* function to query data in the change table. If you enable CDC and set the *supports_net_changes* argument to 1, both functions are available for the CDC instance defined. If you set the *supports_net_changes* argument to 0, or if you do not include the argument, only the *cdc.fn_cdc_get_all_changes_<capture_instance>* is available.

With net changes enabled, if you want to write a query that returns one row in the result set for each changed row in the Log Sequence Number (LSN) range and includes only the final content, even if intermediate changes have occurred, you should use the *cdc.fn_cdc_get_net_changes_<capture_instance>* function.

The *cdc.fn_cdc_get_net_changes_<capture_instance>* function includes the following arguments:

- **from_lsn** Defines the starting LSN number to create the range within which rows should be returned. All rows in the change table with an LSN value equal to or greater than the *from_lsn* value are included in the result set. This is referred to as setting the *lower bound* of the query range.

- **to_lsn** Defines the ending LSN number to create the range of rows returned. All rows in the change table with an LSN value less than or equal to the *from_lsn* value are included in the result set. This is referred to as setting the *upper bound* of the query range.

- **row_filter** Controls which rows are returned and what is displayed in the metadata columns of the result set. The *row_filter* argument can have any of the following values:

  - *All* Returns the LSN number of the transaction in the _$start_lsn column, the value of the operation performed in the _$operation column, and *NULL* in the _$update_mask column.

  - *All with mask* Returns the LSN number of the transaction in the _$start_lsn column, and the value of the operation performed in the _$operation column. If the *UPDATE* operation returns a value of 4, the bits in the _$update_mask column associated with the updated columns are set to 1.

  - *All with merge* Returns the LSN number of the transaction in the _$start_lsn column, and returns a value of 1 in the _$operation column if the row was deleted and a value of 5 if an *INSERT* or *UPDATE* needs to be used to apply the change. The _$update_mask always has a value of *NULL*.

> **NOTE   USING THE *ALL WITH MERGE* OPTION**
>
> This option is designed to improve performance when you don't need to distinguish between *INSERT* and *UPDATE* statements. You should consider using this option if you are also using the *MERGE* operation available in SQL Server 2008.

> **MORE INFO** **MERGE COMMAND**
>
> For more information about the *MERGE* command, see Lesson 2 of Chapter 2, "Modifying Data—The *INSERT, UPDATE, DELETE,* and *MERGE* Statements," in this book.

The table returned when you query the *cdc.fn_cdc_get_net_changes_<capture_instance>* function includes the following columns:

- **_start_lsn** Displays the LSN associated with the commit transaction action of the change.

- **_$seqval** Displays the sequence value to order the row changes that occur within a transaction. All rows in a transaction have the same _$start_lsn value.

- **_$operation** Displays an integer value based on the operation performed and the *row_filter_option* parameter. When you set the *row_filter_option* to *all* or *all with mask*, this column displays the following values:
  - 1 for *DELETE* operations
  - 2 for *INSERT* operations
  - 4 for *UPDATE* operations

  When the *row_filter_option* parameter is set to *all with merge*, the _$operation column displays the following values:
  - 1 for *DELETE* operations
  - 5 for both *INSERT* and *UPDATE* operations

- **_$update_mask** Displays a bit mask representing the columns that are being captured from the source table. A 1 in the mask represents a column that was changed. For *INSERT* and *DELETE* statements, all bits are set to 1.

- **<captured source table columns>** Returns each column from the source table that was captured.

The following query modifies rows in the *FactInternetSales* table. Figure 9-22 shows the result set of the *cdc.fn_cdc_get_net_changes_InternetSales* function once the updates have been executed:

```
USE AdventureWorksDW2008;
GO
DECLARE @begin_time datetime, @end_time datetime, @from_lsn binary(10)
  , @to_lsn binary(10);
-- Set the beginning of the time interval to yesterday to capture all changes.
SET @begin_time = GETDATE() -1;
-- DML statements to produce changes.

UPDATE dbo.FactInternetSales
SET OrderQuantity = 5
WHERE SalesOrderNumber = 'SO43697' AND SalesOrderLineNumber = 1;
```

```
UPDATE dbo.FactInternetSales
SET OrderQuantity = 2
WHERE SalesOrderNumber = 'SO43697' AND SalesOrderLineNumber = 1;

DELETE FROM dbo.FactInternetSales
WHERE SalesOrderNumber = 'SO43701'AND SalesOrderLineNumber = 1 ;

-- Set the end of the time interval after changes were completed.
SET @end_time = GETDATE();
-- Map the time interval to a change data capture query range.
SET @from_lsn = sys.fn_cdc_map_time_to_lsn(
  'smallest greater than or equal', @begin_time);
SET @to_lsn = sys.fn_cdc_map_time_to_lsn(
  'largest less than or equal', @end_time);

-- Return the net changes occurring within the query window.
SELECT * FROM cdc.fn_cdc_get_net_changes_InternetSales(
  @from_lsn, @to_lsn, 'all');
```

	__$start_lsn	__$operation	__$update_mask	ProductKey	OrderDateKey	DueDateKey	ShipDateKey	CustomerKey
1	0x0000002A0000FF6001C	4	NULL	310	20010701	20010713	20010708	21768
2	0x0000002A000100D0075	1	NULL	346	20010701	20010713	20010708	11003

FIGURE 9-22 Partial output from the *cdc.fn_cdc_get_net_changes_InternetSales* function

If you want to write a query that returns rows for all changes that occurred during the specified period, you should use the *cdc.fn_cdc_get_all_changes_capture_instance* function. If more than one change has occurred in a given row of the source table, multiple rows are returned by this function.

The *cdc.fn_cdc_get_all_changes_capture_instance* function includes the following arguments:

- **from_lsn** Defines the starting LSN number to create the range within which rows should be returned. All rows in the change table with an LSN value equal to or greater than the *from_lsn* value are included in the result set. This is referred to as setting the lower bound of the query range.

- **to_lsn** Defines the ending LSN number to create the range of rows returned. All rows in the change table with an LSN value less than or equal to the *from_lsn* value are included in the result set. This is referred to as setting the upper bound of the query range.

- **row_filter_option** The *row_filter_option* can have either of the following settings:
  - *All* Returns all changes that occurred within the range defined by the *from_lsn* and *to_lsn* options. For rows that were modified with the *UPDATE* statement, only the row containing the new values is returned.
  - *All update old* Returns all changes that occurred within the range defined by the *from_lsn* and *to_lsn* options. For rows that were modified with the *UPDATE* statement, both the row containing the values before the update and the row containing the values after the update are returned.

The table returned by the *cdc.fn_cdc_get_all_changes_capture_instance* function has the same columns as those listed previously for the *cdc.fn_cdc_get_net_changes_<capture_instance>* function.

Figure 9-23 shows the results of the *cdc.fn_cdc_get_all_changes_InternetSales* function with the identical changes that occurred for the result set shown in Figure 9-22. You can compare these two figures to see the differences between showing net changes and all changes.

	__$start_lsn	__$seqval	__$operation	__$update_mask	ProductKey	OrderQuantity	OrderDateKey
1	0x0000002A00000FF6001C	0x0000002A00000FF6001A	4	0x000800	310	5	20010701
2	0x0000002A0000100D0075	0x0000002A0000100D0073	1	0x7FFFFF	346	1	20010701
3	0x0000002A000010840004	0x0000002A000010840002	4	0x000800	310	2	20010701

FIGURE 9-23 Sample of *cdc.fn_cdc_get_all_changes_InternetSales* results

When you are building an application to query a change table, you may want to define the rows returned based on the time when the changes occurred rather than on the LSN. You can use the *sys.fn_cdc_map_time_to_lsn* to determine the LSN numbers that you use in the *from_lsn* and *to_lsn* arguments of the *cdc.fn_cdc_get_all_changes_<capture_instance>* or *cdc.fn_cdc_get_net_changes_<capture_instance>* function.

You can use the following CDC functions when querying changed data:

- **sys.fn_cdc_has_column_changed** Returns a 1 or 0 to identify whether the column identified by the mask supplied has been updated in any associated change row. The capture instance, column name, and update mask values are included as input for this function.

- **sys.fn_cdc_increment_lsn** Returns the next LSN in the sequence based on an input LSN value. If you know the upper-bound LSN value for the previous query, you can use this function to define the new lower bound for the range of your new query. You can use this logic to avoid having to know the specific time that the synchronization last ran. You simply need to maintain the LSN values from the previous synchronization period.

- **sys.fn_cdc_decrement_lsn** Returns the previous LSN based on an input LSN value. You can use this function to determine the upper bound of an LSN range defined within a query.

- **sys.fn_cdc_is_bit_set** Uses the ordinal position in the bit mask (the *$_update_mask* value) for a specified column and the bit mask as inputs to return a bit representing whether the input column was updated. You can use this function to append a column to your output representing the update state of a given source column. For example: You are querying the change table and you want to know specifically whether the *GroupName* column was updated in each row returned from the *HR_Department* table. You can use the *cdc.fn_cdc_get_all_changes_HR_Department, sys.fn_cdc_get_column_ordinal,* and *sys.fn_cdc_is_bit_set* functions to add a column with an alias set to 'Group Name Updated' to the result set that displays a 1 when true and a 0 when false.

- **sys.fn_cdc_get_column_ordinal** Uses the capture instance and column name information as input and returns an integer representing the ordinal position of the column in the bit mask.

- **sys.fn_cdc_map_lsn_to_time** Uses an LSN as input and returns the *DATETIME* value of the commit time from the *tran_end_time* column in the *cdc.lsn_time_mapping* system table.

- **sys.fn_cdc_get_max_lsn** Returns the maximum LSN that exists in the *start_lsn* column of the *cdc.lsn_time_mapping* system table. This value represents the last committed change propagated to a change table in the current database. This value does not depend on the capture instance.

- **sys.fn_cdc_get_min_lsn** Returns the maximum LSN that exists in the *start_lsn* column of the *cdc.lsn_time_mapping* system table. This value can change when the cleanup process is performed. You can use this function to determine the low endpoint for the LSN value to verify that your range is inside the CDC timeline.

In addition to the functions to allow you to query the data in the change tables, SQL Server includes stored procedures that you can use to manage CDC.

> **MORE INFO** **MANAGING CDC**
>
> For additional information about using the built-in CDC stored procedures, see "Change Data Capture Stored Procedures (Transact-SQL)" in SQL Server Books Online.

SQL Server Audit

SQL Server Audit provides you with the ability to log information about events and changes occurring on your server running SQL Server. To use SQL Server Audit, you must create and configure at least one SQL Server Audit object for each instance where auditing occurs. You then create specifications for Server Audit, Database Audit, or both, based on a SQL Server Audit object to manage auditing on specific events and objects.

Creating a SQL Server Audit Object

You must create a SQL Server Audit object before you can define audit specifications. You can accomplish this by using SSMS or with the *CREATE SERVER AUDIT* statement.

In SSMS, you can use the Object Explorer and browse to the Audits folder under the Security folder. You can then right-click the Audits folder and select New Audit to create a new SQL Server Audit. Within the audit definition, you can configure the following options:

- **Audit Name** Defines the name assigned to the *Audit* object.

- **Queue Delay** Defines the amount of lapsed time in milliseconds that can pass before the server must process an audit action. The default value is 1 second or 1,000 milliseconds.

- **Shut Down Server On Audit Log Failure** Determines whether or not SQL Server shuts down when auditing fails. You can enable this option if your organization's auditing policies or applicable regulatory requirements, such as the Health Insurance Portability and Accountability Act (HIPAA), the Payment Card Industry (PCI) act, and the Federal Information Security Management Act (FISMA), require you to audit every specified event without failure.

- **Audit Destination** Specifies where the audit information is written. The options include a file, the Windows Security Log, or the Windows Application Log. When you select File for the audit destination, you also need to configure the following options:

  - File Path Specifies the directory where the file is stored. The Database Engine automatically generates the file name, which is based on the *Audit* object name and audit globally unique identifier (GUID).

  - Maximum Rollover Defines the maximum number of rollover files that can be created, except when the Unlimited option is selected. When you enable the Unlimited option for this setting, there is no limit to the number of rollover files created.

  - Maximum Filesize Specifies the maximum file size before rollover begins. You must specify both an integer value and whether that integer should be interpreted as megabytes, gigabytes, or terabytes. When you select Unlimited, the file grows until the hard disk drive is full. If the file fills the hard disk drive completely, logging stops and the server shuts down if the Shut Down Server On Audit Log Failure option is also enabled. The minimum value allowed for this field is 2 MB.

- Reserve Disk Space   Specifies that a file is created at the maximum file size immediately. Otherwise, the file grows as audit details are added to it. You cannot choose this option if the Unlimited option is enabled for the maximum file size.

The following code displays the full syntax for the *CREATE SERVER AUDIT* statement. The options available mirror the configuration options described previously for creating a new *Audit* object by using SSMS:

```
CREATE SERVER AUDIT audit_name

    TO { [ FILE (<file_options> [, ...n]) ] | APPLICATION_LOG | SECURITY_LOG }
    [ WITH ( <audit_options> [, ...n] ) ]
}
[ ; ]
<file_options>::=
{
      FILEPATH = 'os_file_path'
    [, MAXSIZE = { max_size { MB | GB | TB } | UNLIMITED } ]
    [, MAX_ROLLOVER_FILES = integer ]
    [, RESERVE_DISK_SPACE = { ON | OFF } ]
}


<audit_options>::=
{
    [ QUEUE_DELAY = integer ]
    [, ON_FAILURE = { CONTINUE | SHUTDOWN } ]
    [, AUDIT_GUID = uniqueidentifier ]
}
```

After creating the SQL Server Audit object, you must enable it. You can accomplish this by using SSMS or the *ALTER SERVER AUDIT* statement.

Creating a Database-Level Audit Specification

Once you have created the SQL Server Audit object, you can choose to create audit specifications at the server level or the database level. For tracking access or modifications made to data, you create a Database Audit Specification.

You can create a Database Audit Specification by using the *CREATE DATABASE AUDIT SPECIFICATION* statement or by using Object Explorer in SSMS. The Database Audit Specifications folder is located below the *[instance name]\[Databases]\[database name]\Security* folder.

To define a Database Audit Specification, you must define the name of the audit specification, the *Audit* object to which the events will be written, and each audit action that is logged.

There is a wide variety of Audit Action Types that can be configured within each Database Audit Specification. For example, you can specify *INSERT*, *UPDATE*, *DELETE*, or *SELECT* and define on which objects you want to track these commands. You can also specify for which users and roles you would like to have the events logged.

In addition to specifying individual events to be logged, you can specify an entire group of events to be logged. The *SCHEMA_OBJECT_ACCESS_GROUP*, also equivalent to the *Audit Schema Object Access* event class, returns information when an object permission such as *INSERT, UPDATE, DELETE, SELECT, EXECUTE,* or *REFERENCES* occurs. The information provided by this event class reports the query syntax that was issued but does not maintain before-and-after values of updated or deleted data. A complete list of the data columns and the information provided in these log entries is given in the "Audit Schema Object Access Event Class" article in SQL Server Books Online.

> **IMPORTANT** **PERFORMANCE AND AUDITING**
>
> You need to be careful when defining auditing to verify performance effects of the logs. There is a tendency to try and log every event, which may lead to extremely slow performance. Carefully consider the objects on which auditing is required, as well as which events need to be tracked.

Before the Database Audit Specification begins to collect information, you must enable it by using SSMS, as part of the *CREATE DATABASE AUDIT SPECIFICATION* statement, or with the *ALTER DATABASE AUDIT SPECIFICATION*.

> **IMPORTANT** **MODIFYING DATABASE AUDIT SPECIFICATIONS**
>
> A Database Audit Specification must be disabled before modifications can be made to the audit specification.

PRACTICE   Configuring SQL Server to Track Changes

In this practice, you track changes by implementing change tracking and CDC.

EXERCISE 1   Configure and Use Change Tracking

In this exercise, you configure the *ProspectiveBuyer* table to track changes. The application needs to know only when *INSERT*s and *DELETE*s occur on this table. You do not need to include information about columns that are updated.

> **IMPORTANT** **DATA MODIFICATIONS**
>
> In the exercises in this practice, you delete and update rows in the *AdventureWorksDW2008* database. You should make a copy of your tables and work on the copies, or restore the original *AdventureWorksDW2008* after completing the practices from this chapter.

1. Open SSMS, if it is not already open.
2. In SSMS, click New Query to open a new query window.

3. In the new query window, type and execute the following command to enable change tracking with auto cleanup enabled and a change retention period of five days on the *AdventureWorksDW2008* database:

```
ALTER DATABASE AdventureWorksDW2008
SET CHANGE_TRACKING = ON
(CHANGE_RETENTION = 5 DAYS, AUTO_CLEANUP = ON)
```

4. In the existing query window, below the existing code, type, highlight, and execute the following code to enable change tracking on the *AdventureWorksDW2008* database:

```
USE AdventureWorksDW2008;
GO
ALTER TABLE ProspectiveBuyer
ENABLE CHANGE_TRACKING
WITH (TRACK_COLUMNS_UPDATED = OFF);
```

5. In the existing query window, below the existing code, type, highlight, and execute the following code to insert two new rows into the *ProspectiveBuyer* table.

```
INSERT INTO ProspectiveBuyer
    (FirstName, LastName, MaritalStatus, Gender)
    VALUES ('Terry', 'Adams', 'M', 'M');


INSERT INTO ProspectiveBuyer
    (FirstName, LastName, MaritalStatus, Gender)
    VALUES ('Wilson', 'Pais', 'S', 'M');
```

6. In the existing query window, below the existing code, type, highlight, and execute the following code to determine the *object_id* and version information for the *ProspectiveBuyer* table. Make note of the *object_id*.

```
SELECT object_name(object_id)AS 'ObjectName'  , *
    FROM sys.change_tracking_tables
```

7. In the existing query window, below the existing code, type, highlight, and execute the following code to view the information in the change table. If necessary, edit the *object_id* for the *CHANGE_TRACKING_Min_VALID_VERSION* argument:

```
DECLARE @last_synchronization_version bigint
SET @last_synchronization_version
    = CHANGE_TRACKING_Min_VALID_VERSION(389576426);

SELECT
    CT.*
FROM CHANGETABLE(CHANGES ProspectiveBuyer
            , @last_synchronization_version)
            AS CT
```

Review the result set.

8. In the existing query window, below the existing code, type, highlight, and execute the following code to view the row added for Terry Adams in step 5. Make note of the *ProspectiveBuyerKey* for Terry Adams for use in the next step.

```
SELECT * FROM ProspectiveBuyer
    WHERE LastName = 'Adams' and FirstName = 'Terry'
```

9. In the existing query window, below the existing code, type, highlight, and execute the following code to delete the row for Terry Adams and also the row for *ProspectiveBuyerKey* 308. If necessary, modify the *ProspectiveBuyerKey* to match the key from step 8.

```
DELETE FROM ProspectiveBuyer
WHERE ProspectiveBuyerKey = 2060;


DELETE FROM ProspectiveBuyer
WHERE ProspectiveBuyerKey = 308;
```

10. In the existing query window, below the existing code, type, highlight, and execute the following code to view the information in the change table. If necessary, edit the *object_id* for the *CHANGE_TRACKING_Min_VALID_VERSION* argument:

```
DECLARE @last_synchronization_version bigint
SET @last_synchronization_version
    = CHANGE_TRACKING_Min_VALID_VERSION(389576426);

SELECT
    CT.*
FROM CHANGETABLE(CHANGES ProspectiveBuyer
            , @last_synchronization_version)
            AS CT
```

11. Review the result set. Leave SSMS open for the next exercise.

EXERCISE 2 Configure and Use CDC

In this exercise, you configure the *FactInternetSales* and *FactResellerSales* tables for CDC, configure the *FactInternetSales* table to allow access to net changes, and configure the *FactResellerSales* table to only allow access to all changes.

> **IMPORTANT   DATA MODIFICATIONS**
>
> In this exercise, you delete and update rows in the *AdventurWorksDW2008* database. You should make a copy of your tables and work on the copies, or restore the original *AdventureWorksDW2008* after completing the practices from this chapter.

1. In SSMS, click New Query to open a new query window.

2. In the new query window, type and execute the following command to enable CDC on the *AdventureWorksDW2008* database:

```
USE AdventureWorksDW2008;
GO
EXECUTE sys.sp_cdc_enable_db;
GO
```

3. In the existing query window, below the existing code, type, highlight, and execute the following code to enable CDC on the *FactInternetSales* and *FactResellerSales* tables:

```
USE AdventureWorksDW2008;
GO
EXEC sys.sp_cdc_enable_table
    @source_schema = N'dbo'
  , @source_name = N'FactInternetSales'
  , @role_name = N'cdc_admin'
  , @capture_instance = N'InternetSales'
  , @supports_net_changes = 1
    GO


USE AdventureWorksDW2008;
GO
EXEC sys.sp_cdc_enable_table
    @source_schema = N'dbo'
  , @source_name = N'FactResellerSales'
  , @role_name = N'cdc_admin'
  , @capture_instance = N'ResellerSales'
  , @supports_net_changes = 0
    GO
```

4. In the existing query window, below the existing code, type, highlight, and execute the following code to verify your CDC configuration settings:

```
sys.sp_cdc_help_change_data_capture;
```

> **IMPORTANT CDC REQUIREMENTS**
>
> To configure and use CDC successfully, you must verify that the SQL Server Agent service is running.

5. In the existing query window, below the existing code, type, highlight, and execute the following code to update the *FactResellerSales* table and view the changes by using the *cdc.fn_cdc_get_all_changes_ResellerSales* function:

```
USE AdventureWorksDW2008;
GO
DECLARE  @from_lsn binary(10), @to_lsn binary(10);
```

```
-- DML statements to produce changes.
UPDATE dbo.FactResellerSales
SET OrderQuantity = 6
WHERE SalesOrderNumber = 'SO44771' AND SalesOrderLineNumber = 12;

DELETE FROM dbo.FactResellerSales
WHERE SalesOrderNumber = 'SO44771'AND SalesOrderLineNumber = 31;

UPDATE dbo.FactResellerSales
SET OrderQuantity = 4
WHERE SalesOrderNumber = 'SO44771' AND SalesOrderLineNumber = 12;

-- Wait for the capture process to process change data.
WAITFOR DELAY '00:00:10'
-- Set the start and end lsn values to the min and max valid values.
SET @from_lsn =  sys.fn_cdc_get_min_lsn('ResellerSales')
SET @to_lsn = sys.fn_cdc_get_max_lsn()

-- Return the net changes occurring within the query window.
SELECT * FROM cdc.fn_cdc_get_all_changes_ResellerSales(
  @from_lsn, @to_lsn, 'all');
```

6. Review the results and notice that two rows are reported for the updates to the row for *SalesOrderNumber* SO44771 and a *SalesOrderLineNumber* of 12.

7. In the existing query window, below the existing code, type, highlight, and execute the following code to update the *FactInternetSales* table and view the net changes by using the *cdc.fn_cdc_get_net_changes_InternetSales* function:

```
USE AdventureWorksDW2008;
GO
DECLARE  @from_lsn binary(10), @to_lsn binary(10);

-- DML statements to produce changes.
UPDATE dbo.FactInternetSales
SET OrderQuantity = 4
WHERE SalesOrderNumber = 'SO43698' AND SalesOrderLineNumber = 1;

DELETE FROM dbo.FactInternetSales
WHERE SalesOrderNumber = 'SO43717'AND SalesOrderLineNumber = 1 ;

UPDATE dbo.FactInternetSales
SET OrderQuantity = 2
WHERE SalesOrderNumber = 'SO43698' AND SalesOrderLineNumber = 1;

-- Wait for the capture process to process change data.
WAITFOR DELAY '00:00:10'
```

```
-- Set the start and end lsn values to the min and max valid values.
SET @from_lsn = sys.fn_cdc_get_min_lsn('ResellerSales')
SET @to_lsn = sys.fn_cdc_get_max_lsn()

-- Return the net changes occurring within the query window.
SELECT * FROM cdc.fn_cdc_get_net_changes_InternetSales(
  @from_lsn, @to_lsn, 'all');
```

8. Review the results and notice that only one row is returned for each row in the source table, rather than a row for every intermediate modification.

Lesson Summary

- Change tracking is enabled first at the database and then at the table level.
- Change tracking can tell you what rows have been modified and provide you with the end result of the data.
- Change tracking requires fewer system resources than CDC.
- CDC can tell you what rows have been modified and provide you with the final data as well as the intermediate states of the data.
- SQL Server Audit allows you to log access to tables, views, and other objects.

Chapter Review

To practice and reinforce the skills you learned in this chapter further, you can do any or all of the following:

- Review the chapter summary.
- Review the list of key terms introduced in this chapter.
- Complete the case scenarios. These scenarios set up real-world situations involving the topics of this chapter and ask you to create solutions.
- Complete the suggested practices.
- Take a practice test.

Chapter Summary

- You can use the *sp_send_db* mail to integrate e-mail messages into your database applications.
- The SQL Server PowerShell provider allows you to create scripts to automate SQL commands and enumeration of objects on the database server.
- Change tracking and CDC provide you with a variety of ways to implement tracking of data modifications and synchronization with other databases.

Key Terms

- Cmdlets
- Change tables
- Gating role
- Lower bound
- Upper bound
- Log Sequence Number (LSN)

Case Scenarios

In the following case scenarios, you apply what you have learned about integrating Database Mail. You can find answers to these questions in the "Answers" section at the end of this book.

Case Scenario 1: Integrating Windows PowerShell and Database Mail

You are a database developer for Litware, Inc. Your manager has asked you to create a script that lists all user-created tables and views in the *Litware_Sales* database. This script needs to be generated automatically at 5 P.M. each Friday.

The database administrator has configured Database Mail on your server running SQL Server. There is no default public profile in the *msdb* database. The user context from which you are running this step in the job does not have a default private profile associated with it.

Answer the following question for your manager:

- What steps would be involved in configuring a solution for your manager?

Case Scenario 2: Tracking Changes

You are a database developer for Litware, Inc. You maintain an Online Transaction Processing (OLTP) database named *LitwareSales* and a relational data warehouse (RDW) named *LitwareDW*. You synchronize the data between *LitwareSales* and *LitwareDW* every day. Business rules prohibit updates to data once a row is added to the *LitwareSales* database.

You have been asked to determine the best method to track changes on the *LitwareSales* database to optimize the synchronization process. Resources are limited and you want to minimize the amount of disk, processor, and memory resources required for the solution.

Answer the following questions for your manager:

1. What solution best fits the requirements?
2. What options can you set to minimize resource utilization?

Suggested Practices

To help you master the exam objectives presented in this chapter, do all the following practices:

Integrate Database Mail

- **Practice 1** Create and test a variety of e-mail messages created by using different options in the *sp_send_dbmail* system stored procedure.

Implement Scripts by Using Windows PowerShell and SQL Server Management Objects (SMOs)

- **Practice 2** Practice browsing the SQL Server hierarchy and executing cmdlets in a SQL Server PowerShell session.
- **Practice 3** Create a SQL Server PowerShell script to list the columns of a particular table and execute the script by using a SQL Server Agent job.

Track Data Changes

- **Practice 4** Enable change tracking on a database and table. Make modifications to the data and review the information in the change tables to help you understand how different configuration options and different functions allow you to see different results.

- **Practice 5** Enable CDC on a database and table. Make modifications to the data and review the information in the change tables to help you understand how different configuration options and different functions allow you to see different results.

Take a Practice Test

The practice tests on this book's companion CD offer many options. For example, you can test yourself on just the content covered in this chapter, or you can test yourself on all the 70-433 certification exam content. You can set up the test so that it closely simulates the experience of taking a certification exam, or you can set it up in study mode so that you can look at the correct answers and explanations after you answer each question.

> **MORE INFO** **PRACTICE TESTS**
>
> For details about all the practice test options available, see the section entitled "How to Use the Practice Tests" in the Introduction to this book.

Case Scenario Answers

Chapter 1: Case Scenario Answers

Case Scenario 1: Retrieving Data

- Include a sample of an *ORDER BY* clause that references either the order date or completion date.

- Include several queries and sample results that use the *CONVERT* function to display the dates in a variety of formats. Include the names of the format styles in the result set to help the application developer make date formatting decisions.

- Include a query that uses the *DATEDIFF* function in both the *SELECT* and the *ORDER BY* clauses that determines the number of days between the order date and the completed date.

- Include a query that uses the *DATEDIFF* function to find orders that were placed 1 month (*MONTH*), 1 quarter (*QUARTER*), and 1 year (*YEAR*) from the current date.

- Provide information on any *JOIN* operations that may be required due to the database normalization level.

Case Scenario 2: Grouping Data

- Include a sample of a *SELECT* statement using the *SUM* aggregate function to provide the total number of products sold. Provide samples of *WHERE* clauses that can be added to provide information based on different criteria.

- Include a sample of a *GROUP BY* statement that includes the *SUM* aggregate function *ROLLUP* operator.

- Include a sample of a *GROUP BY* statement that includes the *SUM* aggregate function *CUBE* operator.

Chapter 2: Case Scenario Answers

Case Scenario 1: Modifying Data

- The *UPDATE* statement can add the e-mail information and replace the fax number with *NULL*. In addition, the *OUTPUT* clause can store the required information into the *ImporterPropertiesAudit* table.

Case Scenario 2: Using Transactions

Your considerations should include, but not be limited to, the following:

- What is the current transaction isolation level?
- What business rules would affect changing the transaction isolation level?
- How long is each transaction? Are there ways to shorten any transaction or separate the transactions into groups?
- Is all data retrieved from users and verified before starting the transaction so as to avoid user interaction once the transaction has begun?
- Are resources being accessed in the same order in all transactions?
- How many batches are included in a single transaction? Is there a way to minimize this without jeopardizing required functionality?
- Are any locking hints being used within the queries?

> **MORE INFO** **LOCKING HINTS**
>
> A discussion about locking hints and the effects on locking and blocking is beyond the scope of this book. *Microsoft SQL Server 2008 Internals* (Microsoft Press, 2009), by Kalen Delaney et al., covers the topic of locking hints.

Chapter 3: Case Scenario Answer

Case Scenario: Constraints and Data Types

1. Because the table already has data that is not correct according to the constraints that you need to add, you must add the constraints using the *WITH NOCHECK* option (*ALTER TABLE...ADD CONSTRAINT...WITH NOCHECK*). This causes the new constraints to check any incoming data (including updates of the existing data) while allowing the existing data to remain in the table.

2. The largest data type supported by the *IDENTITY* property is *decimal(38, 0)*.

Chapter 4: Case Scenario Answer

Case Scenario: Improving Query Performance

- The report for the data warehouse loads can be accomplished easily by using either subqueries, CTEs, or a combination of CTEs with ranking functions. Because a CTE combined with a ranking function should provide the best performance, you should use this method.

  Iteration across a result set can be accomplished using CTEs, which would be much more efficient than a cursor-based solution. Depending upon the specific business problem, you could use the same method to find load gaps in the data warehouse to solve the problems of finding missing data or filling empty seats. You could rewrite the cursors that are calculating sales figures to use subqueries that can provide running totals as well as aggregate data within a group.

  You can eliminate all the intermediate temporary tables by using derived tables, which can take advantage of the memory available on the machine instead of requiring physical reads and writes to disk.

Chapter 5: Case Scenario Answer

Case Scenario: Improving Application Performance

1. Most of the problems Fabrikam is having stem from poorly designed applications. The applications should not be generating ad hoc queries to submit to SQL Server. The applications should instead follow code encapsulation best practices used throughout the industry. All the database code needs to be removed from the application and moved into stored procedures. The applications then must be rewritten to access the stored procedures. Once a stable release of an application has been achieved that uses stored procedures, you can then begin the analysis and tuning activities that Fabrikam needs. You can tune the stored procedures in isolation from the applications such that any changes needing to be deployed affect only the stored procedures and do not require an application release.

2. You can prevent the accidental deletion of objects on the production server by implementing a DDL trigger to roll back any *DROP* event. However, you also need to address the lack of security and remove administrative access from anyone who is not responsible for managing the server running SQL Server.

3. The complex database code should be removed from the application and migrated into stored procedures, functions, and views, as appropriate. This reduces the complexity of the applications and moves the database code into a format that is more easily maintained and managed.

Chapter 6: Case Scenario Answer

Case Scenario: Tune Query Performance

- To optimize the poorly performing stored procedures, you execute them in SSMS, examine their graphical execution, and consider rewriting their queries as well as redesigning the indexes on the queried tables. To reduce the query execution times for the finance department queries from up to 10 minutes down to a couple of seconds, you most likely need to add more indexes. After adding indexes, test to ensure you haven't compromised performance elsewhere in your applications.

Chapter 7: Case Scenario Answer

Case Scenario: How Should You Store Data?

First of all, there probably is no perfect answer to this question. You most likely need to do prototyping to make sure you get it right. However, from the given scenario, the following points are probably the most important to keep in mind:

- Categories are stored in a table.
- Articles are stored in a table that references the categories table.
- Given that all articles always have a single title, the table should probably be stored directly in a column in the articles table.
- Because the content of an article can contain so many different parts, and those parts probably can be nested inside each other (such as a list inside a cell in a table) and given the fact that the order of the different parts is important, the content should probably be stored in a single XML column.
- Given that what is allowed in the content column probably must be fairly well-defined, you should probably use an XML schema collection to type the content column.

Chapter 8: Case Scenario Answers

Case Scenario 1: Initiating Spatial Data

- For the pallet locations within the warehouse, you should use the *geometry* data type. You should instantiate the spatial data by using one of the *POINT* methods. Because you are defining specific *x, y* coordinates, *POINT* is the best method to use. For the warehouse region functionality, you should use the *geometry* data type. You should instantiate the spatial data by using one of the *POLYGON* methods. Because you want to define a region, a *POLYGON* method allows you to define the coordinates for the outer edge of the region.

Case Scenario 2: Querying a Full-Text Index

1. A custom stoplist needs to be created and associated with the appropriate catalog. In addition, the thesaurus files for the appropriate language need to be edited to include all synonymous words as defined by the business needs.

2. The *FREETEXTTABLE* command provides you with all the functionality required. You need to arrange the result set by descending rank to show the most relevant rows at the top of the result set.

Chapter 9: Case Scenario Answers

Case Scenario 1: Integrating Windows PowerShell and Database Mail

Here is one set of possible steps:

1. You should determine the path and cmdlets that will be required for the SQL Server PowerShell script and then write and test the script.

2. Create a SQL Server Agent job with the appropriate schedule. Use the PowerShell type when defining the job step to be performed. Open or copy your tested script into the job step. In the Advanced tab of the Job Step window, create an output file for the SQL Server PowerShell script.

> **MORE INFO**   **SQL SERVER AGENT JOBS**
>
> For a full discussion about SQL Server Agent jobs, see *MCTS Self-Paced Training Kit (Exam 70-432): Microsoft SQL Server 2008-Implementation and Maintenance* (Microsoft Press, 2009), and Chapter 18 in *Microsoft SQL Server 2008 Step by Step* (Microsoft Press, 2008).

3. Add another job step to send an e-mail message with the SQL Server PowerShell output file attached. Verify that an appropriate profile is defined with the *@profile_name option*.

Case Scenario 2: Tracking Changes

1. Change tracking uses fewer resources and has less overhead than CDC. Because *UPDATE* commands are not executed against tracked tables, being able to see intermediate changes is not an issue, thus removing the need for CDC.

2. Two database-level change tracking settings that can make a difference on the required disk space are the auto-cleanup and retention period settings. Depending on how the daily synchronizations are scheduled and your recoverability requirements, you might want to consider a retention period of between 26 and 50 hours.

Glossary Terms

A

Aggregate function A built-in or user-defined function that provides a calculation on a set of rows or values.

Atomicity When two or more pieces of information are involved in a transaction, either all the pieces are committed or none of them are.

C

Change tables Tables within a database that store modified rows in a database with CDC enabled.

Check constraint A constraint that applies a Boolean expression to rows added or updated in tables to verify whether the update should be allowed.

Clustered index An index that imposes a physical order on the rows within a table. There can only be a single clustered index on a table.

Cmdlets .NET Framework applications that provide specialized functionality within SQL Server PowerShell.

Consistency At the end of a transaction, either a new and valid form of the data exists or the data is returned to its original state. Returning data to its original state is part of the rollback functionality provided by SQL Server transactions.

Constraint A rule applied to a column(s) within a table that is used to validate changes and ensure that data within a table does not violate business rules.

Contract An agreement between two services that defines the message types the services send to accomplish certain tasks. It also defines what participants can send which message types.

Conversation A long-term, asynchronous, and reliable communication channel across which messages are sent by using Service Broker.

Conversation group A collection of conversations that are related.

Conversation priority Sets the relative precedence for Service Broker conversations.

Correlated subquery A query that is embedded within, and references columns from, an outer query.

Cost An internal metric used by SQL Server to determine the amount of processing resources a given query plan will consume.

Cursor A server-side object that allows you to retrieve and process a set of data on a row-by-row basis.

D

DDL trigger A trigger that executes in response to a DDL event.

Deterministic function A function that returns the same value every time it is executed given the same input parameters.

Dialog A conversation between two specific Service Broker services that provides exactly-once-in-order (EOIO) message delivery.

Distributed partitioned view A special case of a partitioned view where the member tables are stored on multiple SQL Server instances.

DML trigger A trigger that executes in response to a DML event.

Durability After a transaction is committed, the final state of the data is still available even if the server fails or is restarted.

E

Event group A set of DDL events within the DDL event hierarchy.

Execution context The security credentials under which a code module is executed.

F

Filestream A property that can be applied to the *varbinary(max)* data type and that makes the actual data reside in a directory structure in the file system instead of inside the database's data file or files.

Filter A component that processes a document to extract the textual information from documents stored in a *varbinary(max)* or image column and then sends that information to the word breaker.

Filter daemon host process (Fdhost.exe) A process that manages third-party components such as filters, word breakers, and stemmers separated from the SQL Server process.

FOR XML A way to make SQL Server return a stream making up an XML document or fragment.

Foreign key constraint A constraint that is used to implement referential integrity between tables (or even within a single table).

Full-text catalog A virtual object that represents a group of full-text indexes.

Full-Text Engine A part of the SQL Server process that manages full-text administrative tasks, handles full-text query execution, and manages the filter daemon host process.

Full-text index An object that contains significant words and their locations within the columns included in the index.

Function A named SQL statement programming object that can be called in either a *SELECT* or *FROM*

clause that returns a single (scalar) value or a value with a table data type, but is not allowed to modify the state of a database or the instance.

G

Gating role A role specified when enabling CDC that is used to limit access to the change data.

***geography* data type** Used to store ellipsoidal (round-earth) data, such as latitude and longitude coordinates.

***geometry* data type** Used to store planar data based on Euclidean space such as points, lines, and polygons.

H

Heap A table without a clustered index. (A heap can still have nonclustered indexes defined on it.)

I

Identity One column per table can be defined as its identity. The IDENTITY property automatically generates a new increased or decreased number for the column when rows are inserted into the table.

Impersonation The process by which a user assumes the security credentials of another user.

Index A physical structure implemented as a balanced tree that is used to speed up query operations.

Indexed view A deterministic view that has a unique, clustered index created against it.

INNER JOIN A join that includes only the rows that are in common in all tables referenced in the *FROM* clause. (See also *JOIN* and *OUTER JOIN*.)

Instantiation The process of producing a particular instance of an object based on the object's properties and methods.

Isolation During a transaction (before it is committed or rolled back), the data must remain in an isolated state and not be accessible to other transactions. In SQL Server, the isolation level can be controlled for each transaction.

J

JOIN A T-SQL operator that combines multiple related tables to define the result set. The *JOIN* syntax defines a column or columns which are common between the tables that are used to correlate the data. (See also *INNER JOIN* and *OUTER JOIN*.)

L

Log Sequence Number (LSN) A number assigned to entries within a transaction log to aid with recovery.

Lower bound Defines a starting Log Sequence Number (LSN) to define a valid range of rows within a change table.

M

Materialized view Another name for an indexed view.

Message Contains information that is sent within a Service Broker conversation.

Message type Defines the name and contents of a message.

Methods Actions an object can perform.

Module A set of code that is stored within a database. The module types supported by SQL Server are triggers, functions, views, and stored procedures.

N

Nonclustered index An index that contains one or more columns in a table that are used to improve query efficiency. If the table has a clustered index, the root level of the nonclustered index points back to the clustering key, otherwise, the root level points to a row in the table.

Noncorrelated subquery A query that is embedded within, but does not reference any columns from, an outer query.

Nondeterministic function A function that might return a different value each time it is called given the same input parameter.

O

Object A collection of properties and methods that provide a defined functionality.

OGC Extended Methods
Methods designed to work with *geometry* and *geography* data types.

Open Geospatial Consortium (OGC) An international, nonprofit organization that develops standards for geospatial and location-based services.

OUTER JOIN A join that includes all rows from an outer table and includes any rows from the inner table that match the join criteria.

P

Page The smallest storage object maintained by SQL Server; a page is exactly 8 KB in size.

Parameter A variable that is passed to a stored procedure or function.

Partition function A function that defines the values that divide a table or index into multiple partitions.

Partition scheme Defines on which file group each partition defined by a partition function should be stored.

Partitioned view A view that utilizes a *UNION ALL* clause to combine multiple member tables of the same structure into a single result set.

Population (crawl) The process of adding data to (populating) a full-text index either during creation or when the full-text index is built.

Primary key A constraint that is set on one column or a combination of columns in a table that must uniquely identify a row in the table. By definition, the primary key cannot contain *NULL* values.

Q

Queue A hidden table where Service Broker messages are stored until they are processed.

R

Recursive CTE A special type of common table expression that has an anchor query, which is the source of the recursion, along with a *UNION ALL* statement and a second query, which recurses across the anchor query, and an outer query, which references the CTE and specifies the maximum recursion levels.

Remote service binding Provides security to dialogs connecting to remote databases.

Route Defines where to deliver Service Broker messages. If not specified, the AutoCreatedLocal route is used.

Row identifier (RID) A numeric value representing a physical location within a heap and page.

S

Scalar function A function referenced in a *SELECT* clause that accepts an expression and returns a single value of a defined data type.

Schema binding An option that is available for views and functions that ensures any dependent objects cannot be dropped unless the view or function is dropped first.

Service The name given to the group of tasks within a Service Broker solution that require messages to be sent.

Service Broker endpoint Used to configure SQL Server to send and receive messages over TCP/IP connections.

Spatial reference identifier (SRID) A reference ID associated with a specific model of the earth. These IDs reference the European Petroleum Survey Group (EPSG) standard identification system.

SQL Full-Text Filter Daemon Launcher (Fdlauncher.exe) A service that starts Fdhost.exe processes when the Full-Text Engine requires them.

SQLCLR A run time inside SQL Server that allows some objects to be created using a .NET language such as C# or Visual Basic .NET.

Stemmer A process that provides inflectional matches to verbs and nouns based on the linguistic rules of the data language defined.

Stoplist A database object that is used to manage stopwords. There is a system-defined stoplist and you can also create your own stoplists.

Stopword A word that is commonly used and adds no meaning to a search, such as a, an, and the. Stopwords

in SQL Server 2008 provide similar functionality to noise words in SQL Server 2005.

Stored procedure A module of code that is stored within a database that provides an API that applications can use to abstract the database structure from application code.

System process ID (SPID) A numeric value assigned to each connection to SQL Server.

T

Table-valued function A function that returns the results as a table data type.

Term The word, phrase, or character string included as input in the full-text query.

Thesaurus XML files that define synonyms for terms in a specific language.

Token A word or character string defined by a word breaker.

U

UNION A T-SQL operator that combines the result sets from multiple queries.

Unique constraint A constraint that is set on one or more columns in a table that ensures the data in each row is unique within the table for that column or combination of columns. A unique constraint allows *NULL* values and therefore cannot be used to uniquely identify a row unless all of the columns defined for the unique index do not allow *NULL*s.

Upper bound Defines an ending Log Sequence Number (LSN) to define a valid range of rows within a change table.

User-defined function (UDF) A function created as T-SQL or as Common Language Runtime (CLR) code. T-SQL UDFs include scalar, multistatement table-valued, and inline table-valued functions.

V

Variable An object that is used to store a scalar value for use within a function, trigger, or stored procedure.

W

Well-known binary (WKB) The binary equivalent to WKT, which is sometimes used to transfer and store spatial data.

Well-known text (WKT) A standard created by the OGC that is used to represent text-based descriptions of geospatial objects.

Word breaker A process that finds word boundaries (tokenizes words) based on the linguistic rules for the data language specified. You can specify the language of the data in the column when creating a full-text index on a table.

X

XML A specification by the World Wide Web Consortium for transmitting and storing semistructured data.

***XML* data type** A native SQL Server data type that can handle both XML fragments and documents as well as untyped and typed (schema-validated) XML data.

XML document XML that is well-formed; that is, it must have a root node.

XML fragment XML that is not well-formed; that is, it does not have a root node.

Index

Symbols and Numbers

@mailitem_id, 381
(number) sign, in standard indentifiers, 91
(double number sign), in standard identifiers, 91
$action variable, 62
$FSLOG directory, 311
%1!, message parameter, 153
%2!, message parameter, 153
%d, message parameter, 153
%s, message parameter, 153
[ ] (square brackets)
  for delimited identifiers, 91
  in LIKE clause, 6
"" (quotation marks)
  defined phrase, 343
  delimited identifiers, 91
.NET Framework, 283
@ (at) symbol, 146
  in standard identifiers, 91
@@ (double at) symbol, 146
@@ERROR function, 39, 154
@@TRANCOUNT function
  determining current nesting level, 156
  retrieves active transactions, 39, 69
@append_query_error, 380
@attach_query_result_as_file, 379
@blind_copy_recipients, 379
@body, 379
@body_format, 379
@copy_recipients, 379
@dialog_handle, 363
@exclude_query_output, 380
@execute_query_database, 379
@file_attachments, 379
@importance, 379
@mailitem_id [OUTPUT], 381
@profile_name, 378
@query, 379
@query_attachment_filename, 379

@query_no_truncate, 380
@query_result_header, 379
@query_result_separator, 380
@query_result_width, 380
@recipients, 378
@sensitivity, 379
@subject, 379
^ (caret) symbol, in LIKE clause, 6
_ (underscore), in LIKE clause, 6

A

abbreviations, in identifiers, 92
accent_sensitivity, 337, 342
ACCENT_SENSITIVITY ON/OFF, CREATE FULLTEXT
  CATALOG command, 337
ACID properties, 67
activation
  CREATE QUEUE command, 360
  Service Broker, 354
Activity Monitor, 72
AdventureWorks2008/DW2008 database, 2
  change tracking in, 399, 401–402
  enabling change data capture (CDC) on, 408
AFTER triggers, 105, 175
aggregate functions
  creating custom, 295–301
  grouping, 20, 22
  overview, 19
  running, 129
aggregate queries
  GROUP BY clause in, 20
  with unequal joins, 129
aliases
  [AS] table alias, 61
  data manipulation and, 9
  defining, in SELECT statement, 31

D

X

Y

About the Authors

TOBIAS THERNSTRÖM has enjoyed the company of Microsoft SQL Server for over 13 years. He currently works with Microsoft in Redmond on the development of the SQL Server Engine. Tobias has been involved in the development of several of the SQL Server certifications provided by Microsoft. He is a Microsoft Certified Trainer (MCT) and cofounder of the Swedish SQL Server User Group (*http://www.sqlug.se*).

ANN WEBER is an independent instructor, consultant, and author from Dublin, Ohio, and she is an MCT, a Microsoft Certified IT Professional (MCITP) on SQL Server, and a Microsoft Certified Systems Engineer (MCSE). Having over 12 years of experience with the various versions of SQL Server, she specializes in classes and projects that center around this product. Ann has worked closely with Microsoft Learning and Microsoft Certification on several projects. Although she enjoys the time she spends as a trainer in the classroom, she also enjoys sharing information through the various white papers and custom courses she has written.

MIKE HOTEK is the vice president of MHS Enterprises, Inc., a U.S. corporation, and president of FilAm Software Technology, Inc., a Philippine corporation. An application developer for about three decades and a SQL Server professional for almost two decades, he has consulted on over 1,000 SQL Server projects over the years and develops products and solutions that span every feature within SQL Server—relational, Extract, Transform, and Load (ETL), reporting, Online Analytical Processing (OLAP), and data mining. He is proficient in over 40 development languages or platforms ranging from Cobol, RPG, Fortran, and LISP to Powerbuilder, Delphi, .NET, and PHP. He has written or cowritten eight books, seven of those about SQL Server, along with dozens of articles for various trade magazines. When he isn't consulting on SQL Server projects, speaking at conferences, delivering seminars, building software, or teaching classes, you can find him behind a lathe in his woodworking shop.

System Requirements

It is recommended that you use a computer that is not your primary workstation to perform the exercises in this book because you will make changes to the operating system and Microsoft SQL Server configuration.

Hardware Requirements

To complete most of the practices in this book, you need a single machine. Your computers or virtual machines should meet the following minimum hardware specifications:

- Pentium III or faster processor, at least 1.0 gigahertz (GHz) for 32 bit and 1.6 GHz for 64 bit
- 512 megabytes (MB) of RAM
- 20 gigabytes (GB) of available hard disk space
- DVD-ROM drive
- A Super VGA monitor with a 800 x 600 or higher resolution
- A keyboard and a Microsoft mouse or compatible pointing device

Software Requirements

The following software is required to complete the practice exercises:

- Microsoft .NET Framework 3.5
- Any of the following Microsoft Windows operating systems:
  - Windows XP Professional Home, Tablet, Media Center, or Professional with SP2
  - Windows Vista SP1
  - Windows Server 2003 Standard or Enterprise with SP2
  - Windows Server 2008 Standard or Enterprise
- Microsoft Data Access Components (MDAC) 2.8 SP1 or later
- Shared Memory, Named Pipes, or Transmission Control Protocol/Internet Protocol (TCP/IP) networking support
- Microsoft Internet Explorer 6.0 SP1 or Windows Internet Explorer 7.0 or later

Resources for SQL Server 2008

Microsoft® SQL Server® 2008 Administrator's Pocket Consultant
William R. Stanek
ISBN 9780735625891

Programming Microsoft SQL Server 2008
Leonard Lobel, Andrew J. Brust, Stephen Forte
ISBN 9780735625990

Microsoft SQL Server 2008 Step by Step
Mike Hotek
ISBN 9780735626041

Microsoft SQL Server 2008 T-SQL Fundamentals
Itzik Ben-Gan
ISBN 9780735626010

MCTS Self-Paced Training Kit (Exam 70-432) Microsoft SQL Server 2008 Implementation and Maintenance
Mike Hotek
ISBN 9780735626058

Smart Business Intelligence Solutions with Microsoft SQL Server 2008
Lynn Langit, Kevin S. Goff, Davide Mauri, Sahil Malik, and John Welch
ISBN 9780735625808

COMING SOON

Microsoft SQL Server 2008 Internals
Kalen Delaney *et al.*
ISBN 9780735626249

Inside Microsoft SQL Server 2008: T-SQL Querying
Itzik Ben-Gan, Lubor Kollar, Dejan Sarka
ISBN 9780735626034

Microsoft SQL Server 2008 Best Practices
Saleem Hakani and Ward Pond
with the Microsoft SQL Server Team
ISBN 9780735626225

Microsoft SQL Server 2008 MDX Step by Step
Bryan C. Smith, C. Ryan Clay, Hitachi Consulting
ISBN 9780735626188

Microsoft SQL Server 2008 Reporting Services Step by Step
Stacia Misner
ISBN 9780735626478

Microsoft SQL Server 2008 Analysis Services Step by Step
Scott Cameron, Hitachi Consulting
ISBN 9780735626201

microsoft.com/mspress

Windows Server 2008— Resources for Administrators

Get Certified—Windows Server 2008

Ace your preparation for the skills measured by the Microsoft® certification exams—and on the job. With 2-in-1 *Self-Paced Training Kits*, you get an official exam-prep guide + practice tests. Work at your own pace through lessons and real-world case scenarios that cover the exam objectives. Then, assess your skills using practice tests with multiple testing modes—and get a customized learning plan based on your results.

EXAMS 70-640, 70-642, 70-646

MCITP Self-Paced Training Kit: Windows Server® 2008 Server Administrator Core Requirements

ISBN 9780735625082

EXAMS 70-640, 70-642, 70-643, 70-647

MCITP Self-Paced Training Kit: Windows Server 2008 Enterprise Administrator Core Requirements

ISBN 9780735625723

EXAM 70-640

MCTS Self-Paced Training Kit: Configuring Windows Server 2008 Active Directory®

Dan Holme, Nelson Ruest, and Danielle Ruest

ISBN 9780735625136

EXAM 70-647

MCITP Self-Paced Training Kit: Windows® Enterprise Administration

Orin Thomas, et al.

ISBN 9780735625099

EXAM 70-642

MCTS Self-Paced Training Kit: Configuring Windows Server 2008 Network Infrastructure

Tony Northrup, J.C. Mackin

ISBN 9780735625129

EXAM 70-643

MCTS Self-Paced Training Kit: Configuring Windows Server 2008 Applications Infrastructure

J.C. Mackin, Anil Desai

ISBN 9780735625112

ALSO SEE

Windows Server 2008 Administrator's Pocket Consultant
William R. Stanek
ISBN 9780735624375

Windows Server 2008 Administrator's Companion
Charlie Russel, Sharon Crawford
ISBN 9780735625051

Windows Server 2008 Resource Kit
Microsoft MVPs with Windows Server Team
ISBN 9780735623613

EXAM 70-646

MCITP Self-Paced Training Kit: Windows Server Administration

Ian McLean, Orin Thomas

ISBN 9780735625105

microsoft.com/mspress

What do you think of this book?

We want to hear from you!

To participate in a brief online survey, please visit:

microsoft.com/learning/booksurvey

...and enter this book's ISBN number (appears above barcode on back cover).

Tell us how well this book meets your needs—what works effectively, and what we can do better. Your feedback will help us continually improve our books and learning resources for you.

Thank you in advance for your input!

Where to find the ISBN on back cover

Example only. Each book has unique ISBN.

Microsoft®
Press

Stay in touch!

To subscribe to the *Microsoft Press® Book Connection Newsletter*—for news on upcoming books, events, and special offers—please visit:

microsoft.com/learning/books/newsletter